PUTTING YOUR PASSION INTO PRINT

Also by Arielle Eckstut

Pride and Promiscuity: The Lost Sex Scenes of Jane Austen

Also by David Henry Sterry

Chicken: Self-Portrait of a Young Man for Rent

Also by Arielle Eckstut and David Henry Sterry

Satchel Sez: The Wit, Wisdom, and World of Leroy "Satchel" Paige

PUTTING YOUR PASSION INTO PRINT

by Arielle Eckstut and
David Henry Sterry

WORKMAN PUBLISHING COMPANY, INC. • NEW YORK

DEDICATION

To Joann Eckstut and Stan Eckstut,
Maureen Moreland and John Sterry,
for always encouraging us to follow our passions

And to all aspiring authors looking to put
their passion into print

 Published simultaneously in Canada by Thomas Allen & Son Limited.

Library of Congress Cataloging-in-Publication Data

Eckstut, Arielle.
Putting your passion into print : get your book published successfully / by Arielle Eckstut & David Henry Sterry.
p. cm.
Includes index.
ISBN-13: 978-0-7611-3122-9; ISBN-10: 0-7611-3122-1 (alk. paper)
ISBN-13: 978-0-7611-3817-4; ISBN-10: 0-7611-3817-X (hc)
1. Authorship—Marketing. I. Sterry, David. II. Title.

PN161.E34 2005
070.5'2—dc22

2005043651

While we had no problem divulging our own missteps, pratfalls and furious anger, it didn't seem fair to air other people's dirty laundry. So we've added the odd "anonymous author story" to our book. To fully protect these anonymous authors, we've changed some details and/or created composite stories. We'd hate to put an abrupt end to anyone's publishing career just to help other people start theirs!

We would like to gratefully acknowledge André Bernard for granting us permission to reprint a portion of his fabulous book *Rotten Rejections: A Literary Companion* (Chrysalis Books, 2002).

WORKMAN PUBLISHING COMPANY, INC.
708 Broadway
New York, NY 10003-9555
www.workman.com

Printed in the United States of America

First printings: August 2005
10 9 8 7 6 5 4 3 2 1

CONTENTS

INTRODUCTION

"Passion is universal humanity. Without it religion, history, romance and art would be useless."

—**Honoré de Balzac**

"Nothing leads so straight to futility as literary ambitions without systematic knowledge."

—**H.G. Wells**

Hello. Welcome. Do you want to see your name on the cover of your very own book but find yourself baffled by the business? Or are you a grizzled veteran of the publishing jungle who's looking to avoid the author-eating beasts this time around? Either way, you're not alone. That's why we've written *Putting Your Passion into Print.*

This book is not about how to be a writer. It is a step-by-step, blow-by-blow explanation of how to take an idea you're passionate about, make a book out of it, get it published and deliver it into the hands, heads and hearts of readers all over the world.

From figuring out the right idea to locating and landing an agent; to selling your book to the appropriate publisher or self-publishing if that's where your road goes; to understanding your contract; to getting P-A-I-D; to actually sitting down and writing your book; to becoming savvy about publicity, marketing and media; to planning and executing a magnificent event where you sell beaucoup books; to planting your flag on bestseller lists: *Putting Your Passion into Print* is your all-in-one guide to publishing.

Sprinkled among all these nuts and bolts are juicy nuggets of insider information from seasoned industry professionals: authors, agents, editors, publishers, publicists, bookstore owners, booksellers and many more.

WHY PASSION?

Passion isn't usually the first item on the list of requirements for writing a book. But here's a fact: Getting a book written, published and read is hard work. And it's even harder if you're writing about something you don't care that much about.

Passion will help you keep on keeping on. And passion is contagious. Whether it's on the page or flowing through your publicity and marketing efforts, passion excites and moves people. More than anything else, passion will help you attract agents, publishers and readers. It will help you sell books. And have fun. After all, what good is any of it if you're not having fun?

Probably the most important reason we decided to write this book is that we are utterly passionate about showing people how to put their own passion into print, whether they want to self-publish a limited quantity of books, go for a fat advance from a big publisher or anything in between. We've seen over and over the joy publishing a book can bring and how it can change people's lives. But it helps to have the right guide dog to help you across the street. We are honored to be your dog.

WHO ARE WE TO TELL YOU ABOUT GETTING PUBLISHED?

For one thing, we're authors who have written books in a wide range of categories: memoir, fiction, practical nonfiction, sports and humor. For another, we've taught Putting Your Passion into Print workshops all across America, culminating in a course at Stanford University that was filled in under five minutes (which goes to show how many people want to write books). Plus, Arielle is a literary agent who worked in New York City, the mecca of publishing, for 10 years before opening up the West Coast office of the Levine Greenberg Literary Agency. She's midwifed dozens of first-time authors, as well as seventh-, eleventh- and twentieth-time authors. She's worked with every major publishing house and sold millions of dollars worth of books.

In addition to being a bestselling author, David has been a professional actor and presentation doctor for 20 years. What do acting and helping people with their presentation skills have to do with writing a book? A lot. We live in a time when the way you present yourself and your book (to a literary agent, a publisher, the media, a bookstore, the public) can be as important as what's in your book. After 25 years of working with everyone from Michael Caine to Zippy the Chimp, and years of hawking everything from Big Macs to Publishers Clearing House, David has learned the art of how to sell yourself, which, in turn, will help you sell your book.

WHERE IT ALL BEGAN

It's strange how often your passion lurks right under your nose but you can't smell it. Or you smell it, but it never dawns on you to write a book about it. In fact, the origin of this book is rooted in an under-your-nose experience that started with the famous Negro Leagues baseball player Satchel Paige.

A lovingly framed poster of Leroy "Satchel" Paige in mid-pitch was hanging on David's living room wall when Arielle, who was David's agent at the time (she's now his wife), first walked into his house. She pointed to the poster and asked, "Who's that guy?"

"Oh, that's Satchel Paige," replied David. "He's been my hero since I was a little kid. He was the greatest pitcher in history. One of the funniest comedians of the twentieth century. And one of the deepest philosophers America's ever produced. He was like Mark Twain, Yogi Berra and Richard Pryor rolled into one."

Arielle looked at David and said: "There's gotta be a book there."

And there was. It was called *Satchel Sez: The Wit, Wisdom, and World of Leroy "Satchel" Paige.* And we wrote it.

David collected nearly every Satchel Paige baseball card, sifted through old newspaper accounts of his exploits, talked to Willie Mays, visited the Negro Leagues Museum, compiled quotes, pictures and stories. Things he would have been doing for fun anyway (well, minus talking to Willie Mays). Only now he was getting paid for it! But if Arielle hadn't pointed out the book to be made from David's love of ol' Satch, it never would have occurred to him to put his passion into print. And if she hadn't guided him in developing the proposal and hadn't had the know-how to present it to the right editors, *Satchel Sez* would never have been born.

Soon thereafter, Arielle took a very important taxi ride. It must be understood that Arielle is a Jane Austen fanatic of the highest order and has been since she was just a tyke. She'd always wanted to write a book about her idol but assumed that since she didn't have a Ph.D. in English Literature, her dream would be forever unfulfilled. Until one day, in the aforementioned taxi, when a friend said, "Wouldn't it be funny if someone discovered sex scenes from Jane Austen's books that had been edited out?" At that moment, a galaxy of lightbulbs lit up over Arielle's head and a little inner voice said:

"There's gotta be a book there."

While she had ignored that little voice many times over the years, Arielle was determined not to let this idea wriggle away. She pored over Jane Austen's books for the umpteen thousandth time, dissecting the intense psychological motivations that drive her marvelously complex characters as they try to find love. Then she created scenes for those characters, writing in the voice of her beloved Austen. Something she would have done for fun anyway.

Arielle put her passion into print, and 18 months later *Pride and Promiscuity: The Lost Sex Scenes of Jane Austen* was born.

WHAT LED US HERE

Writing our books was a blast. And brutally hard. A mental triathlon. There was always so much to do, and so few hours to do it in. But making our books changed our lives. We were invigorated, full of purpose and energy, alive creatively, mentally, soulfully. It was an amazing education. About ourselves. About each other. And about the publishing business. While Arielle had agented dozens of books, we were both author virgins, and publishing had its way with us, for better and for worse. Joy abounded, but naturally there was pain involved.

When it was time to birth our beautiful babies, we asked ourselves how we were going to get people to pay attention to them. Have events in bookstores, we thought, since that's what you're supposed to do. Bookstores informed us that if we could get Mr. Paige or Ms. Austen to come to our events, they would be glad to have us. This presented a seemingly insurmountable problem, since both of our subjects had been dead for many years. We were discouraged, but we didn't panic; after all, we had our publishers behind us, big corporations with sleek publicity machines primed to make bestsellers out of our books.

When we met with our publisher for *Satchel Sez*, we were extremely enthusiastic and overly optimistic. We arrived armed with delectable pastries. We had formulated what we thought was a brilliant marketing scheme.

We'd have Satchel Paige Days at stadiums all over the country. Minor league, major league. We'd have Satchel Trivia Quizzes on the Jumbotron, complete with book giveaways; Negro Leagues Museum tie-ins for merchandising; charity events with Boys and Girls Clubs. We could see it all so clearly. We were raring to go, ready, willing and able to throw our books into our car and drive all over America to sell them one at a time.

Then reality hit us like a shovel. Right between the eyes.

When we went in to talk to the publicity and marketing team, the publicity and marketing team wasn't there. It was only our editor and one guy from publicity. Don't get us wrong, the guy from publicity was a great person. Still is. But he didn't have time to do some elaborate Satchel Paige Day thing at baseball stadiums. He had 10 other books to publicize that week, and another 10 the next week, and another 10 the week after that. And no budget to send us out on tour. No point in touring, really, unless we could somehow resuscitate ol' Satch. Nobody, he told us, would want to come out to a Satchel event in a bookstore. "Baseball events don't work in bookstores," he proclaimed as confidently as he would have said, "The earth revolves around the sun."

Mind you, our publicist did what he was supposed to do, and he did it well. He sent our book out to radio, newspaper and TV people all over America, and he followed up with phone calls. We did probably 50 radio interviews, from National Public Radio to some obscure 100-watt station in Guam (we're big in Guam). Still, we knew where our core audience was. They were at baseball games. So we got a list of all the stadiums in the United States and started cold-calling them. But when we finally got the right person on the phone, he'd tell us it was already too late and ask if we wanted to buy advertising space at the stadium. We tried to convince major league baseball to get in on Satchel Paige Days, maybe on his birthday. Amazingly enough, we got close. But we struck out. We tried to get stadium vendors to sell the book. We succeeded in two places, but we were hoping for 200. We tried to partner with the Negro Leagues Museum. We whiffed once again.

Meanwhile, Arielle was experiencing what was now a familiar frustration with her book. Not having Jane Austen with her in the flesh was proving a formidable obstacle to getting people to come to a bookstore event. Then, on top of it all, her editor, the main champion of her book, moved to another publishing house and her sweet young book was suddenly a miserable orphan.

We felt dumb as a sack of hammers.

Soon thereafter we were at a party, and we accidentally let it slip that Arielle was a literary agent. The word buzzed madly through the room: *There's a book agent in the house!* Arielle was inundated for the umpteenth time. Like a dateless cheerleader at an all-boys high school mixer, she was hit upon all night. As we headed home, we reflected on the seemingly insatiable thirst we'd seen exhibited by the public for the answer to this question:

HOW DO I GET MY BOOK PUBLISHED?

"Aha," we said. We'll do a seminar about how to get a book published! In bookstores. We'll use our own books as examples of how to make a book out of something you love. We'll throw back the curtain and show people the little man behind the scary Wizard in publishing.

Thus was born Putting Your Passion into Print: The Idea.

So we started cold-calling bookstores in the Bay Area (where we live) and all the way up to Seattle. It took dozens and dozens of the coldest of calls, but we finally got our first bite. A booking. At a bookstore in a strip mall in a town you forget even as you're driving through it. But our ball was rolling. We used that booking to leverage others. Boom! We had a 16-bookstores-in-24-days tour.

Thus was born Putting Your Passion into Print: The Tour.

Luckily, we had no idea what we were getting ourselves into. We just tossed copies of our books and promotional materials into our car and off we went. And what an education we got. From people like Mary Gleysteen of the Eagle Harbour Bookstore on Bainbridge Island, Washington, who packed the room full of her smart and lovely customers. And from Maria Muscarella at the Barnes & Noble in Vancouver, who brought all 50 members of her writing group. And from Kate Cerino at Paulina Springs Book Company in Sisters, Oregon, who *did* want to do an event about Satchel Paige and filled her gem of a store with 35 people, almost all of whom had seen Satchel play. (For the full story, see pages 276–77.)

We also visited stores that didn't have our books, hadn't done one thing to let anyone know we were coming and seemed shocked to see us at their door. The worst one was a rainy night in Oregon, when zero people showed up. Zero. And the store didn't even give us a pen or a complimentary beverage. But even this cloud had a silver lining. It was the night of the last game of the World Series, and David was heartbroken about having to miss the early innings. In fact, he'd been secretly hoping we could cut out early—he just didn't think it would be *that* early.

In all, we drove about 3,000 miles. Saw spectacular country. Met amazing people of every ilk. Saw some elk. Sold many books. Witnessed brilliant flashes of wit and imagination. Listened to droning folks who didn't know when to say when. But mostly we were overwhelmed by how many people all over America, from grandmas to teenagers, from businessmen to punks:

- Want to write and publish a book,
- Are starved to have the smoke and mirrors removed from the publishing process, or
- Have previously written a book, watched it die on the vine and are determined to prevent history from repeating itself.

A few months after our tour, a high school friend of Arielle's mentioned our workshop to a colleague who was a producer at NPR's *Talk of the Nation.* Intrigued, and knowing so many aspiring writers herself, the producer asked us to come on the show. It was wild to watch the switchboard light up with calls from every nook and cranny of the country. The segment was such a success that Arielle was asked back for a follow-up interview later that week.

THE PAYOFF

All during our tour, David had kept repeating, like a man possessed, that he thought Putting Your Passion into Print would make for a great book. But Arielle pooh-poohed the idea, coming up with all the lame excuses people use to stop themselves from achieving success and having fun. The only difference being that Arielle's self-doubt was probably even more severe than the average person's because she's a LITERARY AGENT!

Well, just as Arielle was about to put the kibosh on David's idea once and for all, serendipity reared its pretty head. Arielle happened to be meeting with the editorial staff of Workman Publishing (yes, check the spine). Her boss was also in the meeting, and he told Peter Workman about our *Talk of the Nation* appearance. Peter said, "That's a proposal I'd be interested in seeing."

Thus was born Putting Your Passion into Print: The Book.

And it really *was* right under our noses the whole time.

DO NOT SKIP, DO NOT IGNORE, DO NOT PASS GO!

The three most important words in this book are 1) research, 2) write, and 3) network. Your chances of being happily published can't help but go up if you diligently apply these three techniques throughout the process.

RESEARCH

Roaming from coast to coast, talking with book people from the biggest publishers to the smallest, from bestselling authors to writers who have never been published, we've come to the conclusion that three major things stand between you and a published book. Those three things are RESEARCH, RESEARCH and RESEARCH. From the get-go, it's crucial to know what books are out there and to have an idea of who might publish your book, who might sell it and, most important, who will read it and how you're going to get it onto their bookshelves. Research will help you answer all those questions. It will be your guide through every stage of the publishing process, and with a little bit of luck it will help your book rise to the top of the publishing barrel.

If you systematically research every part of the book publishing process, you will be way ahead of your competitors. Most people simply do not do the research it takes to get a book published and sold. Let us be clear that it is *a lot* of hard work to do this research, but if you put the time in, your odds of getting published go from nearly nil to extremely decent.

WRITE

We asked successful authors, "What's the key to a long and successful publishing career?" The overwhelming answer:

Keep writing.

You never know which piece of writing is going to be the one that makes the world stand up and take notice or sit down and shut up. You never know how long it will take to be a great writer or to write a great book. Even if you plan to work with a coauthor, you still need to continually get your ideas down on paper. You fail and you learn. But you can't learn anything unless you're actually, you know . . . writing.

It has been said that writing is not brain surgery. But imagine for a moment that it's as hard to become a successfully published writer as it is to become a brain surgeon. Imagine all the 90-hour weeks young doctors have to put in before they're allowed to practice on their own. You wouldn't let an

THE MAN WHO LEFT NO STONE UNTURNED

There's no better poster boy for the benefits of doing your research than Bob Nelson, author of, among other books, *1001 Ways to Reward Employees.* To learn more about the book business, Bob went so far as to work as a shipping clerk in a bookstore. And that was just the tip of his research iceberg.

After figuring out how bookstores work, Bob researched publishers to suss out who would be best able to package, market, publicize and sell his book. He approached one that had never published a business book because he was impressed by their marketing prowess and their dedication to making every book successful. And once he signed an agreement with the publisher, he didn't sit back and watch. For example, he drafted a 50-page memorandum on what he was planning to do to help make the book a success. He continued researching throughout the entire publishing process as to how he could augment the publisher's efforts.

When *1001 Ways to Reward Employees* came out, Bob traveled to more than 500 bookstores to see what makes people buy a book and what makes them pass it by. He also wanted to understand how and why bookstores order books and what he, as an author, could do to help influence their decision. In each city he visited, he did a follow-up postcard to all bookstore managers, informing them of the media he had done in their market, groups he had presented to, national promotions, and so on. Sound crazy? Then perhaps selling nearly a million and a half books will sound equally insane. That's right. Bob sold way over a million copies of a business book about how to reward employees. Considering the incredibly small number of books that sell over a million copies, this is amazing. But, in Bob's case, it's not even that surprising.

When he hit the one-million-books-sold mark, his publisher threw a party for him. At that party, the president of the publishing company held up a thick file folder filled with information Bob had accumulated about his book in Indianapolis alone! For most publishers, Indianapolis is just a blip on the map, but Bob had done enough media and marketing in that one city to fill a folder larger than what most authors compile for an entire book!

Bob's philosophy? "Leave no stone unturned."

aspiring surgeon cut into your brain after a week on the job, would you? As ridiculous as it sounds, many writers expect this kind of immediate success.

Acclaimed novelist Charles Baxter got a Ph.D. in English and then wrote fiction and poetry while teaching. He finished two novels, neither of which

THE MAN WHO JUST KEPT WRITING

Tamim Ansary has been a writer for 30 years. When he first got out of college, he volunteered at a local collective weekly newspaper where he could write anything he wanted and get it published every week. He didn't get paid for this writing, but he amassed enough clippings to make an impressive showing at future job interviews. In fact, they landed him a job as an assistant editor at a niche newspaper that actually paid him a living wage. He also started sending out fiction to small literary magazines, a number of which accepted his work.

Later, Tamim went to work for a textbook publisher and eventually worked on a textbook program that earned tens of millions of dollars for the company. But his name never appeared on a textbook cover and he didn't get anything out of it except his paycheck and the privilege of working at home. He started freelancing with other textbook publishers and continued to make a living as a writer.

Then, one day, Tamim's wife was browsing through a magazine in a dentist's office and happened to see that a publisher was looking for people with inside knowledge of various countries to write children's books. Tamim got a contract for a book about Afghanistan, his native land. He had no agent, but he got a book with his name on it and eventually even made a little money from it.

Some years later, Tamim completed a novel that an agent liked well enough to represent. And then 9/11 happened. On that horrible day, Tamim sent an e-mail about Afghanistan to a dozen friends, who sent it to a dozen friends, who sent it to a dozen friends, until it landed in the e-mailboxes of millions around the world. Suddenly Bill Moyers, NPR, Oprah and a host of others were asking him for interviews. His agent said, "Give me a proposal to sell, anything, just put something on a piece of paper!" It so happened that Tamim had a thousand raw pages of a memoir he'd been working on for years. He thought about how he could carve a book relevant to the times out of that mass of material and he wrote a one-page description of his book. Titled *West of Kabul, East of New York,* it was snapped up by one of the world's most distinguished publishers. Tamim says, "Getting my book published wouldn't have happened without the e-mail. But it also wouldn't have happened without the raw memoir out of which it was carved, already written and waiting to be used. The moral: Always write."

was published. When he sent off a third novel to a literary agent, the rejection was so resounding that he resigned himself to an academic career. But before hanging up his literary hat he wrote a short story, "Harmony of the World."

That story won a Pushcart Prize, one of the highest honors awarded to a short story, and was included in the 1982 edition of *Best American Short Stories*. It led to a string of book contracts, including one for *Feast of Love*, which has sold more than 200,000 copies and was optioned by Miramax. So do yourself a favor: If you want to be a writer, don't stop writing. No matter what.

Of course, before you even think about stopping, you have to start—a major stumbling block for many of us. We can't tell you how many people we've come across who have fantastic ideas, tremendous enthusiasm, great visions and NO WRITING to show for it. There is just no way your book can change the world or move, touch or make people laugh unless you start writing it.

NETWORK

The Carnegie Institute of Technology has long studied success and has concluded that, even in profoundly technical professions like engineering, only 15% of financial success stems from technical skills. A whopping 85% is due to "human engineering," or people skills. Publishing is no exception. Finding the right agent and publisher, getting mad media love, befriending booksellers and reaching readers are all, in very large part, dependent upon people skills. *Networking.*

For those who embody the shy writer archetype, networking may not be a strong suit. But in this day and age, when much of the small gentlemanly world of publishing has turned corporate, networking is one of your best shots at getting into and succeeding at the publishing game. If the success of your book is 15% dependent on what's inside it and 85% dependent on your ability to network, clearly, you gotta learn to network.

How you network is as crucial as the networking itself. In *Spinal Tap*, one of our favorite films ever, the protagonist laments about the fine line between clever and stupid. There is a similarly fine line between friendly and pushy. If you cross the line, you may shoot yourself in the foot. But just being friendly is often not enough. Make it easy for people to say yes. Be sensitive to what they want and need. That combined with friendly persistence can be a real door opener.

So when you're next face to face with a networking opportunity, don't ask yourself:

"What if they don't want to talk to me?"

"What if I humiliate myself?"

THE KNIGHTS OF NETWORKING

Dynamic duo Keith and Kent Zimmerman have 10 books to their names. In large part, their success is due to their networking skills. Their mantra is "JUST ASK." These guys have made a career out of shutting down the fear factor and approaching people who seem unapproachable. That's how they got an agent, as well as almost all their book contracts. That's also how they got their celebrity coauthors. Scary, intimidating celebrities, at that. Without an ounce of publishing experience, the Zimmermen cowrote a book with the infamous bad boy of punk, John Lydon (a.k.a. Johnny Rotten of the Sex Pistols) and then, without ever having been on a motorcycle, wrote another with Sonny Barger, King of the Hell's Angels. They had a resumé that showed they could write about music, and they had the chutzpah to track down John Lydon and ask him if he was interested in doing a book with them. "We went up to Lydon at a publicity gig he was doing," they recall. "If we had known how difficult people thought it would be to approach him, we probably would have been too scared to do it." But this kind of can-do naïveté can actually be helpful when it comes to getting a book published. Especially when it's paired with the kind of friendly professional persistence these guys practice. As they say, "Whatever you're working on, whoever you meet, can lead to an opportunity. But you've got to be prepared, you've got to be aggressive, you always have to be thinking and, no matter what, you have to ask."

"What if they laugh at me and I'm scarred for life?"

Instead, ask:

"What if this is the person who could make my career?"

"What if I make a friend and ally for life?"

"What if they think I have something really important to share with the world?"

Grasp the opportunity and invite her for a spin around the dance floor. Sure, you may get a no. And then you'll move on. But if you don't ask, you never know what opportunity you'll miss.

PYPIP POP QUIZ

Before we plunge in, we encourage you to take this little test just to see how your knowledge of publishing stacks up.

1. Approximately how many books are published each year in the United States?
   a. 5,000
   b. 50,000
   c. 150,000
   d. 500,000
   e. 1,000,000,000,000,000,000,000,000,000,000,000,000,000,000

2. Bestsellers represent what percentage of Barnes & Noble's total sales?
   a. Less than 5%
   b. Less than 11%
   c. Less than 62%
   d. Less than 84%
   e. Less than 99.99%

3. Which is the largest publisher in the United States?
   a. HarperCollins
   b. Time Warner Books
   c. Random House
   d. Simon & Schuster
   e. The Government Printing Office

4. What is the biggest manufacturing cost for a book?
   a. The printing
   b. The paper
   c. The shipping
   d. The binding
   e. Taking authors out to lunch

5. Bertelsmann, the German company that bought Random House, started out publishing what kinds of books?
   a. Underground comics
   b. Lutheran hymnals
   c. Household electronics manuals

d. Maps of Munich
e. Animal husbandry guides

6. What is the bestselling book of all time, excluding the Bible?
a. *Dr. Spock's Baby and Child Care*
b. *Harry Potter and the Sorcerer's Stone*
c. *Quotations from Chairman Mao Tse-Tung (The Little Red Book)*
d. *How to Win Friends and Influence People*
e. The phone book

7. Which of the following books was originally self-published?
a. *Ulysses* by James Joyce
b. *The Celestine Prophecy* by James Redfield
c. *The Tale of Peter Rabbit* by Beatrix Potter
d. *Joy of Cooking* by Irma Rombauer
e. All of the above

8. On average, how much profit does a publisher make on each book sold?
a. 43%
b. 31%
c. 22%
d. Less than 10%
e. No publisher has ever made a profit on anything, anytime, anywhere

9. What percentage of books earn back their advance?
a. 60%
b. 42%
c. 28%
d. Less than 10%
e. No book has ever earned back its advance, anytime, anywhere

10. The average American buys how many books a year?
a. None
b. Fewer than 2
c. Fewer than 7
d. Fewer than 15

ANSWERS: 1) c 2) a 3) e 4) b 5) b 6) c 7) e 8) d 9) d 10) b

Putting Your Passion into Print
THE PHILOSOPHY

We believe that people can write books about what they love and make money at it.

We believe in really, really hard work.

We believe in having as much fun as possible.

We believe there is no formula for success. We can give you the ingredients and the recipe, but you have to bake your own pie. And eat it.

We believe in putting yourself out into the world. If you don't, the world will generally ignore you.

We believe that those who learn by their mistakes and profit from their errors often succeed.

We believe in keeping your ears and eyes open, in acting upon every opportunity and in deep-sixing that little voice in your head that says you're doomed to painful, disgraceful failure.

We believe in gathering as much information as possible.

We believe that listening is as important as talking and that reading is as important as writing.

We believe that learning the rules is the best way to learn how to break them.

We believe that the more people you help, the more people will help you.

We believe that thick skin is a good thing.

We believe in the power of the please and the thank-you.

We believe that small daily tasks can make big things happen.

We believe that books can change people's lives.

PART I

Setting Up Shop

CHAPTER 1

WRITING THE RIGHT IDEA

"To produce a mighty book,
you must choose a mighty theme."

—HERMAN MELVILLE

It's important not to let the desire to get married interfere with the rational choosing of a suitable mate. So it is with writing a book. While it's great to be passionate about the idea of writing a book, it is imperative that you be more passionate about the actual idea you're exploring. Picking the right idea—which is different from picking a *good* idea—is one of the most essential pieces of the book-writing puzzle. The right idea is one that is so exciting that you're willing to hack away at it for years and years. The right idea is one you are particularly well suited to communicate to your readers. The right idea will make a real contribution—which can include a good laugh or a good cry—to the world. The right idea will get readers to buy and read your book and will inspire all sorts of media to cover it.

Settle on the right idea *before* you start writing. But the very first thing you need to ask yourself, before you even choose an idea, is:

Do I *really* want to write a book?

TO WRITE OR NOT TO WRITE?

Make no mistake about it. Getting a book successfully published is a hard thing to do. And again, like getting married, it's something people rush into, fueled by preposterous fantasies. Let us set the record straight. It's going to take as much hard work, or dumb blind luck, or a combination thereof, to be successful at publishing as it does at marriage.

Even the least labor-intensive book will take hundreds and hundreds of hours of your time, and there's no guarantee you'll ever make a penny, let alone get rich. In fact, your odds of becoming rich in the book world boil down to 1) slim, and 2) none. For every Stephen King (and there is, after all, only one of him), there are tens of thousands of people who write books and make NO money. Either they're unable to sell their projects, or they sell them to publishers who pay no up-front money, or they self-publish and have to dig into their own pockets just to print their books, and on and on. Michael Powell, owner of the famed Powell's Books in Portland, Oregon, says, "I don't think authors ask themselves the hard questions. You can't just hand over the pages of your manuscript and then go to the beach. Writing is the beginning point. Then you have to decide how much energy, money, time you can put into your book." That's why, before you decide to write a book that you dream of getting published, we ask you to consider the following equation:

"The profession of book-writing makes horse racing seem like a solid, stable business."
—John Steinbeck

$$\frac{X (\$)}{Y (\text{time})} = Z (\$ \text{ an hour})$$

Let's say you spend 500 hours on your book. And you make 0 dollars. Now let's do the math:

$$\frac{\$0}{500 \text{ hours}} = \$0 \text{ an hour}$$

Before you start, know that you may make a grand total of nothing. It may actually cost you money to write a book, even if it's simply new cartridges for your printer, not to mention travel, books for research, phone calls, postage, and so on. Now let's suppose you get an advance of $5,000, which can be, depending on the kind of book you're writing, a nice advance:

$$\frac{\$5{,}000}{500 \text{ hours}} = \$10 \text{ an hour}$$

It's important to understand the economics of the publishing world. And important to know that it's much more likely that you'll make $10 an hour pursuing your dream than that you'll become a millionaire, let alone a thousandaire.

PERSISTENCE PAYS OFF

Susan Wooldridge, author of *Poemcrazy: Freeing Your Life with Words*, needed seven years to free up enough time to write her book. Between her kids, her husband, her workshops, her newsletter and her crazy life, she often had only minutes a day to devote to writing. But Susan embraced the ancient Chinese adage, it doesn't matter how slow you go as long as you do not stop. One day, she would just write chapter headings or cross out one line. Another, she'd add page numbers—anything to move forward, to keep her book alive. After seven years, she had more than enough material for a great proposal. Which landed her an agent. Who got her a book contract. *Poemcrazy*, she's happy to report, is now in its 18th printing.

Christopher Paul Curtis took a totally different approach, but also came out happily published. After high school, Christopher went to work in a factory in Flint, Michigan. It was miserable work. He would write in his journal during his breaks to keep from going insane. Still, he didn't consider a career as a writer until his wife encouraged him to take a year off and give it a shot (illustrating the importance of marrying a really nice person). To live on one salary for a whole year was not fun. Having a book after a year of writing was. Christopher submitted that book to a contest, whose first prize was publication by a major publisher. Like Rocky, he didn't win but still ended up a winner. The publisher decided to publish his book anyway, and *The Watsons Go to Birmingham—1963* was named a Newbery Honor Book. And his next book, *Bud, Not Buddy*, won a Newbery Medal, the top prize in children's publishing.

All this means that you're going to need another source of income while you write your book or proposal, unless a) you're a person with a massive trust fund, or b) you work short hours and make large coin. (If you're in either of these categories, please contact the authors; we have some wonderful opportunities to discuss with you.)

Which leads to these questions:

- Do you want to spend many, many hours working on something that may never see the light of day?
- Are kids, partners, job and recreation going to be obstacles that you can get around?
- Do you have the discipline, focus and attention span it takes to make a book and get it published?

- Are you self-motivated enough to grind it out month after month?
- Can you stand being alone in a room staring at a blank computer screen or an empty piece of paper?
- Do you have a life where you can put aside regular chunks of time to work on your book?
- Do you have the desire to shape your life to make the time you need?

Answering these questions with brutal honesty is a smart thing to do before deciding to write a book.

Bottom line: Do you have the skill, the audacity, the brains, the drive, the vavavoom, the zazazoo and the oomph to make a book, find someone to publish it and then convince people to buy it?

If you do, you can have a great time and make some money pursuing your passion and putting it into print. Now it's time to choose an idea. Or rather, The Right Idea.

WHAT *SHOULD* YOU WRITE?

People often set out to write the book they think they *should* write. A chef *should* write a cookbook. A manager *should* write a book on getting the most out of employees. A golf pro *should* write about the perfect swing. If you love what you do and want to share your enthusiasm and expertise, fantastic. But too many people have a miserable time trying to write books when the driving force behind them is one of the following:

- "I *should* write this book because it will give me a bigger profile."
- "I *should* write this book because I need a sales tool at my presentations."
- "I *should* write this book because everyone tells me I should."

Should-based ideas are often unsellable. And many never even make it to proposal stage because it's just too hard to sustain the necessary enthusiasm for something that doesn't ignite your passion. Here's an idea: Try writing a book that makes your heart beat fast with excitement, or that you can't stop thinking about, or that you simply *have* to write whether it gets read by anyone else or not. Even if you're a business person who wants to

HAVING FUN

Have you ever listened to the Car Guys on National Public Radio? You know, Tom and Ray Magliozzi, the nutty brothers from Boston who answer questions about car trouble when they're not laughing themselves to tears? These guys are our poster boys for passion in action. No one could have guessed how wide an audience they'd attract. But these automobile aficionados loved figuring out people's car problems so much, and communicated their joy so thoroughly, that people who didn't even own cars started listening! Now their syndicated show has a huge following. In addition, they've written numerous books and books-on-tape, including *Car Talk, Best of Car Talk* and *In Our Humble Opinion: Car Talk's Click and Clack Rant and Rave.*

Author and award-winning amateur astronomer David Levy also has this ability to spread passion. When he lectures about the night sky, he gets so excited that he dances around the stage like Fred Astaire. Kids and adults alike leave his lectures filled with wonder and never look at the sky the same way again. Levy makes his work come alive, not just because the information he gives is so interesting, but because of the way he downloads his excitement directly into his audience. He could be talking about the newest in shower drains and he would still entertain a crowd! This passion has resulted in Levy's publishing over 20 books on the subject of astronomy—and he doesn't even have a Ph.D.

write a book because you're looking to grow your profile and you need a sales tool at presentations, you still have to find that excitement about your subject matter to make it fly. The best business books, like any other category of book, are fueled by passion.

Once upon a time, a psychologist named Bob Klein went out to lunch with literary agent James Levine to discuss writing a book based on his years of clinical practice—what he thought he *should* write about. As they were looking at the menu, Bob pulled out a long list from his pocket and scrutinized it.

"What's that?" Jim asked.

"Oh, that's my beer list," Bob said. "Wherever I go, I always try a new beer, and I rate it according to color, taste and what food it goes well with."

Jim, a fellow beer lover, asked to see the list. Being the wise agent that he is, the moment he laid eyes on it he said: "There's your book!"

Months later, *The Beer Lover's Rating Guide* was born. It has nearly 200,000 copies in print in two editions and spawned an annual Page-A-Day®

> *"Write something to suit yourself and many people will like it; write something to suit everybody and scarcely anyone will care for it."*
> **—Jesse Stuart**

calendar. Bob is now the envy of men everywhere as he travels the world over, reveling in, analyzing the particulars of and drinking . . . BEER!

Which brings us to our deep, philosophical thought on "should": Should shmould. Write about what you love. Chances are, a lot of other people love the same thing. And, as we said earlier, passion is contagious. If you can communicate your passion, people will be drawn to you and what you write.

ASSEMBLING IDEAS

If you bought this book, you probably have an idea for one of your own. For a moment, humor us and put that idea aside. Get yourself an Empty Book, open to the first page and start writing down the things you're passionate about. Don't restrict yourself; just let fly. Whom do you most admire? Where is your favorite spot in the world? If you have a day off, what do you most want to do? If you could write a book about anything, what would that be?

Because the amazing thing is, you can.

Maybe you're an academic who's on a mission to get your research out to a wider audience than the 10 other people in your field. Maybe you're a businessperson who's carved out your own niche and loves showing others how to do the same. Maybe you have a particular insight into a historical figure. Maybe you have a beautiful, shocking, mesmerizing story that will change people's lives. Maybe you recently read an article that has all the elements of a page-turning plot for the novel you've always wanted to write. Maybe your family history is a sweeping epic that would translate into a staggering book. Whether you're cuckoo for building birdhouses, batty for bodice rippers or crazed for crossword puzzles, don't let your passion go unnoticed.

Get Thee to the Bookstore and the Library

Before we help you figure out which is the best idea for you, we first need to introduce you to your three future best friends: 1) your local bookstore, 2) your local library, and 3) your Internet bookstore. With the exception

THE POWER OF THE SPECIAL PEN AND THE IMPORTANCE OF THE EMPTY BOOK

First, treat yourself to a special pen. We can't tell you how many people have attested to the special-pen phenomenon. Don't ask us why, but special pens make you write better. Second, you need an Empty Book dedicated solely to your project. This notebook should not only inspire in you a sense of fun and purpose but also fit in your bag or briefcase. David carries a hot pink Barbie Empty Book. It makes him feel special. And it's a real icebreaker in awkward social situations.

Take your pen and Empty Book with you everywhere you go. Anytime you have an idea for your project, add it to your book, along with all the bits of practical information that will be crucial to getting your *real* book published.

of those living in the hinterest of the hinterlands, you probably have at least one bookstore and one library somewhere around you. Chances are, you've got a couple. Start spending time in them. And read lots of books—especially in your subject areas.

Many writers underestimate the importance of reading. Without getting into the merits of reading for inspiration, allow us to remind you that reading helps you understand what other readers are buying, shows you how other authors have presented work on similar subjects and lets you discover who publishes books like yours. Reading local and national newspapers will tell you what books are being reviewed and what books are on bestseller lists, while reading magazines like *Publishers Weekly* (the main trade publication for publishing) and its online daily newsletter (see Appendix I) will turn you on to stories about the book business.

Immerse yourself in the business and culture of books. By doing so, you'll start to see if your idea is viable—if it fits into or extends upon what's already out there. While continuing to read, take your quickly filling Empty Book, which is percolating with your ideas, inspirations and passions, and walk into your local bookstore or library. As you enter, take a moment to notice just how many books are there. If you took the quiz in our introduction, you'll know that approximately 150,000 books are published every year in the United States alone. Not to mention the 50,000 books published by our fine Canadian neighbors. To put this into perspective, note that the film industry releases approximately 400 movies a year. The good news is that you have a much greater chance of getting a book published than getting a movie made. The bad news is that once your book is published, the competition is so vast and so fierce that getting noticed will require heaping helpings of hard work and more than a dollop of good luck.

The visual manifestation of this will strike you as you walk into a big bookstore. Look at how few books are displayed with their covers facing out, and how many have only their thin little spines showing. This means that even if your book is lucky enough to land on the shelves of bookstores, it has to rely on its spine to communicate your very excellent idea and your truckload of passion. Again, ask yourself: Is my idea so compelling that a few words on the spine will scream out, "Read me"?

One of the great things about bookstores and libraries is that industry professionals who live and love books often work there. If you're respectful of their time and steer clear when they're busy, you can learn a tremendous amount from them. Marilyn Paige, the community relations manager of the largest Barnes & Noble in Philadelphia, says, "If someone is polite and persistent, and they call me and tell me they're writing a book, and they want 10 minutes of my time to talk about their book, I'm happy to do it. I can let authors know what people are buying. I can help you with spin for your book, give you new avenues you haven't thought of, help you network your book."

"Read, read, read. Read everything—trash, classics, good and bad, and see how they do it. Just like a carpenter who works as an apprentice and studies the master. Read!"
—William Faulkner

If you use your bookstore like your own private library, researching and reading there but never actually buying a book, don't expect to get advice from anyone. Quid pro quo. Buy books, get advice. Being nice also helps a lot.

Down the line, many booksellers and librarians will be deciding whether or not your idea is compelling enough for them to order your book and take up some of their precious shelf space. And unlike agents, editors and other publishing industry professionals, these people are easily accessible. You can talk to them on a daily basis. In the flesh, no less. And for free. So when you go to the bookstore or library, take time to get to know the people who work there. Many bookstores and libraries have a shelf devoted to staff recommendations. Talk to staff about their selections. See who has interests similar to your own. Now, not everyone is as generous as Marilyn Paige, but when the time is right, ask your librarian and local bookseller what they think about your book idea. As Amanda Cotten, owner of Valencia Books in San Francisco, says, "Booksellers also have an in-the-trenches knowledge of what is or is not selling this year."

Remember, this is not the time to try and convince them that your book would do well. This is just a time to listen.

Reduction: Making the Most of Your Strengths

A reduction is a sauce boiled down to its essence, where it's the strongest, thickest and most flavorful. Now's the moment to take the passions you've listed in your Empty Book and reduce them to two or three, tops, from which you'll choose the one idea that best combines your enthusiasm with your ability to write and sell it.

Make a list of the strengths and weaknesses of each idea according to the following categories and questions, which we'll explain throughout the rest of this chapter and indeed the rest of the book:

- ***Potential costs.*** How much will you have to pay for necessary photographs and/or writing by other authors? Will you need to travel?
- ***Competition.*** What other books like yours are already out there? Is the competition overwhelming?
- ***Audience.*** Who will be interested in your book? Is there a big enough audience?
- ***Marketability.*** Why will your book attract attention from the media and the public? What skills and contacts do you possess that would get the word out? Why will anyone want to sell your book?
- ***The "Why me?" factor.*** Why are you the person to write this book? What do you have to say that's new and different?
- ***Salability.*** Why would a publisher, a bookstore and eventually a reader buy your book?

As you weed through your ideas, mix and match them in your no-longer-empty book. Sometimes an idea just needs to be reshaped, combined with something else or left alone to germinate. For example, Alice Sebold had an idea for a novel but chose first to write a memoir, *Lucky*. The memoir was well received, but the sales were relatively minimal. For her second book, Alice went back to the novel, which incorporated many of the same themes as her memoir. That became *The Lovely Bones*, which has sold millions of copies around the world. *Lucky* also benefited from the success of *The Lovely Bones* and became a #1 *New York Times* bestseller.

PERMISSIONS AND OTHER EXPENSES

Will your book require photographs, illustrations, song lyrics, or excerpts from other books or other people's poems? If so, in all likelihood you'll need permission to use them. Permissions usually require money. Your money. Not your publisher's.

That's why it's necessary to deal with the money/permission issue first, before breaking down everything else. This way, you can figure out if your idea is one you can actually afford to write.

For photographs, you may want to start by calling or going to the Web site of Corbis (the largest photo stock house in the world) to find out their going rate for photographs you might use in your book. This will give you a high-end starting point to figure out your costs. The reason for doing this early research is that sometimes permissions can actually cost more than what you will be paid to write your book. And if you get no advance payment, the costs will all be out of pocket. Your pocket.

Also, getting permissions is a huge pain in both the neck and the keister. If playing detective, administrator and accountant is not your strong suits (or if you can't enlist some unsuspecting family member!), you might consider taking on an idea that does not involve permissions.

As if that's not enough, you'll also need to consider other potential expenses. Will you have to travel for your book? Will you have to hire outside help for research? Will you have to buy supplies for your book (i.e., food for recipe testing, yarn for knitting, lumber and tools for a do-it-yourself book)?

DID THE COMPETITION GET THERE FIRST?

Make sure there isn't another book that negates the value of yours. You may have a blockbuster idea that you know will sell a million copies. But if that book's already been done, what's the point? That said, some competition may demonstrate a public desire for your *kind* of book if it hasn't exactly been done before. Spin the idea in an original way, and publishers may look to the sales of similar books as *proof* that lots of readers are interested in your subject.

So, start making lists of books that are similar to yours. Study these books. Get a feel for your competition. Literally. How are they designed? What do their covers look like? How much do they cost? Are they hardcover or paperback?

Internet bookstores are also great for tracking down the competition. A few years ago, if you wanted to do research on similar books, you had to wade through *Books in Print.* Now all you have to do is go to the icon that identifies books similar to the one you're looking at. *Boom*, you've got five similar books. And five more. And five more. Asking around helps, too—at bookstores and libraries, of course, but also at work, school, parties.

Is your book different enough from the competition that a bookseller and a reader will identify these differences simply by picking up your book, reading the description on its flaps or back and leafing through its pages? If not, you'll have a hard time convincing any publisher that your book should be published.

Be sure to write down in your Empty Book the title, subtitle, author(s), publisher and year of publication for each and every book on your list. This will save you time down the line, when you're developing and submitting your proposal or manuscript.

OVERCOMING THE COMPETITION

In May of 1763, James Boswell ran into Samuel Johnson in the back room of a bookstore. At the time, Johnson was one of the best-known literary figures in England, a prickly, difficult man of enormous fame. But Boswell, basically a nobody at the time, was not intimidated. As a result, Johnson took a shine to him and let him hang around. Boswell asked questions. Boswell listened. While Johnson waxed on about, well, everything.

Boswell became passionate about writing a biography of the great man. But he had so much material, and he really wanted to do it right—which meant taking his time. Other biographies popped up. Boswell despaired that no one would care about his—that his moment had passed. Still, his passion burned on. It took him almost 30 years, but he did finally finish his biography. He put his passion into print, and the book became a huge success. It is still in print over *300 years* later, unlike nearly every other Johnson biography out there. Indeed, Boswell's *Life of Samuel Johnson* (1791) is considered by many to be the greatest biography in history.

WHO'S YOUR AUDIENCE?

Yes, you want to pick an idea that will sustain your excitement for years to come, but you want to make sure it's one that piques the interest of readers. So many times, people begin to write books without giving a thought to their audience. The success of any book—whether it be a critical success, financial success or the kind of success that comes in the shape of a letter that says "your book changed my life"—is dependent on its readers. Every part of the publishing process is designed to get your book into readers' hot little hands. That's why you must get a handle on who your audience is and why they would want to read your book. Stand back from the trees and take a look at the forest where your potential readers live, work and play.

> *"The unread story is not a story; it is little black marks on wood pulp. The reader, reading it, makes it live: a live thing, a story."*
> **—Ursula K. Le Guin**

The more specific you can be about your readers, the easier it will be to reach them. As you consider your ideas, picture the people who might buy your book. Make them come to life in your mind:

- What do they look like?
- Where do they shop?
- How much money do they make?
- What kinds of vehicles do they drive?
- Where do they eat?
- Where do they hang out?
- What TV shows and movies do they watch?
- What magazines do they buy?

Discuss your ideas with members of your potential audience and see if they spark enthusiasm. Think of the world as your own personal market research opportunity and see if the audience you think exists really does. This process will help you not only in writing your book, but also in marketing, publicizing and selling it. And if you try and try but still can't find the audience you thought was out there, perhaps you should consider other ideas.

Gynecologist and UCLA professor William Parker was sincerely distraught over how many women were under- or misinformed about their health. But he knew they were seriously interested in learning more. He was determined to write a book for the women who visited his office every day, as well as the millions of others like them whom he would never get the chance to meet. Thus was born *A Gynecologist's Second Opinion*, written with his wife, Rachel, and now in its second edition. His understanding of his audience also ended up helping his practice. Many women, wanting the kind of compassionate care they found in his book, became his patients.

REACHING THE PUBLIC

Once you've got a fix on your potential readers, the next question is, how will you reach them? Two words: publicity and marketing. *The Oxford English Dictionary* says "publicize" means "draw to public attention; make generally known." Can you do this with your idea? Assuming that your idea is based on something of great interest to you, then it's probably fair to say that you're aware of which magazines, TV and radio shows, newspapers, newsletters and the like are interested in the same subject. Make a list of what you already know. Be as specific as you possibly can. For example, write down the names of local columnists who write about similar subjects. Write down the dates of specific relevant columns. After you've exhausted your existing knowledge, it's back to our very first directive: *Research.* If you're writing about interior decorating, start reading interior decorating magazines, watching all the interior decorating shows on TV, checking out all the Web sites and chat rooms on the subject. Pay attention to the differences among them and think about how your book might be featured on each. Again, go after the obvious targets, but be sure to activate your imagination and be perpetually vigilant to new and interesting ways to penetrate the book-buying landscape. For example, when your interior decorating book comes out, maybe you could offer your services to a charity that helps low-income families build homes. Then maybe you could get some local and national media to do a story on it. Stranger things have happened.

Here are some things to think about:

- Is there anything unique about your book that the media might pick up on?
- What publications might you write an article for?

- Which magazines might run an excerpt from your book or do an interview with you? (Think broadly but realistically here. Everyone wants *New York Times* coverage; however, it's better to show a publisher what you have a really good shot at than what you wish for in your wildest dreams.)
- What kinds of organizations might be interested in your book? Do they have publications that might review your book or interview you?
- Are there universities, unions or charities that will cotton to you and your book?
- What kinds of events can you see yourself putting on for your book?
- Is there anything about these events that could be considered newsworthy?

Back to your decorating book: Maybe you could do an event at a home-improvement store where you can show potential readers how to use your techniques and then sell your books at the store. Maybe you could hold a contest for booksellers where the winner receives a free home makeover. Hey, why not?

WHO ARE *YOU* TO WRITE YOUR BOOK?

Now it's time for some honest self-assessment. Do you really have something new to say? Something only *you* can put into words? Neil Sofam, owner of San Francisco's A Clean Well-Lighted Place for Books, says, "The thing I notice with successful authors is that they have a unique voice that communicates to their audience. They touch you in some way. You know immediately who's speaking because they're so distinct." Yes, there are authors who don't seem to have a unique voice yet somehow manage to publish quite successful books. But many, many people spend years and years writing and trying to market books that end up as recycled paper precisely because they've failed to capture their uniqueness on the page. And those who fail often become bitter and frustrated, sliding sadly into desperate lives of drugs, booze and literary criticism.

Which gets us back to your idea. Is it so compelling that a person will plop down $25 of his hard-earned money for a copy of your book? Now is the time to put to good use whatever bits of self-knowledge you possess. Consult your therapist, your inner children, your guru and as many other people as possible. And not just your mother and friends who believe that nothing but sunshine pours out of you.

The more you know in your heart that you are the perfect author for your book, the better your chances of convincing someone else. Remember: Every day, another writer nobody ever heard of gets a deal to publish a book.

WHY WOULD ANYONE BUY YOUR BOOK?

If you feel reasonably satisfied that you've got no major competition, a sizable audience, a good shot at garnering publicity, a whole lotta love for your subject and a good argument for why you're the one to write your book, then you need to ask yourself one last question: Does this book have the potential to sell to a publisher, to bookstores and to readers?

"I never desire to converse with a man who has written more than he has read."
—Samuel Johnson

If you're not sure how to answer this question, you're not alone. Problem is, no one *really* knows the answer to the question "Will this book sell?" Anyone who did would be swimming in money and the envy of all publishing. But because no one does, people in publishing houses are trained to pick ideas apart—to excavate the reasons an idea *won't* work. That's why it's your job to convince them that your book will buck the odds and rake it in. And to make your case, you need to familiarize yourself with what's selling right now, what's sold in the past, and how your idea can be compared and contrasted with successful books in the marketplace. You've got to anticipate any stumbling blocks that might impede the sale of your book and be prepared to counter them. Tit for tat. Lynn Goldberg, CEO of Goldberg McDuffie Communications, one of the leading public relations agencies in publishing, puts it this way: "From the beginning, you must consider yourself an author and think like a publisher. You can't come into the world of publishing a total virgin. The good thing is that with this attitude you're neither helpless nor hopeless."

How do you know what's a hotty and what's a notty? Start by regularly reading the bestseller lists in *The New York Times*, *USA Today*, *Publishers Weekly* and your local paper. Because many bestselling books do not end up on bestseller lists, you'll also need to check out the top-selling books overall and the top-selling books within your category (gardening, mysteries, history, whatever) on online bookstores. Familiarize yourself with what has been successful

THE ART OF BECOMING A LITERARY LION

If you're writing literary fiction, you're probably wondering how in the world you might convince a publisher, a bookseller or a reader to buy your book. Sure, there are trends in the world of literary fiction. But let's face it, literary fiction is a lot harder to pitch than the newest fad diet.

Contemporary literary fiction is, sadly, read by few and doesn't attract the media attention that so many other categories of books profit from. Because it's difficult to get recognition for literary fiction, agents, publishers and booksellers tend to look for what literary journals you've already been published in to determine if you're worthy of representation, publication or room on their bookshelves.

Most people have never heard of these literary journals, even the very best of them, and their circulation numbers are often minuscule when compared to magazines like *Glamour, People* and *Newsweek.* But the top journals (and many smaller journals) are publishing our future literary stars. And those in literary circles look to these journals for a stamp of approval. That's why it behooves all writers of literary fiction to submit writing to respected journals prior to embarking on a book project. This is just what Caroline Leavitt, the author of eight novels including *Girls in Trouble,* decided to do. "I had been sending out dozens and dozens of short stories to little literary magazines and getting nothing but rejections," she says. "As soon as I got a story back, I redid it and sent it out again. Finally, the rejections started getting a little nicer. Instead of form letters, it would be 'Hmmm, interesting. Try us again.' Finally, I got a story published in the *Michigan Quarterly Review.* Two weeks after it was published, I got a letter from an agent in New York City asking if I had an agent and did I have a novel. I was flabbergasted and signed on immediately."

You can see from Caroline's experience just how much weight the best of these journals pull! To find out more about which journals to submit your work to, get yourself a copy of Writer's Digest Books' indispensable annual guide, *Novel & Short Story Writer's Market.*

and what has stayed successful over the years. Go to bookstores and libraries and look at copyright dates. Talk to booksellers and librarians. If you see books about Abe Lincoln popping up on bestseller lists, filling your local bookstore shelves and consistently appearing in the History sections of online bookstores, and you've got a new angle on ol' Abe, then chances are you've got a salable idea. On the other hand, if you're contemplating a subject that can be found only in specialized bookstores, think twice before moving ahead, unless, of course, you're okay with your book being sold in limited outlets only.

Certain stores will not sell your book if it has particular words or situations that they believe will offend their customers. Unfortunately, there is a long and glorious tradition of people condemning books simply because they're controversial or contain language deemed inappropriate. Everything from *Uncle Tom's Cabin* to *Harry Potter* has been banned and burned. So, if you're going to write a book that has controversial situations or potentially offensive language, you might find it more difficult to sell your book to a publisher. However, if your book has these kinds of situations and language, it will also attract a certain kind of audience. You may have to work extra hard to find your readers.

The more research you do, the more you'll notice that certain kinds of books sell over and over. There's a famous story about British humorist Alan Coren, who claimed that the most successful, perennial themes in publishing were cats, golf and Nazis. To put his claim to the test, he wrote a collection of essays entitled *Golfing for Cats.* When it was published, Coren made sure that its cover pictured a cat putting on a green—with a Nazi flag flying above the hole!

What's hot is always changing, so it's your job to know which way the wind is blowing. Research. Bestseller lists. Web sites. Readings. Reviews. Movie deals. Studying the business you want to be part of will help you enter and succeed there.

WRITERS IN SEARCH OF IDEAS

If you've come to the end of this chapter and found that despite your mad skills you've got no salable idea for a book, don't despair. You could look for people to write a book with. A famous local figure who's still unknown to the rest of the world. An expert in a field that you have a particular interest in. Someone you know who has a great idea but no writing skills. Jessica Hurley has written numerous books, including *One Makes the Difference* (with famed activist Julia Butterfly Hill). She got her start by sending her resumé to an author care of the publisher's address. "I had seen the author's gift book series," she says, "and I thought the concept was right up my alley. The author liked the fact that I took the initiative and called me for an informational interview. We hit it off right away, and I started off by making lists of ideas for each of the titles, and then began writing for the series. Eventually, I ended up managing them."

Another way to build up name recognition in the industry without having an idea of your own is to contact a packager. Packagers produce books, taking projects from idea to ready-to-print files. Since they invent ideas in-house, they often use writers-for-hire to complete their projects. They don't pay well (you typically get a flat fee with no royalties), but you'll get great experience and some excellent resumé fodder. And the packager will be the one to worry about the competition, audience, marketing and publicity, so you can just concentrate on writing. Oftentimes, packagers will put your name on the book (though the copyright will probably be in their name), which is a nice added bonus. It's a great way to get your metaphoric foot into the very real publishing door.

CHAPTER 2

THE PERFECT PACKAGE

"There is one rule for business and this is it: Make the best quality of goods possible."

—Henry Ford

Even if you're a professional builder, you still need help building a house. So it is with building a book, only instead of a painter, a plumber and an electrician, you'll need an agent, an editor and a publisher. But to get to any of these people, you must put together a package so perfect that it will make a jaded publishing professional perk up. For nonfiction writers, this means an airtight proposal consisting of everything from a bang-up bio to an outstanding outline. For fiction writers, it means an entire manuscript, along with a few bells and whistles.

Either way, in order to prepare this package, you'll need a steadfast support team, a top-notch title and maybe even a doctor in case your proposal or manuscript gets sick.

SELECTING YOUR DREAM TEAM

One of the ironies of the book business is that while writing is generally a solitary art, the publishing process is all about assembling a great team. Linda Bubon, co-owner of Women & Children First, an independent bookstore in Chicago, says she's noticed a common thread among successful authors: "They involve others in their work. They send drafts out to friends. They solicit advice from friends. They are part of writing groups. They take workshops with other writers. They go to readings and support other writers. They make other people feel that they're part of the process. Writers who never leave their garrets rarely make successful books."

We can't tell you how many times we've heard, "I never could have finished my book without my writing group." Particularly for those writing fiction, creative nonfiction or poetry, writing groups and writing partners can be a great source of inspiration, constructive criticism and support in that we're-all-in-this-together kind of way. Many people have a hard time starting a project (especially one as big as a book), and an even harder time maintaining motivation. So if you have that sinking woe-is-me-I-can't-even-get-started-and-when-I-do-what-will-I-do feeling, find some kindred spirits to march down that long and winding road with you.

"Keep away from people who try to belittle your ambitions. Small people always do that, but the really great make you feel that you, too, can become great."
—Mark Twain

The fact is, it's nigh impossible to be a brilliant writer, excellent editor, superb proofreader, master marketer, salesperson extraordinaire, graphics genius and perfect publicity person all at once. That's why you need to build a team. Your first draft pick, if at all possible, should probably be anyone you know who's actually in publishing. Beyond that, look for people who are erudite, enthusiastic, business-savvy, articulate, selfless readers of books like yours; graphically/visually acute; fab proofreaders . . . and nice enough to tell you when you've got a bit of food on your lip without making you feel like a miserable loser. Start assembling your team early. Prepare to barter for services. According to the Putting Your Passion into Print Etiquette Guide, it's always a good idea to reward people generously whenever they do anything for you.

If you're despairing because you don't know a single soul to fill any of these roles, have no fear. We'll show you where these people are and how to find and woo them. And if all else fails, and you can't find anyone, at least you'll know what all the jobs are so that you can go about doing them on your own as best you can.

Picking Partners: "Help, I Need Somebody!"

Are you a professional-caliber writer? A harsh question, but a necessary one. And if you don't think you can answer it, you may want to turn to your closest friend—or anyone else you can trust to be honest with you.

Unfortunately, neither you nor anyone else in your immediate circle may have the expertise to know whether you've got what it takes. If you're feeling unsure or you're having trouble getting started, staying the course or being a finisher, you might want to bring in a hired gun in the form of a coauthor, cowriter, ghostwriter, writing coach, outside editor or professional reader. These people can help you at every turn, from picking the right idea to starting it up, from finishing your proposal to writing the best book you can.

If you've got the money, hiring a professional could be dollars well spent. Someone who really knows his stuff—and the industry—can give you a major edge over your competitors. This is especially true if you're writing genre fiction such as mystery, romance or true crime for the first time. Genre fiction has hard-and-fast rules that you may be completely unaware of but that a professional writer or editor will know inside out. With a little help, your novel can go from one of promise to one that contains the ingredients of bestsellerdom. All work can benefit from a professional eye, but not to worry if you can't afford one. You'll just have to outsmart (and outresearch) your wealthier counterparts.

What distinguishes a coauthor from a cowriter? A writing coach from an outside editor? Here's a cheat sheet to help you get a handle on the nomenclature:

- A ***coauthor*** brings equal and/or complementary knowledge and expertise to the table. Coauthors may be professional writers, but if so, they usually already have a book or two under their belts and are schooled in the subject at hand. Coauthors generally get equal credit on a book cover—same-size lettering, same line. They typically split all money 50-50, although every deal is different.

- A ***cowriter*** is usually a previously published writer who's in the mix primarily to write—not to provide information or research. Cowriters usually get their names on the cover, but often in smaller type and underneath the primary author's name. They generally split all advance dinero up to a percentage of 50-50, but may get a lesser percentage of royalties paid from books sold. Sometimes cowriters get paid a flat fee broken down into two parts: a fee to write a proposal and then a fee for the book itself if it sells to a publisher. Sometimes cowriters are given a guarantee for a certain amount. And, hold on to your hat, sometimes this guaranteed amount can actually turn out to be more than 50%—even up to 100%—of an advance.

- ***Ghostwriters*** are typically, but not exclusively, hired for celebrity autobiographies or other works "penned" by famous folk. Ghostwriters are brought in to make readers believe that the person whose name appears on the cover has written what's inside the book. Great ghostwriters are able to capture other people's voices with uncanny perfection. Even some mega-bestselling commercial fiction authors use ghostwriters to churn out book after book, without actually having to write them. Nice work if you can get it, being a well-paid author and not having to actually write anything! Naturally, ghostwriters, being ghosts, don't get their names on the cover, but often you can find them in the acknowledgments. Ghostwriters are typically paid up front to write a proposal and are often guaranteed a certain amount of money to write the book. Sometimes they get a percentage of an author's royalties. Often not. Sometimes they're brought in if a deadline is looming huge and the author won't be able to get the book done on time. Or maybe an author is just stuck. Or maybe an author or publisher wants someone to add some panache, punch and pop to a manuscript. If this is the case, hiring a ghostwriter may be just the ticket.

- A ***writing coach*** works with a writer over a period of time, often until the book is sold—or until the money runs out. A good coach will know when to give you a pat on the back and when to give you a swift kick in the behind. She'll hold your hand and midwife your book into the world. She'll help set up a schedule and make sure you stick to it. She'll help you with everything from large structural issues to delicate turns of phrase. She'll help you define and refine what you're trying to say and make sure you're saying what you really mean. A good coach will be a combination cheerleader, taskmaster, master editor, plot guru, devil's advocate, guardian angel and powerhouse motivator. Most writing coaches are paid by the hour, anywhere between $25 and $150 an hour, depending on their level of experience and expertise.

- ***Outside editors,*** a.k.a. book doctors, diagnose, treat and help you fix your book. Many outside editors have worked in publishing and know the ins and outs of proposals and manuscripts. For a fee, the good ones will identify the strengths and weaknesses of a manuscript and suggest ways to correct its flaws and enhance its best qualities. Their fee depends on their degree of expertise, how fast they're expected to get the work done and whether it's a cosmetic nip and tuck or radical open-heart surgery. Hourly rates typically begin at $50 per hour, but a hefty edit of an entire manuscript could cost you $25,000. Again, all fees depend on the editor's level of experience as well as the amount of work involved.

- ***Professional readers*** write evaluations that assess the commercial potential of a manuscript or proposal. They can give you an objective opinion of how your writing will fare in the marketplace—for a one-shot price of between $25 and $1,000. The high end is reserved for professional editors who are hired solely for this kind of evaluation.

Where to Find Your Perfect Partner

If you know you want professional help and you've got money to throw around, you can hire someone who's not only great but has publishing connections. While this won't guarantee you an agent or a publisher, it certainly can't hurt. But whether you have a little or a lot to spend, you can find the help you need by returning to principle #1: Research, Research, Research.

If you're in the market for a writing coach or outside editor, the first place to look is in the acknowledgment sections of published books. What we like about this method is that the published book is proof of the person's expertise. Which is exactly what we don't like about using the Internet. You just don't know if people who claim they're experienced publishing folk really are. So if you venture onto the Web, make sure your shyster detector is switched on. Another great place to look for writing coaches or outside editors is in the continuing education departments of the best universities in your neck of the woods. Many professional writers teach classes in these departments, and many of them work as writing coaches or outside editors on the side.

If you're in the market for a professional reader who won't break the bank, we think your local bookstore is a great place to look for one. Is there someone who's been there a long time? Someone you rely on for recommendations? Who thoroughly knows the category your book falls into? If so, this person will more than likely make a great reader.

If you're looking for a coauthor, cowriter or ghostwriter, start reading magazines and newspaper articles, Web sites, literary journals and books with coauthors or cowriters. And check out *Literary Market Place*, a great place to find industry professionals. Make a list of writers who seem appropriate for your book. Find out everything you can about them. What else they've written. Where they went to school. What their passions are. Many writers have Web sites, which can reveal much about them. The more you know about them, the better it will go when you make your approach. Use your bio, audience, competition, marketing and promo info from Chapter 1 to woo said writer by letter, e-mail or phone call. Even with shallow pockets, if you have a great idea and you describe it well, you'll have a good shot at hooking a professional writer. Why? Because many writers spend their days 1) looking for work, and 2) trying to dream up great projects. Many will forgo up-front money for a bigger share of the overall cabbage if they think something has a good shot at selling to a publisher. And if you team up with an experienced writer, you automatically catapult yourself into the ring of serious publishing contenders.

If you're considering going after an agent before a cowriter, consider this: An agent can often introduce you to a writer. And if you want to get an agent first, proceed to Chapter 3 and have at it. But be forewarned, you better have a big profile, a substantial press kit and a perfect pitch if you expect a callback, especially if you don't have a proposal to show.

Hiring the Right Writers and Excellent Editors

According to the Putting Your Passion into Print Guide to Finding Good Help, you've got to hire top-notch professionals to get top-notch assistance. So, how do you know if you're getting high-end help or low-down bottom-feeders? Naturally, you'll want to ask the typical informational questions: May I have a list of references? How much do you charge? How do you work? Also ascertain the person's previous publishing experience: Have you worked with a major publisher? If so, which one(s)? Doing what, and for how long? Do you have an agent? Do you know any agents, or anybody who knows any agents? What books and/or articles have you written? Have you written and/or sold a book proposal? Do you have publisher contacts to share? Ask for samples of the person's work. Only a true schmo would hire a writer whose writing he had not read.

After you've asked questions, let the writer/editor/writing coach prove to you that he or she is the right person for the job. The best of these people know what sells. They know the language of books. They should be able to give you a sense of why they can or can't help you. And if they can help you, they should be able to tell you exactly how this will happen and for how much. If you're going after a coauthor/writer and you don't have money to pay someone up front, let the person know from the get-go that you're willing to go 50-50 on everything in exchange for no up-front fees.

MODELS FOR SUCCESS

Imagine trying to put together a jigsaw puzzle without a picture. Not impossible, but really, really hard. So it is with a book. Before writing your proposal or manuscript, it helps to have a model—a successful book similar to yours in theme, style and/or approach. You're going to use your model to prove that your book-to-be will succeed. And you're going to learn from your model how to make it so.

When locating a model, there are two rules: 1) Your model must be or have been successful, and 2) Your model must be *similar* to your book in content or form, but not *directly competitive.* A model is all about success by association. For example, if you want to sell a book about Peruvian mud sharks and heart disease, you wouldn't choose as your model a bestselling book about Peruvian mud sharks and heart disease. You might, however, choose a bestseller on Peruvian mud sharks and liver maladies. Or a bestselling book on heart disease and hammerheads. Look, if you're proposing a book that's already out there, editors and agents will naturally question the need for your book. Whereas, if you're proposing a book that's *like* your model but *different* in some key way, it will make them excited to sell your book to those same readers.

If there are no models for your book's success, you have a real challenge. Bookstores shelve their books within particular categories like history, religion and cooking. And within each category there are subcategories. If you take cookbooks, for example, you're likely to find international, vegetarian and quick-and-easy subsections. In other words, if your book doesn't fit into a main category or subcategory, bookstores won't know what to do with it.

To be clear, not fitting into *any* category is different from straddling two categories and residing comfortably in each. A biography of Rosa Parks could fit easily into a bookstore's Biography section as well as the African American, Women's Studies and American History sections. And plenty of books start within an overall category and end up establishing new subcategories in many bookstores. Books on feng shui, which were first published under the general umbrella of home decorating, are a good example of this phenomenon; they got so popular that they now have their own subcategory. But if your book doesn't fit squarely into at least one category, you're probably going to find yourself slamming into brick walls. Because booksellers, particularly large booksellers, don't know what to do with category-free books, they simply don't order many of them. This means that very few publishers will publish them. If you think your book might fit into the "no category" category, be sure to talk to as many booksellers as possible before you proceed.

Similarly, if no books even remotely related to yours have made good money, it's going to be difficult to convince a publisher that yours is about to start a trend. A well-known writer who would prefer to remain nameless was in a publisher's office pitching a book. When he was done and the editor asked him what book of theirs it was like, the writer said it was not like any book they did. The editor gave him a quizzical look and said, "Well, we don't do books like that."

SUPERMODELS ARE NOT BEAUTIFUL AIRHEADS

Paul Davidson wrote a series of letters to America's largest corporations, asking them ridiculous questions or offering ludicrous suggestions about their products. Equally absurd replies returned. Paul suspected that a collection of these letters would make a goofy and offbeat book. He also knew that there was a model for his book in *The Lazlo Letters* by Don Novello (a.k.a. Father Guido Sarducci), a collection of humorous letters to politicians that became a major bestseller in the early '80s and is considered, all these years later, a comedy classic. Paul's book was a terrific twist on the original idea—*The Lazlo Letters* for corporate America.

Paul studied his model carefully, learning from its strong points as well as identifying what he could do better. Which brings us to another important point about models. As helpful as it is to have a good model, you must have the goods to back it up. You want an agent or editor to read your material and think, "Yes, the new *Winnie-the-Pooh!*" or "That's like *Men Are from Mars, Women Are from Venus,* but even better!" Paul had the model and the goods. That's why *Consumer Joe: Harassing Corporate America, One Letter at a Time* sold to a publisher lickety-split.

PERFECTING YOUR PITCH

Every book makes a promise to its readers: to educate, to challenge, to humor, to romance, to inspire, to entertain. What does your book promise?

A pitch must take your promise and deliver it in under a minute. The beauty of a major league pitch is that it contains the juicy essence of your book, it's over in no time at all and it leaves the crowd oohing and aahing in awe. Hey, most people are willing to give you a minute. In that time, you want the person you're pitching to say, "Wow, I can't wait to read that book!" or "I never thought of that before!" or "I know someone who would really love that book!"

A beautifully crafted pitch is a skeleton key that will open many doors. You may want to frame your pitch in Hollywoodese, using something like the following:

> *The Godfather* meets *What About Bob?* = *Analyze This*
> *Jaws* in outer space = *Alien*
> *Romeo and Juliet* in the inner city = *West Side Story*

Here are examples from the publishing world:

> *The Catcher in the Rye* with Asberger's = *The Curious Incident of the Dog at Night*
> *Pride and Prejudice* in modern London = *The Diary of Bridget Jones*
> *Winnie-the-Pooh* meets the *Tao Te Ching* = *The Tao of Pooh*

There are other variations on this theme as well:

> "The _______ with/without _______,"
> "The _______ for _______" or
> "The _______ of _______."

For example, Mark Bittman's *How to Cook Everything* is "*Joy of Cooking* for the 21st century"; Jon Krakauer's *Into Thin Air* is "*Alive* without the cannibalism." If you borrow from a familiar title, you don't have to explain your promise, because people already know what the "it" is. Take this book. We pitched it as "the *What to Expect® When You're Expecting* of publishing." People think of *What to Expect®* as the leading reference book for women who are looking for friendly, in-depth advice on the entire pregnancy process, written by people who have been through it—who know what you'll be feeling because they've felt it. By associating our book with *What to Expect®*, we were promising the same sort of in-depth, in-the-know, full-spectrum advice. The only adjustment our editor had to make was to replace "pregnancy" with "publishing."

No matter how you craft your pitch, it should make the listener want to buy and read your book. Your pitch should entertain and delight, pique interest or give pause, depending on what kind of promise you need to deliver. If your book doesn't fit into a formula, that's fine, too. One of our favorite pitches was for *Why God Won't Go Away: Brain Science and the Biology of Belief* by Andrew Newberg, Eugene D'Acquili and Vince Rause. Here it is: "Did God create the brain? Or did the brain create God? The answer to both these questions is a resounding 'Yes!'" This pitch is quick as silver. It uses intriguing questions and an unexpected zinger of an answer to reel readers in. It makes people want more.

Be careful about putting yourself in the company of great and famous authors. "Early Philip Roth with a dash of Jane Austen" can't stand alone as a pitch. You're sure to turn someone off if you compare yourself to literary giants. Instead, construct a pitch that specifically explains how your book will speak to the audience of those uber-authors: "What happens when the repressed male sexuality of Alexander Portnoy meets the strong-minded, spunky joie de vivre of Elizabeth Bennett? Watch the sparks fly in *The Shiksa of Herefordshire,* a new twist on the old battle of the sexes."

Because the first pitch you develop (yes, there will be more intricate pitches down the road) is only one to three sentences long, those sentences better be jam-packed and drum-tight. A pitch is all about economy. Once you've figured out the words, you've got to practice your delivery. Rehearse on your own, then start pitching everybody, everywhere. Your pitch will be both the backbone and lifeblood of your book from this point through and past publication. You will use it to attract agents, editors, the media, booksellers. And they in turn will use it to sell your book all over the world.

The more often you pitch, the sooner you'll know what works and what doesn't. If people look confused, bored or nonplussed, take this as a clue that your pitch needs fixing. Sometimes it's as simple as reordering your words or trimming some fat. Get feedback. Keep refining your pitch until it rolls trippingly off your tongue. Until people who hear or read it want to be in business with you and your idea. As Valerie Lewis, co-owner of

Hicklebee's in San Jose, California, says, "You have to pitch in a way that eliminates the possibility of getting back the word 'No.'"

GETTING TITULAR: TITLES AND SUBTITLES

America's most famous B-movie meister Roger Corman often used to come up with the title and the poster for a movie *before* the story. And his movies always made money. Corman understood the value of a great title, and you should, too. In some cases, a great title and/or subtitle alone can result in a book sale.

Titles can be metaphoric like *What Color Is Your Parachute?* or practical like *101 Ways to Cook Chicken.* They can be clever like *Lies, and the Lying Liars Who Tell Them,* poetic like *I Know Why the Caged Bird Sings* or silly like *Captain Underpants.* It doesn't really matter how, but your title must make readers want to pick up your book, buy it and read it. And for nonfiction it must express clearly what's inside your book. *Men Are from Mars, Women Are from Venus* is a terrific title because it's clever and intriguing, and it states a point of view that many humans intuitively relate to. It does so in one line. And it lets readers know what they'll find between the covers.

> *"A good title should be like a good metaphor: It should intrigue without being too baffling or too obvious."*
> **—Walker Percy**

Here's one of our all-time favorite titles, which you're going to hear a lot more about shortly: *No Plot? No Problem!: A Low-Stress, High-Velocity Approach to Writing a Novel in 30 Days.* We love this title because it strikes just the right note of freewheeling whimsy and rock-solid information. The subtitle lets people know exactly what the book is, while the main title communicates both the gist and the hilarious tone of the book. A common mistake authors make is choosing a title that has a particular meaning to them but that no one else understands. Choosing a title that sounds good but doesn't clue readers in to what's great about the book is also dumb.

A good technique for finding a title and/or subtitle is to write down all the forms of speech of key words relating to your book. For example, if you want to use the word "receive" in your title, also write down "receiving," "reception" and "receiver." Then put all the words into columns based on their part of speech—noun, verb, adjective, adverb. Play mix-and-match.

When you're looking for a title, get lots and lots of opinions. Write your options on a piece of paper (so your bias is not revealed) and show them around. Go to your support team or writing group. Ask people you think would be likely to buy your book—that includes booksellers and librarians. Have brainstorming sessions. Sometimes the title is lying right there; you just can't see it. But be forewarned: Other people's opinions can confuse matters. Arielle frequently has clients who've settled on a title only to call in a panic and say, "Tom and Dick didn't like it! But Harry loved it! What should I do?" Take the ideas of people you trust, and then go with your gut.

TITLE TORTURE

Rick Beyer had an idea for a popular history book made up of clever, fascinating and little-known stories. Unfortunately, he didn't have a clever, fascinating title to match. He went through approximately, oh, 50 million different ideas, but nothing fit. Just at the point of giving up, Rick said to one of his team members, "Well, there's one I thought about a long time ago, but I don't think it's any good." Hoping for some sort of seed to brainstorm with, she encouraged Rick to say it anyway. "*The Greatest Stories Never Told,*" he said. Not only did she flip her wig over the title, but every publisher his proposal was sent to loved it as well.

The title, a fabulous twist on a common phrase, perfectly captured the idea behind the book. Interestingly, even though Rick came up with this title himself and had always had it in the back of his mind, he didn't have confidence that it was a winner. This is why it's important to share your title ideas. Yes, you'll get a million opinions. But if you've got a great title its greatness will be confirmed by others over and over again.

Indeed, *The Greatest Stories Never Told* sold in a heartbeat and has spawned two sequels. The rest, as they say, is history . . .

THE FACTS ABOUT FICTION

Unless you've recently turned up in the pages of *People* magazine or have already sold a treatment of your unwritten novel to a Big Hollywood Film Studio, chances are you'll need to write the whole enchilada before you start marketing it. This doesn't mean you can't show it to readers a chapter at a time for comments. Just don't start marketing it until you're sure it's as perfect as it can be.

Once you've polished off your fiction manuscript, all you'll need to complete your package is a bio (see pages 54–56), blurbs (page 72) if you can get them and possibly a cover (pages 70–72). If you have a brilliant and/or unusual idea for marketing or publicizing your novel, you'd be crazy not to include that as well. In the meantime, keep reading, because the rest of this chapter touches on all those oh-so-relevant issues that will pop up down the road.

Lastly, we'd like to address the issue of plot synopses. Some editors and agents will never look at such things because they know how difficult it is to boil your book down to a page or two. Others like to scan these first to see if they're even interested in looking at what you've written. Our advice is to include a synopsis if you feel that you've captured the narrative drive of your book and managed to make it seem exciting. If you're unable to do this (and it's particularly difficult with literary fiction), don't submit one with your manuscript. Just wait and see if anyone asks for one.

To master the art of synopsis writing, start reading flap and back cover copy of novels similar to yours. This can be done without leaving home, since most online bookstores include synopses of books.

THE NONFICTION PROPOSAL

Think of writing a nonfiction book proposal as an art form like competitive figure skating. First you must perform the compulsory moves, then you have to dazzle the judges if you want to bring home the gold. And a really snazzy outfit doesn't hurt!

Go back to your Empty Book and look at the page where you identified your audience, your competition, your marketing and publicity opportunities, and why you're the one to write this book. Only now, you're going to put all this information together with succinct, deep and specific information before you wrap it in a nice package with a shiny bow.

Should You Finish Your Manuscript Instead of Writing Your Proposal?

No.

That's the short answer. But please remember that we're talking only about nonfiction here.

There's an old show business adage: Leave 'em wanting more. Publishing is no different. The less information you can give and still make an airtight case, the better. Why? Because publishers, like casinos, live off HOPE. Hope that your book will be reviewed in top-tier newspapers and magazines. Hope that your book will speak to Oprah and, for that matter, that she'll speak for it. Hope that it will quicken the pulses of buyers at bookstores. Hope that it will beat the odds and become a big fat juicy bestseller. Publishers throw a lot of spaghetti at the wall and hope that something sticks. Because when they score a big fat juicy bestseller, they make lots and lots of money.

The chilly reality is that few books get reviewed in top-tier publications, land on *Oprah* or become bestsellers. But you want to keep potential agents and publishers in fantasy mode for as long as possible. Most often this means shorter is better and less is more. If your idea is particularly hot and timely, this may mean going so far as to exclude actual sample chapters from your proposal. However, 95% of the time, publishers are more likely to shell out good money if they read a dazzling sample chapter or two to get the voice and point of view. More than that is rarely necessary. Indeed, it can both harm your chances (if it strays from the agent's or publisher's idea of what the book should be) and waste your time (because the publisher or agent who takes on your project may want you to change large parts of it).

Exceptions to the don't-write-the-whole-nonfiction-book rule: Say you're an English teacher who's writing a popular book about sociobiology. If you have no science background, why would a publisher believe you're qualified to write this book? A proposal alone might not be enough. But maybe you really *do* have something Earth-altering to say. If so, you have a much better chance of convincing people when they can see the finished product.

The other reason to finish a book is simply because, well, you have to. Some people can't complete a part without completing the whole. If you know this about yourself, do what you gotta do. But this doesn't mean you should *submit* a finished book. Instead, follow the guidelines below, picking the best chapters as samples.

Braving the Elements: The Nuts and Bolts of Your Proposal

Good proposals have one thing in common. They convince agents and editors beyond a shadow of a doubt that lots of people will want not just to read your book, but to pay money to buy it. The particular book proposal form we use (our proposal for this book is reproduced in Appendix IV) has been honed over the years by James Levine of the Levine Greenberg Literary Agency, where Arielle is an agent.

The elements include:

- Table of contents
- Overview
- Bio
- Audience
- Competition
- Special marketing and promotional opportunities
- Manuscript specifications
- Outline
- Sample chapters

Each section stands on its own, with its own heading at the top of its opening page. You don't want to begin with a new section in the middle of a page. And no section—with the exception of marketing and promotion, the outline and sample chapters—should be longer than a few pages, double-spaced. And it's best if you can keep the other sections under two. Sometimes a section may be only a paragraph. In other words, keep it short. Keep it tight. Keep it moving.

If you decide to stick with a standard word processing program, you can still make your proposal look better than most. Choose an inviting and readable typestyle (Garamond and Times New Roman are always good stand-bys). Make sure your margins are 1¼" on either side and that your text is unjustified.

We're including an actual nonfiction proposal in this chapter, so you can see what one looks, feels and smells like. We will refer to and analyze it throughout in order to illustrate how to turn your idea into a proposal that will compel people to give you money and publish your book. This proposal was written by Chris Baty for his aforementioned book *No Plot? No Problem!: A Low-Stress, High-Velocity Approach to Writing a Novel in 30 Days*, which can be found at a bookstore near you.

TABLE OF CONTENTS

Start your proposal with the same kind of table of contents that you'd find at the front of any book, including page numbers. This will give an agent or editor a snapshot of your proposal's organization.

Turn the page to see what a table of contents looks like.

TITLE OF BOOK

THE OVERVIEW

Your overview is like what you read on the inside flaps of a hardcover book. It's an extended version of your pitch. It needs to entice and invite while illuminating how your book is unique yet universal, timely yet timeless. It should touch on nearly every proposal part, including your audience and why your book will garner the nation's ovations. Great flap copy is worth its weight in gold. To master this art, read lots of it.

Here's the overview from the *No Plot? No Problem!* proposal:

> When I was 26 years old, I accidentally founded an institution that now produces more fiction than all of America's MFA programs combined.
>
> I blame it all on coffee. National Novel Writing Month (NaNoWriMo) began in a moment of overcaffeinated ambition when I sent out an e-mail to friends, challenging each of them to write a 50,000-word novel in July. Since then, the escapade—chronicled on the *CBS Evening News* and NPR's *All Things Considered* and in dozens of newspaper and magazine articles around the world—has grown to include a high-tech Web site, hundreds of spin-off fan sites and discussion groups, and thousands of enthusiastic participants every year.
>
> Part literary marathon and part rock-and-roll block party, NaNoWriMo is based on the idea that anyone who loves fiction should be writing his own. Not for fame and fortune (though those may come in time). But because novel writing is ridiculously fun once you throw away the rulebook. My rallying cry as NaNoWriMo cruise director (and fellow participant) is simple: No plot? No problem! That low-stress, high-velocity approach has helped tens of thousands of writers set aside their fears and dive headlong into the joys of homemade literature.

> Based on four years of experience as the director of NaNoWriMo, *No Plot? No Problem!* will be a thoughtful, encouraging and fun guide to blasting out a 50,000-word novel in a month.
>
> A resource for those taking part in the official NaNoWriMo event, as well as a stand-alone handbook for year-round noveling, the book will break the spree down into five unforgettable weeks, taking writers from the preparation phase ("If you have children, say good-bye to them now") to the intoxicating highs of Week One, crushing self-doubts of Week Two, critical "plot flashes" of Week Three, and Week Four's victory laps and reluctant reentry into normal life.
>
> Along with the week-specific overviews, pep talks and essential survival strategies, the book will feature checklists, boxed text and anecdotes from myself and other repeat NaNoWriMo winners, i.e., those who completed 50,000 words.
>
> Bursting with can-do literary mayhem, *No Plot? No Problem!* will be the kick in the pants first-time novelists need to jump into the fiction fray, an empowering, creative push from the heart of a wildly successful writing revolution.

Why is this such a good overview? It tells you about the audience, the competition, the market, publicity hooks, even the manuscript specs. But above and beyond all that, Chris makes a profoundly compelling case for why this book will sell. Let's break it down:

1. ***Chris begins with a Big Bang,*** i.e., NaNoWriMo produces more fiction than all MFA programs combined.

2. ***He uses the same playful voice that he plans to use in his book.*** People often write dull, dry overviews, falsely believing that this is like a college assignment where their only job is to get the facts right. Your overview has to be entertaining and informative. Even if you're writing about a very serious subject, you must engage readers.

3. ***You see what an interesting, funny and unusual person Chris is.*** You can tell right away that this guy won't be shy—that he'll be terrific in front of a microphone or camera.

4. ***Chris identifies both a rabid fan base and a wide audience.*** Rabid fan bases often drive a book's success even if their numbers are

relatively small. If you have one, advertise it right up front in your overview, even though you'll repeat it later.

5. ***Chris demonstrates marketing and publicity potential*** by pointing out previous coverage. Even if you've never had any media coverage, be sure to artfully point out how your book is both newsworthy and publicity-ripe.

6. ***It's clear that Chris has thought out every aspect of his book,*** right down to how many words it will be. This reassures publishers that he will be able to pull off what he proposes.

7. ***Chris lets the reader know there's no other book like his out there,*** even though he doesn't say it directly. His voice, and the organization from which the idea sprang, is particular, energetic and hard not to like.

YOUR BIO

Just like your overview, your bio should *not* be a dry, dusty affair. Even more important, it must make the case for why you are the ideal person to write this book and to sell it to the reading public. Whether it's your insider's expertise on a subject, your shockingly compelling life story or your boundless passion for your material, it's up to you to demonstrate why you and you alone are the perfect author for your book. In a page or two. If you've been published, won any awards, been showcased in the media . . . whip all that stuff out. Include any and all information that shows you've got the savvy necessary to publicize and market your book. If you have a Big Time CV, put it in the back of your proposal and pull out the appropriate highlights for your bio. The bottom line is, if you don't toot your own horn, who will?

In one of our seminars, a successful businessman mentioned that he'd been homeless for several years. We told him to put this in his bio because it would show what an unusual and resilient person he is. Can't you just see this story on *Oprah*? Clearly, this is the kind of information you wouldn't bring up in a job interview, but again, it'll set you apart from the hordes of others trying to storm the gates of publishing.

You also want to try and anticipate any problems that publishers may find with your bio. Bill Parker, the gynecologist we mentioned in Chapter 1, has a stellar resumé—great credentials, media experience, the works. He also wrote a proposal that a number of editors said was the best they'd ever seen. But every one of those editors turned the book down. Why? Because Bill was a male doctor writing about women's health. Bill was well aware of this issue in his practice, but he never thought it would be an issue in a situation where he wouldn't be examining anyone. After a second round of submissions, two thoughtful editors (one of whom was the daughter of a male gynecologist) saw beyond this stumbling block and bid on the book. Before publication, Bill opted against a sex change and instead decided to involve his two female partners in the project. As preventive medicine, he mentioned their conributions on the cover. In hindsight, this might have been the thing to do in his proposal from the get-go.

Once again, Chris Baty knew just what to say about himself:

> **Founder and four-time National Novel Writing Month winner,** Chris Baty is the Web's most sought-after writing coach. The 29-year-old Oakland, California, freelance writer has been called "an indie David Foster Wallace with compassion" (*Fabula* Magazine) and has been profiled in newspapers ranging from the *L.A. Times* to the *Chicago Tribune* to the *Melbourne Age,* as well as being featured on NPR's *All Things Considered* and a host of BBC radio programs. When not heading up NaNoWriMo, Baty is usually on the road, covering Louisiana juke joints and Parisian thrift stores for such publications as the *Washington Post,* the *SF Weekly,* the *Dallas Observer* and Lonely Planet guidebooks. His funny, freewheeling style landed him an Association of Alternative Newsweeklies award for Best Music Writing in 2002. Before becoming a full-time writer in 1999, Baty spent several years behind the editing desk, first for Fodor's publications and later as the New York, London and Chicago City Editor for the travel Web site *ontheroad.com.* Baty holds degrees in cultural anthropology and psychology from the University of California, Berkeley, and the University of Chicago. His quest for the perfect cup of coffee is never-ending and will likely kill him someday.

Why is this an excellent bio? It's got awards, it's got Big Names, it's full of writing cred and again it displays in its style a rigor, a vigor, a self-deprecating wit and a sense of rollicking good fun. Let's break it down:

1. ***Chris shows that he's got a wide reach***—he's the most sought-after writing coach on the World Wide Web. He also tells us that he's the founder of National Novel Writing Month, which makes him sound important.

2. ***Information is doled out fast and furious.*** In the very first paragraph, we find out how old Chris is, what he does for a living, that he's been compared to a famous guy and that he's connected to media outlets like the *Los Angeles Times*, the BBC and NPR.

3. ***Chris associates himself with top publications,*** suggesting that his book has a good chance of ending up reviewed and/or covered there.

4. ***He identifies his own style: funny and freewheeling.*** He does this by actually saying it, and by writing his bio in a comparable tone (as illustrated by the inclusion of juke joints and Parisian thrift stores in the copy).

5. ***He establishes his writing and academic credibility.***

6. ***His bio ends with a joke,*** illustrating why it's always good to leave 'em laughing, if you can pull it off.

If, after reading Chris's bio, you feel yours doesn't stack up, do not despair. You, too, can spin a web of magic around your life to make it come up smelling like roses. At first, many people doubt they have anything significant to say in their bio. But if you sit down and make a list of your accomplishments, hobbies and quirks, you'll see an interesting portrait emerge. Have you raised six kids? Did you ever get a hole-in-one? Do you keep chickens in the middle of Manhattan? All these things count as long as they help make the case for your book. One of our favorite bios was written by Dan Kennedy, author of *Loser Goes First.* Dan's book is all about his life as a slacker. So guess what his bio says? "Dan Kennedy lives in New York City." Because, of course, he doesn't have any accomplishments—or so he wants us to believe. Here Dan plays up his sense of humor, which makes perfect sense for his very humorous book.

If you're writing a children's book and are inclined to make a big deal in your bio of how you're a mom or a dad, think twice! Editors get this from every freshman children's book writer, and there's nothing persuasive about it. Just because you have kids doesn't mean you can write for them.

YOUR AUDIENCE

Who's going to read your book? Even more important, who's going to buy your book? Describe your audience—and their motivation to buy—as specifically as possible. Prove to an editor or an agent that people are hungering for your book. There's no better bottom-line proof than the numbers, which is why publishers love them. When Jun Chul Whang, Sun Chul Whang and Brandon Saltz put together a proposal for a book on tae kwon do in 1997, they included the fortuitous fact that there are seven million worldwide practitioners of this particular martial art. Publishers couldn't believe that, given the size of the audience, no major house had ever done a book on the subject. The authors landed a six-figure advance from Broadway Books for *Tae Kwon Do: State of the Art*, in no small part because of the staggering number of practitioners.

What do you know about your audience that a publisher doesn't know? If you say women will be interested in your book, you're not saying much. The question is, which women? If you say women who suffer from depression, then you're getting somewhere. But take it even further. Do they watch *Oprah* or *Ricki Lake*? *Masterpiece Theatre* or reruns of *Friends*? Do they listen to NPR or Howard Stern? Beethoven or Busta Rhymes? Do they read *Real Simple* or *Cosmo*? The latest *Harry Potter* or *The Hours*? Do they drive Range Rovers or hybrids? Do they buy K-Mart or Prada? Are they downhearted baby boomers or despondent Gen Xers? The more specific you can be, the more compelling your argument. Again, it's your job to prove there are readers who will buy your book and to show conclusively who they are. You do this by creating an on-the-money profile of your audience that will blow away even the most skeptical publishing person.

Let's check in with Chris to see how it's done:

The numbers tell the story

NaNoWriMo grew from 21 participants in 1999 to 14,000 in 2002. With a minimum of 25,000 participants expected in November 2003, the built-in market for *No Plot? No Problem!* is sizable, international and annually recurring. NaNoWriMo participants are, by and large, an inexperienced group, excited by the prospect of writing a novel in a month but daunted by the creative and time-management challenges of the endeavor. Participants have already committed a large chunk of their lives to the event; many would be happy to spend a little money on a handbook that would increase the likelihood of a higher return (read: completed novel) on their investment.

The silver bullet: artistic fulfillment made easier

Readers buy how-to books expecting a silver bullet—a magical formula that makes a daunting activity understandable and achievable. This is exactly what *No Plot? No Problem!* delivers: a results-oriented plan for people who want to nurture their inner artists without getting tangled in time-consuming classes or ongoing writing groups. After one week of the *No Plot? No Problem!* regime, participants will have already written 46 pages of their novel. By delivering huge results in a short time, the book will have instant appeal for busy people who want to experience the creative joys of writing, but who have limited free time to devote to the project before the demands of real life intervene.

Also, by framing novel-writing as a short-term, highly accessible activity for everyone, *No Plot? No Problem!* casts its line out beyond the confines of "serious writers," tapping into the vast demographic of people who have no fiction-writing experience but who feel they have a story worth telling. The structured creativity of *No Plot? No Problem!* will reassure first-time writers that they already possess all the skills necessary to write a rough draft, and that the only thing standing between them and their manuscript is a month's labor.

The book will also appeal to those who may not intend to write a novel, but who simply enjoy the thrill of contemplating the project. Studies have shown that 20% of travel guidebooks are purchased by armchair travelers, those who have no intention of buying a ticket to the destination but who appreciate the thrill of a vicarious visit. I anticipate a similar percentage will pick up *No Plot? No Problem!* for its gonzo tone and uproarious depictions of the psychological states writers pass through on their month-long journey to literary fulfillment.

Success stories will reassure hard-nosed, results-oriented book buyers
Though the focus of *No Plot? No Problem!* is on personal achievement rather than fame and fortune, there is no question the low-stress, high-velocity technique laid out in the book has led to some surprising success stories in the world of publishing, allowing several would-be writers to transition into new lives as successful, full-time novelists. These stories, detailed in the book's final chapter, will increase the allure of the book for results-oriented writers looking for a creative on-ramp into the world of publishing.

Why does the audience section of this proposal work? Because it clearly identifies a die-hard, hard-core audience and then branches out to describe several other large yet specific groups of readers and buyers. Let's break it down:

1. ***Chris starts this section off with numbers.*** Right away, an agent and/or publisher will see how many people are ready to buy this book, and why.

2. ***He talks about the power of the silver bullet*** for how-to book buyers and shows how his book delivers such a bullet in no time at all, hence appealing to the I'm-too-busy-to-accomplish-any-artistic-goals person. This indicates a long shelf life and a continuous need for his book, because there will always be those seeking silver bullets for problems they have no time to solve.

3. ***He differentiates his book from the competition*** (books that apply almost exclusively to the serious writer) and so opens up a new audience for himself: people with absolutely no novel-writing experience but the inclination to give it a try. It's a huge leap in numbers when you go from people who desperately want to write a book to people who have thought at some point in their lives that they might want to write a book.

4. ***He closes strong*** by explaining why a person who is faced with a shelf chock-full of writing books would choose his over another, which leads directly to . . .

THE COMPETITION

Identifying your competition has two primary purposes: to prove that no one has published the same book as yours, and to associate your book with books that have been successful. In the first case, you need to state quickly and clearly why your book is *different*. In the second case, you'll want to state quickly and clearly how your book is *similar*. Remember, there must be something compellingly similar about your book and a successful book. Otherwise, the comparison is meaningless and your argument specious.

Go back to your preliminary search of the competition. Get back online to fill in your outline and broaden it out. For example, go to your favorite online bookseller and plug in key words in the search field (like "Tae Kwon Do" and "Martial Arts" if you're doing a tae kwon do book) and see what comes up. Once you've found a book that's a good match, double-click on the title so that you get all its information. Be sure to go to the screen that gives you all the publishing info, reviews, and so on. Scroll down until you get to a feature that says, "People who bought this book also bought . . ."

Following this lead will take you to many other appropriate titles. Aim for at least 5 books and stop at 25. Even if your search leads you to dozens of books, you're not likely to come up with more than 25 that fit squarely into our definition of competition.

SEPARATING THE BIGS FROM THE LITTLES

If you're submitting to a major publisher, it's only necessary to track down titles published by major or midsize companies. Sometimes this can be difficult, because almost every major publisher has numerous imprints that may look like small presses. If you have an actual book in front of you, look on the copyright page. If the book was published by an imprint of a larger house, it will identify the larger house. For example, if the book was published by Riverhead, you'll see on the copyright page that Riverhead is a division of Penguin. To help sort out big from little, see the list of major and midsize publishers and their divisions and imprints in Appendix II.

After you've made your final list, go back once again and ask around at your local bookstore or library. Sometimes librarians and bookstore people may be able to help point you to obvious titles you've missed. In all cases, you must identify the publisher and author of each book and the date it was published. In a short paragraph, describe the book(s) at hand. Say why your book will succeed where the competition has failed, speak to an aspect of your subject that the competition has not or appeal to the same core audience.

Don't trash the competition. You may want to send your proposal to the publisher of one of your competitive books, and if you slag their book, they may not want to play with you.

Call us old-fashioned, but we think it's a very good idea to actually read the competition. That way, you'll really know what you're talking about when you write this important piece of your proposal.

Let's check out Chris's competition section:

Writing vs. writing well

Bookstore shelves are overflowing with tomes from well-known authors quibbling over the tenets of good writing. *No Plot? No Problem!* does not teach good writing. From my work as a writer and editor, I have come to believe that the most valuable writing lessons are self-taught, and that the most beautiful pieces of literature begin as mediocre pieces of crap.

No Plot? No Problem! is essentially a personal trainer in book form, a wise-cracking coach who sits down with would-be writers each night for 30 days and gives them the permission they need to make messes and the encouragement they need to keep going.

A pan-genre approach to taskmastering
Unlike craft-based books, where the author's opinions on timing, semantics and plot development may miss the mark for certain genres, the tactics and strategies of *No Plot? No Problem!* work regardless of novel niche. And unlike the overly broad books for novice writers that cover everything from brainstorming protagonists to handling royalty checks, *No Plot? No Problem!* brings all of its taskmastering to bear on the first and highest hurdle: surviving the first draft.

The miraculous power of a deadline
Finally, where several of the books below give writers assignments on getting started (3 pages a night, 15 minutes a day, etc.), none of them offers a clear-cut stopping point. The value of a deadline—and a contained writing period—cannot be overstated in helping novice writers pull off the mammoth (and at times painful) task of extracting a novel from themselves. The looming 30-day cut-off in *No Plot? No Problem!* helps keep writers motivated, focused and on track.

Along with the range of books that have used the time-tested motivational strategy of a month-long exercise (*30 Days to a More Powerful Vocabulary, The 30-Day Low-Carb Diet Solution, Successful Business Planning in 30 Days,* etc.), complementary titles on writing include:

Immediate Fiction: A Complete Writing Course by Jerry Cleaver (St. Martin's Press, 2002, $24.95). Simple, straightforward advice on everything from plot strategies to book marketing, written in a reassuring tone from the founder of The Writers' Loft in Chicago. Expounds on the joys of messy first drafts and offers the timeless insight "the less you care, the better you write."

Bird by Bird: Some Instructions on Writing and Life by Anne Lamott (Anchor, 1995, $12.95). Inspiring book avoids the quagmire of revision advice and offers humorous insight about the realities of the writing life (including several sections on the utter necessity of not taking first drafts so seriously).

The Marshall Plan for Novel Writing: A 16-Step Program Guaranteed to Take You from Idea to Completed Manuscript by Evan Marshall (Writer's Digest Books, 2001, $16.99). Breaks memorable plots down into a series of formulas and concrete charts, and includes information on how to set up a writing area and manage your time while writing.

How to Write a Damn Good Novel by James Frey (St. Martin's Press, 1987, $19.95). A colorfully written, character-centric guide to the novel writing process. Heavily reliant, however, on prewriting.

How to Write & Sell Your First Novel by Oscar Collier with Frances Spatz Leighton (Writer's Digest Books, 1997, $16.99). A somewhat celebrity-focused book takes novice writers on the inspirational path from selecting a genre to finding an agent.

Why does this audience section work so well? Because it clearly illustrates how Chris's book is different from everything else out there. And again, it does so in a gonzo style. Note that Chris decided to put his "why my book is different" info all up front. This is a great thing to do when none of the books on your list is directly competitive. But if you're writing what you claim will be the definitive book on tae kwon do and there's already a book out there that purports to do the same, you'll have to get very specific about your competition. Let's break it down:

1. ***Chris faces his competition head on*** by telling the reader that he's well aware of the vast number of writing books available. Sometimes writers shy away from the truth because they think the competition will hurt their chances of selling their book. Better to bite the bullet and indicate how your book reinvents the mousetrap for the huge pool of mousetrap buyers always looking for the new best thing.

2. ***He's very clear about what differentiates his book*** from the competition. For example, when he talks about the power of the deadline, he's making a specific case for what his book will offer that no other book does.

3. ***He identifies himself with a well-published category,*** yet explains why his book is unique within the category. When he enumerates all those 30-days books, it makes publishers feel warm and fuzzy because they've sold lots of copies of those books.

4. ***He inspires confidence*** by laying out the list of books thoughtfully and carefully. Looking like you know what you're talking about is often more important than really knowing what you're talking about. Not that we advocate the latter.

5. ***He maintains a consistent tone.*** Throughout, he continues to illustrate the zany style of his personality even as he presents information: "most beautiful pieces of literature begin as mediocre pieces of crap." He makes us laugh with his matter-of-fact demystification of art. We can see even here that he'll be a fun interview and put on a good show at events. Which leads directly into . . .

SPECIAL MARKETING AND PROMOTIONAL OPPORTUNITIES

One of the big buzzwords in publishing these days is "platform." *The Oxford English Dictionary* defines "platform" as "a piece of raised flooring in a hall, or in the open air, from which a speaker addresses an audience, on which an artist gives a performance, or on which officials or promoters of a meeting sit; *fig.* an opportunity to make a speech or express an opinion."

Publishers want to know what public venues you can use to make a speech or express an opinion, because of this undeniable fact: The bigger your platform, the greater your chances of getting attention.

Whether you have a big platform, a small one or none at all, you need to convince an agent or editor that you'll make it your top priority to let the public know about your book. The more creative yet concrete your plan, and the more you can show what *you* will do to spread the good word (as opposed to what the *publisher* can do), the better.

Can you get yourself on radio and television, into magazines and newspapers? Do you write a column for your local paper? Do you have regular speaking engagements? Do you ever appear in the media? Are you affiliated with any large groups? Any specific groups your book will speak to? Do you belong to any trade organizations? Do you have a Web site, or are you going to have one? Does your high school, college or graduate school have an active alumni association with a newsletter or magazine?

This is one place where it pays to let the muse flow through you, without resorting to the obvious or the overly pie-in-the-sky. Everyone knows you fully expect that your book will be reviewed in *The New York Times* and that you're a natural for *Oprah.* But unless you have a concrete plan for making that happen, you run the risk of coming off as a rube.

Are you wondering about Chris's marketing strategy? Here it is:

Evangelical participants as advertisers

The NaNoWriMo participants themselves are evangelical advertisers. The growth of the event—which has never sent out a press release or advertised anywhere—has been due primarily to hyperlinked endorsements from a vast network of participants' Web sites and Web logs. These sites would happily promote a book they felt reflected the zany and unique experience that NaNoWriMo provides every year. The incentive of proselytizing for a good cause is further enhanced by the ubiquitous "Amazon.com Rewards" program, which gives Web logs a kickback on any copies of books sold via click-through recommendations.

The primary sales vehicle, though, would be the *NaNoWriMo.org* Web site. *No Plot? No Problem!* could be sold on the site or offered to participants as part of a "donation package," where a donation to National Novel Writing Month would net the donor a free copy of the book. Each year, around 15% of participants donate to the (otherwise free) event. With 30,000 participants expected in November 2004 (the approximate period of the book's release), *NaNoWriMo.org*–facilitated book sales could range anywhere from one to four thousand units, repeatable annually.

NaNoWriMo groups around the world

There are about 50 NaNoWriMo chapters in the U.S., and 15 groups overseas. These groups meet informally throughout the year to swap manuscripts and support each other's writing projects. *No Plot? No Problem!* would serve as a bible for these groups, and, in the case of a promotional tour, they could be counted on to come out and support the founder of the escapade (and hopefully buy a book or three while they're at it).

The joys of annual coverage

Because it makes for a fun human-interest story, NaNoWriMo is widely covered by TV, radio and print media every year. Most of the pieces on the event feature interviews with local participants coupled with quotes from me on the history and current status of the event. This recurrent media attention will be a boon to *No Plot? No Problem!,* creating an annual opportunity to promote the book long after the first publicity push subsides.

Why does this publicity and marketing section rule? Because it shows concretely that there's a terrific grassroots marketing campaign behind this book as well as real opportunities for local and national publicity. It also indicates that new publicity and marketing opportunities will arise year after year because of the annual nature of NaNoWriMo. Let's break it down:

1. ***Publishers love authors with direct access to a core audience.*** Chris leads with this aspect of his marketing juggernaut, which is just the sort of thing that makes publishers drool.

2. ***Chris ties this grassroots appeal to e-marketing.*** By placing the Web site and the Amazon tie-in so centrally, he lets publishers know that he will be exploiting the awesome power of the Internet, and that makes them happy, too.

3. ***He keeps throwing numbers at them.*** He makes a great case for 1,000–4,000 guaranteed sales a year before the publisher has to lift a finger. Granted, this isn't a huge number in publishers' minds, but it's a nice security blanket. The more you can convince publishers that they will sell books without having to do anything, the better your chances.

4. ***He shows that his audience is worldwide.*** An expanding number of groups that meet regularly in America and internationally will buy his book. By bringing in the international angle, he lets publishers know that foreign sales are likely.

5. ***He makes a compelling case for his ability*** to get both big- and small-time media. Pieces that appear in little papers and on tiny radio stations, as well as on national morning television and NPR shows, are the fuel that keeps the media engine purring. And Chris shows how he can get behind the wheel and drive that baby off into the sunset.

YOUR MANUSCRIPT SPECIFICATIONS

What is the approximate word count of your book? Are there any special design features? Will there be illustrations? Recipes? How many? How long will it take you to complete the writing of the book?

It's no surprise that Chris had a way to deal with all this.

The book's format—part travel guide and part survival kit—will echo the fun, adventuresome feel of the novel-writing process. The book will be 45,000 words long and will contain 36 illustrations.

The completed manuscript can be delivered in PC Microsoft Word format within six months of signing of the contract.

Even in this little section, Chris displays the joie de vivre that dances through his proposal!

YOUR OUTLINE

First off, your outline is not a final commitment. At this stage, it's enough to show that you've got a solid working plan for moving ahead. The outline should contain section and/or chapter headings; beneath each heading, you'll need to write up to a few paragraphs explaining what the chapter contains and how it moves the book forward.

Again, your outline should maintain the style of your book. Every part of your proposal must be a great read. Here's a piece of Chris's outline to give you a sense of how it's done:

Introduction

The author offers a personal history of National Novel Writing Month, explaining both the absurd origins of the event and the surprising, life-changing effects it had on the first group of 21 participants.

Chapter 1

Enlightenment is overrated: Why you should write a novel now—16 pages.

For most people, novel-writing is a "one day" event, as in "one day, I'd like to write a novel." This chapter explores why that day never comes for most would-be writers and offers five reasons why the biggest tasks are best accomplished in a minuscule amount of time.

The chapter opens with a list of common reasons people offer for postponing the writing of their first novel. These include:

"I'm waiting until I'm older and wiser."

"I'm waiting until I get fired from my job, so I'll have more time to dedicate to the book."

"I don't have a quiet place to write."

"My plot ideas are all clichés."

"I'm afraid my novel will suck in unpredictably monstrous ways, and I'll be forced to admit that I'm a total failure as a creative individual."

> The author dispels each of these worries, building a reassuring case for the fact that novel-writing is best undertaken as a month-long, anything-goes adventure, where the stakes are low and the rewards are high for writers of all ages and skill levels.
>
> The second part of the chapter delves into those rewards, including the tremendous boost in creative confidence and a deepened understanding of the hell professional writers endure in creating the books we love.
>
> The final part of the chapter explores the supernatural way a deadline enables achievements far beyond our normal powers, and offers a guarantee for would-be writers: Write for two hours a night, five nights a week, and, over the course of a month, aliens will beam a 50,000-word novel onto your hard drive.
>
> Two supplemental boxed texts for Chapter 1 will provide 1) a gauge of how long 50,000 words really is, including a short list of famous 50K novels, and 2) an overview of the magic number 1,666 (the average daily word quota) and about how long it typically takes writers to reach that goal.

Why is this outline so effective? Chris combines his playfulness with a sure-handed description of exactly what the chapters will cover. Appearing to know what you'll be doing gives publishers a sense of security. Let's break it down:

1. ***Chris has thought through every aspect of the book.*** By addressing the components of each chapter (including supplemental boxed texts), he leaves no one guessing.

2. ***His chapter descriptions are only as long as they need to be.*** The introduction necessitated one sentence; Chapter 1 required several paragraphs. Unnecessarily long outlines are not just boring, they're *dangerous*, and if they feel too much like the real book, without communicating the level of information or interest that the real chapter will hold, the publisher may come away thinking your book itself will be thin. On the other hand, if your ideas are highly complex, take the space you need.

3. ***The outline is fun to read.*** We can't overemphasize the importance of this. Not that "fun" has to be the universal descriptor—heartwarming, authoritative, edgy are all legitimate descriptors for a proposal. But you want your proposal to pop.

Chris also does something out of character that we would like to point out. His impersonal references to "the author" lack the intimacy of the rest of the proposal. Not a big deal, but not in keeping with his voice. As a general rule, don't refer to yourself as "the author" anywhere in your proposal. Either keep it in the first person or call yourself by your given name.

FIRST-PERSON PROPOSAL: YEA OR NAY?

If your book will be written in the first person (as in a memoir, for example), it makes sense to write the proposal in the same first-person voice. This will familiarize publishers with the "sound" of your writing. Problem is, not everyone can write an effective bio in the first person. If you can't blow your own horn, use the third person (it will sound as if someone else is saying how great and qualified you are). If you feel that your proposal will benefit from a first-person voice but you're not comfortable with a first-person bio, change the voice for your bio only. That's okay. The same holds true for your overview and special marketing/promotional opportunities sections.

SAMPLE CHAPTERS

You'll need one to three professional-caliber sample chapters, for a total of approximately 20 to 50 pages. Most writers start with the first chapter—it's harder to get a feel for a book when you jump in midstream. But both page count and chapter choice are ultimately dependent on what you think will make the best case for your book.

While the business end of your proposal is the skin and bones, the sample chapters are the heart and soul. They're what agents and editors will look at to see if you have the goods to produce what you say you can. So while a bad overview can hurt your chances of getting published, bad sample chapters will probably kill them dead.

After you've written and rewritten and rewritten, show the sample chapters to your team. Take heed of all their advice and criticism. Listen with open ears and ask smart questions. But ultimately, trust that little person in your head who's always right. (We won't include Chris's sample chapters here, simply to save some space. But you can go check out his book if you're curious about how it turned out.)

BEST FOOT FORWARD

Most agents and editors have thousands of pages stacked on their desks, which means they probably won't read your proposal or manuscript in its entirety unless they're so taken in by the first sentence, first paragraph or first page that they're spurred on to read more. So make sure each of these is spectacular. Don't count on anyone getting to the "heart" of your proposal or manuscript somewhere deep on page 10. Count instead on having about one minute to capture someone's attention.

Spend as much time as necessary to get your first words right. Study the first sentences of great books for inspiration. Arielle's predictable favorite is the classic opening line of Jane Austen's *Pride and Prejudice*: "It is a truth universally acknowledged that a single man in possession of a good fortune must be in want of a wife." And one of our more recent nonfiction favorite first paragraphs is from Jonathan Kozol's *Amazing Grace: The Lives of Children and the Conscience of a Nation*: "The Number 6 train from Manhattan to the South Bronx makes nine stops in the 18-minute ride between East 59th Street and Brook Avenue. When you enter the train, you are in the seventh richest congressional district in the nation. When you leave, you are in the poorest."

Looks Are Everything

If it looks like a book, if it smells like a book, chances are it will become a book. Again, agents and publishers are inundated by books and book ideas. At parties. At dinners. From family, friends, friends of friends, friends of the family, and family of friends. So the more your document can look like a book, the easier it will be for them to see that it should be a book.

ILLUSTRATIONS

If yours is an illustrated book, it can be very beneficial to hire a graphic designer to do between two and five sample spreads, i.e., side-by-side book pages. This typically costs anywhere from $500 to $5,000, depending on the number of spreads and the designer's level of experience. A major investment. However, an illustrated book is all about how it looks. And an agent or editor who has a hard time envisioning the look of your illustrated book is likely to pass on it.

If you go the sample-spread route, the trick is to make sure your spreads have a finished look like a published book. To achieve a profes-

ARE YOU WRITING A CHILDREN'S BOOK?

One of the biggest mistakes authors of children's books make is to submit illustrations with their text. Even if you think your friend or colleague is a master illustrator, hold off making any sort of recommendation about art until after your book is sold. David Allender, a senior editor at Workman responsible for children's publishing, says, "Including illustrations doubles your chances of rejection. If it's essential, include directional sketches." If you're wondering why submitting art could possibly hurt your chances, here's David's explanation: "Children's book editors are a bit like musicians. We can read the score and hear the music in our head, and that's what's exciting. Typically, pictures drain the life out of the text. Of course, the exception is when there are illustrations that are wonderful. But you have a better chance of getting struck by lightning than submitting this kind of quality illustration."

Another question children's book authors face is how educational to make their books. Steven Malk, an agent at Writers House who has represented many of today's top children's authors, says, "The children's book industry is anchored by schools and libraries, so ideally a book will have a strong life in the retail market while also having the support of teachers and librarians. However, your book can't be purely educational." In other words, don't forget the entertainment factor!

Speaking of entertainment, Steven adds a piece of good news for the world of children's publishing, "A lot more attention is now given to children's books because so many have recently been turned into movies." And when Hollywood calls, the publishing industry runs to the phone . . .

sional look, go to a professional. Not just a graphic designer, but a book designer. Preferably a book designer who designs for major publishers. Thankfully, these people can be found. Their names are often listed on the back flaps of books or on the copyright page, and many freelancers have Web sites. Once you've found a designer, let her know if you don't have a deal yet, and she may give you a better price.

COVER DESIGN

Study book design. Find covers that attract the eye. Go to www.aiga.org and look up the 50 Books/50 Covers Award for the year. If you can design a great cover or know someone who can, go for it. If you don't know anyone with these skills (and most people don't), you can contact schools that have

. . . OR A COOKBOOK?

Let's start with your title. Unless you own an established restaurant or catering business, or you have a title that conjures up images that make people's mouths water, your title must announce the focus of your cookbook. Some classic examples are: *The Cake Bible, How to Cook Everything* and *Bistro Cooking*. And unlike other nonfiction proposals, here your table of contents is key. It serves as an outline, rather than just a page locator, so it has to be thoroughly thought out. Instead of just listing soups, salads, vegetables or whatever, you need to be explicit about recipes in the book—not necessarily every single one, but enough to get an agent or editor hungry and interested. An introduction to the book as well as the introduction to an individual chapter should be included in your proposal. If there are sidebars or other bits that will give your book literary flavor, give samples of these as well. And you'll need at least 10 to 15 recipes with headnotes (the little introductory thoughts you'll find at the beginning of a recipe). Keep in mind that the purpose of a headnote is to let your reader know both what makes this recipe different from others and what makes it something you want to try.

Suzanne Rafer, the editor of such all-star cookbooks as *The Cake Mix Doctor, How to Grill* and the *Silver Palate* cookbooks, says, "I like it when someone can title a recipe well and can give information in the headnote that draws me in. Grilled steak I've seen a million times, but tell me something *new* about grilled steak."

As for photos of recipes, 99% of the time they are *not* necessary and may scare off a publisher who prefers line drawings or no illustrations at all. The exception is when your photos are so exquisite, so professional, that they'd leave Jacques Pepin drooling.

Suzanne adds one last piece of advice: "Even if you're the best chef in the world, you have to realize that it takes a lot of writerly invention and imagination to translate what you do in the kitchen to the page. A lot of people are good chefs but not good writers. If you're having trouble getting what you want to say down on paper, be sure to partner up with someone who can reflect your talent and passion."

graduate design programs. For one of his own books, David found a student who created a great cover for $250.

If you decide to include a cover, here's the catch: MAKE IT GREAT OR NOT AT ALL. If it's not a Grade A cover, it will call you out as a rank amateur. The following books have beautiful, elegant, fun and/or vibrant covers that you might want to check out.

A Natural History of the Senses

The Zuni Café Cookbook

Girl with a Pearl Earring

Divine Secrets of the Ya-Ya Sisterhood

The Worst-Case Scenario Survival Handbook

I Married a Communist (hardcover edition)

Everything Is Illuminated (hardcover edition)

These range from covers that use only color and type, like the graphically intense *I Married a Communist* and *The Worst-Case Scenario Survival Handbook*, to those that elegantly incorporate photography, like *A Natural History of the Senses* and *The Zuni Café Cookbook*, to those that feature a piece of beautiful art, like *Girl with a Pearl Earring*. Yet they all scream: Read me!

The Cherry on Top: Blurbs, Press Kits, Photos and Other Enticing Extras

It's easy to get so caught up in your proposal or manuscript that you forget about additional materials that can be exceedingly helpful in selling your book. Typically, these include blurbs, videotape/CD, press kits, speaking schedules and/or a great photo. But don't stop there. Include any others that you think would get an agent or publisher racing to the phone.

BLURBAGE

What are blurbs? They're endorsements at the front or back of a book, or sometimes inside, by other authors or well-known people. It's slightly shocking how much stock people put in blurbs, but the fact is that a great blurb from the right person can push agents and publishers from on-the-fence to in-your-corner. And while it's not essential to have blurbs in order to sell your proposal, it helps. Just one great blurb can do the trick. If you have a connection to an influential person in your field, or if a well-known writer was your professor in your MFA program, or if you can track down the perfect candidate and help him see why it's incumbent upon him to endorse your work, start making your request now. Many times, you'll get no response, but you'd be amazed what people will do for you if you're respectful of their time and ask nicely.

VIDEO/CD

Have you been on TV, and do you have a professional-quality videotape of yourself? If you've been on TV a number of times, you can cut together a sampling of your best appearances. All you need is a couple of minutes—this is just a tease to show how good you'll be at marketing your book.

Since a great videotape/CD is one of the best sales tools you can have, you might want to hire a professional to tape you if you know you're great in front of a camera but don't have the proof. Again, it must be top-quality. Grainy, handheld, cable-access jobs just don't cut it.

If you happen to have appeared in a TV segment with a long introduction that doesn't include you, cut the introduction out of the tape. People want to see YOU, not an anchorperson. But be sure to keep enough of the intro to identify the show if it's reputable in any way, shape or form.

SPEAKING SCHEDULE

If you speak or hold workshops regularly, include a list of select speaking engagements for previous and upcoming years. Leave out very small venues, unless you're making the point that you will speak anywhere and everywhere, big and small. If, on the other hand, you speak in front of particularly large audiences (500 or more), be sure to include those numbers.

PRESS KIT

It is essential that you gather together any press coverage that you've received over the years, living proof that you or your work has already been recognized. It makes publishers think that someone will want to write about you again. If you can't get your hands on the originals of those articles, do Google and LexisNexis searches. (Sadly, LexisNexis is available only at research libraries and universities.)

PHOTO

If you've been told you take a great photo, then take a great photo. What does a great photo have to do with a great book? Nada. What does it have to do with a great marketing campaign? A lot. If you remember Sebastian Junger's book *The Perfect Storm*, you might also remember the author photo on the back. The guy looks like a supermodel! The joke in the publishing industry was that his photo launched his book. Okay, he wrote a great book. But the photo didn't hurt.

THE VALUE OF GOOD READERS

It is an immutable law of the universe that humans simply cannot, under any circumstances, no matter how hard they try, be completely objective about what they've written. That's why, once you finish a draft of your proposal or manuscript, it's important to let it sit and ferment, marinate and settle. Move away from your work for a bit. This will help with your objectivity. In fact, there's a direct correlation between the amount of objectivity you can achieve and the time you spend away from your material. You can test this by going back and reading things you've written over the years—things you thought were deep and witty and spectacular. You'll be shocked by how *not* deep and witty and spectacular they are.

So, during this marinating/objectivity-enhancing time, get other people to evaluate your writing, to tell you what's wrong with it, what's right with it and how to fix it. The more input you have, the more you'll know about how to make your book better. One of the biggest mistakes amateur writers make is sending out their material before it's ready. It's like feeding someone a cake that's half-baked.

If you subscribe to the theory that Writing Is Rewriting (and if you don't already have a subscription to this theory, buy one now!), you must locate smart, literate, articulate people and then convince them to read your writing after you've finished a draft. Believe us, this is just as hard as it sounds. First of all, where do you find smart, literate, articulate people these days? If you're lucky enough to know any people like this, you know that they mostly have lives that keep them busy. And it takes a lot of time to read a proposal, let alone a fiction manuscript, and make thoughtful, useful comments that will help move your book forward, strengthen plot and characters, and cut away fat.

Friends notwithstanding, where can you find people who will have the time and expertise to help you? Who are they? Where are they? And how can you bend them to your will?

The first and most obvious group to penetrate in your search for quality readers is, of course, other writers. Because if they're smart (and that's one of our prerequisites for a quality reader), they will one day need readers, too. So you'll have an I'll-scratch-your-back-you-scratch-mine type of situation on your hands. But where can you find other writers? At literary events listed in the Events section of your local newspaper. At readings in bookstores. Writing groups. Creative writing classes at colleges, universities and community centers. Writers' chat rooms on the Internet. At poetry readings and coffee shops. Khaled Hosseini, author of the #1 bestseller *The Kite Runner*, read parts of his novel to his writing group and received some excellent advice. "Several members of the group suggested that the beginning of my novel could be better served if I kept the first chapter short (it was initially around twenty-five pages long)," he told us. Heeding their advice, he cut it to one page. "Obviously, not all the suggestions were helpful, but several were. There are always people in a writers' group who are natural-born editors."

Stay away from obsequious sycophants! The last thing you want is people telling you your proposal/manuscript is good when it's not. Be sure to let people know you want the you've-got-a-wart truth.

It's particularly helpful if your potential reader is someone who fits into the profile of your audience. The more specific your audience, the more knowledgable your reader should be. So instead of a general writers' chat room, you might want to find a mystery writers' chat room if you're writing a mystery. But if you're writing a book about knitting, you'll want to track down your local knitting group or the owner of your local knitting shop.

If you feel like you want to hire a professional reader, refer back to the section on writing team members at page 41.

PREPARE YOUR PACKAGE FOR LIFTOFF

Now that your proposal or novel is as close to perfect as it's going to get, it's time to send it out yonder. If your book has a shot at a mid- to large-size publisher of trade books (books for a popular audience), you'll be sending it to literary agents. If it's more than likely to end up at a small, regional or university press, then you're going to be sending it directly to editors.

If literary agents are in your future, proceed to the next chapter. If not, skip ahead to page 120.

CHAPTER 3

LOCATING, LURING AND LANDING THE RIGHT AGENT

"Finding a literary agent is like moving to a new town and having to find a contractor to remodel your house and a mechanic to fix your car all at once. It has a strong element of Russian roulette."

—NATIONAL WRITERS UNION

You've got your title, located your model, perfected your pitch and completed your proposal. And you've come to the outlandish conclusion that you actually want to get P-A-I-D for your work. Now it's time to look for an agent.

But what exactly *is* an agent? People say to Arielle all the time, "So you're an agent? You work for a publisher?" Agents do not work for publishers, they work for themselves or for agencies that house more than one agent. *Good* agents have their fingers on the pulse of the publishing world and are skilled in the art of the deal. Notice the emphasis on *good.* Unfortunately, the thing about agents is that they don't need a degree; they don't have to pass a test or get certified. So practically anyone can be an agent. But there aren't that many *good* agents.

Good agents eat lunches with editors from major publishing houses to find out who's buying what and to discover the passions and pet peeves of individual editors. They know how to find the best publisher for you. They'll help with everything from your title to your bio, to the development of your novel's characters, to basic editing and proofreading, to knowing the competition—even brainstorming with you to come up with the best idea for you to write. *Good* agents will serve as buffers between you and your editor or publisher. They'll come up with publicity and marketing ideas for your book and strategize about getting blurbs for your cover. *Good* agents will make sure you get every thin dime that's owed to you. And they'll tell you when you should take less money and go with a better publisher. *Good* agents don't just sell books; they build careers.

Great agents combine all these traits and are part wizard, midwife and guide dog. They'll show you the tricks of the trade, manage your career, introduce you to all the right people, and guide you and your manuscript through the messy maze of the modern book world.

Bad agents, on the other hand, don't do any of these things, won't return your phone calls and sometimes will even steal your money. Like bad travel agents, they can send you on some really bad trips, or worse, not even get you off the ground. Naturally, there are many more bad agents than good agents. Sadly, when you meet them, it's often hard to tell the difference. But once you've experienced their incompetence, sloth and/or idiocy firsthand, the distinction becomes painfully obvious.

DO YOU REALLY HAVE TO HAVE AN AGENT?

If you're looking to get an advance for your book, you almost certainly will need an agent. And even without an advance (or with a small one) there are many reasons to be agented. However, there are a few exceptions:

- ***Are you a poet?*** Unless you're a Pulitzer Prize winner or a pop icon like Jewel, you stand basically no chance of making any money off your gem of a poetry book. The majority of poets send their manuscripts directly to small poetry and university presses. These publishers rarely offer an advance for poetry manuscripts. The non-Pulitzer, noncelebrity exception to this rule is poetry with a hook or gimmick that allows it to live outside the Poetry section of the bookstore. For example, Hal Sirowitz's *Mother Said* (poems about the truly remarkable rantings of Sirowitz's mother) was published by a division of Random House and distributed widely in bookstores because it could be shelved in the humor section. If you've written poetry that can be shelved someplace other than poetry, look for an agent.

- ***Are you writing a book whose subject is of regional interest only?*** Say you're crafting a guide to the wildflowers of Oregon, a book that would probably be published by a university press within that state or by a local publisher who specializes in books of local interest. In that case, you don't need an agent.

- ***Are you writing for a very limited audience?*** Most agents will not want to take on a book about the history of Lithuanian movie stars or an experimental novel about the life of a brick in Brooklyn or a how-to on breeding and grooming shitzapoos. Let's say there are 2,000 shitzapoos in North America. Even if every single solitary shitzapoo owner and his mother buy your book, you'll still be selling only a fraction of the number of books that a major publisher looks to sell. In this situation, you'll need to go the small-press or self-publishing route. No agent necessary.

- ***Are you writing a complicated book?*** Or one that needs to be packaged with some other product (a CD, a pen, a bracelet)? Most projects of this type are produced by packagers, who will develop the book and sell it to a mainstream publisher much the way an agent would. Finding a packager involves the same process as finding an agent. If this is your sort of project, read on! Just substitute the word "packager" for "agent" as you read.

- ***Are you writing an academic book?*** A treatise on polynomial refractors and their impact on mutating quarks should be published by an academic press. If you ask an agent to sell this kind of book for you, it's extremely likely that you'll get this response: "Huh?"

If you're a published writer who's not happy with your representation, don't drop your agent until you know someone else wants to represent you. Already having an agent is a position of strength you'll want to take advantage of. And be sure not to bad-mouth your current agent . . . it may come back to haunt you. Who knows, the new agent may be best friends with the old one. Or maybe the new agent will think you'll diss her in the future.

Children's Book Agents

Before the advent of publishing conglomerates and the Harry Potter explosion, lots of children's book authors didn't use agents. Not that it would have hurt to have an agent back in the day, but it wasn't a necessity. Oh, how

THE SLUSH PILE

If you're an unknown nobody, your stuff will probably end up in a sad, sorry stack of unsolicited letters and manuscripts—the horribly named "slush pile." Usually read by assistants or junior agents who then pass on any interesting prospects to the appropriate agent(s), slush has been the primordial ooze from which many a bestseller has crawled—a great story come press time! That's the good news. The bad news is that agents get thousands of pounds of slush a year.

Are you starting to understand the importance of researching, networking and making your proposal or manuscript all that it can be?

times have changed. Most major publishers of children's books simply do not look at unsolicited manuscripts. This is also true for young adult novels. If you're set on submitting directly to a publisher, it's essential to find the best editor for your book. Do this using the PYPIP search techniques explicated throughout our chapters. The reason to send your book to a specific person is that most companies have stopped reading slush—the unsolicited letters, proposals and manuscripts that tend to end up in the trash.

Lawyer vs. Agent

A few lawyers sell books to publishers on a regular basis, charging clients an hourly fee instead of a percentage of the book's proceeds. This works only if the lawyer has good connections and if you don't want or need the myriad services that agents often offer, such as editorial development, foreign subagents, hand-holding and more.

Note: A lawyer who doesn't have a thorough knowledge of the business can end up costing you more money than an agent costs, with very little or no return.

LOCATING AN AGENT

People ask in wide-eyed terror how they can possibly find a great agent when agents are as rare as unicorns and there are approximately 17 kazillion aspiring authors. We tell them two things: 1) Without authors, there would be no agents. Let's put that another way: Without authors, agents make no money. 2) *Every single agent in history* has passed on a project by an unknown author that went on to live in the land of bestsellerdom. This is why nearly every agency—whether they admit it or not—looks at query letters. Nobody wants to be remembered as the agent who passed on *Angela's Ashes* or *The Catcher in the Rye.* So, in your quest for an agent, let this be your mantra: THEY NEED ME MORE THAN I NEED THEM!

Proceed now with confidence in your search for a top-drawer agent. For those with no personal referral, about 95% of aspiring authors, fear not! The patented PYPIP system is nearly foolproof. And, of course, it all revolves around Principle #1: Research, Research, Research. You don't want to send your sci-fi epic to a sci-fi loather, your illustrated history of tea to a coffee junkie, or your Christian self-help book to a die-hard reincarnated Buddhist.

Sign up immediately for Publishers Marketplace, an e-source that reports deals daily, identifying the agent who sold the book and the editor/publisher who bought it. Then buy a subscription to *Publishers Weekly* (online so you can sign up for the free daily e-newsletter), and scan for agents and editors who are representing/buying material similar to yours. It's a bit pricey (around $400 for both), but this kind of insider info is invaluable. If you don't have the money, read *Publishers Weekly* at your local library and sign up online for Publishers Lunch, which offers less information than Publishers Marketplace but will begin to educate you in all things publishing. (See Appendix I for ordering information.)

Acknowledging the Acknowledgments

Not every book contains an acknowledgment section, but those that do often hold clues about their road to publication, including the author's agent and editor. We're going to show you how to mine these acknowledgments to help you navigate your own road to publication.

First, retrieve your extended list of competitive titles from your proposal. Then add the books that draw a similar audience as well as those you have strong feelings for or that inspired you. Also go back to your preliminary search of the competition and models, and add these to your list. Now eliminate books that are in direct competition with yours. For example, if you're writing a cookbook on vegetarian Thai cuisine, you do not want to go after an agent who has represented a book on that exact subject. You'd be wiser to choose your favorite vegetarian cookbooks and your favorite nonvegetarian Thai cookbooks as models.

Once you've exhausted your library and your memory, recruise the Internet and revisit your local bookstore and library to complete your list. These visits are especially important for ferreting out those books that didn't make it onto your competition list, but have a style and vision similar to yours.

Once you've located at least 5 to 25 books, take your trusty notebook to the library and/or bookstore. It's time for physical contact with books. After you've got them in hand, look in the acknowledgment sections. See if the author has thanked her agent and/or editor and/or publisher. Make three lists: 1) agents, 2) editors, and 3) publishers. This way, you can call the editor's office to get the name of the agent if none is listed. And these editors and publishers will come in handy later as well. Fishing acknowledgment sections is a common publishing industry trick, but one that few newbies know.

Before you leave the bookstore, check out the agent guides to see if there are other perfect fits who didn't show up in any of the acknowledgment sections.

Going Face to Face

Networking is a great way to meet an agent. While the very thought may activate your wallflower instinct, if you don't face the music and dance you'll make your job a lot harder. Fortunately, there are lots of ways to network: writers' conferences, seminars, readings, MFA programs and more.

WRITERS' CONFERENCES, SEMINARS AND WORKSHOPS

If you've got the dough, go to the hot spots where agents and published writers lurk and linger. Workshops, seminars and conferences are often free when they're presented at a bookstore or library, or when an agent is promoting her own book. The most famous writers' conferences, like Squaw Valley and Bread Loaf, cost a pretty penny—the quality of instruction is high and food and lodging are included. On top of that, you have to factor in your transportation costs, lost work time, maybe extra baby-sitting fees, and so on. Plus, while many are called to these seminars, few are chosen; the acceptance rate at the most prestigious of these conferences can be low. At their best, however, not only will you get to improve your writing skills, but you'll get to meet an agent, live in the same quarters with him for a week or two, take a class from him, go one-on-one and get up-close-and-personal with him. This is a good thing.

As always, inspect and research any and all organizations before giving them your money. Look for conferences featuring agents from reputable agencies. Or, if you hunt down a particularly affordable conference where you don't know the instructors, check out their Web sites and look them up in agent guides (see Appendix I). Go armed with as much information as possible. If an agent/presenter is a nut about nuts and you're writing a history of the peanut, you're in luck.

Local writers' conferences are usually open to anyone who pays. These often last only a day or two, and you may or may not get a lot less personal attention, but you'll usually have at least a shot at a short, private meeting with an agent. The third option is your Learning Annex–type deal—you get a couple hours of a presentation, some Q&A and a card. But face time is possible. Of course, many of these workshops are in your New Yorks and your San Franciscos. But if you do live in the right neck of the woods, or you're willing to locomote yourself, we recommend looking into the possibility. Even if you don't actually acquire an agent, you'll probably ingest some juicy morsels about publishing.

A FINE ROMANCE: MEETING AN AGENT AT A CONFERENCE

Crystal Wilkinson met her agent at a local writing conference, after hearing from other authors that this was how they found theirs. "I had recently had twins, but I thought, *I can do this!* I decided to go to a conference with Richard Wright and Zora Neale Hurston, and I was a nervous wreck. I drove down in a Cadillac I borrowed from the small women's college where I was the assistant director of marketing. I met incredible writers, and I met my agent. I had no idea she was famous. Naïveté can work for you."

As a result of putting herself out into the world, Crystal is the proud author of two published novels: *Blackberries, Blackberries* and *Water Street.* While this is not an easy thing for many, Crystal has sage advice for all: "Just be yourself, and don't be afraid to say you don't know."

READINGS AND OTHER PLACES TO MEET AND GREET

If you're having a tough time meeting an agent in the flesh, try meeting some published writers. Not only is this a great way to become part of the publishing community; it's also a great way to get to agents.

And where does one find published authors? Though often somewhat reclusive, many of them give readings. Get on local bookstore and library mailing lists. Locate lecture series that regularly feature authors. Check out your Independent Booksellers Association regional conferences (they typically occur once a year). Attend any and all readings and lectures, particularly those by an author working in your field. Stay after the reading. And buy the author's book. (More on this later, but understand this: Authors do readings to sell books. They're not supposed to be free workshops or pro bono entertainment. An author whose book you buy will be much more inclined to talk to you.) Try to be last in line at a book signing so no one is breathing down your neck. Ask the author about her publishing experience. See what you can learn. If it feels right, tell the author about your own book. If she's receptive, ask her for advice about finding an agent. Some authors will volunteer their agent's name. If they do, you can use this information in your query letter: "I am writing at the suggestion of AUTHOR X." Copping this information lands you in the "referral category"—an elite position that will exponentially up your chances of landing an agent. Do all this in a sensitive, noninvasive, sweet-natured way. As opposed to a rude, pushy, stupid way.

Many booksellers, themselves, have connections with agents, either because they bring agents into their bookstores to do workshops or because their bookstores are so known in the industry that agents go out of their way to promote books there. Also, many agents have written books themselves and done events in bookstores. The point is, by getting close to your local bookstores, you may even wangle an introduction to an agent.

MFA Programs: Should You Become a Master?

Are you a fiction or creative nonfiction writer? If so, perhaps one of the MFA (Master of Fine Arts) programs is for you. While they can be debt-inducing, they can also be career-launching. The reasons are threefold:

- Well-known writers populate the staffs of these programs. And if one of them cottons to your work, he can introduce you to agents and publishers galore. He can also help you get your writing into important literary journals that will make your resumé thrilling to publishers. Even just a blurb saying how he likes your work can open some pretty heavy doors.

- A prestigious program next to your name at the start of your query letter can light up an agent's eyes. For example, if you attend the Iowa Writers'

Workshop (considered by many the most prestigious writing program around), this will make your query jump to the top of most agents' enormous piles, because agents are scared that they're going to pass up the Next Big Thing. The billions of other queries they've received that week may have avalanched their desk, but this *Good Housekeeping* stamp of approval means your work will probably be worth reading.

- You're immersed in a community of writers with whom you can network, network, network. So if you make nice with your classmates and one of them lands an agent and a book deal, that's one human you know who now can connect you to an agent and publisher.

Because many fiction and creative nonfiction writers don't have the days or the dough to go to school year round, lots of schools have "nonresidency" programs. Bennington, Warren Wilson College, Goddard and Antioch are four of the most respected. (For further information, see Appendix I.) These programs require only a few fortnightly visits a year to campus. The rest of your time, you're on your own.

Agent Roundup

After culling a preliminary more-the-merrier list of agents, do some Sherlock Holmesing. Find out everything you can about each of them. Go to agency Web sites, which often include agent bios. Check out *Jeff Herman's Guide to Book Editors, Publishers and Literary Agents*, which lists personal and professional information about individual agents. Where'd they go to college or high, middle and grade school? You never know, what if you went to the same grade school; wouldn't that make a great opening line? Do they have a dog, cat, horse or snake? Are they a vegetarian, a humanitarian, a contrarian? A sucker for soccer, a football fanatic or a polo pundit? A nature lover, fashion maven, steak freak? A world traveler, car nut, homebody? How does your book relate to them and to their authors?

Although New York is the throbbing heart of publishing, it's sometimes better to have an agent who lives in your neck of the woods but visits the city regularly or worked there previously. An agent who is out of the New York scene may have a better feel for what's going on in the hinterlands than New York agents would have. She may see success written all over your book when someone in the publishing mecca looks down his snobby nose at it.

GRANDÉ AGENTS, LITTLE BITTY AGENTS AND ALL WHO FALL BETWEEN

Querying agents is a little like applying to college. It's great to have Ivy League schools on your list, but you should also include a few good midsize colleges, as well as a safety school or two. Just so you have all your bases covered. Same thing goes for agents. While there's no harm in writing to some Big Shot Agents, don't limit yourself to them.

How do you know how big a Big Shot is? Look at the books an agent represents. If he counts Toni Morrison, Danielle Steel, Stephen Hawking and a galaxy of other bestselling and/or prizewinning authors among his clients, you're in a Harvard/Yale situation. If he's got smatterings of bestsellers and clients with impressive/interesting backgrounds, you're talking good midsize liberal arts college. And if you've heard of only one or two people on the agent's list, or if he has a post office box where an address should be, there is your safety school.

Of course, you can get a crummy education at Harvard and a mind-altering education at a safety school. At the same time, a Harvard degree can help you throughout the rest of your life. So it is with publishing. Working with a smaller agency can be a dream-come-true situation. You may get an agent hungry to make her bones with your book. You may get tons of personal attention. Fantastic editorial input. Or your work can get sucked into that ugly publishing black hole. If you're with a Big Shot, there's no doubt your proposal or manuscript will make editors jump to attention. But there's also the very real possibility that you will be low man on the pole—that you will *never* be able to get the agent on the phone and your work will be sucked into that ugly publishing black hole.

Keep in mind that lots of agents have written books. Read and study these as well.

You will use all this information to personalize your query. For example, a car nut who sells thrillers might be just the right agent for your novel about a vintage Chevy that murders people. Again, an agent who has represented a book directly competitive with yours is not the right agent for you. She will consider this a conflict of interest. And if she doesn't, take a deep breath, sigh in frustration and tell her you don't want her for an agent. However, if she tells you that the directly competitive book is now out of print, she might be perfect.

LURING THE AGENT

Research in tow, it's time to cast your line. Think of your perfectly polished query letter as the bait; your presentation letter as an irresistible lure; and your follow-up letter as the hook.

Go get 'em!

The Killer Query Letter

A smart, savvy, scintillating, personal query letter can get you an agent. Your query letter should be information-packed yet concise, complimentary without being brown-nosey, powerful without being overpowering. Be professional, but make sure the letter reflects the best of your personality and style. Show the agent you'll be great to do business with.

A query letter to an agent has three components: 1) the connection, 2) the pitch, and 3) the bio. Make each one approximately a paragraph long, and try to keep the whole letter to a page.

THE CONNECTION

Why is this agent the right one for you? Use your sleuthing to make your case: you both graduated from Gomer Pyle Elementary School, own three llamas or spent your summers at Camp Wannascalpem. If the agent is also an author, say nice yet honest things about the book(s) she's written. Refer specifically to successful books the agent has represented. Tell her what you dig about the books and why yours is similar yet different.

Most writers don't realize that agents are anonymous pieces of the pie who get no respect outside the industry. How many bestselling authors can you name? Now, how many of their agents can you come up with? Exactly. So anything you can do to make an agent feel acknowledged, appreciated, acclaimed, affirmed and special will go a long way.

We've created three different styles of sample paragraphs that will get just about any agent's attention:

1.

> In researching literary agents, I saw that you represented two of my favorite books, *Poemcrazy* and *Fruitflesh.* I have used these books personally and professionally in my psychotherapy practice. What particularly impressed me about them is the incredible amount of heart they display.

THE MAGIC OF THE REFERRAL

Are you one of the precious few writers armed with an agent referral? If so, and you display the name of the referring person in the first sentence of your letter or on the header of your e-mail, there's a grand chance your query will end up in the hot hands of the agent. If you don't, there's an excellent chance it will end up slushed. *Briefly* explain your connection to legitimize it—"my good friend/colleague/professor"—if, and only if, the connection is more meaningful than your second cousin thrice removed or someone you met for five seconds at a party. Agents often call the referring person to see what your deal is. If there's any way to get your connection to call the agent *before* you send your query, much the better. This is a great buzz builder.

What brave women Susan Wooldridge and Gayle Brandeis are to reveal their lives in such intimate detail! I can't tell you what an inspiration both women have been to my patients and me. I believe that my book, *Writing for Your Life,* shares some of the essential qualities of *Poemcrazy* and *Fruitflesh,* but its roots in my experience as a clinical psychologist make it unique. Because both Susan and Gayle acknowledged you so effusively, and because my book shares many of the same fundamental beliefs as theirs, I hope you'll be interested in reviewing my proposal.

2.

After seeing you acknowledged in *Hooligan Killers,* I logged onto your Web site to check out what other books you represent. I was happy to see so many books that I have on my shelves and that I admire thoroughly. I am a particular fan of *Goalie on a Rampage* and *Midfielders Gone Mad.* But what impressed me the most was your love of Manchester United, as I myself am a Red Devil fan from the days of Bobby Charlton and Georgie Best. At 20, I moved to England and played for Newcastle United's Under 21 Club. I've written a novel about my time as an American soccer player in England called *The Referee Assassin.*

3.

I recently bought a copy of your book *Monkeys in the Bible,* and I read it cover to cover in one night. I loved the chapter in which you had the orangutan come down from the Mount with Moses and the Ten Commandments. I also saw on your Web site that you have agented many popular science

> books, including *Bees Bees Bees* and *Men Are Dogs, Women Are Cats.* I have written a proposal for a book about monkeys based on my award-winning research in Kenya called *My Monkey, My Self.*

REPERFECTING YOUR PITCH

Take the flap copy you meticulously crafted (see page 52) and condense it to one paragraph. For inspiration, go to the bookstore or library and read flap copy and, particularly, the backs of paperbacks, where the whole kit and caboodle is limited to a paragraph or two, tops. You'll see how concise those copywriters have had to be, and how they manage to describe a book—and sell it—in only a few sentences.

Do NOT make your book seem more promising than it actually is. Have you called your opus the next *Da Vinci Code,* when it's no more suspenseful than your average Harlequin romance? Have you compared your book to James Joyce's *Ulysses* when it reads like a sophomoric attempt at stream-of-consciousness writing? If so, you've got trouble, my friend. Do NOT promise a horse and deliver a mule. As Daniel Greenberg of the Levine Greenberg Literary Agency says, "Anytime anyone compares himself to a big bestseller it's a big turnoff. While it's not impossible that there's a real comparison to be made, it raises my suspicion that the person is overhyping himself."

Picking up where we left off with our three made-up author queries, we'll show you a pitch-perfect pitch for each:

1.

> Scientific studies have shown that writing down traumatic experiences immediately boosts your immune system. In fact, your heart rate, brain waves and nervous system are all positively affected by this simple act. *Writing for Your Life* follows 12 women as they write about the seemingly insurmountable challenges they've faced and continue to face in their lives. And it dramatically shows how these women are profoundly changed as a result of daily writing. Each chapter is accompanied by writing practices that any reader can do on her own in order to elicit the same kind of results as the women portrayed in the book. Inspired, inspiring, *Writing for Your Life* will speak eloquently to anyone who's had to fight through adversity and struggle for her dreams.

2.

A supermodel-handsome international soccer star and his pop star girlfriend. A tyrannical, egomaniacal, homicidal national-hero coach. A young stud on the way up with a dark, dark secret. A gambloholic sex-starved referee in deep, deep debt. And a lonely psychopath with an uncontrollable urge to kill—who just happens to be the biggest soccer nut in the world. *The Referee Assassin* is an international soccer thriller that takes ripped-from-headlines events and weaves them into a white-knuckle thriller, culminating in a wild ride of a European Cup that will leave readers screaming, "GOOOOOOOOOAL!" *The Referee Assassin* shoots. And it scores.

3.

When I left to study the candyass baboons of the Burrunguguanaptchinwazazie Plains of western Africa, I was an uptight, unmarried professor with a secret drinking problem and a stack of unfinished academic articles on my shelf. When I returned, I was a hang-loose, loving husband with a profound zest for life, a successful career and an amazing story to tell. And I owe it all to the baboons. While in the wilds of the jungle, I met Zeus, the brooding king of the baboons, struggling to stay the alpha; Madonna, the diva who drove everyone crazy but always came through when the chips were down; and little Tiny Tim, who was born lame in one leg and forced to fight the ultimate Darwinian struggle of life and death. I came away with *My Monkey, My Self,* a book that displays the deep connection we share with our primate friends as well as the many things the animal kingdom has to teach us.

A BOOMING BIO

Take your hot bio from your proposal and pare it down to a paragraph. Remember, this is not a job resumé! This is an enthusiastic review—of you! Let the agent know why you're great. If you've been published, trot out your personal bibliography. If you've won awards, by all means include them. Elucidate how you've got the savvy and the sass to publicize and market your book. Include interesting tidbits about yourself (you were on Canada's Olympic track team in 1980; in addition to being a lawyer, you are also a yak expert; you were Marilyn on *The Munsters*).

And now it's time to read the bios of our three fictional authors that will make their targeted agents get on the horn pronto.

1.

I am a practicing clinical psychologist as well as the founder of the *Writing for Your Life* workshop, which now has over 15 active satellite groups in the United States. Since its inception eight years ago, more than 5,500 people have taken the workshop. I have been profiled in the *Dallas Morning News* and on my local CBS morning show, and have done at least two dozen radio interviews, a number of which were for NPR affiliates. I believe that my experience leading workshops and with the media, along with my willingness to pound the pavement upon publication, will make *Writing for Your Life* a front-list success and a backlist favorite.

2.

When not on the soccer field, I spend my days as a real-life referee, a substitute teacher and a writing instructor at San Quentin. When I was 20, I was a merchant mariner; at 30, I was an emergency room technician; at 40, I was a dot-com multimillionaire in the process of losing almost all of that money; and at 45, I'm the oldest player by 10 years in a Division One intramural league in the Bay Area. I'm tied for the most goals with the youngest player on my team; he just turned 22. I think this says all you need to know about my character. I'm tenacious as hell, and I'm a true team player.

3.

I'm a professor of primatology at Rice University, where I hold the Chippendale Chair in biology. I've included my CV so that you can see the myriad of papers I've had published over the years, most in leading academic journals. I've included photographs of myself with Zeus, Madonna and wee Tiny Tim, as well as clippings from a number of national and local papers in the United States and Canada that featured our story and that served as the seed for this book. I am caretaker of several baboons, one of whom, Zippy, has already made several media appearances and is raring to go again.

Do you want to get a response to your query? Include a self-addressed stamped envelope (SASE). If you leave off the stamp part, you probably won't hear back unless the agent is interested. Include your e-mail and snail-mail addresses, as well as your phone number in case the agent wants to get hold of you ASAP or has lost your SASE (which, sadly, often happens). Yes, agents sometimes get queries with no contact information. Can you imagine?

Multiple Submissions

You've got your agent list. You've got your killer query. Now it's time to launch yourself out into the world. Unless you have a personal referral to an agent or there's one agent who you feel is a perfect fit, you should definitely send query letters to all the agents on your list at once. Many how-to-get-published books tell you not to do multiple submissions to agents. Ignore this feeble advice. Agents can take up to a year to respond. A year! If you wait for each of them, you could easily be dead before you get representation.

If you're sending your query to just one agent because you're sure she's the one for you, be sure to tell her so in your letter. Put a time limit on her exclusive look. Two weeks should be enough time, unless she asks for more.

The great thing about multiple submissions is that, if you get interest from one agent, you can use this interest to prod all the other agents to read your material. And it's not necessary to write in your query that you're multiply submitting. But if you're asked, be sure to tell the truth.

Should You Send the Whole Enchilada?

Do not, under any circumstances, bombard the agent with written material unless you want to get it shredded and trashed. Include a description of what material is available in your query, and then let her tell you what she wants. Some agents want e-proposals, so they don't have to handle any paper; some hate e-proposals. You want to send your material exactly as the agent wants to receive it, and the only way you'll know that is to ask or look up submission requirements on her Web site.

You'd be shocked by how many envelopes and packages float across an agent's desk *every single day*. Thousands and thousands of authors' dream ships sailing by. Make your ship beautiful. Use high-quality stationery. An attractive font. The more elegant, simple and professional the presentation, the less chance you have of bumping up against someone else's taste. Arielle gets lots of query letters on rainbow stationery. She hates rainbow stationery! So she has an instant prejudice against these authors even if they've written excellent proposals. On the other hand, if you're a professional graphic designer, strut your stuff. Top-notch visuals can turn

INSIDE AND OUTSIDE THE BOX

Some years ago, an ambitious but still unknown young writer wanted to have his book represented by a successful New York agent. After schmoozing the receptionist, he discovered that the agent loved sausage, pepper and onion pizza from John's on Bleecker Street. So one day, when he learned from the now friendly receptionist that the agent was eating lunch in his office, the ambitious but unknown young writer sent him sausage, onion and pepper pizza from John's Pizzeria. He had the pizzeria tape his query on the inside of the pizza box, so that when the agent opened his favorite pizza pie box—*voilà!*—there it was. By the close of business that day, the ambitious but unknown young writer had gotten a call back from the successful agent—by thinking outside the box and then putting it in the box!

Today, you can't send food to agents unless it comes directly from the source and is completely sealed; otherwise, it will end up as garbage. But small, tasteful attention-grabbers are usually welcome. For example, are you doing a book on pet grooming? Then a high-end grooming product could be just the ticket. Are you doing a book on quick meals? Then maybe a cool egg timer could be a great add-on. Are you doing a book about the art of seduction? Maybe a beautiful candle would be a lovely gift. The common thread here is that these gifts are useful and not taste-specific, and they are marketing tools, not the mark of a sycophant.

someone on just as much as rainbows turn Arielle off. Or, if your research has unearthed some particular information about an agent, see if you can maximize this knowledge by acknowledging it on your package. For example, if you uncover the fact that an agent is a San Francisco 49ers freak, then a cool Niners sticker on the front of the envelope can be an eye-catching invitation.

For goodness sake, spell the agent's name right! Arielle Eckstut has gotten letters addressed to Arel Ekctuts, Areel Esckstup and Mr. Arilee Etschuck. And while we're on the subject, please make sure the letter you send is to the person named on the front of your envelope. Arielle gets dozens of envelopes a year addressed to her but filled with letters to other agents. Guess where 99.9% of those letters end up? We know it sounds elementary, but make checking the envelope against the letter part of your checklist.

The Fundamental Necessity of the Follow-Up

As important as the query letter is, its follow-up may be just as crucial. You have no idea how many letters get lost. In the mail. Under a desk. In the slush. And once you've made sure your letter has been received, you've got to make sure it gets read. Just because an agent hasn't responded doesn't mean she's not interested. Sometimes she needs a dozen or so gentle reminders.

E-reminders are the least invasive and most effective way to grab an agent's attention. If you don't have an agent's e-mail address, to make contact you must negotiate your way through the first layer of defense: the receptionist.

SCHMOOZING THE GATEKEEPER

Almost certainly, the first person you'll speak to at an agent's office is a receptionist or secretary or intern. These are the people who do the grunt work, get none of the credit and yet are responsible for whether your message finds a place on top of the agent's call list or gets eighty-sixed into the wastebasket.

Be extra nice to the receptionist. Call in the late afternoon, when things are less hectic. Be hyper-aware of the mood in the office. If you hear yelling and phones ringing off hooks, suggest that you'll call back another time. But when the time is right, see if you can strike up a conversation with this individual. See what you can find out about him. There's a good chance he'll be the first one to read your material, and an equally good chance that in a year or two he'll be an agent.

You should keep a separate page in your Empty Book for every agent you're contacting. When you call, note the day and time along with any information that could be valuable down the line. When David was in Hollywood, he was courting a prominent agent. He called and got the receptionist, who sounded miserable. David asked her if she was okay. She confessed that her cat had a tumor. It just so happens that David is a cat lover, so they exchanged cat stories for a few moments. David wrote the name of the assistant's cat in his Empty Book, and the next time he called, the first thing he asked was "How's Max doing?" The assistant couldn't believe that David had remembered her cat's name. More chatting ensued. Three months and 12 phone calls later, David had a meeting with the agent.

If you can develop a relationship with the gatekeeper and the moment feels right, don't hesitate to ask, "If you were me, how would you get my stuff on the agent's desk?" All of a sudden, the person who's been an office underling all day is being treated as an authority. Asked for advice. Humans like to think they're authorities. Humans like to give advice. Use this to your advantage.

THE DID-YOU-GET-MY-LETTER CALL

One week after you send your letter, call the agent's assistant to make sure your letter has actually been received. Use this as a point of contact with the assistant. Again, she might be the first person who reads your letter. BEWARE: She might say, "Oh, what's your book about?" So you better be ready to pitch, baby, pitch (have your query letter handy to help). Make your story clear, exciting and 30 seconds long. Practice before you get on the phone. Then practice some more. When you're sure you've got it down pat, take a few moments and do some more practicing.

If you're using e-mail to send a query, get an automatic "confirmed receipt" if your Internet provider has this function. You won't have to call the agent, yet you'll know when he's opened his e-mail. If you don't know how to do this, find a tech-friend who can help.

Some agencies don't keep a log of what query letters have been received because they simply get too many. If you call an agency and you're told they don't keep track of queries, don't act steamed. Just thank the receptionist and ask if you should send another.

THE DID-YOU-*READ*-MY-LETTER CALL

This one calls for delicacy. David, an avid agent hunter for over 20 years, thinks it's best to call the agent or assistant once every couple of weeks to follow up. Arielle, on the other hand, being an agent for over a decade, hates people calling her to find out about query letters. She believes the one did-you-get-my-letter call to the assistant is enough. Or that an e-mail to the agent is okay. But she believes that persistent calling should be reserved for the months *after* the agent has received the material he requested. What we both agree on is that you never, under any circumstances, want to be a pest. Pushy is bad. Tenacious, friendly, charming, sweet, thoughtful, kind and professional are good.

LANDING THE BIG KAHUNA

Now that you've located and lured some agents, it's time to reel one in. Some writers may have a number of nibbles to work with. Some one. Some none. However, your chances of landing the right agent go up if you systematically apply the guidelines that follow.

Eureka: An Agent Calls!

You wait and you wait, and you wait and you wait. Maybe a week, maybe a year. Then, all of a sudden, you get a call from an agent. Someone's interested! If you've got the money, send the requested material overnight delivery. (REMEMBER: Have your materials ready and waiting before your query goes out.) Or, if appropriate, ask if you can e-mail your proposal. Whatever you do, get something off immediately so you're still on the agent's mind when she gets your package.

Next, call every other agent you queried and let them know that you have interest from another agent. This should vault your query to the top of their lists. With any luck at all, these calls will produce more requests for your material.

Once you've sent out your proposal or manuscript, it's follow-up time again. This time, David and Arielle agree: You're going to have to be persistent—and nice and funny and patient—for the long haul.

Agent Grilling

As Smokey Robinson's mother so wisely advised, "You better shop around." Or, put another way, you want to find out who you're hopping into bed with before you do the hopping. So, even if an agent says she's ready to sign you up as her client, stop doing your happy dance long enough to figure out what you're getting into.

The thing is, some agents will never talk to you after they sign you. They will not return your calls. They just want to sell your material. In most cases, this is not the kind of agent you want. You want an agent who loves working on proposals, getting books out into the world and building writing careers. Many agents are also talented editors, and part of the joy of their job is shaping material. This can be enormously helpful in selling your book. You want this to be the start of a long, fruitful relationship, not a dark,

SOUNDING OUT SOLO AGENTS

Many agencies are one-person operations. This can be great—you're more likely to get personal attention—but you need to know exactly what you're getting yourself into. Barbara Moulton, who opened her own one-person agency after years as an editor at HarperCollins, says, "You want to know what qualifies the person to be an agent. Is she a publishing defector? That's usually a good sign. But always check the agent's background."

Here are other essential questions to ask a solo practitioner:

- When you're on vacation, are you available to take my calls if an emergency comes up? If not, do you have an assistant who's capable of taking care of business?
- Do you sell rights to books around the world? If so, what is your commission?
- Will you be able to sell serial rights to my book?
- Do you have the ability to sell film and TV rights? If so, what is your commission? Do you work with a TV/movie-selling co-agent? If so, who?

The answers to these questions are very important, as you'll discover throughout the rest of this book.

harrowing nightmare. The point is, you have to find the right person for you.

Here are some key questions you should ask an interested agent:

- What other books like mine have you sold?
- Do you help develop material?
- Will contact be primarily with you or your assistant?
- Will you help me promote my book when it comes out?
- Are you a member of the Association of Authors' Representatives?
- Do you have client and editor references I can call?
- What publishing houses do you work with on a regular basis?
- How many books have you sold in the last year?
- Are you known for selling a particular kind of book (business, science, African American, romance, literary fiction)?
- How experienced are you when it comes to negotiating terms of a contract?

It's perfectly legitimate, logical and human to ask: "How much can you sell my book for?" But be forewarned that the answer, e.g., "big bucks," might be the opposite of what you want. In fact, if an agent gives you the "big bucks" answer, don't take it with a grain of salt; take it with several shakerfuls. No agent can possibly give you the real answer to this question. Books that look like bestsellers often sell for pocket change. Esoteric, quirky tomes sometimes sell for six figures. You just never know. When authors ask Arielle this question, her stock answer is: "Somewhere between $5,000 and $500,000."

An Embarrassment of Riches: When More than One Agent Is Interested in Your Book

Suddenly you're in the enviable position of choosing among several agents. Maybe one agent is young, hungry, attentive and inexperienced, and another is super-high-powered but impossible to get on the phone. Whom to choose? Again, what do *you* need? A hand-holder? Then young and hungry is the one for you. Are you more of a "show me the money" type? Then high-powered might be the solution, especially if you've written a book with big potential. Make a pluses-and-minuses list based on your interview questions. Are the

EENIE, MEENIE, MINIE, MOE . . .

A first-time writer who wishes to remain nameless found herself on the horns of a choosing-between-two-agents dilemma. Both seemed great, though for very different reasons. The less experienced agent completely understood her book and was delightful to talk to and not in the least intimidating. He flew out to meet with the writer and was accessible to her at all times. He made editorial suggestions that made perfect sense to the author. However, he didn't have a client list packed with Pulitzer Prize winners and bestsellers, like the super-high-powered agent. But the super-high-powered agent asked the writer to change her book from nonfiction to fiction. Asked her to change it from a dark, literary story to a light, fluffy one. As flattered as the writer was by the super-high-powered agent's interest, and as awed as she was by this agent's client list (which included two of her all-time favorite authors), she simply couldn't live with these kinds of changes to her book.

In the end, the writer went with her gut and signed with the younger, hungrier agent. Turns out her gut was right. Her agent got her a two-book, six-figure deal. And she was never scared to pick up the phone and call him.

pluses things you care about? Are the minuses less important? If so, that's the agent for you.

If you want to write for a niche audience, it really helps to have an agent who knows that particular world and the players in it. If she specializes in your category and wants your project, odds are she'll sell your book.

But the macrocosmic question is less about whether the agent will help you with your current book than whether she'll be able to help you build a career. If you envision a next book that is *not* in the agent's area of specialty, then you've got a tough decision. It's hard work finding another agent, and most agents want to represent all your work. If you do plan on writing a different kind of second book, this is something you should discuss with the agent from the get-go. On the other hand, if you want to continue to work in this area, your agent may well be the perfect partner. Point being, while you're looking at the trees, don't lose sight of the forest.

The Lone Suitor Scenario: When Only One Agent Is Interested in Your Book

It can be tough if you're not entirely sold on the sole agent who wants to work with you. On the one hand, if the agent can sell your book, at least you'll get your work published. And if you then go on to write a second, it'll be easier to find another agent with a published book topping your resumé. On the other hand, an ineffective or nasty agent can spoil your chances of getting published. Your book may never make it out of the agent's office, or it may go to all the wrong editors, or you and your work may become associated with an agent who sends out bad material. Or she may be a hellion to deal with. But on the whole, it's almost always better to have an agent than to have none at all.

Back to the Drawing Board

We don't know any writer who hasn't been slapped by the cold hard palm of rejection. Often repeatedly. If you have a hard time dealing with rejection (and who doesn't?), you may want to go directly to Chapter 5 to help shore yourself up against the inevitable. Once you've soothed the savage whatever, evaluate the feedback you've received. If several agents tell you the same thing, it's certainly worth addressing their concerns. However, you may get no feedback at all. In that case, you have to reassess the commercial viability of your project and/or the writing while keeping your sense of humor as activated as possible.

If you still feel your project is salable and the writing is professional-caliber, go back and repeat the steps you've already taken: do more research, come up with more agents and submit to them. If you do this several times and still get nary a nibble, it's probably time to think about 1) going with a smaller publisher, in which case you won't need an agent, 2) self-publishing, or 3) hiring a trained professional to help make your work more marketable.

JOHN HANCOCKING: SIGNING AN AGENCY CONTRACT

Almost all agents, whether they're working solo or as part of a larger agency, will have you sign an agency agreement. Specifics may vary, but a standard agreement includes:

- The agency's commission (on advances, royalties and sub-rights sales)
- A description of how the agency charges for out-of-pocket expenses (if it does)
- The agency's obligations to you, and vice versa
- Conditions for termination

Most agencies charge a 15% commission on advances, royalties and most subsidiary sales, except for foreign rights. For these, 20% is standard, because the agent works with co-agents who split the commission. So in actuality, while you're paying more, your agent is getting less. The smallest agencies can charge up to 30% commission on certain sales (such as foreign rights), because they use a middleman to connect them to a subagent and each party gets 10%.

Many agencies charge for out-of-pocket expenses like postage, overnight delivery and messengers. It's perfectly fine to ask for a cap on expenses or to be notified if expenses go beyond a certain point.

It's important to remember that in life just about everything is negotiable. If any part of an agreement is confusing or simply feels wrong to you, be sure to ask if it can be eliminated or changed. If this is not possible, make sure you're satisfied with the agent's explanation of why it's in the contract.

THE HOLLYWOOD AGENT

Unless your agent works at a large agency with its own film/TV department, you're more than likely working with a separate film and television agent to sell these rights to your book (if you're going to sell them at all). Many agents have set up relationships with Hollywood agents, known in the book biz as co-agents. Some literary agents have exclusive relationships with co-agents and some work with a variety of them.

If you think you've got a hot film or TV property on your hands, you'll want to get hooked up with a co-agent sooner rather than later. Sometimes a movie/TV deal can be made just on the basis of a proposal. And if you and/or your agent can swing this, it will bring much-needed buzz and glamour to your work, and your stock will rise like a thermometer on a hot summer day.

If you don't have a literary agent, or don't have one who works with other Hollywood agents, you need to find your own. Using the PYPIP agent-hunting techniques outlined in this chapter, make your list of appropriate Hollywood agents and approach them with the same vim and verve you did a literary agent. Illustrious producer and personal manager Marion Rosenberg of the Marion Rosenberg Office has this advice: "The trick is to find a way in. Put together your blurbs and reviews and define your approach as to why you think your book would make a great movie. Present it in simple, straightforward terms and help the buyer know how to sell it. 'This is a perfect Catherine Zeta-Jones/Michael Douglas movie.' People have short attention spans, and they're extremely busy. Make sure your presentation is professional—neatly typed, spell-checked and bound—and be persistent."

When you're dealing with Hollywood, you want to look for agents who have worked with similar writers or with actors, directors and producers for whom your material would

If the agent doesn't make you sign a contract and you're comfortable working this way, that's fine. It's much easier to walk away from this type of deal. But protect yourself by getting a signed letter stating how much commission the agency will take on your advance, royalties and sub rights so that there are no surprises down the road.

Contract Red Flags

Most agency contracts are straightforward and harmless. A few are not. Here are the main red flags to look out for:

1. Do *not* sign with an agent who charges a fee for his services. Most agents charge for their out-of-pocket expenses, but no one should

be appropriate. If, for example, you think Brad Pitt is the perfect star for the film version of your book, you can send it directly to his agent or his production company. Good news: This means more choices for you. Bad news: The moats surrounding Hollywood are even wider and deeper, and full of scarier monsters, than those surrounding the land of publishing. More good news: Players in Hollywood, even more so than those in publishing, are terrified of missing out on The Next Big Thing. So if you can convince them that you've written the next "it" book, you've got a chance of cashing in. Still more good news: Hollywood people are easy to find. The Screen Actors Guild (SAG) will give you the name of any actor's agent, and the Directors Guild of America (DGA) will do the same for directors. Producers have their own companies, and these are listed in the *Hollywood Creative Directory.* Ideally, you want to pitch to managers, development people and agents. But even a sharp, ambitious assistant can open a door for you if you develop the right relationship with him.

If you're having trouble making contact with any of the people on your list, try to reach these folks through their managers or publicists. Agents, production companies, DGA and SAG will often provide contact info for both. Managers and publicists are generally more receptive to taking calls than agents are.

Yet another way to reach Hollywood is through scouts. These middlemen do just what their name suggests: they scout out material for studios and production companies as well as foreign publishers. Scouts are listed in *Literary Market Place (LMP)*, a great resource guide for all things publishing, which you can find at your local library. If you can convince a scout that you've got a hot Hollywood property, she can get it into the hands of people who, in all likelihood, you could never get on the phone.

charge "development" or "reading" fees (see the Association of Authors' Representatives listing in Appendix I for more information). If someone proposes this to you, don't walk away. Run.

2. Do *not* sign a contract that locks you in for a set amount of time and doesn't allow you to leave. Your contract should state that either party can walk away with 30 days' notice.

3. Do *not* sign a contract that locks your next book up with that agent (also known as an "option book"). You should be free to work with any agent you choose on your next book without having to pay a commission to the agent who represented your first one.

Knowing that some agents try to take advantage in their contracts, many writers wonder whether they need a lawyer to look everything over. If you happen to have access to an affordable and competent lawyer who specializes in publishing law, it certainly can't hurt. But if it means spending money you don't have or don't want to part with, then we don't recommend hiring a lawyer. The reasons are two: 1) Most lawyers don't have publishing experience, so they end up asking for pie-in-the-sky clauses, which leads to the fact that 2) The contract doesn't change (no agent would make such outlandish requests) and you've spent an arm, a leg and half a lung.

WHAT'S NEXT?

If, by the end of this chapter, you've found your agent match, please proceed to the beginning of the next chapter, "Demystifying Submission," to learn all about how to work most effectively with your agent, as well as how to navigate the shark-infested waters of the submission process.

If you've decided to pursue a small or university press, walk straight ahead to page 120, because you no longer need an agent.

CHAPTER 4

DEMYSTIFYING SUBMISSION

"If you have built castles in the air,
your work need not be lost, that is where they should be.
Now put foundations under them."

—HENRY DAVID THOREAU

If you've done your work and you submit your book properly, you're likely to get some publishing love. Michael Powell, founder of Powell's Books in Portland, Oregon, says, "I believe nearly every book that deserves to be published gets published." Heartening news indeed.

If you've signed with an agent, this submission period will involve working with her to hone your proposal or manuscript to the point where she thinks it's good-as-it-gets. If you have a proposal that's all set to go, it will involve setting up a strategy for the submission and sale of your work. This is also the period when the honeymoon with your agent usually ends, and you're going to have to learn to navigate the rocky roads of marriage and get the most out of your new partner.

AGENT RELATIONS: SNARLING SNAFUS AND SCARY SILENCES

Now that you and your agent have moved from courtship into a meaningful relationship, you need to get your proposal or manuscript submission-ready. You may have material that's ready to go as is, or you may discover you have a lot more to do than you expected. Either way, this is when you climb into the trenches with your agent. Whether the agent is an attentive, caring hand-holder or an unavailable, self-centered knuckle-rapper, there are four major areas that can make or break your relationship.

Sweet Appreciation

We've talked about how agents get so little professional love from anyone outside publishing. Consequently, those precious few drops of appreciation from you can go a long way. Most of us don't do nearly enough appreciating in our lives, but here's a circumstance where there's a direct correlation between sincere appreciation shown and benefits reaped. A lot of writers don't even quite know what their agents do, so naturally they don't know what to thank them for. Here's a list of potential thank-yous:

- ***"I know how busy you are. Thanks for getting back to me."*** Many writers labor under the mistaken impression that they're the only clients in their agent's stable. Clients who act annoyed if their agent doesn't get back to them immediately make the agent never *want* to get back to them. Appreciation beats annoyance in any agent's eyes.
- ***"I know how busy you are. Thanks for reading my material."*** Reading material carefully takes a long time and requires much concentration. One novel can take eight hours to read. Even just skimming a proposal or manuscript takes time. Agents are on the phone all day, which means they have to read at night and on the weekends, when they'd rather be relaxing or pursuing their own passions.
- ***"I know how busy you are. Thanks for your thoughtful comments."*** Ditto above. Thoughtful comments are not dropped off by the Thoughtful Comment Fairy. They take a long time to develop and can't be done with the phone ringing off the hook.
- ***"Thanks for taking the time to explain the process."*** Assume that most agents have at least 25 clients (and many have 50 or more). Assume that at least half these clients are first-time authors. That's a lot of time spent explaining the ins and outs of the business and answering questions. If you and every other first-time author the agent represents ask half an hour's worth of questions a week, that's at least six hours total—almost a whole day per week.

Great Expectations

Unless you're not quite human, you have expectations about what will happen to your proposal or manuscript. Your agent will drop everything as soon as your proposal or manuscript comes in, give you brilliant notes immediately, sell your book to a great editor at a great publishing house, then sell the film rights, the foreign rights, the audio rights, and on and on.

Go ahead and dream. Part of the fun of this whole process is imagining bestseller lists (#1, of course), a translation into Croatian and a Pulitzer Prize. However, it is your duty to manage your great expectations and not dump them all over your agent. Making your agent into a beast of burden is one of the quickest and easiest ways to alienate her.

Expectations often do not reflect reality, which is why, at the beginning of your relationship, it's a good thing to ask your agent which of your particular expectations are legitimate and which are poppycock. For instance, are you expecting daily, weekly, monthly check-in calls from your agent? Are you expecting a return call within the hour, the week, the decade? Are you expecting the agent to read your 500-page manuscript within 24, 48, 100,000 hours?

As these numbers illustrate, some people's expectations are simply unmeetable, while others are sickly self-defeating. If you find out at the beginning of the submission process exactly what your agent can and cannot do for you, then you can adjust your expectations accordingly. Ultimately, this is all about . . .

Maximizing Communication

Over and over, we hear writers say: "I'm so scared of my agent, I avoid calling whenever possible." They haven't learned that lack of communication equals bad news for their book. Good agent-client relationships are made up of honest, thoughtful, reasonable, respectful communication, with a dash of humor thrown in to lighten the load. The more you respect the agent's time, expertise and effort, and the better you articulate what you want and need, the more you increase your book's chances of getting out into the world successfully. An agent who genuinely enjoys working with you is sure to be a better salesperson for your book.

Many writers and authors feel so lucky to have found an agent that they're terrified to stand up in the boat, let alone rock it. As a result, when they do have a legitimate problem or just a series of reasonable questions, they tend to err on the side of mum. If you're the mummish type, here's an important rule of communication: Ask. Compile your list of questions carefully and make sure you catch your agent at a moment when she's not crazy with the heat. How do you know? Same rule: Ask.

Especially when you're starting out in publishing, it's often better to admit you know nothing, even if you know something, than to pretend you know everything when you don't know anything at all. Just preface a question with "Excuse my ignorance, but . . ." and you'll most likely get a thorough, plain-English explanation. Temper your natural ignorance with sweet humility and watch people flock to your side.

On the other end of the bell curve are complainers who are never pleased, no matter what their agents do. They demand constant attention with useless, irrelevant, I'm-talking-just-to-hear-myself-speak questions and comments. Agent-wise, we strongly advise against nagging . . . unless you want to see your book buried under a massive stack of manuscripts in your agent's office.

Many people assume all sorts of outlandish scenarios about why their agent hasn't called them. They get sucked into the ass/u/me vortex, wherein assuming makes Asses of U and Me. If you're sensing a problem or you're simply in the dark on an issue, what do you do? Ask.

DO: "Is this is a good time to talk?"
DON'T: "I need to talk to you right now."

DO: "Am I calling too much?"
DON'T: "Why haven't you returned any of my calls?"

DO: "Have I overwhelmed you with material?"
DON'T: "It's been three weeks since I gave you my material, and I haven't heard a thing."

DO: "Have you lost interest in this project?"
DON'T: "I'm taking your malicious indifference to mean you're no longer interested in my project."

DO: "Do you have a lot on your plate right now?"
DON'T: "Why do you hate me?"

Some of these questions can be terrifying to ask. That's why we advocate rehearsal. Replay the conversation in your head, then act it out with a friend who plays your agent. We understand that this may sound ridiculous, but being prepared can alleviate flop sweats, jitters and tongue ties. Bottom line: It's much better to know where you stand (and to move on, if necessary) than to stew in your own juices, or worry yourself sick, or ass/u/me all kinds of scenarios that make you feel like the loser of the universe.

THE SADDEST SCENARIO: WHEN YOUR MATERIAL NEVER GETS SENT OUT

An alarming number of authors sign with agents who never send their work out. Or never *say* they've sent their work out. This maddening situation sometimes takes place even when an agent has exhibited all the telltale signs of enthusiasm: warm handshakes; weekend phone calls; kind, quickly returned e-mails.

What gives? For one thing, in almost all such situations, the author, out of fear, ignorance or a combination thereof, has never called the agent to follow up. Big mistake. Imagine entrusting a baby-sitter with your newborn only to find out she sat in front of the TV all day and left the baby wet and crying in the crib. Wouldn't you say something? Of course you would! Well, you put a ton of time and love into creating your baby of a book, so don't let it languish in dirty diapers! Speak up. The book you save may be your own.

If you've done all the asking you can do and you're still confused, unsure or disheartened, it might be time to tell your agent how you feel—if you can do it without attacking him.

DO: "I know you're busy, so please let me know the best way for us to communicate."

DO: "I feel that I haven't edited my material enough, but I'm unsure what to do. Please let me know if I'm asking for too much help."

DO: "I feel that you've lost interest in this project. I'd rather know now if that's the case, so please be up front with me."

Yes, of course, problems will come up and things will not go as planned. No matter how much you prepare for every contingency, you will be unprepared. But at least, if you've asked all you can ask and you've said how you feel, you'll know you've given 110%, which is, in the end, all a person can do.

If you call your agent several times over the course of, say, a month and you get no return phone call, no e-mail, no timeline and no editorial feedback, it's probably the moment to start looking for another agent.

The Dangers of Being an Affirmation Junkie

If you're a self-assured, well-balanced, healthy-egoed person, you can skip this section altogether. But if you're like the rest of us, you'll want to not only read it more than once, but maybe even make a needlepoint out if it.

It's natural to want your agent to affirm the value of your project, your talent . . . you. And a lot of agents are very good at supporting their clients and providing positive, encouraging feedback. But a lot simply don't have these skills or are utterly uninterested in anything that smacks of cheerleaderism. It's a shortcoming, but if you get stuck with an agent who can't support you this way, it will be up to you to find your affirmation elsewhere.

Look, an agent doesn't have to be warm and cuddly to sell a book. In some cases, a cold and prickly agent can get more money and make better deals. Don't let your emotional needs overcome your business savvy. If you have an agent who's stand-offish but does a great job selling your book to a reputable publisher, it may not be your best-case scenario but it's good enough.

"I WANNA HOLD YOUR HAND"

Defined by the *OED* as "giving close guidance or moral support," handholding is only one step beyond standard affirmation—but above and beyond the agent's call of duty. Many agents will do some hand-holding, but frankly it's an unreasonable expectation. You should expect expert advice on all things related to the publishing of your book. You should hope to receive positive feedback on good work well done. But a desire for more than that is a symptom of neediness—a dangerous country to be from. If you inhabit it for too long, your agent may break off all diplomatic relations with you and sometimes even declare war.

SAME-PAGING

From the get-go, your agent may indicate that your project needs minor or major (or anywhere in between) changes. But sometimes an agent will tell you nothing but how great your work is until *after* she's signed you. Then she'll tell you everything that's wrong with your manuscript. Don't be surprised if you start to feel that what was once Enthusiasm Central now sounds like Reservation City. This change in attitude might get your antennae twitching, but don't assume the worst. Your agent might have signed you up without carefully reading your proposal (this can happen especially if the agent wants to make a quick offer of representation). So, when she told you that you needed to do very little work, he may not have been dishonest, just not fully informed.

Whether or not your agent was up front about the amount of work you needed to do, you'll now want to be sure that you're both on the same page editorially. This means getting the clearest set of directions possible. Start with a conversation. Take notes. Ask questions—even the ones that seem utterly obvious:

- What specifically did you like about my material?
- What specifically stood out in it? What did you find particularly strong?
- What did you feel were the problems?
- Are there specific sections that you feel need strengthening?
- Is there anything that you feel should be added?
- Is there anything else I need to do to make my material ready to sell?
- Do you have the time to mark up my material so I can see exactly what you're talking about?

If you're preparing to submit an illustrated book, ask your agent a few additional questions: Do I need sample spreads? If so, what quality do they need to be? Do I need to make changes on my existing spreads? And do I have to print more than one copy?

Alan Burns, cocreator of *The Mary Tyler Moore Show*, was once told by an executive that his script needed to be "40% funnier." This kind of generic criticism is brutally useless. Find out specifically what you need to do to make your manuscript as great as it can be. If, say, you've written a humor book and your agent tells you that the story on page 7 isn't funny, find out what in particular isn't funny about it. Maybe it's simply that the ending falls flat and is totally fixable. Or maybe it feels out of place and would be better suited to a later chapter. Or maybe a character you're describing doesn't come off as real. The point is, if you don't get specific feedback, you're left with "not funny," which could lead you in any number of directions that fail to address your agent's concern. Also, specific criticism can sometimes clarify in your own mind exactly what you wanted to say, even if you don't agree with the comments.

If your agent can send you an edited, marked-up copy of your proposal or manuscript, all the better. But we still encourage a conversation, because even a marked-up submission may hide more general concerns. And the agent may not have taken the time to tell you what she liked best about your work, which is just as important as what she didn't like.

Lastly, you may want to ask your agent if she thinks you can get the job done in one more draft or if it's going to take a number of passes. Some agents will go back and forth on a proposal numerous times. Liz Perle, author of *When Work Doesn't Work Anymore* and a former editor and publisher herself, says, "My agent was really tough on my proposal. I think I redid it twenty times. Sometimes I didn't agree with him, though, and I had to balance what he thought would sell with what I wanted to write."

Having a sense of how far you are from a finished proposal or manuscript will keep your expectations in check and your frustrations at bay. If you know early on that it's going to go back and forth between the two of you for a few drafts, it's a lot easier to bear. And, as Liz Perle made clear, you have to maintain your own core convictions about your work and communicate any discomfort you may have with your agent regarding dubious changes.

If you have a minimum dollar amount you need to write your book, figure this out BEFORE you or your agent goes out to sell it. Calculate costs for your time, permissions and illustrations, travel and research. Make it a bare-bones-honest-to-goodness-bottom-line-minimum amount, not what you fantasize about in your dreams or what you think your agent should ask for. Daniel Greenberg of the Levine Greenberg Literary Agency says, "Trust me, agents eat off their 15%. They have every incentive in the world to get as much money as possible. You don't need to re-incentivize them."

SENDING YOUR BRAVE LITTLE BOOK OUT INTO THE WORLD

The actual submission process produces excitement and anxiety in equal measure. Will my book sell? To whom? How fast? For how much? Or will it never ever sell? All these questions are on every author's mind. Unfortunately, no one can tell you if your book will sell, but we can help you get enough clarity to quell some of your agita.

Who Will See Your Book?

Agents submit your proposal or manuscript to editors within a publishing house or to the publisher himself. Submitting your book to the right editor is key to selling a book, just as submitting your query to the right agent is crucial to landing representation. There is an art to putting together a most excellent submission list. And good agents know how to land a deal—often by sending your material to someone who either specializes in or has a deep personal interest in your subject. And it certainly helps if your agent knows the editor personally. Agents spend countless hours having expensive lunches and sipping drinks with editors, getting to know their likes, dislikes and personal passions, so that when it comes time to submit your proposal they know just who to send it to.

Within each publishing fiefdom, most editors stake out territories. So while there may be numerous nonfiction editors within a house, there will probably be only a couple who patrol the science provinces, another couple who rule the roost of health, and a couple who command the kingdom of cookbooks. But knowing who those editors are is not enough. If you've written a medical book about breast cancer, say, you want your agent to send it not only to one of the health editors, but to the one whose mother is a breast cancer survivor.

How *Many* People Will See It?

Sometimes an agent will get a project that is simply perfect for one particular editor, who just happens to work at the perfect publishing house for your book. Sometimes an agent will be unsure about a project. In either situation, the agent may send the proposal or manuscript on an exclusive to one person. In the first case, she believes she has a good shot at a fast and high-priced sale. In the second, she's testing the waters, seeing if she needs you to continue working on your proposal or manuscript—seeing if she has the right bait and she's casting in the right river.

An agent may also submit on a not-quite-exclusive basis to a few editors. Maybe she thinks three people feel like particularly good fits. Or maybe she wants a few professional opinions on the commercial value of your work.

At the other end of the spectrum, your agent may go hog-wild and do a large multiple submission, which can mean sending your book to anywhere between 15 and 30 editors. This allows a much wider range of opinions on how big a market there is for your book and can possibly create more competition for it. More Peters, more Pauls, maybe even a few Marys.

Big and small submissions have their pluses and minuses. Small allows you the leeway to learn from editors and to change a proposal or manu-

HOW TO HELP YOUR AGENT DURING SUBMISSION

In Chapter 3, we had you look at *Publishers Weekly* and publishersmarketplace.com as well as the acknowledgments of books similar to (but not directly competitive with) yours for the names of editors and agents who might be interested in what you're writing. We asked you to put the editor names aside for later. That later is now. While agents should have their fingers on the publishing pulse, they can't know what everyone is up to. Revisit your editor list and gently pass on the names to your agent. You might have a few suggestions that your agent hasn't thought of; besides, it's good for your agent to know which editors' books you admire. Just as you used information about books your agent represented to gain her interest, so your agent can do the same with editors, who will love to hear that you're a fan of a book they've sweated over.

script without having burned every bridge. And since exclusives are given for anywhere from a day to a couple of weeks, they can also make an editor act fast. On the minus side, submitting to one editor at a time can take forever. The waiting can get painful. But probably the chief disadvantage is that you can't create a competitive environment. And if you accept an offer from an exclusive, you never know how much money you may have left on the table. Then again, you might get someone to put all his chips on the table in order to take your book off it. Large submissions allow for maximum competition and can drive up the price of a book. But if it turns out your proposal/manuscript has problems that you and your agent did not see, you may find that you can fix them but have no place left to go.

YOUR AGENT PITCHES AND FIRES

Your agent has your completed proposal or manuscript. She's made a submission list of editors who she thinks will be hungry for your book. She then, more than likely, writes a cover letter with her version of the same pitch you've been working on since day one. Because a well-crafted cover letter can really sell your book, make sure your agent has all the information she needs to write one that's a killer. Some agents don't write cover letters and only do a telephonic version of your pitch. And some do both in order to gauge editors' interest and get them salivating for your work before it arrives.

Your agent will then send out your proposal or manuscript. Overnight delivery or messengering can be cost-heavy, and typically you'll have to reimburse your agent for that expense. We think it's worth every penny since it makes your work feel urgent and important. Ask your agent how she's sending out your book; if you can afford it, tell her to same-day or overnight it.

A CORNUCOPIA OF CONGLOMERATES

Your agent may be sending your book out to 30 editors but only 8 publishers. How, you may ask, can this be? These days, every big publishing house is owned by a larger company whose holdings go beyond books. Many of these companies have bought up numerous other publishing houses and umbrella'd them under one huge roof. For example, Random House is owned by Bertelsmann, which also bought, among others, Crown, Knopf, Doubleday, Bantam and Dell. These are now called divisions. And within each division, there may be a number of imprints. For example, the imprints within the Crown Publishing Group include Clarkson Potter, Harmony and Three Rivers.

Your book can be simultaneously submitted to several different divisions and imprints within the same company. In fact, it's often essential to submit your book to numerous divisions and imprints if you want to get a bidding war going. That's when things get really tricky. Some publishing houses let their different divisions/imprints bid against each other; others do not. For example, if your agent holds an auction, Random House allows for competing bids within its walls as long as one outside house is part of the auction as well; Penguin does not allow for competing bids. But don't worry your pretty little head about such things. That's what your agent is for!

THE AGONY AND ECSTASY OF "INTEREST"

You open your e-mail inbox. There's a message from your agent. A publisher is interested in your book. Take a minute to rejoice. But don't start spending your future advance. An excruciating amount of time may go by before an offer is made. The interested publisher may want to meet with you. Then you may receive so much inconsistent feedback that your head will spin. And sadly, sometimes interest does not result in a sale. But steel your resolve and gird your loins, because this is where the real fun begins . . .

Face Time with Your Potential Publisher

Once there's interest in your project, meeting with publishing teams—from potential editor, to publicity people, marketing and sales, all the way up to the publisher—may serve you well. Indeed, some agents, eager to have you meet with editors, may ask you to arrange a trip in conjunction with your proposal being sent out. They will then let editors know when you will be in town so that they can set up meetings. Often these meetings can fan the flames of desire for your book. As Kathy Pories, an editor at Algonquin, says, "When we're trying to decide whether to publish a book, the personality of the author is a factor: how are they going to present themselves to the world?"

Can't make the trip to meet with a publisher? Then ask your agent to set up a phone call.

For some writers, it's scary to think about taking a trip into the cut-throat madness of the book business. If, after careful consideration, you do not feel physically, financially, emotionally, verbally, mentally and/or sartorially equipped to sell yourself and your book to a roomful of hardened publishing pundits, you may do yourself a disservice by presenting yourself in the flesh. If you have doubts about your performance potential, discuss them with your agent before she starts contacting editors about a meeting. The fact is, if you're not a presentation-friendly author, you can actually cause more damage than good by revealing that now. Understand that most books sell without the author meeting the publisher. And have no fear, you can improve your presentation skills before you'll be called upon to speak publicly about your book.

That said, it's just as important to check out your editor as vice versa. The editor is like a parent to your project. Imagine that you got the chance to pick your own mom and dad and decided not to meet them before you made a decision. Madness! So we suggest trying to look your future editor and publishing team square in the eyes, shake their hands and get a good measure of them. Even if you don't get to choose your editor in the end, take notes on everyone. The information you gather in these meetings can help you later on. You can often pick up what kind of hesitations a publisher has about your book or you. And if you address these early, you'll be happy later.

If you have a good rapport with your agent, it's great if she can come with you. She can be just the social lubricant needed to ease you into an informative and lucrative meeting.

"WHAT SHOULD I WEAR?"

Before you meet with a prospective publisher or editor, it's prudent to properly prepare. On the fashion front, follow this easy rule of thumb: Wear what you would wear if you were talking to a big-haired host on a TV show. And if you even suspect that you're fashion-challenged, do yourself a favor and get some help. Unless your book is some glam-fest, always go for elegant over flashy. And be sure to wear an outfit that makes you feel comfortable. You don't want to be fidgeting with a too-short skirt or fussing with an uncomfortable necktie. If you have any doubts, ask your agent for advice. Just knowing an industry professional thinks you look good can help you feel pretty, witty, handsome or wise.

WORKING THE ROOM

Successfully working a room is a tricky thing to do. Practice with your friends. Your agent. Your office chums. You want to be energized but relaxed, a good talker but a good listener, confident but not cocky, intuitive but well prepared, eager but not pushy, funny but not shticky. And whatever you do, no matter what you say, display your passion. Remember, passion is contagious. Agents often see publishers who have been riding the fence about a project get won over by an author's passion.

Have your pitch down stone-cold. This way, you'll be able to deliver it with an energetic yet conversational ease. You must understand that you live and die in publishing according to how good your pitch is. If an editor hears a juicy description or a marketing hook that he can repeat to the publicity people who chat up talk-show producers—and then to the special marketing people who get corporate guys to bulk-buy books, and then to the sales force working to sell your book to booksellers large and small—your book will most likely get published. You want an editor humming your pitch as he leaves the office. Make sure it's a catchy tune—easy to remember, and totally you.

Get a card from every single person you meet at the publisher's—not just the editor, but the publicity, marketing and salespeople. Immediately after you do your rounds, send thank-you notes. Then squirrel these cards away in a safe place so you can take them out and nibble on them later.

You also want to have good questions ready to ask (writing them down is incredibly helpful). Why? 1) You need as much information as possible to make an informed decision about who is the best publisher for you. 2) You

PERFORMERS ONE AND ALL

Have you written something that you can dramatize powerfully? If so, put together a three-minute reading and test it out on your agent. Then ask him if he thinks a reading would dazzle potential publishers.

Regina Louise wrote a proposal that caught the attention of over half a dozen top publishers, but Arielle knew she had another card to play. Regina is stylish, engaging and powerful; she also happens to be a scintillating performer. That fact, combined with her riveting and very personal story about surviving 34 foster homes as a child, made her a force to be reckoned with. So Regina memorized about three minutes of her work and opened her publisher meetings with this short dramatic presentation. Each reading produced the same effect: a cartoon-like bugging out of publisher eyes. Everyone saw immediately what a star she was—that she was going to be a great promoter of her book, that she would captivate an audience in a bookstore, in front of a microphone or on camera. Regina, an unknown writer and salon owner who'd never been published before, received a two-book, mid-six-figure deal. Her first book, *Somebody's Someone*, launched her career not only as a writer, but as a sought-after speaker as well.

want to be in the power position. If you're the one asking the tough questions, it will feel as if you're interviewing them, not vice versa.

Below is a list of starter questions to ask an editor, although it's imperative that you come up with ones that are appropriate to your particular project.

- What other books have you published that are similar to mine? Have these been successful? Why or why not?
- What changes do you foresee in the content or direction of my book?
- What are the weak points and how would you fix them?
- What are the strong points and how can I make them better?
- What kind of publicity/marketing plan do you envision for my book?
- How do you like to work? Do you like to receive a complete manuscript or to get several chapters at a time?
- When do you see my book coming out, and why?

Listen. Aggressively focus in on what the editor has to say. Take notes so you can compare editors after your whirlwind of meetings.

How Long Must You Wait?

Of all the excruciating waiting you'll endure in the publishing business, the period between submission and offer (or rejection) will make you feel like a pregnant woman who's three weeks overdue. It's important to prepare yourself because this so-close-yet-so-far waiting can be brutal. Sure, your book can sell super quick. Within a week or two, you can have a publisher and—take a breath—a delivery date! But if you find yourself a month or even six months into a submission, it doesn't mean that your book won't sell.

So what should you do to quell the willies of waiting? Many authors believe their best course of action is to call their agent every hour on the hour to get a progress report. We advise in the strongest terms possible that you NEVER do this. One of the greatest calls an agent ever gets to make is the one that starts: "Hello, I got an offer on your book." Have no fear, as soon as your agent has good news, you'll be the first to know. If, after a few weeks, you haven't heard anything, it's okay to send an e-mail saying, "Any news?" Then, please, do yourself a favor and leave it at that. You can do this every few weeks. If any rejections have crawled like sniveling pigdogs into your agent's office, ask for copies of the rejection letters. They may prove helpful later. If, after a few months, there's not a bite, it's time to have a conversation with your agent. Ask her what she thinks isn't working. Is there any consistent feedback? Should you start reworking your proposal or manuscript? Also ask if she's gotten any positive feedback and what exactly it is. You want to be sure not to eliminate anything that editors actually liked.

Can't get a clear answer from your agent about when she sent your proposal out? Ask for copies of the cover letters for your files. This way, you can track how long your work has been out in the world.

I LOVE IT! I HATE IT!

It couldn't be more common: two smart, successful editors with opposite opinions of your work. At Arielle's agency, there's a story that's become a favorite office joke. James Levine sent out a proposal that he was tremendously excited about. The first call came in, and the editor said, "Jim, the writing here is marvelous, but I just don't think there's an audience for this idea."

SWEET VICTORY

Damian McNicholl sailed through the process of finding an agent but found himself submission-stymied. His novel, *A Son Called Gabriel,* fit squarely into the category of literary fiction and had both gay and Irish themes running through it. Fortunately, in recent years a number of novels with these themes had done extremely well. Unfortunately, publishers seemed to think a novel with these themes would never do well again. He got the "it's been done before" rejection letters. The "gay themes don't sell well" letters. And the "novels like this are getting increasingly difficult to sell" letters.

The really frustrating thing was that Damian was getting juicy compliments about his writing—he could fill the back of a book with blurbs culled from his rejections.

His agent then made some submissions to midsize houses. And while these went out, Damian got busy. He decided that if, for some reason, the second round didn't drum up an offer, he would do a third round with small publishers who specialized in literary fiction. He sent an e-mail a day, tailoring each according to which publishing house he was writing. One of the houses was Greycore Press, which had recently published a book to acclaim that had been rejected by all the big houses. From the reviews the book received, Damian could tell that this small press was proud of picking up on a book that the big guys had missed. So he opened his letter by saying that he, too, had been turned down by the big boys but believed he had a very good book on his hands. Lo and behold, the publisher responded excitedly and asked to see the manuscript.

The last of the rejections were trickling in from the midsize publishers when Greycore offered Damian a deal—but with a catch. His novel wouldn't be published for

Then the second call came in, and the editor said, "Jim, the idea here is terrific, and there's clearly a huge audience, but the writing isn't strong enough." Crazy-making? Absolutely. Unique? Absolutely not. There's simply no accounting for taste. The only thing you can do is learn what you can and then move on. Incidentally, Jim ultimately sold the book for three-quarters of a million dollars and then promptly sold the film rights for half a million more.

FIRING BLANKS

If your agent doesn't get a bite on the first round, it's important to re-express your appreciation of all he's put into the project thus far. Remember, your agent has been working for free up to this point. He doesn't make a cent until you do.

another two years. Then the publisher mentioned another option: her distributor, Client Distribution Services, was starting a publishing arm called CDS Books. She proposed seeing if they would copublish. After many more months of sorting stuff out, CDS was on board and tickled pink. In fact, they were so thrilled that they decided to publish it on their own as a lead title to launch their literary fiction list. Damian then thanked his lucky stars that no big publisher had made an offer! He was going to be the star of this new company, which was known for its top-notch sales force.

Damian is happy to say his agent stayed the course, negotiating a great contract for him, despite the fact that he got no advance. In the end, the relentless full-court-press teamwork paid off in spades. In fact, even as we write this, CDS Books is launching a major publicity and marketing campaign for *A Son Called Gabriel*—a campaign as good as any that established literary fiction authors receive with the big boys. This campaign has included a large galley mailing to traditional trade book editors, editors at gay and lesbian and Irish American magazines and radio shows. To top it off, the American Booksellers Association Book Group of independent booksellers has made it one of their monthly selections—a major coup for literary fiction.

And the early reviews—like Damian's rejection letters—rave about his stunning writing! Damian says, "I have a personality that never gives up. Even at my lowest point, I believed that what I'd written deserved to be published. You just have to systematically explore all the opportunities that exist. I think the key is to remain positive and well-mannered throughout the entire process. Leave any arrogance behind."

If you sense that your agent is rapidly losing interest in you and your project, it's important to ask up front if he plans to cut bait or try to do some more fishing. If he says he's willing to continue but you hear some serious waffle in his voice, you have several options: 1) You can approach smaller publishers on your own. 2) You can try to find another agent. (This choice is recommended only if you've had a nightmare experience thus far with your own.) 3) You can, in addition to expressing your sincere appreciation, ask your agent what you can do to improve your proposal/manuscript to make it salable. Do not count on much agent participation at this particular point in the process. Once an agent has received a lot of rejections on a project, its luster can fade. Unless he has an undying passion for your work, it will be difficult for him to call up the same enthusiasm he brought to begin with (assuming he actually brought any enthusiasm). But lack of agent participation doesn't mean all hope is lost. A little of the right advice can sometimes fix your ship. Maybe your agent can suggest a book doctor or editor if the rejections you've received have to do with editorial problems. (You might also want to jump ahead and read our next chapter about making the most of rejection.)

If your agent agrees to cast out his line again, find out the strategy behind his submissions. Are they to divisions of the bigger houses that haven't seen your work yet? Are they to second-tier publishers who pay less money but are very good at what they do? Are there smaller or university presses that might be a good fit for your work?

If, on the other hand, your agent tells you he's not sending your work elsewhere, reassess. Is this really the end of the line? Or just for this agent? Once your book has been submitted by an agent and remains unsold, it can be very difficult to find another agent unless your first agent did a very small submission or has a reputation as a loose cannon or an idiot. If you do decide to change seahorses in midstream, be sure you know exactly who your book was submitted to (again, get copies of all letters, both submission and rejection) and ask your agent for suggestions about who you should submit to on your own. Maybe he can give you a list of small publishers who would be appropriate for your book. Ask if he knows any editors at these houses. And ask if he'd be willing to negotiate the deal with a smaller publisher if you get an offer from one. If you decide to fish in a smaller pond, see the directions that follow for submitting your book on your own.

SENDING YOUR BOOK DIRECTLY TO PUBLISHERS

If you've decided to submit directly to publishers, you're going to have your best shot at smaller, independent houses. In fact, not all independent publishers are that small. Yes, some are mom-and-pop operations and have published only a few books. (In the publishing industry, a "small press" is defined as a press that publishes fewer than 12 titles per year.) But independent presses also include university presses, midsize presses and a number of stars in the industry, including Chronicle Books, the top gift book publisher in the industry; W.W. Norton, known far and wide for its anthologies; and Workman, the publisher of this very book.

Stacks of bestsellers and tons of bestselling authors have been published by independents. Tom Clancy's *The Hunt for Red October* was first published by the Naval Institute Press. *Chicken Soup for the Soul* and its dozens and dozens of offshoots are ladled into the world by Health Communications, an independent press operating out of Deerfield Beach, Florida. And it's not a fluke that these books became bestsellers. Independent publishers may be small, but they're not necessarily small businesses. In fact, independent publishing is a $29.6 billion industry. In addition, although it may seem stranger than fiction, less than a third of independently published books are being sold in bookstores. We'll discuss why in a moment.

Are you determined to send your work directly to a big publisher? Then make sure you have the name of a specific editor to send your proposal or manuscript to. Otherwise, it'll be shredder bound. As always, this entails doing your research. Your two best bets are looking in acknowledgments and checking out Appendix I for books that list editors' names along with their individual interests.

Why to Consider Working with an Independent Publisher

These days, many writers prefer independent publishers to the big guys. Here are some of the best reasons you should seriously consider working with an independent:

- ***Special love, tender care.*** Independent presses are likely to give you more personal attention than a publishing behemoth, and to view you as a valued player during each step of the publishing process. Many independent publishers are looking for long-term relationships that help to build writers' careers.

- ***Big-time front-list attention.*** Let's say you're published by a division of Random House. The chances of being one of the few new books that are given the most attention are slim, even if the publisher paid a nice chunk of change for your book. So when it's time to publicize and market your book, you may be sadly disappointed over the amount of attention it receives. Because independent publishers are dealing with smaller lists of books, your book has a chance to get some front-list enthusiasm and attention, which can go a long way even if resources may be limited.

- ***Long shelf life.*** Because they usually publish far fewer books than the big boys, independent publishers do their darnedest to keep each book in print for the long haul even if it hasn't had killer sales right out of the gate. You can't underestimate the importance of keeping your book in print. There's nothing more frustrating, heartbreaking and revenue-reducing than putting your passion into print, only to have it languish sadly on remainder tables a year later. Also, you never know when it will suddenly become relevant. A major worldwide event or your relentless promoting could bring your book into the spotlight and turn it into an "instant" best-seller. But if the book is out of print, you're out of luck.

- ***Specialization.*** Most independent publishers specialize in a particular area. Guess what Motor Books publishes? What about Travelers' Tales? Or Collector Books? Specialized publishers know how to get your book into the hands of your audience. They're chummy with the media people who cover your subject, and they sell into non-bookstore venues that specialize in your area. They know how to get sports books into stadiums, cookbooks into kitchen stores and dog books into pet stores. Less than a third of books published by independent presses end up in bookstores precisely because they sell directly to their sweet niche audiences.

Scared an independent press won't lend your book the credibility it needs? Think bookstores and reviewers may pooh-pooh your book? Our research indicates that when a title is being considered, the size of the press doesn't matter as much as its reputation. So, if prestige is a concern, check if a publisher's books are sold in the chains and in your local independent bookstore. Track down reviews, news stories and other periodical features to ensure that major media outlets pay attention to a particular publisher.

Why Not to Consider Working with an Independent Publisher

As compelling as the reasons are for going with an independent publisher, difficulties can ensue. Here are some of the downsides:

- ***Smaller advances.*** Unlike the big conglomerates, independent publishers generally pay less money for advances (in the $1,000–$3,000 range), if indeed they pay any at all. While some occasionally pay five- or even six-figure advances for a book, you are more than likely going to make your money on royalties, which only accrue once your book is out in the marketplace.

- ***Lower royalties.*** Standard royalty rates for independent presses run about 10% of net (this is approximately 5% of the cover price). Most major publishers start their royalties at 7.5% of the cover price for paperbacks and 10% for hardcovers. This lower royalty is due not to greed on the part of independent publishers, but rather to the reality that most don't have in-house sales representatives. This means they have to pay extra fees to get their books distributed to bookstores and other retail venues.

- ***Small to nonexistent marketing budgets.*** A big publisher who gets behind your book might sink thousands of dollars into marketing and publicizing it. This isn't even a remote fantasy with many independent publishers.

- ***Potential distribution problems.*** Because almost no independent publishers have their own sales force, they have to use commission sales reps, distributors and wholesalers to sell their books to stores around the country.

  Commission reps work independently and are paid a commission by the publisher based on net sales. These reps typically have long-established relationships with their publishers and retailers. Surprisingly, this is not always the case with in-house sales groups, where turnover is traditionally higher.

  Distributors are companies that employ a group of sales representatives who go out seasonally and tell bookstores what publishers have coming up. Both distributors and commission reps represent several publishers at once but, like in-house sales reps, cover a defined geographic area.

  Some small publishers don't even have sales reps and depend solely on sales outside of bookstores and/or Web sales and/or wholesalers. Wholesalers do not actively go out and sell your book. Rather, they make your book easily available to bookstores—often only on a local basis. If you want your book sold in bookstores, your publisher should, at the very minimum, work with wholesalers.

  Bottom line: If you want sales in bookstores across the country, you'll want to be sure your publisher also has commission reps or a distributor.

Jan Nathan, head of the Publishers Marketing Association, the leading organization for independent publishers, breaks it down: "You will

GOING WITH AN INDEPENDENT PUBLISHER: THE GOOD AND THE BAD

Shawna Kenney is the author of *I Was a Teenage Dominatrix*, about her very interesting after-school job. If you're conjuring up an image of a mean lady who inspires terror in everyone she meets, you'd be describing Shawna's exact opposite. Shawna is a sweet, warm, inviting person who promotes relentlessly and loves working with a team. That's why going with a respected, midsize independent publisher made sense for her. According to Shawna: "My publisher allowed me complete artistic freedom in choosing a cover. . . . I know their salespeople and can call or stop by whenever I like." She also liked their extremely equitable contract and how they continued to feature her book in their catalog well after publication.

Not to say that her experience was flaw-free. Shawna says, "Due to their small size and a more laissez-faire attitude than the majors, I learned that sometimes things run well behind schedule. For example, my book was reprinted almost six months later than the date stipulated in the contract, due to the owner's illness." She also was left to handle most publicity and marketing on her own. Fortunately for Shawna, she's a PR whiz, so the lack of backup was something she learned to live with. And her experience overall was exceedingly pleasing. The book was very well received critically and has been optioned to be made into a Hollywood movie, while her fan base has grown at well-attended events all over the country.

probably not have the potential for a hundred thousand in sales your first year, but you'll have a long-term partner in your independent publisher and be treated like a star." "Long-term partner" and "star" are not words ever to be taken lightly by a writer. Upon hearing them, many a backlist author from almost any one of the big New York houses would be sorely tempted to jump ship.

While independent presses tend to focus more on nonfiction than on fiction, a number specialize in genre fiction, ranging from sci-fi, mysteries and romance to literary fiction and poetry. Unfortunately, whether the house is big or small, fiction is particularly challenging to sell. But not impossible. If you're having a difficult time finding a home at a major publisher for your novel, it's still worth pursuing independents, university presses or self-publishing.

Not Your Father's University Press

Traditionally, the mission of most university presses has been to publish important books with little or no concern for marketplace demands. That's still true, but over the past 10 years, as more and more individual publishers have been bought by conglomerates, something's changed. The quality of general-interest submissions at university presses has gone up. Opportunistic agents and authors realized that as major publishers were becoming more conservative, university presses were launching books in categories they traditionally left unexplored. It turns out that top-notch books without blockbuster potential or top-notch authors whose books never broke into bestsellerdom were being frozen out of large publishing houses. University presses grabbed the opportunity and began publishing these excellent books and authors, many of whom have dedicated audiences. True, these books don't bring in megaprofits, but they're doing well enough to take care of the bottom line of a university press.

Nowadays, over 50% of university presses' lists are made up of trade books. You'll see university press books covered everywhere from *The New York Times Book Review* to *USA Today*. No longer do people expect stiff, stuffy tomes on the Fluctuation of Market Trends in Postindustrialized Patagonia. Rather, you'll find memorable memoirs, titillating histories, even fabulous fiction. This is not your father's university press!

In addition, many university presses have specialty areas into which your book may fit perfectly. And unlike many other independent presses, university presses often handle literary fiction. The University of Wisconsin Press, for example, has one of the best gay and lesbian lists in the country. It also publishes highbrow mysteries, travel, popular history, even cookbooks. Raphael Kadushin, an editor at the University of Wisconsin Press, says, "We've probably had better luck with smaller literary books than the big New York houses. We regularly get reviews in *The New York Times* and other national exposure." So, if you can live off a smaller advance and you find a university press that knows just how to publish your book, this can be a better choice than a large house.

Another good time to go with a university press is if you're an academic who's written a popular book but would like the prestige of a university press behind you for career purposes. This is especially true if your book has the possibility of being adopted for classroom use. University presses are even better at getting their books into classrooms than a lot of the major trade houses.

Talk about a good news/bad news situation. Good news: University presses are now another venue for excellent trade publishing, giving you more choices in a world of conglomerates. And they offer all the advantages of independent publishers. Bad news: They're relying more and more on agents for material. This was unheard-of a decade ago, and the result is that it's less and less likely your book will be able to climb out of the slush pile. The exception to this rule is a book with regional appeal. Most university presses have a regional publishing program (in fact, some university presses are devoted primarily to regional publishing), and they're more likely to read direct queries if done professionally.

Approaching the Independents

If you read the chapter on finding an agent, some of the following information will ring a bell because you'll be using the same PYPIP techniques to find the right publisher. Again, research. Which independent publishers do books like yours? Revisit your local bookstore and library and log onto an Internet bookstore. Amanda Cotten, owner of Valencia Books in San Francisco, says, "Booksellers often know which publishers tend to publish which books and may be able to help you with which ones to approach, especially the small local publishers."

There are independent publishers for virtually every category. But it's up to you to find out which publisher is a good fit for you and your book. Track down appropriate publishers. Study them. Find their books. Read them. Check the acknowledgments to see who's thanked. Does it look like there was a good relationship between author and publisher? If so, write down their names.

There may be only one independent publisher that's *exactly* right for you, but a number of other houses that look good, too. Let's say you're writing about teen pregnancy. You learn that Morning Glory Press of Buena Park, California, publishes books solely on the subject of teen pregnancy. An obvious place to start. But your research should uncover a number of other independent publishers who handle parenting and teen titles that should be added to your list. And if you're writing about the history of race car drivers from Oxford, you'd probably start by looking at Motor Books, which has an office in Oxford, England.

Once you've researched the appropriate houses, it's time to write your query letter. A query letter is best addressed to a particular editor and is made up of three essential elements: 1) *Why your book is right for the publisher's list.* This is where you display your hard-earned knowledge of the press you're approaching. Talk about the books the editor herself has worked on and make a personal connection. This will lower the letter's chances of ending up in the dreaded slush pile. 2) *Your pitch.* In order to write the best possible pitch for a particular publisher, you want to study the copy on the back and jacket flaps of their books and write your pitch in their style. 3) *Sell yourself.* Let them know why you're the perfect person to write this book—and why you'd be a smashing addition to their list.

If you can find the e-mail address for a particular editor or for the general acquisitions editor, all the better. Send your query via e-mail and attach your proposal or, if you're writing fiction, a piece of your manuscript.

It's now time to put a two-week tickler on your calendar. When that tickler tickles, it's time for a follow-up. You can do this every two weeks. For more information on the art of the follow-up as well as more query letter information, see Chapter 3.

If a publisher asks you to send your proposal/manuscript, we recommend overnighting or messengering your material. It's the top-priority factor, thus lessening your chances of getting lost in that vast morass of paper. Plus you'll have a record of receipt.

If you'd like to submit your proposal/manuscript to more than one publisher, send queries simultaneously. It's okay to send out multiple submissions even if a publisher wants exclusivity. Publishers can have exclusivity when they give you a contract. But if they ask, you should be honest. Then, the second you get a nibble, contact all queried publishers and let them know another someone is panting after your book. Since you don't have an agent to represent you, you'll have to leverage interest. And one of the best ways to do this is to let everyone know someone else wants to take you to the prom.

Again, if your personality is suited to the task, try to meet any and all interested publishers, as well as their staffs. Scope out their organizations. Are they so small that you'd be better off self-publishing? Or have they been doing this for years and know just how to do what they do? Whether you get to meet with them or not, there are two major questions that you must ask all interested independent publishers.

SUBMITTING TO HOLLYWOOD

If you have a movie-friendly book, you need to determine the best time to go out with your material. *When* you send your book out will, in part, decide whether your book will be made into a movie and how much money you'll be paid for it. Some books will benefit immensely by being seen first in their complete form, as opposed to a proposal, so people can grasp the whole breadth of your story. On the other hand, some high-concept ideas scream movie from the moment they're put down on a page, and just the promise of what you'll deliver will make some movie mogul plop down a huge chunk of change. A well-known film agent once told Arielle, "There are good reasons to sell your book fast. And there are good reasons to sell your book cheap. But there are no good reasons to sell your book fast and cheap." Unless, of course, you're dying for cash or think the chances of your book being made into a movie by anyone else are super thin.

No matter whether you choose to send your book as a proposal, a manuscript, a bound galley or a finished book, you've got to pick your moment to infiltrate Hollywood. Should you send it when there's still a halo of hope hovering over your unpublished book? Or should you wait until you have something concrete and exciting to dangle in front of Tinseltown? This is a tough call and one that only you, your agent and your sixth sense can make. But be sure to follow trends and developments in the film world. Is the highest-grossing movie of the moment in the style of film noir? Is your book also written in a noir style? Have there been a string of sci-fi flops? Is your novel science fiction? Then hold off.

1. ***Who is your wholesaler?*** Ingram, the biggest wholesaler in the country, has shut the door on any publisher with fewer than 10 titles in print. If Ingram won't buy books from your potential publisher, the only other major player is Baker & Taylor, whose main customers are libraries. Unless your book is suited primarily for libraries or is of local interest only, this is deeply problematic.

2. ***Who is your distributor?*** Do you have commission reps? If your potential publisher has no distributor, you've got trouble, my friend. Distributors, through their sales reps, introduce your book into stores all over the country. If, however, your book's main sales channel will be outside bookstores, e.g., at flower shops, judo centers or golf courses, and your potential publisher sells directly into these sales channels, then

Remember the scouts we talked about in the last chapter? If your book has movie potential, it's very likely to land in a scout's hands, whether you put it there or not. It's the scout's job to discover what's new and exciting before anyone else. Scouts create relationships with a whole host of editors who tip them off when something promising comes in. This can be good news if they get their hands on your work and pass it to the right people at the right time. But it can be bad news if they pass it on to the right people at the wrong time. If a studio or producer rejects your book before it has a chance to blossom, it will be hard to get them to revisit it later, when it's in full bloom. If you have an agent with good relationships with the scouts, she can help manage this relationship so that you're protected against premature exposure.

You also shouldn't automatically assume that your book is *not* right for Hollywood. Rosalind Wiseman's *New York Times* bestseller *Queen Bees & Wannabes*, a sociological exploration of the hierarchy of adolescent girls, has no plot, no heroes. Not a likely candidate to be made into a blockbuster Hollywood movie? Guess again. *Queen Bees & Wannabes* was turned into the #1 box-office hit *Mean Girls*. FYI: Rosalind's next book, *Queen Bee Moms and Kingpin Dads: Coping with the Parents, Teachers, Coaches, and Counselors Who Can Rule—or Ruin—Your Child's Life* (written with Elizabeth Rapoport), was sold just as the movie was hitting screens all over America. We're sure you won't be surprised to hear that it went for a very pretty penny.

you're okay. In fact, many independent publishers make their bread and butter by selling to specialty stores like these. You just have to be clear about where you think your book has the best chance of selling and whether or not you or the independent publisher can successfully get it there.

If an interested publisher wants you to pay a fee to get published and says you have to give up all rights to your work, with no royalties, RUN SCREAMING FROM THE ROOM AND NEVER LOOK BACK! This is not a real independent publisher. This is a vanity press. A publisher who doesn't actually put money in your pocket shouldn't be taking it out, then keeping all the proceeds. **(For more on vanity presses, see page 354.)**

AND IN CONCLUSION . . .

If you've generated a lot of interest in your project, it's time to celebrate profusely. With gusto.

If your first round didn't go well, despair not. Many books remain unsold on their first, second or even third submission, then go on to lead long and happy lives. If your work is submitted to 15 publishers, all 15 of them may reject your work; then, on the next round, your book can be the subject of an intense bidding war. In the end, it ain't over till you say it's over. Channel angst and anger into action. This action may be figuring out how to mend your proposal/manuscript or coming up with an alternate publishing plan like developing a platform first, going back to finding an agent or possibly self-publishing.

New bait, new rod, new pond . . . you never know. At the end of the day, it's up to you to keep casting your line. If you're finding rejection hard to bear (and who doesn't?), move on to the next chapter. It's important to remember that, time and again, it's the patient fisherman who catches the real whopper.

CHAPTER 5

REJECTION SECTION

"Can't act, can't sing, can dance a little."

—HOLLYWOOD STUDIO HACK, REJECTING FRED ASTAIRE

There's no more heartrending story of rejection than that of John Kennedy Toole, author of *A Confederacy of Dunces.* In 1969, three years after the novel was rejected by Simon & Schuster, Toole had become so despondent that he committed suicide. Toole's grief-stricken yet incredibly determined mother asked everyone she could think of to read the book. Seven years of rejection later, she got it into the hands of novelist and professor Walker Percy. How could he say no to this poor woman with her deceased son's unpublished manuscript? With great dread, he began the thick tome, hoping it would be horrible so he wouldn't have to read the whole thing. At the end of the first page, he sighed in dismay. Unfortunately, the book was too good to quit reading. As he read on, he groaned. It was so good, he was going to have to read the whole thing. Halfway through the book, he realized he was holding a novel of immense value. In fact, *A Confederacy of Dunces* went on to win a Pulitzer Prize.

If only Mr. Toole had maintained his mother's faith and resolve. Imagine the career he might have enjoyed, the books he might have written.

If you write something that you want someone else to publish, YOU WILL ALMOST CERTAINLY BE REJECTED. It's not a question of *if.* It's a question of *when.* Virtually every great author has been rejected. In fact, as far as we're concerned, you can't be a great writer until you've been rejected. James Joyce's *Ulysses,* voted the best novel of the 20th century by The Modern Library, was rejected over and over again, deemed by many "learned experts" to be unpublishable. Jane Austen, J.D. Salinger, Vladimir Nabokov. Name your favorite authors and you'll find a trail of rejections scattered behind them. So if the greatest writers have been bashed, pilloried, dismissed, railed upon and savaged, what makes you think it should be any different for you?

Unfortunately, we humans hear the roar of rejection hundreds of times louder than we hear the whisper of praise. Lance Armstrong, the great cycling champion, described riding down a mountain during the Tour de France. Even though there were thousands of people cheering loudly, he found that all he could hear was that one booing, jeering jerk screaming, "YOU STINK!" Obviously, no matter how many great things people say about you, it's hard not to focus on that one voice saying you're no damn good. And it's even harder, of course, when no one at all is saying anything nice about you. This is the time to keep the cheerleader on your team close at hand. It's also a good time to devise a strategy for dealing with rejection. That's what this chapter is all about.

REJECTION RULES

Humans can get used to anything. Muhammad Ali once devised a strategy called the rope-a-dope, in which he tucked his head behind his gloves and let his opponent pummel him until the sap wore himself out. Ali would then pounce back and win the bout. Rejection can make you feel like a human punching bag. But if you hang in there long enough, you just might triumph in the end. Below are some coping strategies to help you bear up.

- ***It's only one person's opinion.*** All agents and all editors have stories about bestselling books they've turned down. Books they thought were downright terrible, books they thought had no market. Or simply books they didn't feel strongly about one way or another. The problem is that agents and editors have only their own experience on which to draw. Maybe they've always been carb fans and thought the Atkins diet was not only distasteful but ridiculous. Think of all the bestselling books that don't appeal to you—that you just don't get and that you can't understand why others are reading. Or, conversely, the books you love that never made it big. The point is, there simply is no accounting for taste.

- ***No one wants to give you your first job.*** Everyone wants to give you a job after you're already successful. A couple of nutty brothers wrote a script that was made into a movie, and suddenly they had the ear of some Hollywood muckety-mucks, all of whom wanted to know: "Where's your next script?" The brothers had been working on a big, crazy science-fiction idea that they wanted to direct themselves. But the idea was so huge and unusual, no one would give them the money for it. No one would risk giving them their first directing job on a film so large and strange. So they wrote a smaller, easier-to-make movie, much of which takes place in one apartment. Because the budget was so small, and the movie was so good, it made money. So now those Hollywood muckety-mucks, who wouldn't give them money to make their crazy science-fiction movie before their success, were more than happy to give them $70 million. The nutty sci-fi film? A little movie called *The Matrix*.

- ***No one knows what's going to sell.*** In a study done at the Wharton School of Business about predictors of success in trade publishing, it was shown overwhelmingly that no amount of number crunching or objective quantifying analysis can predict what will be successful. The best predictor of a book's future success is an agent's or editor's or publisher's gut instinct. Unfortunately, it appears that the guts of those in publishing are particularly unprescient. So, no matter how many people tell you that your manuscript has no value, understand that a large percentage of those people have no idea what they're talking about.

- ***Let no nabob shake your faith in your writing ability.*** Yes, listen intently. Yes, be open to making the changes necessary to mold your manuscript into a lean, mean fighting machine. But don't let the "nattering nabobs of negativity" shake your belief in your own ability to succeed. As Saul Bellow put it, "I've discovered that rejections are not altogether a bad thing. They teach a writer to rely on his own judgment and to say in his heart of hearts, 'To hell with you.'"

- ***It takes only one.*** Your book can be rejected by hundreds of publishers and/or agents. But all it takes is one publisher or one agent to make your dream come true. Joe Quirk wrote five novels and collected 375 rejection letters before he got published. After finishing his fifth novel, he sent the first chapter to *Harper's* magazine. He got back a form rejection letter. Scribbled across the bottom were the words "Give it a rest, pal." You'd think at this point he would have done just that. Instead, he soldiered on and a month later found an interested agent. Shortly thereafter, his book was sold. We're happy to report that *The Ultimate Rush* went on to become a national bestseller.

TO LEARN OR NOT TO LEARN

Can you learn from your foul and brutal rejections? Are there consistencies from letter to letter? Is it obvious from these rejections that you haven't made particular points clearly enough? Does your ending fall apart? Or is there a weakness in your writing (stiff, purple, meandering) that is directly addressed or alluded to?

Most people get so caught up in the rejection that they don't see the gift the rejecter is giving them—free advice! Imagine what you would have had to pay this fancy agent or editor if you hired her for an evaluation. Granted, often you just get a form letter, but sometimes you don't. And the letters that contain advice can help you transform your work from a pile of dusty paper into a book. Rainelle Burton, author of *The Root Worker*, says, "Many writers either become devastated when they get a rejection letter or don't submit their work out of fear of being rejected again—often because they take it as a personal rejection. Some of the best advice on how to shape and rewrite my book—and one of the book's strongest characters—came from agents' rejection letters. I paid attention to what they said the book needed, took their advice and sent it back. I ended up with a stronger, better novel."

Here are three real rejection letters from editors to an agent, all regarding the same novel. Taken together, they illustrate what you can and can't learn from a rejection letter.

1.

Thanks for sending me ______. Although I can certainly see why you are so taken with this, I'm sorry to say that I didn't share quite the same level of enthusiasm.

2.

Thanks for giving me a look at ______. The world portrayed is fascinating, and one senses that the portrayal is authentic. I found the development of the story a little too bare, though, and I longed for more texture and complexity. For this reason, I'm going to pass.

3.

Thanks so much for showing me ______. This novel was a really tough call for me. I was very drawn to its sensitivity, its depth and the elegant and sparse language that captured the lives of such interesting people. I was completely

> transported into a world so very different from mine, and yet so complex and poignant. Overall, I found the story itself to be engaging, deft and extremely touching. However, my main problem with this novel was the fact that I did not feel acquainted with the main characters until halfway into the story. I just didn't know them well enough to care as much as I felt I should until I was well into the book. For this reason, I'm passing on _____.

Letter #1 is a great illustration of what you *can't* learn from a rejection letter. Even though the editor says, "I can see why you're so taken with _____," she gives no information to back this up. She then goes on to say she doesn't share "the same level of enthusiasm." Why? We have no idea. From this letter, we can't even tell if the person actually read the novel. This is an utterly worthless rejection and should be used as lining for the birdcage.

Letter #2 is also quite "bare"—the word used by the editor to criticize the book. But at least she gives a little bit of detail about why she's passing. As she says, she longed for "more texture and complexity." By itself, it's a little hard to know exactly what this means. What kind of texture and complexity is missing? Is there not a strong enough sense of place? Is the plot thin? Are the characters cardboard? But, when coupled with Letter #3, you can start to put the pieces of the puzzle together to reveal what exactly this novel may be missing.

Letter #3 shows that the editor also has a problem with the story being bare, though she doesn't put it in the same words as the writer of Letter #2. Instead, she says it took too long to get to know the main characters. Okay, now we've got something. There is a lack of character development up until the midpoint of the novel. Might a dose of texture and complexity help? Once you've gleaned this kind of information, you can go back into your work and see 1) if you think the criticism is on target, and, if so, 2) how you can fix your book.

While it can be difficult to hear criticism, it can be equally difficult to hear praise. As we said, we humans tend to hear rejection roar and praise whisper. But the kind words contained in a rejection can help clarify what works—important if you don't want to make unnecessary changes to your proposal or manuscript. Even in the worst-case scenario—that you don't sell the work in question—these kind words can guide you to your next project by pinpointing your strong suits as a writer or your affinity for a particular subject. For example, a single chapter or character may grab the attention of agents and editors. Maybe this chapter or character can be expanded into a book itself.

Praise is also a balm for pain. It's proof that you're not busting your buns in vain. And if you don't let yourself hear this praise, it's going to be very difficult to plod on.

If you reread the second two letters, you'll see a solid helping of praise. Letter #2 says the world portrayed in the novel is "fascinating" and "authentic." Two *major* successes for any fiction writer. And Letter #3 is the kind of rejection letter you long for (an oxymoron, we know). It's filled with praise and adjectives you'd want to pull out and use as blurbs on the back of the book: "engaging," "deft," "extremely touching." And it should definitely make the author hopeful—the editor lets him see how close she came to making an offer on the book. So close that the author could resubmit the manuscript if he goes back in and addresses the editor's concerns. All in all, this letter is cause for celebration. If you get one like it, don't mope around the house thinking how close you got. Go out with friends and toast the great writer that you are!

Of course, some rejection letters are just plain ridiculous. One of Arielle's all-time favorite rejection letters included the line "a novel should not be written in the first person." Go quick! Rip *The Catcher in the Rye* from your shelves and fling it in the garbage! Or there are David's favorite kinds of rejections—the ones that dismiss an entire category of books: "Football books don't sell!" "Cancer memoirs don't sell!" Or, as a famous rejection of George Orwell's *Animal Farm* stated, "It is impossible to sell animal stories in the USA." Statements like these are continuously disproven, and when they are, publishers rush to do dozens of books in whatever category they've just lambasted (most of which fail because they aren't nearly as good as the book they're copying). These kinds of rejection letters are for prominent display on your wall of fame or for placing in a favorite scrapbook. As for the educational value of such letters, they teach you only one thing—that publishing is a ridiculous business inhabited by fallible individuals who often can't tell a bestseller from a pointed stick poked sharply into the eye.

Bottom line: Do not ignore your rejection letters and/or choose to simply let them get you down. Please, play through the pain; you can't hit the game-winning home run unless you're up at bat.

The Art of Taking Criticism: "Thank You, Sir, May I Have Another?"

The art of taking criticism can be as difficult to learn as not falling off a rolling log. Our instinct is to become despondent and defensive when we hear negative things hurled at us . . . even when they're being said politely. This is why it's often better to keep ears open and mouth shut when people are telling you what's wrong with your work. No one wants to hear that his child is ugly. But, unfortunately, it may be true. The great thing is, you can actually make it more beautiful.

If you're lucky enough to have the opportunity to talk to your rejecter in person, on the phone or via letter or e-mail, DO NOT BE DEFENSIVE. Instead, ask your rejecter what you might do to improve your work, as well as what he liked about the work. If, for example, someone happens to e-mail you to reject a proposal he requested, don't just delete the e-mail and eat a pint of Häagen-Dazs. Take the time to compose a thoughtful reply so that you can get as much information as possible about why the rejecter rejected your work. Here's the kind of exchange that you'll want to shoot for, in this case with an agent:

Rejecter e-mail #1: *Thanks very much for submitting your work, but this project just isn't right for me. I wish you the best of luck with it.*
Author e-mail #1: Thank you very much for taking the time to read my material. I really appreciate it. I'm wondering if you could give me some specific feedback so I know what I need to work on. Can you tell me what did and didn't work for you? And what you think I need to do to improve the proposal?

Rejecter e-mail #2: *The writing isn't strong enough. It's too stiff and academic. I think it would be a good idea to work with an editor or to bring on a writer.*
Author e-mail #2: Do you have any suggestions for someone I might work with? If I go ahead and hire either an editor or a writer and rework my proposal, would you be interested in taking another look?

Rejecter e-mail #3: *Yes. But I'd like to see an introductory chapter if you resubmit. And Bud Krupke, a freelance editor, might be a good fit for you.*
Author e-mail #3: Thanks so much for your helpful advice. I will pursue either an editor or a writer and get back to you with a revised proposal and new introductory chapter once I feel that I've addressed your concerns fully.

As you can see, this rejection went from a shutout to an open door. And even if the rejecter had said "no thanks" in the end, this writer would still have learned that her writing was stiff and that her submission package was missing a piece—the introductory chapter. And the writer got a great referral of someone to work with. This exchange also gave the writer a chance to make it clear that she would be great to work with. She listens well and is willing to put in the necessary work to polish the proposal so it's publisher-ready. Agents and editors hate it when they have to read a second draft of a proposal or manuscript that's essentially the same as the draft they've already read. By clearly stating that she won't get back to the agent until she's fully addressed the agent's concerns, she lets the agent know that this will not be the case with her book.

So the next time your work is criticized, try the open-minded question approach. It's preferable to the slinking into silent self-loathing one.

If you happen to get a rejection over the phone, be sure to have a pen and paper handy before you ask a single question. Then write everything down. Memory can be a harsh and faulty companion.

Many times it will not be possible to face your rejecters. Many times you will hear nothing at all from them, as if a giant black hole has sucked up your manuscript and swallowed it. Sometimes you will get a form letter. If this is the case, we have a suggestion. Turn these wicked pieces of paper into art—a collage or a poem. Or, if it's cold and damp, build a roaring fire and watch it burn, baby, burn.

How to Deal: Developing Thick Skin

David was a professional actor for 20 years before he became an author. So naturally he was rejected tens of thousands of times, by everyone from titans in the industry to the lowliest bottom-feeders. Thus he became the Raja of Rebuff. The Sovereign of the Snub. Master of the Cold Shoulder. And to David, a rejection proves only one thing: that the rejecter is the biggest moron in the world for not understanding what a brilliant, astonishing, amazing specimen of humanity he is. He looks at each rejection as a badge of honor. And he's got his own little conspiracy theory going about rejection. Only after he's accumulated a sufficient number of rejections will he be rewarded with an offer.

Hallie Ephron, coauthor of the Peter Zaks mystery series, agrees that a stubborn streak is crucial: "The difference between unpublished and published writers, talent aside, is sticking with it. Don't give up after you get rejected by four agents—a good friend of mine was rejected by 48 before she found one who then promptly sold her book within two weeks."

Unfortunately, a large percentage of us feel as if the word "loser" has been permanently branded on our foreheads when confronted with rejection. Unlike David, we stew in the juices of our limitations rather than taking the "no limits" point of view. So, if you're one of the majority, it's a good time to reread the rejection tenets and then to come up with a mantra that comforts you. Bestselling author Barbara Kingsolver says, "This manuscript of yours that has just come back from another editor is a precious package. Don't consider it rejected. Consider that you've addressed it 'to the editor who can appreciate my work' and it has simply come back stamped 'Not at this address.' Just keep looking for the right address."

We know a writer who imagines himself commiserating with James Joyce and Herman Melville about what it feels like to be rudely rejected. Similarly, many writers find it helpful to get together with others to swap war stories. Sometimes the stinging nettle of rejection is soothed by voicing it to others who've been similarly stung. And the great thing is, the worse your rejection, the more entertaining, funny and interesting your stories will be.

These methods may sound hokey, but it's amazing how helpful hoke can sometimes be. So before you throw this book at the wall (another helpful venting technique), at least try commiserating, or ranting, or making badges of honor out of your rejections, and see if it makes you feel better. If it doesn't, we have a surefire technique for one and all. Type up a number of rejections of famous books and pin them up in your work space. These are great spirit buoyers. Here's a good starter list taken from the wonderful book *Rotten Rejections*, edited by André Bernard:

The Deer Park, by Norman Mailer:
"This will set publishing back 25 years."

The Diary of Anne Frank:
"The girl doesn't, it seems to me, have a special perception or feeling which would lift that book above the 'curiosity' level."

Barchester Towers, by Anthony Trollope:
"The grand defect of the work, I think, as a work of art is the low-mindedness and vulgarity of the chief actors. There is hardly a 'lady' or 'gentleman' amongst them."

Carrie, by Stephen King:
"We are not interested in science fiction which deals with negative utopias. They do not sell."

Catch-22, by Joseph Heller:
"I haven't really the foggiest idea about what the man is trying to say. . . . Apparently the author intends it to be funny—possibly even satire—but it is really not funny on any intellectual level."

The Spy Who Came In from the Cold, by John le Carré:
"You're welcome to le Carré—he hasn't got any future."

Lady Windermere's Fan, by Oscar Wilde:
"My dear sir,
I have read your manuscript. Oh, my dear sir."

Lolita, by Vladimir Nabokov:
". . . overwhelmingly nauseating, even to an enlightened Freudian . . . the whole thing is an unsure cross between hideous reality and improbable fantasy. It often becomes a wild neurotic daydream . . . I recommend that it be buried under a stone for a thousand years."

TAKING ACTION

If you've ever had someone close to you die, you know too well the frenzy of activity that follows the death of a loved one. Calls need to be made, the funeral planned, the flowers ordered. And in this flurry of to-do lists lies a certain kind of relief. Well, rejection is like a very, very small death. And here, too, the pain can be lessened by action. Fortunately, there's a lot you can do—rethinking, revising, resending. But no matter exactly what action you take, be sure to draw on the passion that begot your project. That passion is what took you this far, and it's what will help you move through rejection.

James Bradley, author of the #1 *New York Times* bestseller *Flags of Our Fathers,* which was rejected 27 times before it was bought by a publisher, said this in an interview: "When someone says 'no,' the most important thing you can say to yourself is . . . 'Next!'"

PART II

Taking Care *of* Business

CHAPTER 6

LET'S MAKE A DEAL!

"The best way to make a good deal is to have the ability to walk away from it."

—BRIAN KOSLOW

Your agent calls. A publisher with great taste has made an offer for your book. Or maybe several publishers with equally great taste have made offers. Maybe your agent has just held an auction, and she's calling to tell you which lucky publisher is the highest bidder. Maybe you've submitted your proposal or manuscript directly to a publisher, and they've just called to say they want to publish your book.

Excitement reigns! You rule! Savor this moment. Then take a step back. You may be inclined to jump at the first offer. Don't. This is the time for a calm head and cool nerves. This is the time for strategic evaluation of your options so you can make the best possible deal with the best possible publisher.

THE SELLING OF YOUR BOOK

Some deals move with the speed of a glacier. Some deals happen lickety-split quick. Some initially sizzle, then quickly fizzle. Some crescendo only after fits and hiccups.

Almost all offers come in one of three ways: 1) preemptive offers, 2) auctions (either round-robin or best-bid), and 3) individual offers. Preempts and auctions occur only if there's competition. If you've submitted your book directly to publishers, you'll more than likely be dealing with individual offers.

If you have an agent, it's tempting to want her to make the hard decisions for you. Your agent is there to present you with options and to get you the best possible deal. But ultimately you're driving the train. If you're clear about what you want, you'll go a long way to preventing derailment and resentment.

The Preempt

Preemptive offers are made in the hope of eliminating the competition. That's why most publishers will let a preempt sit on the table for only about 24 hours. They don't want the author shopping their offer around.

Like everything else in life, accepting a preempt has its pluses and minuses. Here are the pluses:

- A publisher who preempts is a publisher who is really passionate about your book.
- A preempt may be the best offer you get.
- No matter how many birds are in how many bushes, this is a bird in hand.

And now the minuses:

- If you accept the offer, then you can't use it to breed other interest.
- Another publisher might have given you more money, so you could end up leaving money on the table. Bad place to leave money.
- Another publisher might be a better match for you and your book.

If you're lucky enough to be on the receiving end of a preempt, try to at least talk with the editor who's making the offer. Or, if you're in the same city and you feel up to it, go meet the editor. Carefully pick your agent's brain. Emotions run high. Methodically compile an organized list of questions (see pages 115–16).

Auction Action

There are two kinds of auctions in the book world: *round-robin auctions* and *best-bid auctions*. Both occur by phone, fax or e-mail at a preordained time and date. In a round-robin auction, people often start low and end high, whereas in a best-bid auction each editor has to do just that: pony up his one best bid. Only if two publishers make the same highest bid will they be given a chance to give another best bid.

In round-robin auctions, all editors make first-round bids (with the exception of floor-holders). Whoever has the lowest bid in the first round makes the first bid in the second round, and on and on. Each offer has to top the previous bid by a minimum percentage, typically 10%. So, if someone makes an initial offer of $10,000, the next bidder has to come in at $11,000,

ONE MAN'S CEILING IS ANOTHER MAN'S FLOOR

Sometimes an editor will make a preemptive offer that isn't as sumptuous as you or your agent would like. Your agent may then ask this editor to take a floor in an auction. If you've ever been to a live auction, you may have noticed that someone had submitted a first offer prior to the start of the auction, below which no bids can go. This is a floor. However, in publishing, it has an additional significance. When a floor is accepted, the editor who holds it sits out of the auction. Once all bids have been made, the floor-holder then gets an opportunity to make one final topping bid that typically has to be 10% higher than the last bid.

Floors are great because they guarantee the sale of your book for a predetermined sum of money. But floors can discourage other publishers from participating in an auction; no matter how much they bid, they don't have the option of making a last offer.

the next at $12,100, and so on. However, someone may choose to make a bid that exceeds 10% above the current offer. This is a strategic move that editors make in order to try and knock out the competition.

This bidding goes on until only one editor is left standing. If the auction has a floor-holder, he is now allowed to come back and top the final offer. Whoever makes the highest bid wins and gets the honor and privilege of publishing your book. Or, at least, this is an auction at its simplest. In reality, money is just the largest of many points considered in an auction. Other points that are considered include format (hardcover vs. paperback), rights (worldwide vs. North American), royalties, publicity and marketing commitments, and more. We'll get to these matters shortly.

To give you a sense of how an auction actually works, let's imagine that Crown (a division of Random House), William Morrow (a division of HarperCollins) and Putnam (a division of Penguin) are bidding on your book. Their initial bids for round one are as follows:

Crown: $25K
William Morrow: $40K
Putnam: $40K

Crown, the low bidder in the first round, then makes the first bid in the second round, which must be 10% higher than the last round's highest bid. Since William Morrow and Putnam placed the same bid, the agent typically contacts the person who called first and let's him know where the action stands. So our second round goes as follows:

Crown: $44K (the minimum bid)
William Morrow: $49K (they round up from the minimum bid)
Putnam drops out

Third round:

Crown: $53.9K
William Morrow: $61K

Fourth round:

Crown: $75K
William Morrow drops out

You can see that Crown made a risky move in the fourth round, offering more than was required in order to try and knock out the competition. The strategy worked.

Note that if there had been a floor in this auction, the editor who held the floor could have topped the $75K bid by 10% and bought the book for $82,500.

One of the beauties of a round-robin auction is that in a short time you can watch your money grow by leaps and bounds. Another is that the initial lowest bidder can come out on top. One of the downsides of a round-robin auction is that money is the controlling factor. Sometimes the underbidder may be your first choice, and this can lead to unpleasant feelings. Another downside is if one house is willing to pay a lot more than the others. Let's say one house was willing to pay as much as $100K whereas everyone else will not go above $50K. This means that if everyone's initial offers are low, your book could end up selling for $55K.

SIFTING WHEAT FROM CHAFF: THE RIGHT PUBLISHER FOR YOU

Your publisher can make or break your book. If the publisher is excited and gets behind it, your chances of getting reviewed, going on tour and generating that elusive, all-important buzz rise exponentially. In 2002, for example, Little, Brown was publishing a novel about a dark and brutal subject. But everyone in the house was passionate about this book, so they sent promotional copies everywhere and talked about it to everyone. The sheer force of their efforts, combined with the quality of the book, created a blizzard of big-time buzz. That book hit the ground sprinting, and in almost no time it hit the million-copy mark. The book was the aforementioned *The Lovely Bones* by Alice Sebold, and it became the bestselling novel of 2002. Yes, it's an excellent book, but it's about a very difficult subject, and if it hadn't been handled with such relentless passion by Sebold's publisher, it could have died on the vine. So, if you have a choice of publisher, choose carefully.

If you're lucky enough to have more than one publishing suitor, you're in a position to be able to actually choose the one who's best for your book.

If you haven't already met with interested editors and you don't live in the same city as the publisher(s) who made the offer(s), ask to speak to all editors by phone (see page 177 for pertinent questions to ask). You can learn volumes by speaking to an editor.

Remember to send classy, funny and/or sweet thank-you notes to anyone you meet or speak with. Not only is it the polite thing to do, but as a result an editor may remember you and look out for your next book.

Once you've met with or talked to editors, go over your notes to ascertain their enthusiasm levels. Sometimes the publisher you thought would be least likely to make an offer shows up with the bucks and a passionate letter of intent. Maybe a publisher you loved made an offer, but it's half what another publisher offered or not close to what you'd like the book to sell for.

What about the different styles of editors? Is one quiet and demure? You're in the honeymoon phase now. Imagine this person when the bloom is off the rose. When she's displeased. Or even when she's pleased but doesn't show it. Again, know thyself. Do you need a lot of sweetness and light? Do you think this editor will be able to provide that? Quiet and Demure isn't bad as long as you can live with it and the publisher does a great job with your book. But if you need someone who's going to be demonstrative and supportive, you're going to have a hard time with quiet demurishness. It's important to keep in mind that personality does not necessarily reflect talent. You may find yourself with an unexpressive editor who will edit your book to perfection and champion it relentlessly. Let your gut instinct and your listening skills, coupled with each editor's track record, be your guide. Also, consult with your agent, whose experience should help guide you.

Or maybe there's an editor who can't stop telling you how fantastic your book is. Maybe you feel a deep personal connection with this editor. You both have cockatoos and spend your spare time creating rubber-band balls. Maybe this editor's ideas aren't as strong as Quiet and Demure's, but you just know that this person is going to be your friend for life and a dream to work with. Again, ask your agent for advice.

Beware of the editor who comes on gangbusters, only to disappear when push is coming to shove. Don't get swept away by someone who promises the moon and stars and then doesn't have the wherewithal, desire or resources to deliver. Separate the rush of enthusiasm from the actual facts of what he's really putting on the table. You may also want to ask for a list of books he's edited so that you can quietly check out the acknowledgments he's received.

What about the publishing company as a whole? Are they, as a group, excited about your book? Have you heard anything from the marketing, publicity and sales departments? If you met with the publishing company, did anyone from marketing, publicity or sales show up? Keep in mind that once your editor edits your book, it's going to be handed off to the publicity and marketing departments. Then to the sales force—the people who are actually going to sell your book. It's crucial to have the whole house behind you.

Another reason to evaluate the whole house and not just the editor is that editors in publishing change jobs as frequently as teenage girls change boyfriends. The editor you fall in love with may be there for only a part of your book's journey through publication. You want to be sure that the enthusiasm for your book doesn't leave with her.

LESS MONEY, BETTER PUBLISHER?

If you have a family to feed, or rent to pay, or a body to clothe, you'll be tempted to take your highest offer. But don't make the mistake of confusing more money with more love. It might seem slightly insane, but publishers often give huge advances for books that they pay little or no attention to when it comes time to publish them. This can be due to a regime change, a lackluster finished manuscript or a slow sales start. So you could pay off your mortgage but end up with a book that doesn't do as well as it should have, and your book may be viewed by publishers as a disappointment because of lack of sales. If you want a long career as a writer and/or you'd like to see your book on the shelves in 2, 4 or 24 years, a smaller advance with a publisher more committed to your book and better suited to selling it may be the way to go.

SHARING A VISION

Remember Tamim Ansary? The guy who wrote the e-mail about Afghanistan heard round the world? He was in the fortunate position of getting to choose among a number of first-rate publishers. He had fruitful, in-depth conversations with each. One of the conversations was with a publisher who has a list of hits as long as your arm. This publisher immediately offered up a pretty pile of money. But Tamim had a sense that as savvy as this publisher was, she ultimately envisioned a different book from the one he wanted to write. He turned down the offer and accepted a lower one from a publisher who shared his vision. His book, *West of Kabul, East of New York*, published by Farrar, Straus & Giroux, became a bestseller and is now taught at colleges and universities around the country.

But what exactly makes a publisher "more committed" and "better suited"? Our definition includes:

- A track record in publishing your kind of book
- Enthusiasm from top to bottom, side to side, stem to stern, foot to mouth
- An editor who loves your book
- An established edge in prestige, attention, design or anything else that's important to you and the health and wealth of your book
- A desire and ability to go the extra mile to get your book into readers' hands

If you accept a smaller advance from a better publisher who pushes your book the right way, to the right people, it could end up selling a lot more copies. Selling a lot more copies would 1) ultimately put *more* money in your pocket, 2) make you a hotter commodity, and 3) help you sell your next book. If your book is brought out by a great publisher and makes a big splash in the world, your stock will soar, making everything you produce worth a little bit more.

What if you're leaning toward one editor in particular and/or don't like a particular editor? In that case, let your agent know right away. She'll probably want to hold a best-bid auction, not a round-robin.

But sometimes you won't find out that the editor or publisher who makes the highest bid is just not right for you until the round-robin auction is over.

Maybe another editor writes a passionate letter about why he's the right match for you. Maybe another makes a marketing commitment in her contract. Maybe another will give you a large first payment and you really need the money. If you feel that your book will fare better with an underbidder, it is your prerogative to choose that house instead. For understandable reasons, this will anger the highest bidder in almost all cases. But if you're worried about a grudge against your future work, know that people tend to forget old slights if your next book has the sweet smell of money wafting over it.

ONE LONELY OFFER

Often only one brave publishing house will be willing to take a chance on you and your book. Sometimes this one offer is made by the publisher you like the best and for the money you want. But sometimes the publisher may not be your first choice or deliver top dollar. While some authors choose the "I'll wait to see what better comes along" route, we'd like to say this: Would you rather have a xeroxed proposal/manuscript in your filing cabinet or a book in your local bookstore? Yes, you want a great publisher with a great track record and a great editor. But you also want a book.

ONE SAD OFFER, ONE BESTSELLING BOOK

When Geoffrey Moore's book *Crossing the Chasm* was sent out to publishers, it received only one offer for an underwhelming sum. At the time, Geoff was a consultant at a prestigious high-tech consulting firm. But he wanted to set up his own consulting practice and thought a book would help to establish his credibility, since he wasn't well known in his industry. His hunch was right. He took the offer, and *Crossing the Chasm* went on to be not just a bestseller, but a business classic—required reading in business schools and corporations worldwide. Since then, Geoff has written three more bestsellers. He's known all over the planet as a guru of high-tech marketing. And all it took was one wee offer.

"IS THAT ALL THERE IS?"

Jerry Stahl, author of the bestselling memoir *Permanent Midnight* and the bestselling novel *I, Fatty*, says it best: "My daughter's thirteen, and I need to find a better place to live and pay for her college down the road—neither of which I could do by devoting myself to what amounted to the rather expensive hobby of writing books." Because advances rarely translate into

JE REGRET TOUT

Katy Butler, a well-known journalist who has written for the *San Francisco Chronicle*, *The New Yorker* and numerous other publications, put together a terrific proposal for a book about the politics of sexual violence. Fellow writers, experts in the field and her agent all said the proposal had "big book" written all over it. Indeed, Katy received offers from editors at two major houses: one a veteran editor, the other a big shot with her own imprint. Both offers were healthy, but they weren't the kind of "big" money she was expecting for her "big book." Nor did she feel they would adequately cover her expenses for the two years it would take to write the book. So Katy turned both down. "I really wish I had taken one of those offers," she says. "In retrospect, I could have easily rearranged my life to live more cheaply."

The good news is that Katy has since hooked up with a leading academic in her field and is writing a new proposal that she believes will reach an even wider audience. "I feel like I learned a valuable lesson," she says. "This time, if I get an offer from a good publisher and if it's at all feasible, I'll take it. I'm ready to get my name on a book in stores."

a minimum wage and considering how much time you'll most likely spend on a book, you often have to make the difficult choice to take an offer that will not support you in the style to which you are accustomed. In fact, your advance may not support you in any style at all.

If the final offer you get doesn't meet your minimum, you or your agent can go back to the publisher and explain your situation. Sometimes seeing an actual budget will make publishers come up with a little more cabbage. Or you can apply for a grant or look for corporate sponsorship. This will almost certainly take lots of work and tons of time. But it can also pay off.

In the end, of course, it comes down to how badly you want to do your book, and what you and the market will bear. Maybe you decide you can't write the book for the money offered. Maybe you can then use the experience you gained to develop your next project, which will get you a larger advance. If you can sell a different project first and it does well, your original proposal will become more valuable. But if your goal is to get a book in bookstores, as bank-breaking as it may seem, this might be your chance. We know a number of people who turned down the only offer they received, and every single one of them has regretted it. If you can find a way, suck it up and get your book out into the world; you never know what it will lead to.

FINDING A COWRITER OR DUMPING THE ONE YOU HAVE

An editor or publisher may want to buy your book but insist on another writer. What to do? Every situation is different, but they all come down to what you're willing to give up and what you must hang on to. The studio that bought Sylvester Stallone's script for *Rocky* insisted that someone else play the lead. But he had written the script for himself, so he refused. In the face of much browbeating and angry posturing, Sly would not relent. The studio did. And the rest is history. He got to be a movie star.

But not all publishers will relent. Sometimes they'll tell you and your proposal/manuscript to go away if you don't do exactly what they want. How much does it mean to you to write the book? Are you sure you're capable of writing the book? Soul searching and a lot of consultation with your agent, friends and colleagues are required here.

In other cases, an editor or publisher may want to replace the writer you're already working with. This is potentially a *Sophie's Choice* moment. Only you can assess your level of commitment to your writer. Perhaps you want to buy him out and cut him loose. Perhaps he's your best friend and you'd never toss him aside. Either way, get as much info as you can from the publisher. What's the problem with the writer? Who's being thought of as a replacement? Talk to potential writers with an open mind. Sometimes an experienced writer with an established track record is just the person to turn your book into a wild success. Sometimes loyalty to your writer, or your own writing talent, must be honored. Your call.

NEGOTIATING NUGGETS FOR AGENTLESS AUTHORS

Many people feel daunted when they have to negotiate for themselves. Especially when they're in a new business and don't know the lay of the land. How do you put a value on your passion? Or accept someone else's value that may seem paltry or downright insulting? How do you know if a contract is fair when your contract looks like a bunch of gibberish? Every deal is different, but here are some guidelines to raise your comfort level and to help you avoid getting saddled with a nasty contract:

- Rrrrrresearch, baby! Know the terrain. Have you been reading the deal sections of *PW* and Publishers Lunch? Have you Googled your prospective publisher's backlist to see if you can get some dirt on their deals? Do you have a sense of what books like yours are selling for? Amass as much info as you can, so you don't act like the neophyte that you may be.

- Let the publisher make an offer first. Don't fall into the trap of naming your dollar before they do, because most authors either greatly under- or overvalue their work. That being said, a publisher may try to lowball you or give you a crappy contract. And if you've ever been lowballed, you know how painful that can be. So don't just accept a first offer.

- Use your agentless-ness to your advantage. Ask lots of questions: "What are the highest royalties that you've given in a contract?" "What's the range in advances that you give?" "Will you guarantee an advertising or publicity budget?" "What's the most free copies you can give me?" You may discover answers that an agent never would have. Agents are so used to operating within the industry standards that they know not to ask for the unaskable. Thing is, sometimes the unaskable can get you the ungettable.

- Prepare a budget. Demonstrate your costs so your requests don't seem like they're coming out of thin air, left field, the blue. Do you have research, permission or travel costs? Do you need to take time off from work or hire a baby-sitter? Be specific.

- If you can, hire a lawyer with publishing expertise. They'll know what's kosher and what's hooey. Also, they can act as your negotiator, creating that cushy business buffer between you and the publisher that often allows people to ask for what they really want.

- Can't afford to hire a lawyer? Join The Authors Guild. The Guild distributes official contract guidelines and offers a written contract review which provides specific suggestions and comments, though it's not exhaustive, nor will they speak on your behalf to a publisher. As they say on their Web site, "While the Guild does not negotiate individual member agreements, we are willing to answer members' specific inquiries to aid

MILLION-DOLLAR BABY

We know three enterprising fellows who came up with an idea they thought was worth some money. They made a prototype, and lo and behold, one of the behemoths of their industry beckoned. They were pleased as punch and happy as clams. They were sure they could get enough money to put down payments on country homes. They convened to come up with the dollar amount. They made a pact. They were dreaming big, and they decided they'd ask for the whopping sum of $30K, $10K each. They wouldn't take a penny less. Granted this was 25 years ago, but to them it was major coin. Furthermore, they were determined not to let the big boys push them around. They were going to go in, control the meeting, name their price and walk out triumphant.

The day of their meeting arrived, and they walked into the conference room in their Sunday best, cocksure and ready to rumble. Before they had a chance to name their deal-breaking, drop-dead number, the Head Honcho talked about how much he loved their prototype and went on to say that his company wanted to make an offer. "We're prepared to offer you one million dollars," he said. "But we can't go a penny more." Dumbfounded, the three industrious fellows had no idea what to say next. Their plan hadn't anticipated this turn of events. So they just sat there in slack-jawed astonishment until someone mumbled a faint "Uh . . . yeah . . . cool."

The moral of this story? He who offers first often comes in last.

them in securing the best deal possible." Lastly, the Guild has contract seminars around the country. Sign up for one now! (See Appendix I.)

As difficult as it may be, if you don't ask, you most certainly will not receive. Stand tall, be firm, keep your sense of humor. In the end, you may not get what you want, but hopefully you'll get what you need.

GET IT IN WRITING: THE DEAL MEMO

After much brouhaha and folderol, you've finally decided who's the right publisher or the decision has been made for you. You've accepted an offer. But it's always a good idea to get it in writing that you have a deal in place before the contract gets executed and signed, which can take months. The best way to do this is with a deal memo, confirming the basic points of the offer you've accepted. This memo should include the advance, royalties, territory, payout, rights, delivery date, bonuses (if any), option information and every other pertinent part of your contract. In order to understand exactly what you're agreeing to or asking for, read to the end of the next chapter.

Some agents do deal memos. Some don't. Some do them some of the time. Some do them all of the time. If your agent isn't the type to do deal memos, it's not necessary to insist. Just make sure you understand the basic points of the deal so that you can check that your contract jibes with the original offer. If you're negotiating a deal on your own, you can ask the publisher directly for a deal memo or you can draw one up yourself and send it in. (E-mail is fine.) Here's a sample of a deal memo to give you an idea of what you'll want to include:

Territory: North America.

Advance: $75,000.

Payout: $37,500 on signing, $18,750 on delivery and acceptance, $18,750 on publication.

Royalties: Hardcover: 10% for the first 5,000 copies, 12½% for the next 5,000 copies, 15% thereafter. Paperback: 7½% flat.

Sub rights: Publisher retains audio and first serial. 80/20 split on British rights, 75/25 on translation.

Bonus: $10,000 earn-out bonus. Must earn out within one year of publication. Bonus applied to advance.

Option: 30-day option on next proposal, to begin after delivery and acceptance. No matching clause.

Title: Mutual agreement on title.

Cover and jacket: Consultation on cover and jacket copy.

Now put on your eyeshade, roll up your sleeves and channel your inner CPA. It's time to dissect your contract.

CHAPTER 7

CONTRACT FACTS

"A verbal contract isn't worth the paper it's written on."

—SAMUEL GOLDWYN

People spend years and years and hundreds of thousands of dollars learning how to read contracts. If you're interested in understanding the full nitty and complete gritty of contracts, go to law school. While we're not going to teach you about force majeure (not to be confused with horse manure), we will give you basic guidelines and red flags to look for in dealing with a book contract. The basic purpose of a contract between you and a publisher is the granting of rights regarding your work. Usually a publisher wants to claim as many rights as possible while paying as little as possible, so part of your agent's 15% is earned by making sure you get a fair shake. If you don't have an agent, read this chapter carefully. We also suggest that you buy a copy of *Kirsch's Guide to the Book Contract.*

If all things legal make your eyes glaze over or bring on a severe case of nitpickerism, heed the words of Dennis Dalrymple, former head of contracts at Warner Books and current contract consultant: "Approach your contract carefully, but don't be paranoid."

AN ASKANCE GLANCE AT YOUR ADVANCE

An advance is exactly that. Cash advanced to you before your book starts making money. The point of an advance is to allow you to write your book unencumbered by the need to make money elsewhere. In reality, however, advances are typically based on the publisher's projections for the first year of revenues, so they vary wildly in size. This means your advance may not cover your expenses, unless you live in the woods and eat nothing but shrubs and berries or have kind and wealthy relations.

An advance is formally referred to as an *advance against royalties.* To explain how this works, let's take a quick trip through the economics of a book. Say you receive a $20,000 advance. Say the price of your book sells for $20. Say 10% of the cover price of your book goes to you, which means you earn $2 for every book sold through regular retail channels. This 10% is called a *royalty.* However, you won't get a check in the mail after your first copy is sold, since you first have to earn out your advance. This means that you must apply your share of the earnings to the amount that was advanced to you. In this case, 10,000 copies of your book will have to be sold at retail in order for you to earn out. Then and only then will you start receiving one of the loveliest things an author can get: a royalty check.

The equation below illustrates how the sale of one book impacts your royalties in the preceding example:

$20K (advance) – $2 (sale of one book) = $19,998 (left to earn out)

If you're writing an illustrated book or a cookbook with photos, try to get a separate art budget that is NOT part of your advance (typically, you are expected to pay for photographs or illustrations). This way, you'll have a lower advance to earn out.

One of the most frequent questions we hear from first-time authors (often with voices aquiver and terror in their eyes) is this: "If I don't earn out my advance, do I have to pay it back?" Imagine their relief when we say: Heavens to Betsy, of course not! All advance money is yours to keep even if you end up selling only three books. If you took our quiz on pages 13–14, you know that only 10% of all books earn out their advances. That being said, if you don't finish your book, you *will* be responsible for paying the money back.

Payout: "When, Oh When, Do I Get My Money?"

We wish we had a dollar for every time an author has asked us this question. So here's the skinny. Almost all advances are paid out in chunks. Typically, you get one chunk when you sign your contract, another chunk when your manuscript is accepted and the last one when your book is published. However, sometimes there are more payment dates in the schedule, and sometimes there are fewer. For example, a percentage of the money may be released on delivery of only half the manuscript or on publication of the paperback version of a book if its first release is in hardcover.

In general, publishers try to spread out their payments over as long a period as possible. Here are a few typical ways advances are made:

⅓ on signing of contract
⅓ on delivery and acceptance of manuscript
⅓ on publication date of book

¼ on signing of contract
¼ on delivery and acceptance of manuscript
¼ on publication of hardcover
¼ on publication of paperback

½ on signing of contract
½ on delivery and acceptance of manuscript

The last scenario, comprising only two payments, is less common than the others, especially when you're talking about advances in the high five or six figures. Once you get into these numbers, a publisher is sure to break up the money as much as possible in order to hold on to it longer. But according to the PYPIP Guide to Financial Success, it's important to get as much money up front as possible—unless there are major tax implications. Let's say, for example, that your publisher wants to pay you in thirds. See if you can get them to change the payout to ½, ¼, ¼. With this arrangement, if your book gets canceled or your pub date keeps getting delayed, you've got more of their money in your pocket. And generally speaking, it's always better to have money in your own pocket than in theirs.

If you're being paid upon paperback publication, make sure it's spelled out in your contract that you receive that portion of the advance either at that time OR within 12 months of hardcover publication, whichever is earlier.

"When, Oh When, Do I *Really* Get My Money?"

Pay attention now. After you make your deal, it may be months and months before you actually have cold hard cash in your hot little hand. Between agent-editor haggling, corporate bookkeeping lethargy and the check clearing through the agent's bookkeeping system, it's not unusual to wait three to six months to get paid. Sometimes more.

Similar snafus can affect the timing of your other payments. Say a publisher makes an offer of $10,000 on January 1, 2010. In your contract, it says you will be paid in thirds. Taking the six-months rule, you'll get your first $3,333.33 check on July 1, 2010. Now let's say you have a delivery date of May 1, 2011. You hand in the manuscript on time and your editor takes two months to read it and get back to you. You then take another month to get changes back to your editor. She takes another month to read the revision and asks you for a few more minor changes. So it's October 1, 2011, before you get your delivery and acceptance check of $3,333.33. Your book is not coming out until October 1, 2012. So your final check of $3,333.34 will not be in your hands until almost three years after the offer was made.

Here's how your contract and payment calendar would look:

January 1, 2010: offer made
July 1, 2010: payment due on signing of contract
October 1, 2011: delivery and acceptance payment made
October 1, 2012: publication payment made

YOUR PUBLICITY NEST EGG

If you were lucky enough to get an advance for your book, we recommend that you set aside money RIGHT NOW toward marketing and publicizing your book. Every penny helps. If you can put aside $25,000, fantastic. If you can put aside $2,500, that's good, too. Start small; think big.

If you didn't get an advance and you aren't going to go into debt writing your book, start adding to the publicity piggy bank. See if you can stash away even a thousand bucks by the time you finish your book. It may be a small nest egg, but if you use it right, it'll help your book fly.

With some small publishers who have cash-flow troubles, you may wait much longer for a check than your contract stipulates. If you're signing with a smaller publisher, ask to have it written in your contract that you must be paid within 30 days of each payment date. This way, if they don't pay you for months, they're in breach of contract and, in the worst-case scenario, you can cancel your deal and take your book on to greener pastures.

Bonus Bounty

If you're dissatisfied with your advance or you simply want to see additional royalty dollars, it's always good to ask for a bonus. Bonuses typically come in two forms: bestseller bonuses and earn-out bonuses.

First of all, let's be clear here. A bonus in the book world is not like the bonus an employee gets at the end of the year for work well done. It's just more money added to the pool of money you already have to earn out—the equivalent of an added advance check.

Bestseller bonuses usually revolve around hitting the *New York Times* bestseller list—the holy grail of publishing. A typical *New York Times* bonus is based on where a book appears on the list. For example, if your book hits the #1 spot, you get more money than if it hits the #10 spot. Sometimes you get a one-time bonus for hitting the list. But more than likely you'll get a certain amount for each spot and for each week, up to a specified cap. And, typically, your book must find its niche on the bestseller list within a year of its publication (this usually limits the bonus to the hardcover edition only).

Here are some standard *New York Times* bonus numbers:

(i) $2,500 per week for each week the Work occupies any of the #6–#10 positions,
(ii) $5,000 per week for each week the Work occupies any of the #2–#5 positions, and
(iii) $10,000 per week for each week the Work occupies the #1 position.

The aptly named *earn-out bonus* is given if your book earns out its advance or sells a certain amount of copies within a certain amount of time, typically a year. For example, if you earn out your $25K advance in the first year, you could be given an additional $10K advance. The beauty of the bonus is that it puts more cash in your hands but doesn't require the publisher to take huge risks. In other words, it's a win-win situation.

THE REALITY OF THE ROYALTY

A royalty, despite its rather kingly connotation, is simply a payment you receive when a publisher sells a copy of your book. This royalty varies greatly, depending on three major factors.

- The format of the book, e.g., hardcover, paperback, illustrated, four-color
- The buyers, e.g., independent bookstores, mass merchandisers, QVC
- The terms on which the book was bought

Anything special the publisher adds to your book—color, glossy paper, a page that folds out, stickers—naturally adds to the production costs. And when your production costs go up, the publisher will want to lower your royalty. Royalties on four-color (industry language for "full-color") books or books with special features can have their royalties cut in half. The good news is, if your book does well, the initial production costs (which are the highest) go down as you sell more copies.

Below you will find standard royalties throughout the publishing industry for a typical sale. These are NOT for unbelievablycheapbooks.com sales, mail-order sales or other sales that vary from the publisher's standard asking price. Compare your contract with these numbers. The royalties pertain only to one-color, standard-size books. And they are based on the cover price.

Hardcover	Trade Paperback	Mass-Market Paperback
10% to 5,000 copies	7½% for all copies	8% to 150,000 copies
12.5% to 10,000 copies		10% thereafter
15% thereafter		

What's the difference between the two kinds of paperbacks? The ones you see on supermarket racks, with pages made from newsprint paper, are called *mass-market paperbacks*. The pricier, often larger ones, filled with nice paper, are called *trade paperbacks*. Not only do they look different and cost more, but they're sold differently. Mass-market paperbacks are often sold through special distributors, as a magazine would be, and trade paperbacks are generally sold through regular book channels.

Riding the Escalator

Often a publisher will reward you with a higher royalty rate if you sell more than a specified number of books. This is called an *escalator*. For example, if you sell more than 50,000 copies of your book, your publisher might be persuaded to go from a 7½% trade paperback royalty to an 8% royalty. The sale of large numbers of books means an increase in profit margins and more samolians for your publisher, who can then pass some of them on to you.

It's always good to try and get escalators written into your contract. But it can be particularly crucial if your advance is small and you think you're going to sell a lot of books. In this way, you'll be able to make up for your small advance with more money from long-term sales.

It's also a common practice for publishers to reduce a royalty if they do a reprint of a limited number of copies, giving the author what's called a *small printings royalty.* Often, this is the only way they can manage to keep books in print. If your contract stipulates such a reduction, see if you can make it for the smallest number of books possible (most publishers will agree to 2,500 copies or less for one-color books). And be sure that it can occur only once a year and no earlier than two years after publication.

THE SIZE OF YOUR ROYALTY

Many authors are aghast when they discover that they receive only between 5% and 15% of the sale price of their book, while the publisher keeps between 85% and 95%. However, it might be more shocking to learn that the publisher sometimes earns even less per book than the author does. If your book sells for $15 and the average wholesale price is $7.50, then the remaining $7.50 has to cover all the publisher's costs. These costs include your initial advance, your royalty, the production costs (e.g., paper and binding), shipping costs, paying for any outside staff who will work on your book and a very large overhead.

Illustration Escalation

Say your publisher wants to start your trade paperback royalty at a lower-than-average 5% because your book is four-color. (He may also want to figure the royalty on net receipts rather than retail price. Fight that one if you can.) Four-color books are so expensive to produce and print that it takes longer for publishers to earn back their money, hence low beginning royalties. But that doesn't mean you can't ask for an escalator that rewards both parties if the book does well. Here's a suggested escalator:

5% for the first 25K copies
6% for the next 25K copies
7% for the next 25K copies
8% thereafter

Even half a percent can make a big difference if your book sells a lot of copies. Let's suppose your book retails for $20 and you sell 100,000 books. If your royalty is half a percent higher, this will mean 10,000 more dollars in your pocket. If you sell a million copies, that's $100,000. What? It could happen!

Flying Without a Net: Calculating off "Net Price"

Some publishers, especially small ones, work off net price, not list price. Typically, net is approximately 50% of list price. So typically your actual royalty will be twice the standard royalty on list price. For example, if your book sells for $10 and you're getting a 7½% royalty on list price, then you will receive 75¢ for every book you sell. If, on the other hand, your royalty is based on net price, i.e., $5, you should receive a royalty of 15%. That's 75¢ a copy as well. Same money. Different math.

The Ouch! of Deep Discounts

The book business has changed immensely in the past decade. Whereas chains like Wal-Mart and Costco used to account for a small percentage of overall sales, it has recently been reported that they now account for over 50% of all books sold. These chains and many others are offered what are called "deep discounts" by publishers when they order very large quantities of often nonreturnable books. They then offer the consumer deeply slashed prices on these books. The problem with deep discounts is that, in turn, your royalty is significantly reduced. The upside is that you can sell many more copies of your book. Most deep discounts are around two-thirds of the prevailing royalty rate. But the math can be confusing, so make sure you're in this range. Most authors overlook deep discounts because they don't know what they are and find them confusing, which can result in the loss of lots of money.

DELIVERY: THE FIRST STEP TOWARD ACCEPTANCE

Delivery and acceptance are two very distinct yet interconnected activities. The delivery of your book is self-explanatory—it's the moment you hand over the finished manuscript to your publisher. And the delivery date that you put in your contract should not be arbitrary. There are two major points to consider when deciding on your delivery date.

THE EARLY BIRD MAY *NOT* GET THE WORM

It's not impossible that you will have to finish your book before your contract is done. Talk about an act of extreme faith, but sometimes this will be in your best interest. Let's say, for example, your book is about Christmas. Chances are, you're going to want it to come out a month or two before. If you sell your book in September and want it to come out during the holiday season of the following year, in all likelihood you'll have only a few months to write the book. If you factor in the three to six months before you see your first check (let alone your last), you may have to finish your book before a check is even in the mail, never mind in your hands.

If you find yourself in this situation, 1) make sure you get a deal memo before you start, and 2) do not turn in anything before your contract is signed, the check has cleared and the money is in your pocket. If, for some reason, the publisher doesn't like what you've written, they can just decide to cancel the contract. And that means all work and no money for you.

Also, don't be shy about asking your publisher or your agent to put a rush on the contract and check due to the time constraints. This is possible no matter what any naysayer tells you. Even the biggest publishers can get you a check in a day if they want to. The trouble is, what often is a huge deal to you is insignificant to them.

1. ***Realistic time frame.*** Be conservative. Give yourself more rather than less time. You simply cannot believe how quickly time flies once you've got your contract. And, as we said, a check may take months and months to land in your hand. If you can't start working on your book until you receive that check, then add another four to six months to your delivery date.

   If you don't give yourself enough time and you end up being late, you will be in breach of contract and your book deal can get CANCELED. While publishers are used to unrealistic deadlines and are often willing to extend delivery dates, you need to realize, going in, that they have the right to cancel if you don't meet your deadline. Of course, nobody wants a canceled book.

2. ***Publication date.*** Discuss with your publisher and consider carefully when you want your book to come out, and work back from there. For example, if you want your book to come out in time for Mother's Day, ask your publisher to give you the latest date you can hand in your book and

still get it into stores in plenty of time. Sometimes this will necessitate having to work fast. Make sure the schedule is doable. Do not under any circumstances agree to a delivery date you can't meet. Also understand that while everyone wants to get published as soon as possible, most publishers need at least nine months to do the preparation it takes to launch a book properly.

The Beauty and Power of Acceptance

While delivery is self-explanatory, acceptance is not. "Finished" can mean many things, especially where your manuscript is concerned. Is this a sloppy first draft? Or an incredibly polished ready-to-publish manuscript? Or (more likely) something in between? How close your manuscript is to actually being publishable will determine, in large part, whether or not it's accepted.

Typically, you and your editor will go through at least one round of revisions before your manuscript is "accepted." During this time, you may be required to make minor cosmetic changes or do radical surgery on your entire book. But at a certain point, with any luck at all, your editor will say to you that the manuscript is ready for the copy editor. The moment your book is handed off to the copy editor (barring any red flags from your publisher's lawyer) is often the moment your book is considered officially accepted. At this point, your check is released from its gilded cage so it can fly merrily to you. Now it's time to pop that cork and celebrate!

If you need to get permissions for your book, you must deliver these with your completed manuscript in order for the work to be accepted. Your publisher may give you a little leeway, but don't count on it.

Unacceptability

Unfortunately, some manuscripts are just not acceptable. Be sure you're protected in this sad, unlikely but not unheard-of event, because you could end up having to pay back your advance for no good reason at all.

AVOIDING A "BAD HAIR" CANCELLATION

Your contract will most likely stipulate the circumstances under which your work can be rejected. You want to be sure that your publisher can *only* reject your work for editorial or legal reasons. This means the publisher can't cancel your book because of changing market conditions, because they disagree with your politics or because they don't like your new 'do. The only reason they can cancel your book is because the manuscript is editorially unacceptable or you're guilty of something heinous like plagiarism. Rejection for editorial reasons is still vague enough to cover a wide range of issues: for example, the writing isn't up to professional standards, the structure is a mess or they simply don't like the way it's written. But if you have this clause in your contract, and your publisher decides to cancel your book because another book has just been published on the same subject, they have to let you keep your entire advance. Sometimes publishers claim they're rejecting a work for editorial reasons, but in reality they're canceling the book because of changing market conditions, political views or bad hairdos. If this is the case, you have grounds to sue your publisher.

Bottom line: If you don't add "for editorial reasons" to your contract, a publisher can cancel your book on the slightest of whims. In this salt-in-the-wound situation, you will not get the rest of your advance money, you'll have to return the money you've already received and you won't get your book published. Bad bad bad.

THE SANITY CLAUSE

Your contract should include a clause stating that your editor must respond to your manuscript within 60 days of delivery. He doesn't have to accept the manuscript, but he has to give you feedback. If he doesn't, you and/or your agent can force a response. Many contracts stipulate that if you hear nothing within 60 days, you must write a letter to the publisher, demanding a response. You still probably have to wait awhile, but it's a lot better than having the editor sit on your manuscript for six months or a year.

FIRST PROCEEDS PROCEDURES

If your book is canceled for reasons within the bounds of your contract and you've already been paid any money, the *First Proceeds clause* stipulates not only *that* you must repay the money, but also *when*. Ideally, your contract should say that you need only repay your publisher out of the proceeds of a sale to another publisher. Many contracts, however, now state that you have to repay all monies within 12 to 18 months regardless of whether you're able to resell your book. This means that 18 months after a publisher rejects your manuscript, you have to pony up the dough. In reality, however, most authors do not repay this money—mainly because they don't have it to repay. Sometimes publishers will go after authors to get their money back. Sometimes they won't. This is dependent, naturally, on how big a stash of cash is involved. But if you wish to publish another book and you owe money to a big publisher because they canceled your book, you probably won't be able to do business with them again until you pay back the money you owe. So, if you're unable to secure first proceeds only out of a sale elsewhere, try to make your time limit as long as possible.

COPYRIGHT OR COPYWRONG?

Always retain the copyright to your work. Some publishers write in their contracts that they "may" register an author's book. Some say in the contract that they own the copyright. Neither situation is acceptable. Under all circumstances, you want it stated in your contract that the publisher *shall register* the copyright in your name.

If you're writing a book for a packager, with a corporation or even in certain situations with a coauthor, you may be signing a work-for-hire agreement. In such an agreement, the writer does *not* retain the copyright. In addition, the writer may receive negligible royalties or none at all.

THE MANY FACES OF SUBSIDIARY RIGHTS

Along with the standard rights to publish your book, your contract will also contain *subsidiary rights*. These rights (known in the industry as "sub rights") are those that are secondary to the primary rights granted to the publisher: rights to the hardcover and/or paperback version of the book that is sold in the United States (or wherever the primary publisher is). Sales of the work in a different format—whether it's an audiobook, a TV show or a large-print edition—are considered subsidiary rights. Sales of the work in a different territory like the United Kingdom, Japan or Brazil are also considered subsidiary rights, typically covered under the "foreign rights" section.

Your contract will stipulate what percentage of each sale of a subsidiary right goes to you and what goes to your publisher. The typical splits between you and your publisher are as follows (the first number represents your share of the pie, the second represents the publisher's):

- First serial (the appearance of part of your book in a magazine just before or coinciding with its publication): 90/10
- Second serial (the appearance of part of your book in a magazine after publication): 50/50
- Book club: 50/50
- Permissions (the use of part of your book by another author): 50/50
- Paperback: 50/50
- Special editions: 50/50
- Foreign-language translation: 75/25 (50/50 for four-color illustrated books)
- United Kingdom: 80/20 (50/50 for four-color illustrated books)
- Textbook: 50/50
- Large-type edition: 50/50
- Electronic book (commonly called an e-book, an electronic version of the entire book, which can be sold via the Internet or a special provider): 50/50
- Electronic version (an adaptation of a book, which may use some of the text and/or illustrations, or additional text or illustrations as well as video or sound added): 100/0
- Audio recording: 50/50
- Commercial and merchandising: 100/0
- Performance (film, TV, stage): 100/0
- Storage and retrieval: 50/50
- Calendar: 50/50

We believe you should retain certain subsidiary rights in totality (those marked with a 100/0 split). If you don't keep these rights, they will almost certainly languish and die a sad and lonely death at the hands of your publisher. You and/or your agent have the power to do something with these rights and the chance to make some additional dough. The one exception here is commercial and merchandising rights. If you happen to have a publisher who wants to pursue these rights, give them the option for a limited time period (one to three years).

There are also a number of other sub rights you should consider retaining. These include:

- First serial rights
- Foreign rights
- Calendar rights
- Paperback rights

The benefit of retaining all these rights is that if you or your agent can sell them, 100% of the proceeds goes directly into your pocket. But each of these rights has its sticking points.

In order to successfully sell *first serial rights*, it's necessary to have contacts at magazines and newspapers who could publish a section or chapter of your book. If your agent has these contacts, great. If you're a journalist who makes your living selling magazine articles, you may want to hold on to them as well. But even so, remember that the typical split here between you and your publisher is 90/10 in your favor (although you won't see that 90% until you earn out your advance). Better to let your publisher keep 10% and take care of all the xeroxing and mailing of your manuscript, because these costs may well exceed the 10% you held on to. And if your or your agent's only contact with the magazine business is a weekly reading of *People*, you should certainly let your publisher hold on to first serial rights. All large publishers have a department devoted solely to subsidiary rights. Of course, this department may have to deal with literally hundreds of books, so unless yours is one of their leading titles, its chances of getting the level of attention needed to actually make a first serial sale are slim. But slim is better than none. And if you do have magazine connections, you can work in conjunction with your publisher to sell these rights.

Whether or not to retain *foreign rights* can be a particularly difficult decision, because there can be much money involved. Many agents have what are called subagents in countries around the world to help sell these rights. But once again, if neither you nor your agent has the contacts to sell your book abroad, there is little point in holding on to foreign rights.

Whether you or your publisher retains foreign rights, you should know about the power of scouts to help with your foreign sales efforts. These middlemen are employed by publishers around the world to look for titles appropriate for their lists. By getting your proposal/manuscript into the hands of scouts (who are listed in *LMP*), you may increase your chances of foreign sales.

Calendar rights are significant only if you're one of the lucky few with a book that can be transformed into a calendar. Does your book have witty aphorisms that are perfect for a boxed calendar? Does it have gorgeous photos that would translate into a knock-your-socks-off wall calendar? If not, pursuing publishers that produce calendars won't be worth the energy.

Paperback rights are relevant only if your book is coming out first in hardcover, and important only if your book is with a midsize/independent publisher. The reason is that midsize/independent publishers often sell the paperback rights to large publishers, whereas larger publishers more often than not publish both the hardcover and paperback versions themselves. If, for example, your book is coming out in hardcover with a university press and it does particularly well, it's very likely that it will sell in paperback to a large publisher like Simon & Schuster or Penguin.

A large publisher who buys the paperback rights to your book pays your publisher an advance and royalties, half of which gets applied to your own advance (if you received one) and royalties. The problem with allowing your publisher to retain the paperback rights is best displayed in the following numbers: Say your paperback rights sell for a $50,000 advance with 7½% royalties. Say your book sells 75,000 copies at $15 per copy, or $1.13 per book in royalties. Since you get only 50% of the take, you end up with approximately $42,000 in your pocket. However, if you had held on to the rights, you would have received the full 7½% royalty, resulting in $84K in your piggy bank. But if you don't have an agent, selling paperback rights can be very tricky. Your book has to do well enough for publishers to be coming to *you*, or for you to interest an agent who can sell the paperback rights.

THE RANCOR OF RETURNS

It's hard to believe how publishing works, so listen up. Let's say a bookstore orders 10 copies of your book. Your publisher then sends 10 copies of your book to said bookstore. The bookstore pays for those 10 books. The books then go onto the shelves. Sometimes they're not all sold. These melancholy books can then be *returned* to the publisher, who has to give the money back or credit the bookseller.

How does all this affect you? It may be written in your contract that the publisher can withhold the money for a "reasonable" number of projected returns. So, while the bookstore may have sold 10 copies of your book, your publisher can withhold money against future returns—what's called in the business a *reserve against returns.* Most of the time, this is not more than 25% of your royalties. But it can be more. Try to ensure in your contract that the publisher can withhold no more than 20% of your royalties against returns. Also, try to ensure that the publisher cannot withhold your money for more than two royalty periods (one royalty period equals six months).

WARRANTIES AND INDEMNITIES: PUBLISHERS COVERING THEIR ASSE(T)S

You wouldn't plagiarize, would you? That's good, because most publishing contracts have a paragraph requiring you to *warrant* that the writing you say is yours really *is* yours. And just in case it's not, you also have to *indemnify* (protect) your publisher from damages in case an aggrieved party sues. This indemnification applies even if you unintentionally err. So, if you're researching a topic and copying down material created by others, be extra sure to keep track of your sources so you can give them proper attribution. And make sure those working with you do the same. If a research assistant or secretary forgets to put quotation marks around a passage taken from another source and you accidentally use that passage as your own, you are liable.

While you almost definitely will not be able to change anything in your contract related to warranties and indemnities, it's incumbent upon you to understand what you're getting yourself into. There's a whole world of people with way too much time on their hands and way too much bitterness in their hearts for you to make a mistake in this area.

Few authors are sued over their books. But those who are can certainly benefit from insurance. Most big publishers include you in their insurance policies. And some smaller houses will add you to theirs if you ask. But if you're with a house that doesn't have insurance and you don't want to spend the time investigating insurance policies, here's some advice to live by: Don't write anything libelous and don't infringe on anyone else's copyright.

AUTHOR COPIES: "YOU MEAN I HAVE TO BUY MY OWN BOOKS?"

Think you get unlimited free copies of your own book? Think again! The number of free copies you receive is written into your contract, and there's a good chance you'll get as few as 10. This means, if you want to give copies of your book to friends, relatives and folks you meet along the way, you will have to buy them. That's right, not only will you have to write the thing, but you'll have to pay good cash money for your own book! The good news is, you get what's called an *author's discount*. This, too, is stipulated in your contract. Most publishers give you a 50% discount, although some go as low as 40%.

Some publishers will also agree to give you many more free copies of your book for promotion and marketing purposes. One of the ways you can get these additional copies written into your contract is to provide a list of great contacts to whom you'll be sending your books. It's not unreasonable to ask for as many as 250 copies. If you can't get this stipulation, don't worry. Your publisher will often send books to the media or other important folks who will help get the word out—though "important folks" don't include your second cousin.

If you or your company plans to buy large quantities of your book (say, over 1,000 copies), you might be able to get the publisher to give you a larger discount (under the category of "special sales"). Similarly, if you expect your own connections to result in direct sales to a company or companies, you might be able to increase your own royalty on these sales. Be sure to negotiate this discount at the time of the initial offer.

COVERING YOUR COVER

Do whatever you can to get the *right of consultation* on your book's cover, as well as on your interior design, flap and catalog copy. Not that consultation means all that much. In essence, it means that your publisher can show you each of these things, get your comments, say thank you very much and give you the big kiss-off. But at least, if you get to review these pieces, you have the chance to ask and fight for changes.

Your contract should say that you and your publisher will *mutually agree* on a title or that you get approval on the title. Hopefully you're going to be saying this title for the rest of your life. And you don't want a bitter taste in your mouth every time you do.

OPTIONS FOR YOUR OPTION

Most publishers want first dibs on your next proposal or manuscript (especially if your first book does well). This is what's known as an *option.* Options allow your current publisher to have an exclusive time period to decide whether or not to pursue your next project. All options should be limited to:

- Your next book of nonfiction *or* fiction (whichever your current book is)
- A book written solely by you, if you are the sole author of your current book, OR a book written solely by you AND your coauthor, if you cowrote your current book
- A detailed proposal only, if you're writing nonfiction

The option period should begin as close to delivery and acceptance as possible. If it can begin at delivery and acceptance, that's great. But some publishers will make you wait until your book comes out before you can show them a new proposal or manuscript.

Once you submit your option book, your publisher should have no more than 30 to 45 days for an exclusive look. If no decision is made within that time, you should be free to shop it around.

Finally, you want to make sure your contract has no *matching clause.* A matching clause stipulates that you cannot enter into an agreement with another publisher for your option book if your current publisher matches the next one's offer. If your publisher doesn't make a satisfactory offer within 30 days of receiving your proposal/manuscript, you should be free to move about the cabin at your leisure.

THE RULES OF ACCOUNTING

Your publisher should send you royalty statements at specified intervals (at least twice a year) on specified dates. These statements should be sent whether or not a payment is due at the same time.

An accountant of your choice should also be allowed to examine the publisher's books at least once a year in case you feel there are errors in the statements. Your contract should stipulate that the publisher will pay for the examination as well as all monies owed within 30 days in the event that the accountant finds errors greater than 5%.

It can be a frustrating and difficult thing, but understand that publishers do sometimes "lose" sales of thousands of books. This, of course, can mean thousands and thousands of very real lost dollars. It's certainly not an everyday occurrence, but more than one author has had to sue his publisher over discrepancies in actual sales vs. reported sales. If you're concerned about the accuracy of the numbers on your statement, check with booksellers in your hometown and around the country. Keep an eye on Amazon to see how your book is selling. If you know you've sold books but negligible sales keep coming up on your royalty statements, you may have a problem. (See pages 348–50 for more.)

SIGN HERE, PLEASE . . .

If you're a writer and you don't deal with contracts on a daily, weekly, yearly or even once-in-a-blue-moon basis, you may let your excitement overshadow your obligation to pay close attention to your contract. Do not fall into this trap. Working closely with an agent and/or lawyer, go over your contract with the finest of fine-tooth combs. You don't want to be one of those poor dweebs you read about who signed an odious contract and made a big pile of money for somebody else, only to keep a wee sliver of it for himself. Au contraire. You want to be the writer who was savvy enough to get all the t's crossed and all the i's dotted. The one who got to keep the money.

If you don't have an agent, you should definitely have a lawyer. And even if you do have an agent, you might want to have your publishing contract looked over by a lawyer who knows the ins and outs of the publishing business. Anyone else will more than likely be a waste of money.

CHAPTER 8

WRITE AWAY!

"I think I did pretty well, considering I started out with nothing but a bunch of blank paper."

—**Steve Martin**

Some writers write only when caffeine-saturated, while others demand distilled water. Some vampirically shut all the shades; others need a room with a view. Edgar Allan Poe is rumored to have written with a head full of opium. Isabel Allende is said to light a candle and write until it goes out. Carolyn See, *Washington Post* book critic and author of numerous books, takes the practical approach. She writes 1,000 words every day.

The important thing is to write whichever way suits you. This may mean following in someone else's footsteps or inventing your own mad ways. While we can't help you put pen to paper, we can help you break down your big scary book into a series of small friendly tasks—from filling in a Master Calendar so you can pace yourself and avoid burning out, to the nourishing and use of your outline, to the creating of your first draft, to the inevitable and seemingly endless revisions and rewritings, to that wonderful moment when you're done.

SAME-PAGING: GETTING SIMPATICO WITH YOUR EDITOR

Many of the principles that apply to working with your agent also apply to working with your editor, only more so. If you feel the need (and maybe even more so if you don't), go back and revisit pages 104 to 110, where you'll find everything you need to know about appreciation, expectation, communication and affirmation.

Before you write your first word, arrange a meeting or phone conversation with your editor to establish the guidelines of your working relationship as well as the direction of your manuscript. This is where you need to get as much information as possible about the kind of book your editor wants. If, unbeknownst to you, your editor has a different idea of what your book should be, you could be in serious trouble when you hand in your manuscript and she asks you to do massive rewrites or, horror of horrors, rejects your book. To avoid such a fate, prepare a solid list of questions. Like all good questions, yours should be both practical and substantive. Here are some general questions to ask your editor, but it's important to develop additional ones that reflect you and your beautiful project:

- What would you like me to know about how you and this process work before we begin?
- Do you want to see chapters as I finish them? Or would you prefer to see a completed manuscript?
- Do you prefer telephonic or electronic communication?
- Do you have any general or specific editorial suggestions before I start? Is there anything in my argument/presentation/information/plot/characters and/or tone that needs work? Did you see any stylistic problems in my sample writing/manuscript that you would like me to work on?
- How closely should I stick to my outline? If there are changes in the outline, would you like me to keep you in the loop about them?
- What is the ideal pub date? Are there certain key holidays or events you want to plan my book release around that will affect my deadline?

Now is the perfect time to riffle back through any rejection letters you might have filed away. Study them carefully, with a detachment that allows you to take in the truths contained in the rejections you accumulated like so many cherished battle scars. And now that you've got a book contract, take a moment to gloat over how foolish all those rejecting editors were!

Your editor's responses will give you a lot of information about her. Are her fingers going to be deep in your pie? Or will she simply support you? Or neither? All this info will be important as you navigate the seas of publishing.

But no matter what your editor is like, when she talks, listen aggressively. Odd how hard this is to do sometimes. Write down all suggestions. Thank your editor for taking time out of her busy schedule to formulate her comments. Really think about them. Ask your friends, allies and agent for their opinions. Then formulate a thoughtful, smart, professional response.

Once you feel that you and your editor have agreed on the direction of your book, it's time to start breaking your tasks down and making a schedule.

GETTING YOUR DUCKS IN A ROW SO YOU CAN START QUACKING

To do something as monumental as writing a book, it helps to see it as a series of small, doable tasks. Break it down. How long is your book? How fast do you write? When is your deadline? When do you want to be finished with your first draft (which is a different question from when you want to hand in your completed manuscript)? Consider that before you deliver a draft to your editor, you should have it read by your team, your agent and other assorted readers so you can use their comments to rewrite before you hand in your manuscript. You may want to do this several times; it can take readers weeks or even months to read and intelligently evaluate a manuscript. Then factor in your rewrite time. Sometimes a large hairy rewrite. When you're estimating, assume you'll have to do more rather than less work.

Then you need to consider whether there are photographs or illustrations to find or make, permissions to obtain, research to do or people to interview. It may seem slightly ridiculous to methodically organize an artistic activity like writing, but doing so can bring comfort and freedom. You'll know where your milestones are, when you're moving ahead of your deadline and when you're falling behind. As the great Yogi Berra said, "It gets late early out there." And you do not want to be scrambling around as your deadline looms, panicked, frantic, sleep-deprived. Generally speaking, people do not do their best work under these conditions.

Making a Place to Write

Before you sit down and make a schedule, create a work-friendly environment. If you're the kind of person who craves quiet, make sure you have a work space without distraction. If you're someone who craves commotion, find a café or a community center where you can work. Try to arrange your life so you have several hours every day when you don't answer the phone. This may mean getting up at five in the morning or staying up until five in the morning.

Many years ago, Erma Bombeck was an unknown housewife with less than no time to herself. But she really wanted to write. She wanted to write so much that she made herself a little desk area in the kitchen where she would grab 15 minutes here and 15 minutes there. She turned her desire into a wildly successful publishing career, writing about the everyday trials and tribulations of being a mom and a wife in America. Crystal E. Wilkinson, author of the short-story collection *Blackberries, Blackberries*, further attests, "You have to make writing a part of your daily routine, like brushing your teeth and having dinner. You have to train your loved ones to accept your writing as part of your routine. If you do, they will. I have twins, so if I can do it, anyone can. In the end, though, either you want it bad enough or you don't."

Understand that while writing is certainly time spent at the computer or with pen in hand, it's also time spent thinking about your book between writing sessions. As Agatha Christie said, "The best time for planning a book is while you're doing the dishes." Perhaps you could use the time spent commuting to iron out plot problems. When you're lying in bed at night, figure out what your characters are wearing, what their parents were like, what their hobbies are. Use workout time to smooth out the bumps in your thesis and the chinks in your arguments. While you're making dinner, think about how to present the various elements of your subject in a new, original, easy-to-understand way.

The Art of the Schedule

Let's suppose you plan on writing a 500-page manuscript. Say you write two pages a day and you have a year to finish your book. This means it will take 250 writing days, or about eight months. And you have to assume you won't be able to write every single day. So you should probably aim to get a first draft done in nine months. That will give you plenty of time to get people to read your draft and give you brilliant comments, and for you to do your award-winning rewrites.

Breaking it down further, this schedule means you have to do 55 pages a month. Given the fact that a page equals 250 words, you will have to write

13,750 words a month. That's around 3,437 words a week. If you write 5,000 words a week for two and a half weeks, you'll have almost enough for your whole month. Then you can either forge ahead or go back and rework what you've done. If things are going slowly and in three weeks you've got only 7,500 words, you know you need to put your life on hold a little and churn full steam ahead.

"When I start a book, I always think it's patently absurd that I can write one. No one, certainly not me, can write a book 500 pages long. But I know I can write 15 pages, and if I write 15 pages every day, eventually I will have 500 of them."

—John Saul

To keep on track, it's important to construct a motherboard, your Master Calendar, which will lay out all your deadlines from here through launch and beyond. Buy or make yourself a big one-year calendar. You will need to be able to change and modify it. A lot. A big white erasable board and colored erasable markers could be just the ticket. Or maybe a big blackboard with many hues of chalk.

You can use your Master Calendar not only in the writing of your book, but in its marketing, publicizing and selling as well. Your Master Calendar won't let you overlook any of the many important details. It's nigh unto impossible to stay on top of everything, but if you're meticulous about updating this calendar and consulting it regularly, you can stay one step ahead of the typhoon that will soon be your book.

First, mark out a year's worth of months, with plenty of room to write in. Make sure there's extra room above and below each month to make notes to

BY WHATEVER MEANS NECESSARY

Khaled Hosseini had a great excuse not to write a book. He was a full-time doctor. He had no time. Nonetheless he was bound and determined to write a novel. "I would get up at four," he says. "I'd read the paper, have my coffee and then start writing by four forty-five. I'd write until about eight. Then I'd go in and work my shift. Luckily, in residency you learn how to function on very little sleep." Khaled found that there were few distractions at that time of morning, and he was able to finish his novel. His book *The Kite Runner,* set in Afghanistan, is now a #1 national bestseller that has sold over a million copies and has been optioned to be made into a Hollywood movie.

yourself. And it's best if you can see the whole year at a glance. Mark your start date and your deadline. Then determine your various interim deadlines. Where do you need to be by the end of the first month? In six months? Nine months? A year? Lay it all out for yourself very clearly. In number of words, in number of pages. If you're doing interviews or research, jot down when you'd like each completed. If you need to acquire permissions, add these to your schedule. If your book contains original illustrations or photographs, set up deadlines for these as well.

Search and Research

If you're writing a book that requires extensive research, do yourself a couple of favors. First, leave lots of time. Second, document your research meticulously.

Doing research is like mining for gold. It takes time and patience to hack all that rock just to find one gleaming nugget. And you never know when your next hack will be the one that strikes that rich beautiful vein. That's why it's very hard to make a schedule around research. You could take a three-week trip to Bali and come back empty-handed. You could spend an afternoon at your local public library and find everything you need. That's why it's critical to stuff in sufficient padding when you're making a research schedule. If you haven't done a major research project before, talk to authors who have. And remember, when it comes to research, a great librarian can be worth her weight in the aforementioned gold.

THE SWEETNESS OF DOCUMENTATION

Keep track of everything. Whether you're gathering information from historical documents, interviewing people, or getting pictures and articles from the Internet, magazines and/or books, write down *all* pertinent information: publications, exact dates and times, photographers' names, page numbers. Everything. It's best to keep all this information in one log, so that you always know where to find it. This can be in your Empty Book, if there's room, or in another empty book altogether.

This log will hold valuable information for your footnotes and for tracking permissions. When we wrote our book about Negro Leagues baseball player Satchel Paige, we did a lot of research in libraries across the country. Much of this involved making xeroxes from microfiche. We naïvely didn't write down the names or dates of the publications, thinking we'd somehow remember them when we got home. Naturally, we couldn't remember a thing. We thought we'd have to spend thousands of dollars making a second trip back to these libraries to get our information straight, but luckily we were able to do heavy detective work from home to figure it all out. Still, we wasted countless hours by not keeping careful records. Clearly we violated one of the most essential PYPIP rules for success: Don't be stupid.

If interviews are required for your book, the best way to document them is to tape them. Always test your taping technique before you go to an interview, especially if you're taping for the first time! Also, be sure people know when they're being taped. And don't deceive anyone by pretending to turn the recorder off when you're leaving it on.

Keith and Kent Zimmerman have spent years and years doing taped interviews, first as journalists and then as coauthors for famous folks. Their advice is as follows:

- End the formal interview before you run out of tape, and keep the mike hot so you can get some great off-the-cuff remarks.
- Try not to interrupt. Silence brings extra insight as your subject attempts to fill up the spaces.
- Transcribe your own tapes. You were there. Nobody you farm it out to can re-create that experience. You can also do subtle rewrites, cleaning up grammar and syntax, as long as you don't in any way change the meaning or language of what was said.
- Change rooms every so often when conducting interviews. Familiarity breeds complacency.

THOU SHALT NOT MAKE STUFF UP OR COPY FROM OTHERS

This may seem obvious, but again, say it we must. If you're writing nonfiction, DO NOT claim that something that isn't true is true. And with fiction and nonfiction, DO NOT use other people's words without crediting them properly.

In recent years, a number of plagiarism scandals have involved some of our most beloved historians. Often these cases turn out to be more about sloppiness than bad intentions. But in a court of law, plagiarism is plagiarism. Which brings up another essential point. DO NOT be sloppy. A world of people with nothing better to do is just waiting to prove that something in your book is wrong. And if someone proves one thing in your book is wrong—whether done intentionally or not—it destroys your credibility. If there's one thing you don't want destroyed, it's your credibility, as this often leads to public disgrace and humiliation, and sometimes having to pay back all the money you made from your book.

So if you're doing research and copying information directly from a source, put quotes around it so you know which words belong to you and which belong to someone else. Then be sure to get permission for any quotes that exceed "fair use" (see page 186 for details). Better yet, if you're working in Microsoft Word, use the footnote function as you work. Word is a great tool because it syncs all footnotes even if you move material around.

The Art of Locating Art

In order to know what a schedule for art entails, you first have to figure out exactly what art you need. If you need a photographer or illustrator to create original art, and your publisher is not helping you locate such a person, head straight for your local library, bookstore and magazine stand. The children's sections of bookstores are great spots to start looking for illustrators, even if your book is for adults; since nearly every book is illustrated, you can often find someone whose style appeals to you. The next place to look is *Communication Arts* photography and illustration annuals, the sources that advertising agencies, publishers and others use to track down illustrators and photographers. These sources are helpful because they include each artist's contact information.

Once you have about half a dozen people you're keen on, check if they have their own Web sites. You want to see as much of each artist's work as possible to make sure his style fits yours. Often, you'll spot an illustration or photograph in a magazine that looks perfect. But when you go to the artist's Web site, you'll see that piece was the exception to a style, not the rule. Hone your artist list down to three to five names. Usually, you'll be able to track these folks down through the Web or the original publication where you first spotted their work.

Original illustrations and photography can cost thousands and thousands of dollars. But if an artist is excited about your project and feels it will help his career and be fun, you may be able to swing a deal. How would your project benefit an artist? If the artist has never worked for your publisher (or any publisher, for that matter), you will be opening a valuable door for him. This is particularly important if you have a publisher known for illustrated books. Many illustrators and photographers bang their heads on publishers' doors until they're lumpy with knots, so often they'll take a pay cut just to have an in. Not that you want to undercut the person you hire. As we all know, you get what you pay for. But beware: An illustrator or photographer with no book experience might be in for a shock when he discovers how low fees are in publishing compared to those in the advertising world. For example, a photographer can make $10,000 in one day when shooting for an ad, as opposed to $10,000 for an entire book's worth of photographs. You want to make sure he doesn't give you an automatic "no" just because the fee you can pay is not commensurate with what he typically receives. Explain the publishing pay scale and the benefits of having illustrations or photographs in a book. If the artist won't agree to your offer, and you don't have anything more to give, consider giving him a small percentage of the royalties.

In terms of setting a price for art, work with your editor and/or agent to determine fair market value and go down from there. In most cases, it's better to negotiate a flat fee for all art than to pay for it piece by piece.

Your project may be of personal interest to an artist. Say you're doing a cookbook on pastas from the Ligurian region of Italy. Maybe your top choice for an artist has ancestors from that part of the world and has always wanted to go there. Once again, doing your research, making a personal connection and showing the value of your project are paramount in bringing a top-notch artist on board for a price you can afford.

Don't have the money for a professional illustrator or photographer? Art schools are great places to find very talented people at very low prices. Some students will hand over their work for nothing in exchange for getting their work published. But be careful here. While the price may be right, the work might be subpar. If you can, meet several times with the artist to make sure he's reliable and conscientious as well as talented.

If original art is not necessary or appropriate for your book, you can look for existing art in any number of places. Do you need historic photos? Period illustrations? Vintage advertisements? Contemporary photos? Japanese anime? Cave drawings?

If you're looking for anything old, libraries and historical societies are great places to start. The Library of Congress is one of the greatest resources for artwork because its archives are so huge and its prices are extremely affordable.

If you're looking for contemporary photographs (or classic photos by famous photographers), there's no easier pit stop than a stock house, which owns thousands of images. Corbis and AP are great places to start and are accessible via the Web. Put in a search word and you'll probably find hundreds of potential images at your fingertips. However, Corbis and other high-end stock houses can be stiff, price-wise. That's because they'll do the research for you and come up with fabulous images for you to choose from. Their permission process is simplicity itself. And you can pay for everything on a credit card. But watch out: They also have a cumbersome fee structure. Corbis charges based on the size of your first printing. And then recharges you for every subsequent printing. This can really add up. AP charges less but doesn't have nearly as many images as you'll find in the Corbis library.

No matter what your source, it almost always makes sense to buy as many images as possible from each one; you stand a much better chance of getting a lower price per image. Even Corbis discounts their prices when you buy a lot from them. If you ask, that is. Never just accept the price someone quotes you. Haggling, if done with humor and intelligence, can be both fun and profitable. Because in some cases a picture may be worth not only a thousand words, but a thousand dollars as well!

Permission Slips: Decoding Copyright Laws

If you want to reprint something that was not created for your book, you very often need to get written permission from the person who owns the copyright to the work. Before a major publisher will publish your book, they must have all your permissions in their possession. If they don't, they'll ask you to take the material out of your book. If you won't, they won't publish your book. They don't want to be sued. And neither do you.

Making a schedule for permissions is tricky because you never actually know what you're going to use in your book until you write and edit it. Books often change significantly from first draft to last. A picture or poem you think is essential early on might prove to be meaningless fluff when the book is laid out. But that's usually quite late in the game.

So don't start getting permissions *too* soon, because you don't want to waste your time or money. However, since it often takes a while to track down a pesky permission—and *all* permissions should be handed in with your finished manuscript—we suggest the following process:

1. ***Break your permissions into three piles.*** Definites, Maybes, Unlikelies. Track down all information for the Definites as early as possible. Get prices and any necessary forms. This will help you guestimate total costs and figure out how much you'll have left over for the Maybes and Unlikelies.

2. ***Don't pay for a thing until you're sure what's going in your book.*** This way, you won't spend money on a Definite that turns out to be an Unlikely.

WHAT DO YOU NEED PERMISSION FOR?

To start with, you will almost certainly have to obtain permission for more than two lines of a poem, more than one line of a song or more than a few lines of a book or essay. You will also almost certainly have to obtain permission for a photograph, illustration or painting. One exception to this rule is the use of text in the *public domain.* All works published before 1923 are now in the public domain, but works published after this date fall into a number of different categories. If you're unsure whether something you want to reprint is in the public domain, we encourage you to go directly to *The Chicago Manual of Style* (which has over 30 pages on the subject) or to the Library of Congress to ask for help.

And no permission is necessary if the piece you're reprinting is considered *fair use.* Here's where things get really complicated. There is no actual measure of fair use. As the *Chicago Manual* says, "Use of less than the whole [poem, essay, chapter or such] will be judged by whether the second author appears to be taking a free ride on the first author's labor. As a rule of thumb, one should never quote more than a few contiguous paragraphs or stanzas at a time or let the quotations, even if scattered, begin to overshadow the quoter's own material. Quotations or graphic reproductions should not be so long that they substitute for, or diminish the value of, the copyright owner's own publication. Proportion is more important than the absolute length of a quotation: to quote five hundred words from an essay of five thousand is likely to be more serious than quoting five hundred words from a work of fifty thousand." In other words, it's okay for us to quote 122 words from the *Chicago Manual* because thats a tiny percentage of its total word count (the book could double as a doorstop). However, if you took 122 words out of a 200-word poem, you *must* get permission to reprint it—unless, of course, it's in the public domain. And don't forget, composers' and poets' estates are notorious for going after people who abuse copyright law.

If you've tried without success to track something down, don't despair. One author we know used archival magazine footage from the 1940s in her book. The magazines were no longer in print, and it became clear that it would take an enormous amount of work to track down anyone who could grant permission for use. So she checked with her publisher, and they agreed that she did not need to pursue these permissions. If, for some reason, she was contacted by one of the sources, she would negotiate a fee at that time. If you decide to take a similar tack, check with your publisher to make sure they're okay with the associated risk.

HOW TO GET PERMISSION

To acquire a permission, you need a form specifically made for this purpose. This is called a permission form. It states *what* you're reprinting, *in what form* you're reprinting it, the *territory* you're reprinting it in and in *how many books/editions* the material will be reprinted. This form will be a legal document between you and the person/company who owns the material you want to reprint.

It's always better for your permission form to cover nonexclusive world rights in all languages and for all editions of your work. Sometimes this will not be possible or will be prohibitively expensive. If, for example, you can afford to acquire only the North American rights and you don't predict any foreign sales of your book, then stick with the North American for the moment. But if you're lucky enough to sell foreign rights down the road, you'll have to go back to the source and pay for these additional uses. The same rule applies to different editions. If you can only afford to buy the rights to reprint something for your hardcover edition, then you'll have to go back if a paperback edition comes out. Sometimes you'll even be asked to state the number of books being printed for a particular edition. The more copies, the more you'll be expected to pay.

You should be able to get a standard permission form from your publisher. In case you're self-publishing, we've included a form in Appendix III for your convenience.

THE PANGS OF PERMISSIONS

Acquiring permissions requires the patience of Job and the persistence of a pit bull. When she began writing *A Thousand Years over a Hot Stove,* a book with more than 100 photographs and illustrations, Laura Schenone was ill-prepared for the amount of work permissions required. Not to mention the pounding her pocketbook took in the process. Laura says, "I wish I'd had a better understanding of those permission fees at the outset and how they work with print runs—a huge issue with an illustrated book."

Laura was presented with an unexpected challenge. Many of the people she was dealing with would sell her rights only for the first printing of her book. "My editor told me this would be 7,500 copies," she says. "When I bought the permissions, I wanted to up this number to 10,000 or 15,000 copies to be sure I was covered. But sometimes the fees as much as doubled."

Laura's story illustrates the importance of understanding permission costs before signing a deal or even developing a project. That said, Laura couldn't be happier that she wrote her book, permissions and all: it went on to win a James Beard Award, the Pulitzer Prize of food writing.

Once you have a form in tow, the next step is identifying the owner of the material you want to use. If you're looking for permission to reprint material from a book, first go to the copyright page to find out who originally published it. For example, if the material is in a paperback edition of a book, you may find that a different publisher did the hardcover; if so, you'll need to go there to secure permission. Or, let's say you're using an essay from an anthology. It may have first been published elsewhere, perhaps in a magazine. The copyright page will list the source you need to contact.

If you need permission to reprint song lyrics, you can go directly to the Web site of the American Society of Composers, Authors and Publishers (see Appendix I). Click on the tab "ACE Title Search." Then click "search the database." Fill in the search field with a title, writer or performer. At the bottom of your search result page, you'll find the information about the publisher/administrator. These are the people you'll need to go through to obtain permission.

Sound like a pain? It is. But there are worse pains in life.

Once you've found your source, it may take you what seems like a billion phone calls to track down a real person. When you do, be sure to get a name and e-mail address as well as phone and fax numbers. Keep this information in your Empty Book. Do not under any circumstances count on permission givers getting your permissions back to you in a timely fashion. Repeated follow-up will probably be necessary. Gently remind the owner(s) of the material that you need your permission form signed and returned. You might even have to send another form because the original has been "misplaced" or was "never received."

Don't necessarily assume you will have to pay anything. Some kind souls will give you the piece of material you're seeking free of charge. But even if you get someone's permission for free, you still need his signature on your form.

EVERYMAN POWER: THE PAUL DAVIDSON STORY

As you may remember from Chapter 2, Paul Davidson wrote a book containing dozens of letters he penned to the customer service departments of America's biggest corporations, along with their responses. When he sold his book, the publisher informed him that he would now have to get permission for EVERY SINGLE letter from EVERY SINGLE company that wrote to him. Many of these letters didn't put the companies in the rosiest of lights. And yet, if he wanted his book published, by hook or by crook he had to get these corporations to sign release forms.

What's a guy to do? After tracking down the correct contact people, Paul got on the horn and trotted out his excellent sense of humor. At first, many company representatives didn't believe that it was in their best interest to sign. But Paul made them laugh until they gave in. One time, he had his wife call and leave a message for one of the most stubborn of the bunch, saying that their marriage was taking the brunt of Paul's hunt for permissions and would they please, please, help save a sacred union. In the end, fewer than a half-dozen companies refused to sign permissions. In Paul's words: "It was an arduous process for a non-lawyer, but it turned out to be greatly successful because I was, indeed, not a lawyer. By coming across as an 'everyman author,' companies seemed more apt to help." Now his book, *Consumer Joe: Harassing Corporate America, One Letter at a Time*, is sold in Jamba Juices around the country. Why? Their tongue-in-cheek letters addressing Paul's ideas for a delicious Tuna Melt Smoothie were in his book. In fact, Jamba Juice was one of the first companies to realize that it was good business to have some fun and join Paul's party.

You may be surprised to learn that your publisher will most likely not lift a finger to help you with permissions. However, in some extreme instances, if you've tried and tried without success to secure a permission, your publisher will step in at the end and facilitate. In the big houses, people trained to do such things can assist in a pinch. But DO NOT count on this. Often the publisher just won't let you use the material in your book. Case closed. End of story.

Do not rest until every single permission has been tucked nicely into bed. It's easy to forget about a dangler, and this could lead to trouble down the road.

Lastly, make copies of your permissions before you send them to your editor. Put these copies in a very safe place. You're going to have to credit all sources at the back (or front) of your book. The more organized you are now, the easier this task will be later.

GETTING STARTED

Ernest Hemingway's first rule of writing was "Apply the seat of the pants to the seat of a chair." That's another way of saying something that many people have difficulty grasping: If you want to complete your book, you have to write it. And starting is almost always more difficult than keeping it going. Something about inertia, and bodies in motion remaining in motion.

But whatever you do, don't wait for inspiration to write.

Just write.

> *"Every day, every day, I write the book."*
> **—Elvis Costello**

When you write, it's crucial to turn off the critical part of your brain. The snarky part that snarls, *Who would ever want to read this pitiful drivel? Who do you think you are anyway, trying to write a book and get it published?* When you hear that voice (and you will hear that voice), you have to find a way to push the mute button. Nothing will stop you colder, deader and flatter than the nobody-loves-me-everybody-hates-me-I-think-I'll-go-eat-worms voice. As Samuel Johnson said, "Keep always in your mind that, with due submission to Providence, a man of genius has been seldom ruined but by himself."

There are many techniques for dealing with this voice. One effective method is to consciously acknowledge it. Try saying some variation of this:

RESISTING THE TEMPTATION TO WRITE THE PERFECT SENTENCE

Many writers want to write the perfect sentence right out of the chute. And if they don't have the perfect sentence, they feel as if they can't go on. It's extremely difficult to write a great book this way. It's hard to write any kind of book this way.

Try this: Write the best sentence you can at this particular moment.

Then move on.

That's right. Just move on.

The PYPIP Guide to Sentences clearly states: Never sit with one sentence longer than five minutes. Writing can be like quicksand. If you struggle, you just sink faster. Give in, accept the fact that you're stuck and come back later to fix it. Tonight. Tomorrow. Whenever. You'll be amazed how often the fix seems obvious. Or more often still, it becomes obvious that you can just throw the sentence away.

We know a man who wants to be a great writer. He wants to write a perfect book, full of perfect sentences. If a sentence isn't perfect when he writes it, he considers it a miserable failure. So, after years and years of writing and rewriting, he has yet to reach page 51 of his manuscript. If you find yourself bedeviled by a piece of your writing, put a moratorium on it. Do not allow yourself to go back and look at anything until you've completed a first draft.

"I'm afraid nobody will want to read my book."

This alone will keep your brain from doing what it was doing: crashing your hard drive. Then you can restart your brain, like rebooting a frozen computer, with a new, different, better thought. Something revolving around your passion.

If this seems hopelessly dorky to you, fine. Make up your own technique. But keep moving forward. Always keep writing your book, even if it seems like the lamest piece of dreck ever. Get that first draft done. Then you can start shaping your book. Making it great. Developing characters, strengthening arguments, jettisoning hackneyed metaphors, sharpening wit.

As you move forward, it can be helpful to look back through work you've already done. One of the best places to look is your outline.

If you're having trouble getting started, try automatic writing. Just write whatever comes into your head, even if it has nothing to do with the subject at hand. No matter how trivial and idiotic it may seem. Laundry lists, grocery lists, childhood rhymes. Whatever. Just the act of writing will often prime your brain's pump.

Nourishing Your Outline

Some authors like to make elaborate outlines and plot out their books in their entirety before they write word one. Others just start writing, and whatever book comes out is the book that comes out. Many fiction writers make notes on index cards as they do their research, carefully filling in each scene with each character's motivation, what the locale looks like in detail, how the scene moves the plot forward. Some writers could care less.

Naturally, most writers are somewhere in between. But we're big proponents of outlining. Here's why:

1) If you're writing nonfiction, you probably included an outline in your proposal. Feeding and watering it as you write will undoubtedly make it easier to organize your book, see where it's going and where it's been.

2) It's easy to get off track when you're writing. Sometimes going off track can lead you to new and exciting places. But sometimes it can be a huge waste of time. If you have an outline, you can see if your new ideas make sense, and if they do, where exactly they fit. Maybe you're on a tangent that slots perfectly into chapter 10, not chapter 2. That's much easier to see with an outline in place.

"I was working on the proof of one of my poems all the morning, and took out a comma. In the afternoon I put it back again."
—Oscar Wilde

3) When you get stuck, an outline helps you see the big picture and gives you other avenues to explore. If chapter 4 isn't flowing, you can move on to another and come back to the bugaboo later.

4) Making an outline is also a good way to break down a book into its smallest elements. In this way, an outline can help you focus on the individual twigs that you can easily gather in building the nest of your book. The more minutely detailed your outline, the easier it is to visualize and thus write your book. Think of your outline as a living, breathing, evolving thing. Continually revise and update it to reflect changes. Having a good, detailed outline will help you slide right into your first draft.

First Drafting

You have to write a first draft. It doesn't have to be good, but you have to get it done. Anne Lamott, author of the fantabulous writing book *Bird by Bird*, puts "SHITTY FIRST DRAFT" on top of everything she starts, to remind herself that's exactly what it should be. Once you complete the first draft, you can tell people:

"Yeah, I just finished my first draft."

Nothing quite matches the relief you'll feel when you can say that. Then, once you've finished celebrating the completion of your first draft, you can go back and make it just right.

Writing Is Rewriting Is Rewriting Is Rewriting

As with all clichés, there is utter truth in the statement that writing is rewriting. The way to perfect your writing is not through sitting on a sentence for an eternity, but by doing multiple drafts of your book. Sentence by sentence.

One of the most important parts of rewriting is cutting away the fat. Go through and fine-tune your manuscript with a fine-tooth comb. Do this many times, always looking for stuff you can lop off. Eliminate redundancy. Streamline every chapter. Every paragraph. Every sentence. Every word.

"To write is to write is to write is to write is to write is to write is to write is to write."
—Gertrude Stein

Occasionally you may have to kill the baby. Sounds gruesome, true, but it's an apt description of what it feels like when you take a piece of your book that displays the full range and depth of your writing brilliance, cut it out and then discard it on the junk heap where old manuscripts go to be buried. It's important not to fall so in love with a piece of writing that you lose sight of the big picture. As Colette said, "Sit down and put down everything that comes into your head and then you're a writer. But an author is one who can judge his own stuff's worth, without pity, and destroy most of it." The only modification we'd add is: Save the baby you've killed. Store it away somewhere safe. Someday you may be able to perform mouth-to-mouth on it and bring it back to life in another book, where it can dazzle the world.

Do not rest until you've transformed your manuscript into a thing of beauty. Then read your book from stem to stern, cover to cover. Do you repeat things? How is the pacing? Does it lag at times? Did you rush through information that needs more development? Do you repeat things? Did you cut away from a scene before the drama was fully played out? Are your characters consistent? Is your prose too slick or too flowery? Too choppy or fragmented? Do you repeat things?

Fools Rush In: Turning In a Great Manuscript

Assume you have only one shot with your editor, readers and reviewers. It's a bit like going out on a job interview with a company you want to work with for the rest of your life. You wouldn't show up looking all dopey with some nasty hair and bad shoes. If you have your own best interest in mind, you'll take the time to look as spiffy as possible. So it is with your book.

Many, many writers do themselves the disservice of presenting material that is just not ready. They assume their editors will wave a magic wand and fix their manuscript. In this day and age, a lot of editors have neither the time nor, frankly, the skills required. But, most important, you want your editor to jump for joy upon finishing your manuscript. What you don't want is for him to sit around and stew over how much work he's going to have to put into it. Leslie Meredith, an executive editor at The Free Press, puts it this way: "Why would you hand in something that can be turned down—that isn't your best book? You want your editor to be an advocate of your book, not to be tied down with a laborious revision. And you don't want your book to get a reputation as a problem."

"You know you've achieved perfection in design, not when you have nothing more to add, but when you have nothing more to take away."
—Antoine de Saint-Exupéry

Ironically, one of the best things you can do for your writing is not write for a while. Once you've completed your first draft, give it a rest. Get some distance from all those words your brain coughed up. When you go back to them, many of the problems you struggled with will be easy to solve. You'll find the perfect words to replace the ones that never sounded right. And you'll discover that distance is a miracle worker when it comes to structure. It's like a Magic Eye poster; where before you saw only dots, now you'll see a fully formed picture.

So, please, don't be the fool who rushes in. We beg you *not* to turn in your book until you:

- Rewrite until you can rewrite no more.
- Get some distance by letting your book sit for anywhere from a week to a month.
- Have many readers of all different kinds evaluate your book.

THE DANGER OF TURNING IN A NOT-SO-GREAT MANUSCRIPT

We know a writer who received a hefty advance for his novel. He was in the very unusual position of having sold a novel on the first 100 pages only, and his editor pushed and pushed to get the finished manuscript, ASAP. He was a fast writer and was proud as punch when he turned in his manuscript ahead of the rushed schedule his editor had him on.

A week later, his agent called and told him the publisher was rejecting his manuscript and canceling the deal. The writer was in total shock. He assumed that after he turned in his furiously fast first draft, he'd be working with his editor, getting notes, doing rewrites. But because he gave in to his editor's pressure to turn the manuscript in NOW NOW NOW, because he didn't rewrite until he could rewrite no more, his deal got killed and he got to keep only a pitiful pittance of his advance. Cue the violins and pass the hankies.

This writer has since gone on to write several books, all of which have been published. His secret? Handing in a clean, professional manuscript.

- Rewrite some more.
- Read your manuscript out loud, from beginning to end, to make sure it flows and doesn't harbor mistakes.
- Finish off with a couple more rewrites.
- Make sure typographical and grammatical errors have been corrected.

MORE READERS

After you've gotten distance and rewritten, it's time for more readers. As we said in Chapter 2, good readers don't grow on trees. You have to unearth ones who have the skills, time and desire to read and comment intelligently on your work. Reader candidates include your agent, fellow writing group members or writing partners, and the larger network of writers/authors you've cultivated over the book-writing process. Friends, family and acquaintances who can read and talk reasonably well are also good people to pursue. These people may be more excited to read your work because they've never been asked to do such a thing before. Presented correctly, it can be a novelty and make people feel special.

Have you invested a lot of time in developing your relationships with local booksellers? If so, you might want to ask a bookseller or two to read your manuscript. But heed the advice of Linda Bubon, co-owner of Chicago's Women & Children First: "Be humble. Don't make demands. I'm more likely to respond positively to someone who is a regular customer. Who attends programs and book groups. Who has an interest in literature outside their own writing."

Asking people to be readers can be awkward for a writer. Look, it takes a lot of time to read a manuscript, and we all know that it's hard enough finding the time to eat and sleep these days, let alone read 300 pages. But it also means exposing yourself, making yourself vulnerable. Will your readers like it or loathe it? Or, worst of all, will they find it utterly average and ultimately unpublishable? Many writers, when forced to face these fear-based feelings, decide not to pursue readers. This is a mistake. If you're writing a book for the general public, this means OTHER PEOPLE ARE GOING TO READ IT! And it's better to get feedback now than to encounter crippling criticism later.

Getting the Most Out of Your Reader

When you work with a reader, maximize your time by putting together a list of questions. Some writers prefer to dole out the questions after the read has been completed, because they don't want to color their reader's point of view. These questions should be extremely general ("Was my story suspenseful to the end?") and extremely specific ("Is the dialogue on page 52 between the killer whale and the drowning muskrat really believable?"). And always ask: "What did you like best (or least) about my book?"

Why the questions? Many readers will simply say, "I really liked it," and call it a day. This is not helpful. You want as much information as possible about your manuscript. Once you've sussed out its strengths and weaknesses and gathered as much specific info as you can, ask your readers for ideas about how to fix any problems.

After all that writing and rewriting, your perspective will be skewed. If your readers can articulate problems and solutions, they'll have done you the immense favor of letting you see through new eyes.

Here's a list of general questions to ask your readers:

- Did the book deliver its promise?

- Was anything confusing or awkward?

- Was the information easy to understand? Was any information missing?
- Did the arguments make sense?
- Where does it flow? Where is it choppy?
- Was there enough humor?

For fiction writers only:

- Are the characters and the dialogue believable? Do you care about these characters? Are you rooting for them to succeed or fail?
- Did the plot make you want to keep turning the page? Where did the story lag? Are there scenes that should be taken out? Scenes that need to be added?
- Was it suspenseful? Predictable?
- Was the end satisfying?

It's Critical to Take Criticism

Whether you think you're after praise or not, you are. If you're human, that is. And while you may ask for criticism, when you actually hear it you may wish you'd never asked. Learning to take criticism early on is great preparation for rude reviews that may attack or belittle you and your book, often for no good reason at all. Good to toughen the hide before the slings and arrows start flying.

The first rule of taking criticism, especially when you've asked people to take their precious time to help you, is to listen instead of defending yourself or your work. If, after serious consideration, you have questions about someone's criticism, that's all well and good. Ask civilly for clarification. But wait until you've had time to calm your emotional beast. Avoid all sentences like "What kind of stupid comment is that?" and "What was the last thing *you* wrote?"

> *"It's my experience that very few writers, young or old, are really seeking advice when they give out their work to be read. They want support; they want someone to say, 'Good job.'"*
>
> **—John Irving**

READING RIGHT OUT LOUD

After you've sucked all the advice you can out of your readers and made your edits, take the time to read your manuscript out loud. That's right, your whole manuscript. You'll be surprised to discover how you're able to hear sentences or passages that sound awkward. Reading your book aloud will also give you a sense of scenes or sections going on too long, straying off point, coming across as boring, bad or unclear. Your voice will also naturally find the points of emphasis. And your manuscript will be all the better for reflecting your own personal rhythms.

MORE ON OUTSIDE HELP

Even if you're working with an editor at a publishing house, you might need outside help *before* you turn in your manscript. This depends, of course, on 1) what kind of person your editor is, and 2) what kind of shape your manuscript is in.

If you've received little or no help from your editor and you anticipate a light edit, you might want to hire an outside editor/book doctor. Why? We've said it before and we'll say it again: Your book has ONE shot in the world. You want to give it every opportunity to succeed.

But how do you even know what kind of editor you've got? This is where showing your editor a chapter or two (or three) can come in handy. See what kinds of comments you get back. Are they thorough, interesting, thoughtful and reflective of a deep knowledge of what you're trying to do? Even your first conversation with your editor can reveal a lot about her editing skills. Did she give you concrete suggestions, ideas and comments? Did she seem to have a clear vision and real understanding of your book? If your answer is "no" to all of the above, then you can put money on the fact that your editor is probably not going to do the kind of editing you need.

Now, what if you're having a really hard time with your manuscript? You just can't get things to gel. Your readers are reinforcing your fears that your manuscript isn't very, you know, good. Or you've taken the requisite time off, come back and still can't see clearly where to go from here. This may be the time to bring in an outside editor. While readers can help you identify problems, they more than likely won't be able to tell you how to fix them. A good independent editor can. Hiring extra help is shame-free. Many professional writers do it. Your job is to produce a great book. No one cares how you do it. The Free Press's Leslie Meredith puts a tremendous amount of time into editing her books, but still encourages authors to hire freelance editors because 1) clean manuscripts will excite your editor and make her a full-on advocate for your book, and 2) clean manuscripts allow her to get great sample material around to her colleagues right away so that others can get excited, too.

An outside editor can be an editor who's worked in the publishing business and is now independent, or someone who works for a publisher and is moonlighting. An outside editor may also work as a professional reader or a writing coach. So be specific about what you think you need. (See Chapter 2 for more details.)

Unfortunately, high-caliber, state-of-the-art editors can cost a pretty penny. Well-known editors with great track records can make thousands of dollars, depending on how much work they have to do. And some of them *are* worth their weight in bestseller lists. But if you don't have the bucks, and you feel you need some truly objective and professional advice, then go with the professional reader option. A smart local bookseller may be just the trick (a nice bonus for paying a local bookseller is that he'll be all the more invested in your book when it comes out).

DON'T LET RUNNING OUT OF TIME DRIVE YOU OUT OF YOUR MIND

After all the writing, rewriting, editing, reading, time off and personality-induced paralysis, is it any wonder that writers have problems hitting their deadlines? Plenty of powerful people in publishing will tell you that deadlines mean nothing in the book business. And while there is a great deal of truth in that statement, it is not entirely accurate.

Most publishers plan their lists 9 to 18 months ahead of time. There's an art to these lists; they want their seasonal catalogs to be well balanced. Naturally, it takes a lot of juggling and planning to pull this off. If you've written a reference book on mental health, your publisher will not want to put out another reference book on mental health in the same season—or maybe even the season after that. And one of the ways they plan their catalogs is by looking at due dates. So, if they think your book will come out in the fall of one year, they'll make sure the other mental health book won't come out until a year later. Watch the trouble that ensues when you hand in your book six months to a year late.

The good news is, unless your book is time-sensitive, your publisher will probably be happy to give you an extension on your deadline with enough advance notice and time to juggle things around. In fact, your editor could be so swamped that she wouldn't mind postponing your manuscript one little bit! But, if you get an extension, be sure to get a written amendment to your contract. That way, if your editor leaves or anything else untoward happens, your publisher will still have a contractual obligation to honor.

If you need an extension, don't underestimate the time you require. Publishers lose confidence in authors who repeatedly ask for extensions. And a publisher who isn't happy with what you've been sending in so far can use a request for multiple extensions as a reason to cancel your contract. As one successful author told us, "I was having a terrible time getting my book done. I was new to the book business and slightly clueless. Well, my editor left the company, and all of a sudden I was an orphan. So when I was late with my manuscript, they canceled my contract. Just like that. Believe me, I've been very careful about meeting deadlines ever since."

POSTPARTUM DEPRESSION

We've made the "book as baby" comparison before, and we'll be making it again. But if there is one moment when your book feels especially babylike, it's when you hand it in. This is when you'll feel the pangs of postpartum depression. You've birthed your baby, and now you no longer have control over its fate. You are left to wonder how it will fare in this cruel yet beautiful world.

Or, worse yet, you've birthed a baby that's nothing like the gorgeous one you imagined. That's how it may seem, anyway. We're here to tell you that this, too, shall pass. If one moment you can't imagine a worse book in the history of time, know that this will be matched by a moment when you can't imagine a better one. These mad mood swings are all part of the giddy process of making a book.

Just keep in mind that nobody put a gun to your head and said: Be a writer.

If somebody did, you should contact the authorities immediately and have this person dealt with harshly.

"If there is a special Hell for writers, it would be in the forced contemplation of their own works, with all the misconceptions, the omissions, the failures that any finished work of art implies."

—John Dos Passos

ONE LAST THING BEFORE YOU TURN IT IN

Before you submit your manuscript, give it one more final dress inspection. Make sure that its hair is combed and its shoes are nice and neat. That pages are in the right order, contact numbers are correct, and chapters begin and end correctly.

And remember, writing your book may be the most difficult thing you ever do. But that doesn't mean it can't be fun. If you take an organized methodical approach, you can minimize the difficulty and maximize the joy. And let your passion come shining through.

CHAPTER 9

WORKING WITH YOUR PUBLISHER

"I am a publisher—a hybrid creature: one part stargazer, one part gambler, one part businessman, one part midwife and three parts optimist."

—Cass Canfield, chairman of the board, Harper & Brothers, 1945–55

In days of yore, publishing was known as a Gentleman's Business. Run by Gentlemen. Individuals. Families. Yes, they wanted to make money, but they would also produce beautiful books whether they thought they produced a profit or not. They wined and dined their clients. Threw lavish parties. Made a habit of martini lunches.

You see very little of that these days, although some smaller publishers still hold to the traditions of yesteryear. Maybe not the martini lunches, but the ethos of a family business where long-term relationships are valued alongside the bottom line. If you've signed a contract with a publisher like this, your experience may vary wildly from that of authors who have signed with a larger house. Today, the big publishers are owned by major corporations staffed by thousands of people who have no idea who you are or what your book is about. Welcome to your corporate publishing team—at best, a sleek machine where each department works in tandem to maximize your book's chances for success. At worst? The right hand won't even know what the right hand is doing.

Which brings us to one of the most important things you can do to help your book succeed: you must turn your name into a face. When your book goes from being a bunch of squiggles and symbols on a piece of paper or computer screen to being the product of a real person with a face, dreams, talent and passion, most people will feel differently about it and you. Many times, this can mean the difference between someone making that follow-up call that gets you an article in a leading magazine or pitching your book extra hard so it gets reviewed in *The New York Times*, is available in stacks at bookstores around the country or has a cover you'd like to be judged by. It's your job to be the best team player you can possibly be. Sometimes that means ruffling a few feathers. Sometimes it means taking one for the team.

EDITOR 101

As we mentioned, large and midsize publishing houses have many departments. These include sales, marketing, publicity, art, accounting, and so on. The department your editor belongs to is, appropriately enough, called the editorial department. Editorial departments, like other tribal societies, are hierarchical. At the top of the totem pole is the publisher (who also runs marketing, publicity, sales), then comes the editor in chief, then sometimes the editorial director, then executive editors, then senior editors, then editors, then associate editors, then assistant editors, then editorial assistants. The most powerful and successful editors work their way up the totem pole and often become editorial directors, editors in chief, publishers or heads of their own imprints.

> *"Some editors are failed writers, but so are most writers."*
> **—T.S. Eliot**

Every publisher is different, of course, but nearly all editors, regardless of rank, acquire books and are thus known as *acquiring editors*. In most cases, they find a manuscript or proposal that they think will sell and that fits their company's list of books, and then take it up the editorial ladder to what's called an editorial board or acquisitions meeting. There, they try to convince all the other people in editorial (plus, possibly, people from marketing, publicity and sales) that the manuscript or proposal is worth buying. This is undoubtedly how your opus got acquired, unless the publisher or editor in chief acquired it and decided to edit it himself or hand it off to an editor.

No matter what her position, every editor works differently. Some are very hands-on. They get all the way into your manuscript and go line by line, syllable by syllable. They make sure the voice, the rhythm, the plot and the information are what they should be. From micro to macro, from soup to nuts, they will try to massage your book from zygote to bestseller.

Some editors make only broad changes.

Some editors will change barely a word.

Most fall somewhere in between.

Ultimately, it's up to you to get the most out of your editor.

Your editor is also your primary point person, your liaison to every other department. She can be a great cheerleader, shepherd of your complaints, pumper-upper of sales/marketing/publicity. Or she can actually stunt the growth and development of your book. Bottom line: You want to do everything you can to make sure your editor never hesitates to go to bat for you.

Early in your relationship with your editor, ask her to keep you abreast of key dates in the publishing process. Of particular importance are the launch meeting and sales conference, which we'll get to later in this chapter.

Walking a Mile in Your Editor's Moccasins

Publishing people are, generally speaking, underworked and overpaid. No, wait, reverse that. Overworked and underpaid. And the epitome of this overworked/underpaid dichotomy is the editorial staff. Editors are often people with multiple degrees from top universities who have forgone higher-paying jobs because of their love of books (or because they have liberal arts degrees and have no idea what to do with them). They stay late and often give up their nights and weekends, hauling home large stacks of manuscripts.

Most editors are also master multitaskers. These days, they're forced to acquire more and more titles every year with the hope that a few will actually make money. And in addition to acquiring and editing numerous books at the same time (yours will certainly NOT be the only book your editor is working on), they are also required to go to numerous meetings, return phone calls and e-mails and put out the inevitable fires that rage in any modern publishing house. Why are we telling you this? Because we want you to think twice before assuming the worst when a phone call isn't returned pronto.

Acquiring Editorial Love

While it's crucial to be on the same page with your editor from the get-go, it's also important to keep up an ongoing dialogue. When you start working with your editor, it's a bit like going on a blind date that you hope will end up in marriage. It will probably be a bit awkward at first, especially if you don't feel a personal connection, but as you continue dating you want to establish an increasingly comfortable rapport—a relationship where ideas flow freely and easily. If this doesn't happen, don't panic. Many writers confess in hushed tones that they walk on eggshells around their editors. Your editor doesn't have to be your best friend. She just has to be your professional ally.

Often your relationship with your editor will not heat up until you hand in your manuscript. Then what happens? The whole publishing machine starts gearing up to produce your masterpiece. As word spreads that your long-awaited work has finally arrived, excitement swells through the various departments and Oprah starts calling. Right?

Wrong.

Almost certainly, this next phase of your relationship with your editor involves . . . WAITING. After that, you'll probably have to . . . WAIT. Then, most likely, there'll be more . . . WAITING.

The Waiting Game

The period between handing in your manuscript and hearing back from your editor may make you feel like an old-fashioned father-to-be stuck in the waiting room. However, instead of pacing through a few hours of labor, you will in all likelihood be treading that linoleum for at least a couple of months. Even though most contracts spell out the "waiting" period, many editors far exceed it. This is an utterly brutal time in any writer's life. Your book—indeed, your whole writing career—is hanging in the balance. Will it be the next National Book Award winner? Or shredder fodder? Gwen Macsai, NPR commentator and author of *Lipshtick*, a collection of humorous essays, says this about the waiting period: "I loved my editor, and he was extremely attentive at first. Then he fell off the face of the earth. I sat there thinking: 'He hates me' . . . 'He hates my work' . . . 'If he hates me, he should just tell me he hates me and stop leaving me hanging like this!' It makes you crazy and chips away at any confidence that you have."

To avoid the pain and suffering of the waiting period, we advise making your presence politely felt. Resist the impulse to pop your head into the delivery room every hour, but don't disappear entirely from your editor's life. A friendly postcard or hello every couple of weeks is perfectly acceptable.

TWO MONTHS AND COUNTING

Has it been over two months, maybe even six, seven or eight months, and you've still heard nothing? First of all, this situation is not as uncommon as you might think, so don't immediately assume the worst. As a general rule, it's almost never a good idea to freak out. Your editor may have gotten in 10 books all at the same time and is simply unable to address yours. Maybe the others are time-sensitive or written by celebrity authors who get star treatment.

Most contracts stipulate that your editor must provide editorial feedback within 60 days. If the editor does no such thing, most contracts require you to send a letter to the publisher asking for a response. But this protocol isn't always followed. For example, you may have a very good relationship with your editor and feel uncomfortable going this route. If your book is time-sensitive, however, at the very least it's necessary for you or your agent to get your editor to commit to a date by which your work will be edited. Figure out the last possible date when your manuscript can go to the printer and work back from there.

Even if your book isn't time-sensitive, you don't want to give the impression that it can constantly be moved to the back of the bus. By asking an editor to commit to a date, you're forcing her to be accountable. It's important to get this date in writing. This way, if your editor is not able to deliver, you or your agent will have ammunition if you need to go up the publishing ladder.

In these situations, it's always better to have your agent carry the big stick so you can walk softly. Obviously, if you don't have an agent, it's up to you to do both. And if your contract does have the 60-day stipulation and you continue to hear nothing, sending a letter demanding editorial feedback is the way to go.

You don't even need to ask, "Have you read my manuscript?" And do try to suck all desperation out of these communications.

On the other hand, if you haven't heard from your editor in over two months, you may have a problem on your hands. Be sure to stay in contact with your agent, if you have one, about the state of your manuscript. Your agent can nudge in a way that you can't. And if there's a problem, you want to know about it as soon as possible. Your agent may be able to pick up trouble on his radar long before you can.

If you're agent-free, stay on top of business in a professional and annoyance-free manner.

Hearing from Your Editor: "You Want Me to Change *What*?"

At last, the waiting is over. Your editor has read your manuscript and is ready to proceed. Unless your manuscript needs enormous work, you will probably receive a letter stipulating the overall changes your editor would like you to make, in addition to line-by-line edits.

Your editor has an objectivity about your material and an insight into the book business that you almost certainly do not possess. Be thankful for both. On the other hand, you have a depth of insight into your material that your editor does not. DO NOT automatically agree or disagree with your editor. Some writers just blindly follow their editor's instructions. Others take the drama queen approach and seem hell-bent on having a series of emotional arguments. We do not advocate either of these approaches. Emily Loose, a senior editor at Penguin Press, has this advice: "Take a few days to respond to editorial feedback. Then read it over several times so that defensiveness isn't your first reaction."

> *"No passion in the world is equal to the passion to alter someone else's draft."*
> **—H.G. Wells**

If you just say "yes" or just say "no," you deprive yourself of going through the process of exchanging ideas. Instead, calmly and carefully formulate your response. Where you agree. Where you disagree. Where you have questions about what your editor meant. Often a confusing piece of information can be transformed into a brilliant insight by the simple act of asking a simple question. From this sort of collaboration can come a great book.

As you go through your editorial letter and line-by-line edit, jot down questions you have. Use your friends, allies and agents to clarify and refine your questions before you address your editor. They may see things you don't. A reader or agent may confirm an observation of your editor's and illuminate the point in different words. Carefully lay out your ideas before you have a conversation with your editor. Maximize your editor's time. We're not advocating short, curt conversations. We're suggesting that you go to your editor with a serious, well-informed, intelligent list of questions and comments that can be a springboard for a fruitful dialogue that will make your book good, better, best.

Ideally, this is a time to meet with your editor face to face. Oftentimes you can get information from her demeanor and her tone of voice that you could never get in a letter. And every scrap of information is valuable.

"WHOSE BOOK IS THIS ANYWAY?"

Sometimes you will come to an impasse with your editor. From plot to argument to character, from the general to the specific nature and tone of your book, there are countless ways you may disagree. When it comes to the details, most editors will bow to the author. But an editor who sees fundamental problems that will impede your book's success is more likely to hold fast. Try to be open to suggestions even as you stick to your guns. It's almost impossible not to react emotionally in these situations and to feel that your editor is a chowderhead who's totally missed the point. Instead of pouting or railing, decide whether to knuckle under or make a case for why the manuscript should stand as is.

Sometimes the suggestion an editor makes is NOT the right one but will lead to changes you would have never thought of on your own. Sometimes an editor can be flat-out wrong. But even an editor's insensitivity to your work can help you clarify what you want to do. This is a time to formulate an argument that convinces your editor of your position. If this doesn't work, then you have to decide whether to ruffle feathers or roll with the punches. Either decision comes with a price.

If you take one for the team and make the necessary changes, hopefully your editor will appreciate the fact that you're playing ball and be more likely to get behind your book with enough enthusiasm to help make it a

BLIND FOLLOWING

One author, who wishes to remain nameless, sold her proposal to an editor she really liked and who seemed to understand exactly what she was up to. However, when they started working on the first few chapters, her editor steered her in a whole new direction. The author told us, "I followed my editor's advice because I respected her and wanted to please her. But all along I kept thinking that this was not the book I signed on to write, nor was it a book I knew how to write." The author plodded along. When she turned in her final book, her editor was extremely displeased. The author tried to explain that she had only been following orders, but by this time it was too late. "I could see that there was no hope of repairing the relationship or the book," she said. "I knew I'd have to find another publisher. Fortunately, my agent convinced the publisher to let me keep the money already advanced. But I was devastated. And I wish with all my heart that I had just written the book I wanted and knew how to write."

success. But by taking one for the team, you also run the risk of creating a book that you don't like. Will this still be a book you'll be proud to have your name on? Remember, it will never be your editor's name on the cover.

With that in mind, ruffling feathers may be your best option. But better to be a dove of peace than a bird of prey.

GOOD COP, BAD COP

Your agent has mounds more experience than you do and can be far more objective about your work. This is why it's good to use your agent as a sounding board to figure out which issues are important and which ones you should let slide. Sometimes what seems to you like a boulder can be turned into a pebble.

If you both agree that it's time to speak up, let your agent be the bad cop. One of the skills a good agent acquires is the ability to get what a client needs without alienating the team. Your agent may already have a relationship with your editor and can speak the language of publishing, articulating what you want better than you can. In addition, most editors don't want to anger agents. They depend on them for the best projects and want to keep them happy.

If you do call in your agent, we suggest following the advice of Mauro DiPreta, an executive editor at HarperCollins: "What an editor doesn't like is a passive-aggressive author who says yes or gives an implicit yes and then has his agent come in and say, 'What he said isn't what he meant.' Either let your agent handle a situation entirely, which I have no problem with whatsoever, or speak up and say what you really think."

Just be sure to save your agent for a time when you've come to an impasse and need a good Sherpa to help you over a perilous crevice.

GOING OVER YOUR EDITOR'S HEAD

Few people enjoy having someone leave a footprint on their scalp. But there's always the chance that you or your agent can finesse going over your editor's head to get the ear of his boss, convince her that you're right *and* make your editor look good.

What? It could happen.

Before you make the decision to stomp on someone's head, though, think carefully. Make sure you've exhausted all other avenues. Be extra sure that the thing you're fighting for is crucial to the success of your book. And once you've made the decision to jump rank, tread quietly. Be humble, be charming, lie on your back and show your belly. Do whatever you have to do, but make it as easy as possible for your editor to save face. Jennifer Josephy, an executive editor at Broadway Books, suggests that you go to your editor before you go above her head to let her know that you'll be doing so. This allows for one last opportunity for rapprochement and also will not leave you feeling like a snitch. Jennifer suggests this script: "Say to your editor, 'I'm feeling frustrated by our communication, so I'm afraid I'm left with no choice but to go to a higher authority unless we can resolve this amicably.'" But she also cautions: "Unless violence is about to ensue, you will have to work with your editor through your publication date. Publishers will only very rarely switch editors on a project, so it's imperative to keep communication open at all times." Even if that communication means going to your editor's boss.

Again, your agent can really help.

The fact is, there *are* circumstances where you need the aid of a more senior person. You may have an editor who's young and inexperienced. Smart, dedicated and hardworking, yes, but without the experience, time and/or contacts to give you what you need to make your book great and profitable. Or you may get stuck with an editor who's just plain incompetent. If you and your agent, after due consideration, come to the conclusion that you've been shackled with such a dud, remedy the situation by whatever means necessary and as quickly as possible.

Build a concrete case with specific examples of your editor's poor performance. This way, if you do need to go over someone's head, it'll be clear why you're doing so. It's also important to point out your editor's positive qualities. This will soften the blow and make it clear that you're a reasonable, thoughtful person and not a lunatic.

TAKING YOUR BOOK TO ANOTHER PUBLISHER

After receiving Graham Greene's manuscript for *Travels with My Aunt*, his American publisher cabled, "Terrific book, but we'll have to change the title." Greene responded, "No need to change title. Easier to change publishers." If your editorial differences absolutely cannot be resolved, it's time to consider taking your book to a new publisher. That means returning the money to your current publisher without knowing if there's another taker. Obviously, this option is fraught with peril. But on the plus side, if you sense things are only going to get worse and that your publisher might

PACKING UP AND MOVING ELSEWHERE

One well-known writer, who has asked for anonymity, sold her book at auction for a hefty sum to a most excellent editor at a top-notch publishing house. The start of their relationship was nothing short of a lovefest. But when she handed in the first half of the book, things changed. To begin with, she had to wait several months to get a lick of feedback. And when the feedback arrived, it made her heart sink. Her editor did not have one single positive thing to say.

The writer had heard only the very best things about this editor, so she figured it must be that her writing simply wasn't very good. She hired an outside editor to help her get the manuscript in tip-top shape. In the meantime, her editor at the publishing house never returned her calls, and all the good feelings that had passed between them early on in the process seemed like distant history. Finally, it was time to hand the book in, and all she could do was hope for the best.

Lo and behold, the months ticked by. Not a word. No return phone call. Her agent did a bit of nudging here and there, but still no response. The writer was now not only distraught but furious. She had spent day and night of an entire year getting her book finished and a good deal of money on outside help to make sure it was as good as it could be. She decided that if she didn't get back an edited manuscript at the six-month point, she would move on.

And that's just what she did. After a call from her editor but still no edited manuscript, she just knew that this person was no longer her advocate. When she took a step back, she remembered her book's auction. Many people had wanted this book. And after all her work, there was sure to be someone who still would.

Turned out she was right. Her agent resubmitted her book to a half-dozen hungry editors. And within two weeks of pulling her manuscript from this publisher, she got a commensurate offer from a lovely, very enthusiastic editor who edited the manuscript within two weeks of a signed contract. Clearly, sometimes yanking a book can be the best thing that ever happened to it.

be getting ready to reject your manuscript, your preemptive move will make it easier to resell. The fact is that once a manuscript has been rejected, it's very often perceived as tainted. It's kind of like breaking up with someone before he gets the chance to break up with you. It's powerful being the rejecter. Only trouble is, you run the risk of being perceived as "difficult." That's why you need to come up with a good answer to the question: "What happened?" Your answer needs to indicate that you are the active party, without calling your ex a bad name. The most popular reasons seem to be "creative differences," "not seeing eye to eye" and "wanting to go in a different direction." Of course, you will want to take one of these phrases and make it your own.

Before you make any move regarding a change of publisher, have many long, thoughtful conversations with your agent. If you don't have an agent, try to talk to other people in the business or to other writers to help you make the most informed decision. Either way, work out an exit strategy along with a plan for what to do next.

Leaving your publisher should be like removing a bandage. You want to do it quick and clean. The sooner you can find your book a new home, the better. You want to spend as little time as possible in publishing limbo.

CANCELLATION (GOD FORBID)

A tiny percentage of book contracts get canceled. So it's unlikely, but, yes, it could happen to you.

After you (and your agent, if you have one) have exhausted all avenues of discussion and negotiation, you may have to accept the fact that your publisher is cutting you loose. It may be your fault. Or it may have absolutely nothing to do with you.

If you've missed your deadline, if you handed in a manuscript that's not up to professional standards or if it doesn't deliver on the promises made in your proposal, your book can be canceled.

On the other hand, if your editor leaves or gets fired, if your publisher decides to go in a new direction or if something unforeseen happens in the world, your book can also be canceled.

The first thing authors want to know is: *Do I have to give the money back?* If your manuscript has been rejected within the terms of your contract (for example, if you've missed your deadline), then technically you do have to return your money. If, however, you can show that the cancellation had little to do with the terms of your contract, you should be able to keep what you've been given thus far. Even in the first case, your publisher in all likelihood will not sue you for the money (depending, of course, on the size of the advance and the degree of animosity between the parties). But if you're able to resell the book, then you will almost certainly have to pay back any money you've received.

RESELLING YOUR REJECTED BOOK

If you're a fan of the online humor Web site and newspaper *The Onion*, you probably know their #1 *New York Times* bestseller *Our Dumb Century*. And if you've read the book, you'll find it very hard to believe it was canceled by its original publisher.

Our Dumb Century was originally sold to Hyperion, the publishing arm of Disney. The authors received a six-figure advance and wrote a fantastically funny and furiously scathing satire that their editor loved. However, the higher-ups at Disney thought the book was a bit *too* scathing. And they were particularly upset by the page stating that a Nazi propaganda cartoon was cocreated by Hitler and "pal" Walt Disney. Hyperion demanded that the unsavory bits be eliminated. *The Onion* refused. So Hyperion decided not to publish the book.

Clearly it was up to professional standards. It was exactly the book the authors said they would write. So *The Onion* got to keep their advance money. *And* sell their book again to another publisher. Which they did, in a major bidding war for three times the amount Hyperion originally paid. They also had the benefit of the story getting written up everywhere from the *Washington Post* to the *Dallas Morning News*.

Now, that's sweet revenge!

The good news is that you will own all rights to your manuscript once again. Which means you will have the opportunity to resell your book. The bad news is that your manuscript, as we indicated earlier, may be seen as soiled if it's already been through one company and spit out unpublished. This is why it's particularly important to revisit your proposal or manuscript before going out with it. You never know, but if you take into account everything you've learned, you could end up with more money the second time around.

THE MOTHERLESS CHILD

The publishing business is populated with too many books that have lost their parents and been abandoned, cut adrift in a heartless world with no one to protect them. If the editor who purchased your book leaves your publisher, your book will become known as an "orphan." Unfortunately, editors have a glorious tradition of changing jobs more often than a nervous girl changes outfits before her first date. So don't be shocked if this happens to you. As Phil Bashe, author of over a dozen books, says, "It's been ten years since I started and finished a book with the same editor. Two books ago, the original editor was fired several months into the project; a second editor resigned after a week on the job; and the senior editor who inherited the book was canned just three weeks before publication. It's pretty maddening, especially when you've had a good rapport with editor number one, then have to build a rapport all over again with number two."

Yes, Phil's situation was extreme, but he illustrates perfectly the worst of authoring an orphan. Editors asked to take over your project rarely have the same passion for your book as the editor who acquired it. This means you'll have lost your primary advocate, a loss that can prove calamitous. If this happens to you, resist tossing your manuscript into a dumpster. Instead, win her over. How? If there's one thing editors love, it's authors who are easy to work with. (Let's hope you made a reputation with your last editor as a marvelously collegial person.) Maybe your new editor isn't gaga for your subject. But you may have other things in common. Or perhaps, with your controlled and intelligent passion, you can make her see how cool your subject is.

In fact, sometimes you can stumble into a better situation with a change of editors. So if your book becomes an orphan, assess your situation before taking action.

If, however, your new editor turns out to be a wicked stepmother, here are your options: 1) Slog on, cursing your fate, swallowing your rising bile. 2) Have an open, honest conversation about the editor's commitment to your project. Find out where you stand and what can be done to improve your situation. 3) Cut the cord and find a new parent within your publishing house. This is best done with the help of an agent, if you have one. 4) Cut the cord and find a new publisher. Numbers 1 and 4 should be your last options, used only in the most extreme and dire situation; it's not easy to find a new home, and it's hard to swallow bile.

The Hand-Off: What Happens Next?

Ring. Ring. It's your editor. Your book has gone into production. What does this mean? It means, barring a legal review (which some books must go through in addition to copy editing), your book has been accepted by your publisher! At this point, you're 99.99% certain that your book is really going to be A BOOK! While it's being groomed, your editor will be discussing it with other members of your publishing team. This is why it's so important for your editor to be a big fan of you and your book. If you've made a great book and you've been a joy to work with, this information will pass from department to department. So your relationship with your editor affects not just the editing of your book, but the entire publishing process.

THE ROLE OF YOUR COPY EDITOR

The next person on your road to the land of finished books is the copy editor. A copy editor focuses only on your spelling, punctuation, grammar, consistency of language and other important nitpickings such as fact checking. Depending on the complexity of your manuscript, this work can take from a week to a month or more. You will then receive a xerox of your copy-edited manuscript, which you will need to go through carefully, approving or disapproving every comment and correction. Typically, you have a week or two to do so—more for a long or complicated book. Don't leave this to the last minute. Reviewing your copy-edited manuscript is painstaking work and can take many, many hours. You may disagree with a whole host of changes, which may require some back and forth with your editor (you almost never have direct contact with your copy editor). On the whole, however, most people are delighted by the cleaning, buffing and polishing a good copy editor bestows on their manuscript.

Can you hear the distant drums? It's now, depending on your particulars, 9 to 18 months until your Pub Date.

MIXED REVIEWS

If you're an author who plays with language and sentence structure, or who writes in dialect, you will want to pay very close attention to your copy editor's corrections to be sure they don't diminish the zazazoo of your writing. Raymond Chandler once wrote to his editor: "Will you convey my compliments to the purist who reads your proofs and tell him or her that when I write in a sort of broken-down patois which is something like the way a Swiss waiter talks, and when I split an infinitive, god damn it, I split it so it will stay split." On the other hand, James Michener was so pleased by the work his copy editor did on his books that he sent her a round-trip ticket to Paris.

CORRECT YOURSELF

Once you've returned your copy-edited manuscript with your comments and revisions, you won't be invited to make any other significant changes.

The manuscript will now be sent to a typesetter and turned into page proofs, a set of which will be sent to you for your approval. At this juncture, you just want to be pointing out errors in typesetting and making small, last-minute adjustments.

Making major changes on page proofs is a no-no for two reasons. First, making extensive insertions and deletions opens the possibility for introducing new errors, which may or may not be caught at subsequent stages in the process. Second, your publisher needs to start figuring out the number of pages for the entire book, including acknowledgments, index, and so on. This is because most books are manufactured by binding together signatures of 16 or 32 pages. If the total length were to run over from, say, 272 pages to 278 pages, your publisher would have to go up to 288 pages (not likely) or cut six pages (not pleasant). So, at this stage, adding and deleting more than a paragraph or two can be highly problematic.

If you *must* make major changes (and we mean *MUST,* as in something in the world has changed that makes information in your book incorrect or you're going to be sued, not *must* as in a turn of phrase that's causing you to lose sleep), ask your publisher for a clean copy-edited manuscript before your page proofs arrive. This way, you can figure out ahead of time which changes you must make.

If you feel compelled to change large sections of your book after the type has been set, most publishers will charge you if the changes exceed 10% to 15% of the total manuscript (printer's errors aside). This is stipulated in almost every contract and can cost a pretty penny. While the cost is a good enough reason not to make changes after the copy-edit stage, another is that those made at a later date just generally annoy everyone at your publisher's. The sections that you change have to be copy-edited, and you can potentially affect the schedule. All in all, you're making more work for people.

A GALLEY IS NOT IN THE HULL OF A SHIP

While you're checking your page proofs, the printer may be turning them into *bound galleys* with pages cut to size. If you're the lucky recipient of bound galleys, their arrival is an exciting time because now your book actually *looks* like a book.

The drums are getting closer. It's now approximately six months until your Pub Date.

To be clear, bound galleys do not include any of the changes you make to your proofs. And these bound galleys will go to a number of book reviewers. However, all bound galleys have a prominent label instructing reviewers not to quote anything from the text without checking it against the finished book, which will contain all revisions. Reviewers are aware that bound galleys are uncorrected proofs and should check all quotes and facts in their reviews against finished books.

THE BLAD

If you've written a book that will be printed in full color, you won't be seeing bound galleys. You'll review page proofs, maybe more than once (particularly if it's an art book and you're the "expert" who must check for the accuracy of the color). And often the next thing you'll see is a *blad* (an acronym for "book layout and design"), which is usually a pamphlet-size sampler of your book. This blad will be sent to the reviewers and media people who need an early look. So if there's a particular spread you think will help sell your book, be sure to let your publisher know as soon as you turn in your manuscript. Blads are also used for more highly designed but text-driven books. If your book fits into this category, you'll want to pick appropriate spreads in this case as well.

THE MOTHER OF ALL MEETINGS: THE LAUNCHING OF YOUR BOOK

Remember when we said your editor would be talking to various departments about your book? Well, now these talks have escalated into meetings during which the marketing, publicizing and selling of your book will be much discussed. A plan will start to materialize in these meetings and will be nourished, fed and fussed over until . . . THE LAUNCH MEETING!

The Players

Whether it's in a basement in Biloxi or in a high-rise overlooking the skyline of Manhattan, your launch meeting will in many ways chart the entire course of your book's introduction to the world. This is where your editor will formally pitch your book to key members of your publishing team. Depending on the size of your publisher, this can be anywhere from a guy and his cat to a dozen or more key players representing numerous departments. If your book is with a larger publisher, this meeting will probably include:

Your publisher

Your editor

Your publicist

The head of publicity

The head of marketing

A representative from e-marketing/publicity

The head of sales (along with the divisional heads who sell to chains, independents, etc.)

A representative from special sales

Sub-rights representatives for first serial and foreign sales (if relevant)

Your editor you know. But if you're like most of the world, the rest of these monikers are nebulous. And yet these are the people who will either make the world pay attention to your book or not.

The publisher. Your publisher is the big kahuna, le grand fromage, the master and commander of your publishing ship. Publishers have certain godlike qualities—they're in charge of everything and everyone. If you can get them excited about your project, your chances of succeeding rise meteorically. Your publisher almost certainly has great contacts and knows the right people, or at least some of them. A word of praise about you and your book purred into the right ear can be the tipping point for its success. So if your editor walks into the launch meeting full of enthusiasm, expertise and passion, this can only help your chances of turning your publisher into your cheerleader.

Publicity and marketing. First of all: What the heck is the difference between these two departments? While the line can be blurry, here's a general rule of thumb: Publicity is when you get it for free; marketing is when you have to pay for it. For example, an article in *The New York Times* is publicity and an ad in *The New York Times* is marketing. Being on *Oprah* is publicity; sending a life-size cutout of yourself to everyone on Oprah's staff is marketing. Having your book end up on the bedside table of Tony Soprano is publicity; paying for it to be there as product placement is marketing (which more and more often is the case).

Generally, you'll have much more contact with the publicity department than with the marketing people. In fact, you'll probably be assigned your very own publicist, whereas you may never—or only fleetingly—speak to anyone in marketing. Why? Because publicity is often dependent on you as a speaker or interviewee, or as the subject of an article or TV/radio segment. Marketing, on the other hand, involves disseminating information about you and your book through stuff they have to pay for. Think ads, brochures, flyers, postcards and baseball caps.

Sales. The sales department consists of people who, you guessed it, sell your book to retailers. Larger publishing houses have their own sales people who sell to independent bookstores, chains, online merchants such as Amazon or bn.com, mass merchandisers, catalogs, warehouse clubs, gift stores, department stores, and nontraditional outlets ranging from clothing stores to car washes to sporting goods emporiums. Often these houses have a separate department devoted to making what are called "special sales." This department sells to corporations and other nontraditional booksellers. There are also regional sales reps. So one sales rep may cover the whole of Northern California and another Southern California.

Smaller publishers use distributors or commission reps to sell their books. These are simply hired sales forces.

The sales force goes out seasonally to sell the books on the publisher's upcoming list, which means that each book on the list will receive between a few seconds and a few minutes of attention. As short as this sounds, it's enough time to persuade a bookseller to place an order if the pitch is powerful. Once again, a short but informative pitch can win the day.

Sub rights. The subsidiary rights department consists of people who try to sell secondary rights to your book. The two sub rights most likely to be discussed at launch are first serial and foreign rights. If you've retained foreign rights, then only serial rights are relevant. In terms of serial rights, don't get too excited. This doesn't mean you're going to be gracing a box of Wheaties anytime soon. It only means that a portion of your book will be reprinted in a magazine or newspaper. In days of yore, newspapers published the likes of Charles Dickens in installments. Nowadays, it's very difficult to have your book serialized, because magazines and newspapers are devoting fewer and fewer pages to reprinted material. However, a reprint from your book in the pages of anything from *Ladies' Home Journal* to *Rolling Stone* can really help your launch.

Foreign rights can also add up to a tidy sum and can make you feel very worldly without having to leave your living room. In all midsize to major publishing houses, there are people who try to sell your book overseas. In most cases, the person handling your foreign rights will be selling your book through subagents rather than directly to foreign publishers. Many small publishers also use subagents.

Preparing for Liftoff: How You Can Affect the Launch Meeting

Most authors are blissfully ignorant about how important their launch meeting is to the emotional, physical and financial future of their book. Your editor now has to deliver his version of your road-tested, sweetly honed pitch. If he does a good job, everyone will leave that room understanding beyond a shadow of a doubt why, and to whom, your book is going to sell. Even if it's not "their kind of book."

Understand that this meeting will in large part determine your publicity and marketing budget. Whether you go on tour. Whether ads will be bought. How hard the various players are going to push your book. Luckily, you marked the launch meeting on your Master Calender. So, like good scouts, you and your editor are well prepared. In fact, you've given your editor all the information outlined below.

PUBLICITY

Blurbs for your book can go a long way toward inspiring your team members. Especially if they're from well-known people they respect. If your editor can come into the launch meeting with one or more meaningful endorsements, suddenly you're a bona fide author. In addition, your editor should be armed with a top 10 list of *potential* endorsers to see if anyone in the room is connected to any of them. A great blurb can not only excite your publisher, but may help them decide to send you on tour.

These days, fewer and fewer publishers are supporting author tours, questioning their cost effectiveness as a publicity and marketing tool. But if you feel that a book tour would be a boon to sales, you need to provide your editor and publisher with compelling reasons as to why such a tour will be successful. Even more importantly, you need to show them through the sheer force of your personality and your passion that they would be crazy NOT to send you on a book tour. Concretely, you need to let them know what your event/reading/speaking engagement would consist of and your ideas for getting lots and lots of people to show up—one of the most difficult parts of a book tour. If you're already speaking around the country, this will make their decision that much easier (especially if someone else is footing your travel bills!).

MARKETING

Are there essential materials you need to help get the word out? Postcards or other mailings? Widgets or doodads that might sell your book in a fun and interesting way? Does it make sense to take an ad out? Why and where? Do you want to hold a fun-filled contest? Can you plaster posters all over your city?

Lay out creative marketing techniques that suit you and your book. And if you want free things to give away, you'll have to convince your publisher that these things won't just be thrown in the trash.

SUBSIDIARY RIGHTS

Give your editor a list of book chapters that you think could be serialized, along with publications where it would make sense to place them. This will make the people who handle first serial rights very, very happy. As you can imagine, they don't have time to read each book and then think about which chapters are best to excerpt.

For the foreign rights people in the room, be sure you've supplied your editor with supportable information on why your book might sell to specific countries. Your editor should also have copies of any articles that have been written about you abroad. Do you speak any languages fluently? Do you travel regularly to any particular countries? If so, make sure your editor knows about these selling points.

SALES

One of the most important tools you can provide to the sales force is the proper positioning of your book. This means comparing your book to other successful but not directly competitive titles. By describing the bestselling lineage of your book, you'll be identifying your potential audience. It's another way of saying that people who bought these books will also buy your book.

SPECIAL SALES

Provide your editor with a list of places or companies apart from bookstores where your book has a reasonable chance of selling. (Take a look back at your proposal, where you may have listed such companies.) If you can come up with contacts at these companies, this will greatly enhance your chances of penetration. For example, if your book mentions Jamba Juice, as Paul Davidson's *Consumer Joe* did, maybe you can convince them to sell it. As he did.

PREPARING YOUR BOOK FOR CATALOGING

Next stop: your publisher's catalog. This is your book's coming-out party, which is why you want to make sure it's the belle of the ball. A great catalog entry can be the difference between minimal orders and big piles of them. Libraries, independent bookstores, gift stores, trade shows/display rooms and universities all look at catalogs to help them make their ordering decisions. There's even a chance that some enterprising Hollywood movie producer or scout may browse your publisher's catalog, looking for their next huge blockbuster, quirky independent film or HBO series.

Generally speaking, your catalog entry will include eight or nine nuggets of information from publication date and price to cover image and author photo. We'll take you through each of these elements so that you can help your book have a splashy debut.

A Pub Date Is Not a Social Engagement in a Bar

Catalogs are often organized according to season. So what's the best time of year to publish your book? With some books, it's obvious. A Christmas book needs to be out no later than October. A baseball book must be stocked in stores before April. A book about Abe Lincoln should be published on his birthday—and shipped to bookstores at least a month before.

Picking the right date and season can really help you generate publicity and make marketing much easier. If the nature of your book does *not* suggest an obvious publication date, you and your editor will want to look for a natural tie-in. If your book is about Mae West, maybe you can release it on the anniversary of her birthday. If it's about an African American historical figure, perhaps your release date should be during National Black History month. If it's about supermodels, maybe it should come out during Fashion Week.

If you're still at a loss, study seasonal publishing patterns. Certain books do better in certain seasons (beach reading in summer, diet books at the new year). Study bookstore display tables to see what books are put out when. Booksellers love promotions associated with certain months or holidays: March Madness, Presidents Day, Father's Day. You name it, most bookstores will have books related to the theme of that month or day. See where your book will fit in.

On Lincoln's Birthday, media outlets around the country are looking for new and different ways to talk about Lincoln. They almost certainly won't be so interested in talking about your beach book. The fall is a particularly difficult time to publish a book unless your publisher is putting hefty support behind you. This is because publishers release the bulk of their big, blockbusting books in the fall. All in time for holiday sales. If you've written a health reference book, you'll have a hard time getting any attention in November when the press is concentrating on gift-giving.

The fall season may be a difficult time to launch a book, but it's nigh unto impossible if it's an election year. Unless your book happens to be about politics. Make sure to keep the presidential election in mind if you're planning a fall publication.

Most publishers are juggling so many books that they may want to put yours where they have a slot, as opposed to where it would best be published. Although you might not have much say in your pub date (especially if you're with a large publisher), let your publisher know your thoughts about the best time for your book's publication—and why. If your book is about guacamole and you heard through the avocado grapevine that June is about to be made National Avocado Month, make sure your publisher knows. If you think you can get those elusive but lucrative avocado speaking engagements during this month, let them know that, too.

Titling and Subtitling

Sometimes the title on your proposal will appear on your book when it hits the shelves at Borders. More often than not, it won't. Sometimes you will feel the change is an improvement, and sometimes it will feel like the utter ruination of your book. To ensure the latter never happens, every author's contract should include either "approval" or "mutual agreement" when it comes to titles. But even with this insurance, sometimes publishers bully authors into titles they absolutely abhor. What to do if this happens to you? While Gallup hasn't done a poll, it seems that about half the time the author is the one with the good instincts and half the time the publisher is the one with the good instincts. So you must determine whether your feelings of loathing toward the new title are in the best interest of your book or you simply got used to your old title.

Below are some common traps that authors fall into:

- ***"I've shown it to X number of people, and they all hate it."*** Never *tell* someone your title. Even if you don't start your sentence with "I hate this title, but what do you think?" most people can hear the drip-drip-drip of negativity in your voice. If you're going to ask for people's opinions, then *show* them the various titles by typing them out on a page. That said, unless you're able to show a very large number of people or a small number of influential people (like booksellers), telling your publisher that your friends hate it means nothing.

- ***Fixation on one word or phrase,*** especially if it's essentially irrelevant or based on some personal dislike. Just because a word makes your hair stand on end doesn't mean it might not be a great word in your title. Again, think about your potential readers. You're not going to be the one buying the book.

- ***Snippy, combative belligerence.*** Enough said.

Publishers have their own share of unhelpful comments:

- ***One muckety-muck doesn't like it.*** Therefore, it won't fly regardless of what anyone says. It's shocking how much power one higher-up can wield. This is a very frustrating situation because, depending on how big and hot the bigwig hotshot is, there's virtually nothing you can do about it.

- ***People in sales, marketing and publicity are making the decisions.*** Another tear-your-hair-out situation. While the people in these departments certainly have experience and information that you don't have, many of their decisions are made without actually reading the books under discussion.

- ***Snippy, combative belligerence.*** Enough said.

If you've sorted out what's best for your book, and you feel you must go up against your publisher, take a deep breath and see pages 239–40 on how best to do this.

Catalog Copy: Making Your Book Sound Exciting

Some people can spin beautiful phrases that make books feel simply irresistible. One of these people may or may not be writing your catalog copy, but often it's written by your editor or her assistant. Since you've been honing your pitch for months and months, you'd be crazy not to work with the person writing your copy to make sure that it really is excitingly enticing. As you may remember from our discussion of contracts in Chapter 7, we recommend that you be ensured consultation on your catalog copy so that you're guaranteed at least a look before it goes to press.

The Cover of Your Book

A great cover can make the difference between your book popping off the shelves and languishing on the remainder table. William Shinker, publisher of Gotham Books and an industry veteran, has these words hanging in his office: "The man who said, 'Don't judge a book by its cover,' never sold a book in his life." Take these words to heart.

The cover in your publisher's catalog may or may not be the final cover that appears on your book. That being said, most of the time it will bear a close resemblance, whether you like it or not.

Most publishers want to minimize your involvement in the cover design. They accomplish this by barring you from meeting with the art director or designer. This can be maddening, but you can still be heard. To begin with, do NOT wait to receive a cover before you state your ideas. Ask your editor from the beginning to let you know ONE MONTH BEFORE work begins on your cover. Make it clear that you would like to communicate with the designer.

Many designers appreciate input. What they don't appreciate are comments like "I hate it" and "It sucks." If you get to the designer of your cover before he's spent a lot of time on it, he'll be more open to your suggestions (and you won't have to think of a euphemism for "yuck").

Early on, start amassing images that are as close as possible to what you're looking for. This includes specific typestyles, covers from other books, artwork, photography and color palettes. Be sure your personal preferences

LIVING WITH A COVER YOU HATE

Before Arielle sold *Pride and Promiscuity,* she had a professional designer create a beautiful proposal for her. Since the book is a parody of Jane Austen, she wanted the design to evoke Regency England, and to that end they researched authentic borders and typestyles. The result was a work of art that welcomed the reader into the world of Jane Austen.

When the book was sold, Arielle made it abundantly clear to her large corporate publisher that she wanted to be involved with its design. She thought that by hiring a professional and by letting the publisher know that she herself had extensive design experience, her publisher would welcome her into the design process. She also assumed that she would have extra pull since she was an agent. The publisher had LOVED the design of the proposal. In fact, the interior of the book was almost an identical copy of what Arielle's designer had done.

Unfortunately, Arielle's designer had not worked on a cover. But considering the enthusiasm for the design and the research that had gone into it, Arielle assumed that the cover would be consistent with the interior. She gave her publisher the appropriate typestyles and general design ideas and then asked to meet with the art director. She was told this was not possible. When she asked if she could have a phone conversation, she was told of a blanket policy prohibiting authors from talking to or meeting with the art director. Hoping for the best, she let it go. In the meantime, she sent her editor concrete

do not stand in the way of the success of your book. Just because you love a particular image doesn't mean it communicates your book's contents. As Sydne Waller, the book buyer at Chapter 11 Books in Atlanta, Georgia, says, "I do judge a book by its cover. And the cover should reflect what the book really is. I just read a book that had a cover that looked like it was a Chick Lit book. In fact, it was a murder mystery. A good one, too. But it was off-putting."

When you've been given the heads-up that it's design time, color-copy all relevant images and send them to the designer with a lovely yet detailed note describing the tone and look that you're after. You should discuss your thoughts with your editor and agent beforehand to make sure that you successfully translated your ideas into helpful art direction. If you can't articulate your vision, you'll be wasting the designer's time. If you can prove your design salt to your editor, she'll be more likely to remove the road-block between you and the art department.

ideas about the design, including the name of an illustrator who was perfect for her book. The publisher did not like that illustrator but sent Arielle samples from another first-rate illustrator. Arielle liked them and, wanting to seem like a team player (and secretly hoping she could "buy" herself some more involvement), sent a nice note to the art director via her editor, thanking her for bringing on such a talented artist.

Shortly thereafter, Arielle was shown a "preliminary design" for the cover. It had a distinctly Victorian look—a style utterly different from the Regency feel she had established in the interior. She made sure to be very upbeat and appreciative in her response to her editor, but was also firm about the changes she wanted. Turns out "preliminary design" was a euphemism for "totally finished." Barely anything was changed. As the daughter of two designers and as an author who had put so much effort into giving her publisher specific information, Arielle was beyond frustrated. Still, faced with making a huge stink and alienating her publishing team, she decided to simply live with it.

But wait! There's a happy ending. David happened to mention Arielle's book while at a dinner with his fine, smaller, more collaborative British publisher. The publisher loved the idea and bought the U.K. rights. The art director at her British publisher actually knew the difference between Victorian and Regency England. Arielle got to sit down with him, brainstorm, share her thoughts. And, with her help, he created her dream cover.

If you get a cover back that doesn't reflect your vision, then it's time for constructive criticism. *Constructive* is the operative word here. Be specific about what you don't like. The more specific, the more likely your request for changes will be met. It's also helpful to show your cover to those in the know. This could mean graphic designers who can give you feedback in design-speak. Or local booksellers whom you've befriended. John Evans, co-owner of Diesel Bookstore in Oakland, California, says, "Because we see things at the moment of sale, we have a really good idea about what kinds of covers sell. At Diesel, once a season a local publisher brings their design people through our store to look at our displays." Publishers listen to booksellers because they're at the front lines. And a criticism from a bookseller can be just the ticket to getting your cover changed.

If all else fails and you're stuck with a stinker, it may be time to make a stink. (For tips on stink-making, see pages 238–40.)

Michael Powell, owner of Powell's Books in Portland, Oregon, suggests putting a blurb on the FRONT of your cover—not just on the back. If you were lucky enough to get a great blurb early, be sure to suggest this to your editor. (For more on getting blurbs, see pages 72 and 246–47.)

INTERIOR DESIGN

A catalog will include your book's cover but not the interior design (unless it's an illustrated book, in which case an interior spread might be displayed). If you want a certain look for the interior, this is the time to put forward your ideas. Once again, study the interiors of books you love. Do you want something ornate? Do you want something simple? What typefaces do you want? Icons? A second color? Sepia tone? Artwork denoting each new chapter?

YOUR SPINAL COLUMN

The spine of your book, like its interior design, will not appear in the catalog. But it is an integral part of the design process and one you'll want to pay very close attention to. Why? Because much of the time it's the *only* part of your book that potential readers will see. The *only* visual enticement. The *only* information they'll get. And yet spines are too often a virtually ignored afterthought. Sometimes they're so visually dull that they disappear into the bookcase as if they're camouflaged. Sometimes there's only a title, when in fact the subtitle contains the most important information. And sometimes the type is so small that anyone over 50 won't be able to read it without a spotlight and a magnifying glass.

The size of your spine will certainly help determine how much information it can contain. But even thin spines can have visual pizzazz through color and typeface that entice a reader to wonder what's inside.

A number of years ago, a very talented designer had the idea to put a piece of the cover image on the spine. This has spawned a slew of fantastic designs, the best of which practically beg readers to pull the books off the shelves. One of Arielle's all-time favorite spines is by designer John Gall. It incorporates vibrant colors, a bold typeface and a piece of the cover imagery in perfect balance. This spine belongs to the book *Che: A Revolutionary Life* by Jon Lee Anderson. Check it out.

Categorization: Where Will Your Book Live Best?

Imagine your lavishly illustrated soul food cookbook ending up in the African American History section of a bookstore. Or your book about cannibalism coming to live in the Cookbooks section. Sound ridiculous? It happens. You'd be shocked by how many books are categorized incorrectly and, as a result, die sad, lonely deaths in a section where no one would think to come visit them.

Even a subtle mistake can mean a loss of sales. Let's say a customer wants to buy your book about Passover. He goes to the Religion section and finds a subsection on Judaism, where there are many books on Passover. Naturally this is where he looks. But your book has been shelved with the general religion titles. "Oy," he sighs. "I guess they don't have that book on Passover I read about in yesterday's paper." Like so many of us, he doesn't ask for help but picks up some inferior book written by your bitter rival.

Make sure your category is correct right from the get-go. The first time you'll see it will probably be in the catalog. If you're in the wrong category there, be sure to tell your editor immediately.

Your category may also be listed on your flaps or back cover. This tiny detail is how most bookstores decide to shelve their books. To prevent your book from being trapped in the wrong neighborhood, check out comparable titles to see what category they're in. And let your publisher know right up front what you think your category should be.

On the copyright page of a book, you'll also notice an additional list of categories filed with the Library of Congress. These categories will determine where libraries across the country shelve your book. They will also give library-goers a cross-referencing system that will help them find your book. According to David Williamson, cataloging automation specialist

Sometimes you carefully pick your category and your book STILL ends up buried in the wrong section of your bookstore. For example, Borders does not have a Biography section. This means that even if your book is categorized as a biography or memoir, it will be shelved according to what Borders deems your theme to be. If you write a memoir about depression, it might end up in the Psychology section. Memoir buyers don't usually think to go to this section to buy memoirs. But there's simply nothing you can do. If this happens to you, take a deep breath, go home and scream: "SERENITY NOW!"

in the Acquisitions Bibliographic Access Directorate of the Library of Congress, "Unless we [the librarians at the Library of Congress] are totally wrong in our subject analysis, we do not accept requests for subjects. We are cataloging for our needs." That said, "subject analysis" relies on a publisher's submission of subject materials for Cataloging-in-Publication data. Every time a publisher fills out the CIP forms prior to a book's publication, the publisher and author are really being given a chance to sway catalogers like David Williamson. The CIP is the cataloger's first look at the upcoming book (it may include a proof or material such as title page, table of contents, preface, samples) and should lead to a perfectly proper categorization. So, if you want your cookbook, *Festive Recipes of the Napoleonic Wars*, categorized under Napoleonic Wars as well as Feasts and Festivals of Europe, you and your publisher had better boldface and underline those subjects in your CIP application. (For more information on CIPs, see the *Chicago Manual.*)

Format: Hard, Paper, Trade or Mass

Hardcover, trade paperback or mass-market paperback—different formats hold different associations for people. Hardcovers often spell prestige, while mass-market paperbacks scream supermarket.

Most of the time, authors and their publishers agree on a format from the get-go. But sometimes publishers will pull the old switcheroo. You might find that your publisher wants to publish your first novel as an *original trade paperback.* Nowadays, however, this is a common practice and one that may save your book from oblivion—especially if your audience is in their teens and twenties. Most people in this age group don't have $25 to shell out for a hardcover. Yes, you'll more than likely miss out on a review in *The New York Times*, which favors hardcovers. But what good does a review do if your readers can't afford to buy your book?

Do you need a lower retail price with a high-class look? Then you might want to suggest a paper-over-board format to your publisher. Paper-over-board is an unjacketed hardcover, with the cover image printed directly on the front. Ty Wilson, a buyer at Copperfield's in Sonoma County, California, says, "Paper-over-board is a great option that I feel is underutilized. It looks very good, and we can sell it on the new hardcover table."

A FAULTY FORMAT

A writer we know wrote an excellent reference book. He was an unknown author but a well-known writing teacher in his neck of the woods, and he had come up with a unique book within the writing reference category. Because it filled a hole in a category that has evergreen sales, the writer and all his fellow writer pals were convinced the book would have a good long life.

Mid-priced trade paperbacks dominate this category, so the writer was shocked when his book was listed as a hardcover in his publisher's catalog and priced at $25.95. Because he was a neophyte, he didn't say anything. He figured his publisher knew best.

He went ahead and booked all sorts of events. Hundreds of people attended these events. But when it came time to buy books, only the older and wealthier ponied up. One or two younger people would shuffle over when the event was finished and apologize for not buying a book, saying they couldn't afford it. Too many said they'd have to wait until his book came out in paperback.

Now the writer was really concerned. If he didn't sell enough hardcover copies, his publisher might never put it out in paperback. And yet he couldn't sell enough copies precisely because it *wasn't* in paperback! He soon discovered that a number of writer friends had had similar experiences. One had written a hip memoir geared to high school and college graduates. At one of her events, more than 150 people listened to her speak but only two bought books. All the twenty-somethings stood in line so they could talk to her, but they had no money. More than half asked when her book would be out in paperback.

After hearing this story and others, the writer took matters into his own hands. He gathered all sorts of comparable titles, forwarded all the e-mails he had received regarding the price and wrote a letter to his publisher explaining his experience. The publisher decided to bring the book out in paperback much sooner than planned, and the book was soon selling at a brisk pace.

Publishers generally know more about the marketplace than their authors do, but that doesn't mean they're always right. And a mistake in format can make a significant difference in sales. So, if your publisher changes formats or if you realize that the original format they chose doesn't make sense, don't sit back because you assume the publisher knows best. Just as you search comparable housing sales when assessing the value of your home, the best way to convince a publisher of the value of a particular format is through the success of comparable titles.

Cover Price: What Is Your Book Worth?

How much should your book cost? Usually your publisher won't consult you about cover price, because frankly what do you know about pricing books? Unless you've spent time working for a bookstore, the answer is probably very little.

Some books merit high prices. For example, Taschen America published *GOAT (Greatest of All Time)*, a 700-page, 10-inch-thick, 74-pound, lavishly illustrated book on Muhammad Ali that retails for $3,000! But most of the time you won't want to price yourself out of your category or audience. To find out what's standard, do your own research.

Publishers sometimes have to put a higher cover price on a book than those of comparable titles that sit next to it on the shelf in order to cover production costs, especially on illustrated books or books with special add-ons like spiral binding or pocket folders. But if yours is the only book about Chihuahuas that's over $21.95, and your potential buyer, Chihuahua lover that she is, knows that she's never bought a book on her favorite pet for more than $20, she may decide to let yours go. In addition, if a price is too high, some chains will order fewer books or none at all.

Some publishers believe that going slightly under the average cover price is the best route. But if your book is priced as if it were destined for a remainder table, that can be a turnoff to buyers as well. Many people are wary of "bargain books" unless they already know the author's name. The other difficulty with lower-priced books is that if a book is under a certain amount, warehouse clubs like Costco and Sam's, as well as QVC, won't take it because they need a certain return on their investment.

All in all, the pressures to move the price of a book up or down are quite complicated, and what might make no sense to you may be very well thought out by your publisher. These complications shouldn't turn you off from doing your own research, though. You have more time than your publisher has to study your particular category or models for your book, and this may lead to discoveries that are well worth sharing.

More Publicity and More Marketing

If your book was given a two-page catalog spread, an announced first printing of 50,000 or more and a long list of publicity and marketing commitments, you can be pretty sure your publisher is pulling out all the stops. If it got one page, a 25K first printing, a five-city tour and a few other nice publicity and marketing promises, this is good, too. But regardless of what your book's catalog copy says, don't count on it being 100% accurate. First printings are almost always exaggerated. Publicity and marketing information is also typically pumped up because publishers want to make booksellers think they're really getting behind a book. In reality, however, a first printing listed at 25,000 could easily end up as 15,000. A five-city tour can rapidly become a tour of your living room. And the entire publicity and marketing campaign can disappear faster than you can say Oprah Winfrey.

On the other hand, if there's precious little info about publicity and marketing and no initial print run listed, you can be pretty sure your book is at the bottom of your publisher's barrel that season. But don't despair, this is where *most* books find themselves.

No matter which scenario applies to you, your entry in your publisher's catalog is important because it introduces your book to the world and signals how your publisher sees it. The good news is, once you know where you stand, you can figure out the best way to hit the ground running.

The Author Photo: Putting Your Best Face Forward

If the publisher wants your photo on the front cover of your book, it's their responsibility to pay for that photo and to set up a photo shoot. Unless you're movie-star pretty or really famous, this probably won't happen. Most of the time, your photo will go in the back of the book and you'll be required to provide and pay for your own photograph. At your own cost. As tempting as it is to ask your loving but decidedly amateur husband or your next-door neighbor's well-meaning but untrained cousin to snap a shot, DO NOT take this approach. Your author photo can be a huge sales tool. Get a good one. (See pages 257–58 for more info on achieving the perfect photo.)

SIX MONTHS TO GO!

Approximately six months before the publication of your book and preferably before sales conference, if you have the money and the personality, meet with key players at your publisher. Mauro DiPreta, an executive editor at HarperCollins, says, "If possible, an author should come in for a meeting with the editor, publisher, publicist and anyone else who can attend.

If it's six months before your pub date and you still feel nervous about meeting your publisher, you should start getting help with your presentation skills. See page 260 for info on media coaches and presentation doctors.

This way, you can come up with a publishing plan together. The result is almost always that the publishing team comes away more focused."

DO NOT expect your publisher to take the initiative to set up this meeting. If you have an agent, let him set it up. If he's willing and able, by all means bring him with you. Your agent's presence will help reduce the intimidation factor, and hopefully he'll know the right questions to ask to maximize your time with your publishing team.

Remember when we said how important it is to turn your name into a face? Well, now is the time to do just that. Because this may be your ONLY opportunity to meet many of the people who will be instrumental in making your book successful, to pick their brains, to use them as sounding boards for your ideas and to inspire and excite them.

You want to walk into this meeting with your pitch on your lips and your plan in hand. If you wrote a proposal, review your competition, publicity and marketing sections. If you didn't, see Chapter 2. Continue refining ideas you can present to all departments that will help them do the job of selling your book.

A great way to open your meeting is to pass out goodies from the best bakery in town. This may sound obsequious, but it shows that you want to give as much as you want to receive and it gets people on a nice sugar high.

Once you sit down, ask everyone for a card so you can refer to people by name throughout. Trot out any new endorsements you've received; as we've said all along, everyone loves endorsements, and this should get things going on a positive note. Calling on all your style and passion, fully communicate your killer, can-do, leave-no-stone-unturned attitude. If you're spending time on the marketing and publicity of your book (and you should be), let everyone know what you've accomplished and what you plan to accomplish. Have you set up speaking engagements? Have you made contact with journalists? Written magazine pitches? Take your publishing team through the marketing, publicity and sales opportunities that you've created. Make them see that they have a seriously organized, dedicated, driven, passionate, articulate, good-humored, reasonable author on their hands.

After you've talked about what you've already done, it's a perfect time to bring up what you'd like to happen. A great way to do this can be through a top 10 wish list. Again, this is not so different in concept from a where-do-I-want-to-go-to-college list. Every entry on the list should be someplace you'd really like your book to end up. But it should be a combination of safeties, solid choices, obtainable dreams and maybe one "reach." And every entry on your list has to make sense. You have to be able to logically support your inclusion of an ad in *Essence*, a first serial in *Yoga Journal*, a foreign sale to Norway. You can make wish lists for, among other things, the media, bookstore appearances, blurbers and events.

The last, yet possibly most important piece of your plan is, as always, your pitch. You want everyone to see what a bang-up job you do with your delivery. And you want to make it extra easy for anyone in that meeting to go out and do a superb, brief, yet utterly exciting pitch of your book to anyone anywhere anytime.

MEETING ABSOLUTELY EVERYONE ON YOUR TEAM

Sometimes an author has the opportunity to meet far-flung members of his publishing team. Michael Perry, author of the memoir *Population: 485*, about returning to his small Wisconsin hometown and becoming a volunteer EMT, did just this when he toured HarperCollins' distribution center in Scranton, Pennsylvania. It turned out to be a truly moving experience. As he says, "Most people think of books in terms of editors and writers, but all the angst-ridden typing in the world does no good if someone doesn't move the books from point A to point B. During my tour, I met everyone from the folks who handle telesales to customer service to the technicians who put the books in the boxes. For a while, we stood beside a forklift and talked about deer hunting. Perfect. They gave me a cake with the book cover reproduced on the frosting, several neat gifts and, perhaps coolest of all, my own monogrammed safety belt in case I ever need to run up the forklift to fetch a pallet of my books. Man, that made me smile."

While very few authors get (or create) the opportunity to meet *all* the folks who make publishing happen, it's still important to recognize that your team most likely has individual players you never even knew existed. And all these players are helping (or not helping) your book reach readers. So if you get to meet any of them, spread good cheer. Michael did just that, and it helped generate buzz within his team as well as in the publishing trade journals.

If your agent comes with you, try to arrange to have a quick bite or drink together after your meeting. Review what was accomplished and what still needs to be done. Ask your agent for feedback on your performance. What are your strengths? What do you need to work on?

As soon as you get home, send thank-you notes to everyone who sat in on the meeting (another good reason to make sure you get cards). Personalize them as much as possible by using the notes you made during your meeting. Regina Louise, author of *Somebody's Someone*, happens to own a hair salon along with being a writer. She took note of everyone's hair type and sent each person a special hair product along with a thank-you note. This practical yet thoughtful gift really made an impression on her publishing team.

Can't do an in-person meeting? Then put together a written version that informs your publishing team in writing of all your present and future efforts.

THE SALES CONFERENCE

Three to six months before your book comes out, your publisher holds a sales conference. Basically everyone who has anything to do with the selling, marketing and promoting of your book will be attending this conference. The ideas from your launch meeting will be solidified here, and a grand plan will emerge.

During the sales conference, your editor or publisher will pitch your book to the *entire* sales force, usually in under three minutes. Annik LeFarge, a senior editor at Crown, says, "Our sales force hears 600 to 800 books at one meeting. The sales conference is ultimately, in most cases, where the sales force gets swept up by the enthusiasm of its colleagues and becomes passionate about selling certain titles. For every book, they have to think: *How do I sell this? Who is the audience?*" Many of the biggest publishing houses no longer invite editors to these meetings, which means your biggest advocate may not be there when the sales force decides, *Wow! I can't wait to sell that one!* Or not. Hopefully you've spoon-fed your pitch to your publishing team so that it rolls trippingly off even the dullest tongue.

Again, the more ammunition you give your publisher about your audience, comparable books and what makes your book exciting and salable, the easier it will be for the sales force to storm the castle. And this goes back to your pitch, which you've been working on for months and months and months.

Tipping the Scales

Hopefully, your sales reps will leave the conference stoked about your book and armed with your *tip sheet*, which includes the basic specs of your book (title, subtitle, ISBN, pub date, and so on), plus all of the marketing and sales information that is not on the catalog page: comparison titles, audience and what other similar books that audience bought. Please note how much of the meat of the tip sheet comes from information you've been developing from Day One. Your tip sheet is the most important tool your sales force will use when going out to sell your book.

Some authors volunteer to write their own tip sheets. If you're up to it, ask if your editor would like you to provide one. Regardless, the better your pitch, the more accurate your comparison titles and the firmer your grasp on who will buy your book, the easier it will be to create your tip sheet and the easier it will be for the sales force to sell your book. Elise Cannon, director of sales at Publishers Group West, says, "I think positioning is most important. I need '*The Graduate* meets *The Texas Chain Saw Massacre.*' I spend a really good amount of time prepping my sales call, getting the right comparison book and its sales figures." Getting the *right* comparison book is the key here. Carole Horne, senior buyer of the Harvard Bookstore in Cambridge, Massachusetts, says, "The comp title has to be valid and make sense. Otherwise, you can do more harm than good."

Most authors don't get into the book business so they can talk about comp titles, positioning and tip sheets. Yet these are necessary to selling your book far and wide. That's why you want to get as involved as you can in the presales process. Otherwise, you'll only find yourself complaining later.

Your Sales Reps Hit the Road

Starting as early as six months before your book is published, your sales reps begin their quest to convince booksellers to order your book. Some of these reps sell to bookstores within a particular region, say, the Pacific Northwest. Others sell to one or more national accounts, like Barnes & Noble or Amazon. But from the largest chains to the tiniest mom-and-pop bookstores, your sales reps get approximately 30 to 60 seconds to spin their magic for you . . . and for every single other author on their list.

And here's the rub: Your sales reps have to give an honest account of the promise of your book and how it delivers, because at the end of the day all they have is their reputation. Elise Cannon says, "You must establish credibility with an account. You have to tell them what you truly believe. You can't lie. Lying wouldn't serve anything." Linda Bubon, co-owner of Women & Children First in Chicago, adds: "For me, it's all about relationships. Many of the reps I work with have stayed in their jobs for 15 or 20 years. When they say, 'I've read this book and I know you can sell it,' that makes a big difference."

The health and success of your book is shockingly dependent on how well your sales reps pitch and how many books these booksellers buy. In fact, the results of these pitches (especially the early ones to places like Barnes & Noble and Borders) will, in some ways, determine such things as your publicity and marketing budget, whether or not you get to tour on your publisher's dime and the size of your first print run.

Just because you have little contact with your sales reps doesn't mean you can't let them know you're not just an ISBN. Time again to pull out your thank-you notes. Ask your editor if you can send notes to the reps, and more than likely she'll cough up the names or send them along for you.

MAKING A STINK: WHEN TO GET MAD AND WHEN TO SHUT UP

Gene Wilder, the brilliant writer/actor, was making a movie with the equally brilliant filmmaker Mel Brooks. Wilder had written a scene that he thought was very funny. Brooks had a very different opinion and wanted to cut the scene out of the script. But Wilder would not let it go. He shot down all of Brooks' objections as he worked himself into a lather over what a hilarious scene he'd written. Brooks was finally worn down by the sheer force of Wilder's passion. He still thought the scene stank, but he agreed to film it just to shut the man up. Guess what? Wilder was right. The movie was *Young Frankenstein*. The scene was a musical soft-shoe shuffle involving Frankenstein's monster doing "Putting On the Ritz." To this day, that scene brings down the house.

You, too, will encounter many situations in which your desires will come in conflict with those who are members of your own team. It's very difficult to know when to make a stink and when to shut up. Sometimes when you put your foot down, it ends up in your mouth. Sometimes the squeaky wheel really does get the grease. Again, weigh all the circumstances carefully before you take any action. Sometimes it's worth bruising a few egos, cracking a few whips and kicking a few keisters to get everything right. Sometimes it will make all the difference between your book being successful and languishing in obscurity.

But sometimes it won't. People often pick the smallest, most insignificant things to fight about. Things that in the grand scheme of life don't amount to a hill of beans. And they end up being seen as a big braying irrational ass that nobody wants to work with. Distinguish between these two radically different yet occasionally very similar situations.

Sometimes you can make a legitimate request in the wrong way and, as a result, get refused. Sometimes, no matter how hard you try or how patient and sweet you are, it becomes clear you are not going to get your way.

MAKING A STINK STICK

Michael Moore wrote *Stupid White Men* before the 9/11 attacks. After 9/11, his publisher told him he would have to eliminate what she considered to be unpatriotic pieces of the book. Michael said he stood by every word and would not make changes. There were already many, many copies of the book sitting in a warehouse, but his publisher refused to release them. In fact, she wanted him to buy back the copies of his own book. But he would not bow to her pressure. He thought this might be the death of his book, but he knew he had to take a stand.

It just so happened that Michael had a speaking engagement lined up in New Jersey when all this came down. He told the story of how his publisher refused to release his book. Turns out there was a librarian in the audience, and she was outraged. She started an e-mail campaign to fellow librarians, who then contacted Michael's publisher, demanding that the book be released. The press got wind, and it became a huge story. Due to public pressure, Michael's publisher was forced to release his book. Of course, it went on to be a huge international bestseller.

This story has two morals: 1) Stick up for what you think is right. 2) Always be nice to librarians.

Before you decide to cause a big fuss, consult with your allies to be sure they agree that this is a battle you need to fight. In the end, make certain this is something you feel passionate enough about to go to the wall. Although you don't want to make this a habit. The wall is hard, and it can hurt you.

Have you appropriately made your stink but there's still no sign of that special something you were promised? Have you followed up with concerned calls and e-mails and had your agent step in on your behalf but you're still getting no love? Then it's time to get proactive. If you have the money, spend it on a plane ticket. Put on your best outfit. Go into your publisher's office and convince them with solid evidence and sincere passion to step up to the plate. If you spring into action instead of just being a complaining ninny, you'll be sure to receive a much better response.

If they still won't budge, and you've done everything short of the old horsehead in the bed, then you just have to acknowledge that you've got a subpar partner and move on. But don't be afraid to ask for what you want. You'll be amazed by how effective you can be if you do it the right way. And, as always, doing it the right way means less complaining and more solid, research-based requests that your publisher can actually respond to. Bruce Harris, former vice president of Crown and former publisher of Workman, put it this way: "What I hate: cursing, whining authors who are unable to be a part of the team. Particularly those who demean the professionalism of our team. What I like: authors who are willing to listen to professionals, who appreciate the work that's being done on their behalf and who are always willing to do more on behalf of their books."

ENJOYING THE RIDE

Yes, there will be turbulence. But no matter what, try to have fun. And remember, you're not alone on this journey. The most important thing to do is to write a good book, but getting it published is a team effort. Some members of your team will be working behind the scenes to ensure a successful trip. Others will be right there with you, making sure you enjoy the ride.

Now it's time to make your book fly. So buckle your safety belt, put your seat in the upright and locked position, and jump the gutter . . .

CHAPTER 10

PREPUB PUBLICITY AND MARKETING

"To be prepared is half the victory."

—Miguel de Cervantes

Your book is finally in production. Listen closely, and you'll hear a faint ticking. That's the sound of time marching toward destiny, when it's finally (cue drum roll) . . . YOUR DATE OF PUBLICATION. Time to get busy. But why? Can't you start planning your publicity and marketing once you have an actual book in hand? Won't your publisher handle all that stuff? Won't everyone just go out and buy your book because it's so great?

NO, NO and NO! A large part of your publicity and marketing effort must be made long before publication. And most of this effort will come from you.

SELLING YOURSELF

We often advise authors to pretend their publisher is their printer—and that's all. That way, they won't be disappointed when their publisher disappoints them.

The thing is, all the work you did figuring out your audience and crafting your pitch is going to serve you over and over again as you publicize and market your book. Now it's just a matter of putting your skills and information to work. And just as you made writing a part of your daily life, now you must make the promoting and marketing of your book an ongoing activity. Nine months to a year before your pub date, try to spend half an hour every day promoting your book. Then at three months before your pub date, try to up the ante to an hour a day. At three weeks before your pub date, up the hours to as many as you can handle. By the time your blessed pub date rolls around, you will have made great strides toward working your book into the collective conscious and unconscious. This sounds like a lot of work, and it is, but it's the kind of work that nearly every successful author needs to do. Kathy Pories, an editor at Algonquin Books, put it this way: "A lot of successful authors seem to be good problem solvers. They don't view their publisher as a maternal entity. They're always thinking about who their book will appeal to. They're engaged. They don't wait around for someone else to do something."

If you've never written a book before (or a book on your particular subject), it can be very difficult to know how to create any sort of plan. That's why it's important to start studying successful marketing and publicity strategies for other books, as well as for movies, products and anything else that involves spreading the word. Don't just read the book section or entertainment stories in your local paper. Dig into the business section and then try *The Wall Street Journal.* Listen to NPR and surf the Web for trends and information that will help you generate interest in your book. Go to events. Study how authors present themselves. What works and what doesn't? What do successful authors have in common? What mistakes do you see authors make? Which of your ideas will make people passionate about your book? All of this information will help you get a publicity and marketing plan percolating. It will spark ideas that you will mold into a full-fledged strategy.

But before you do anything else, pull out your Master Calendar. Make sure your pub date is correct, because we're going to give you some tasks to perform and some ideas to use for publicizing, marketing and selling your book that you should mark on your calendar now. This way, you have a shot at making a dream launch on your Pub Date.

Handy Handouts

After your book goes into production, no matter what you do or where you go, you need to have something in hand that will make everybody you meet really want to read your book. It can be a business card, a postcard, a bookmark, a baseball card, a one-page promotional sheet. Just make sure it's something that's easy to carry and easy for people to take with them. Create an electronic version of your handout that you can e-mail to people.

DOODADS AND WIDGETS

If you've got a little extra cash on hand, come up with something amusing to spread the word about your book. Can openers. Monogrammed chocolates. Dog collars. Yo-yos. Cool T-shirts. Baseball caps. Collapsible drinking cups. Refrigerator magnets. Decals and stickers. Whatever it takes to make an impression on people. Dan Kennedy wrote *Loser Goes First*, a book in part about his failed dream of becoming a rock star. To promote his book, he created "backstage passes" modeled after the real things. Not only were they a fun and unusual handout, but they also made him feel like the rock star he'd always dreamed of being.

Lay out your handout in a way that's appealing to the eye but includes all the necessary information. Your handout will be ever-evolving and will eventually find its form in a press release, press kit, postcard and/or interesting objet. Don't make too many to begin with, because you'll need to update them without feeling as if you're wasting your money. The first version will inevitably be on the skimpy side and consist only of your book's title and subtitle, your name and bio, your flap copy, publisher, pub date and contact information. Eventually, however, it should also contain your cover, blurbs, reviews and ISBN. As each new piece of information comes in, update that handout. Show your handout to your editor and/or agent to make sure it's up to professional standards.

As soon as you've got a finalized cover, it's worth asking your publisher if they'll pay for postcards containing your book's information. Quite often they will. And if someone else is footing the bill, get as many as you can. It costs almost the same amount to produce 200 postcards as to produce 2,000. This way, as you go through life, whenever anyone asks you what your book is about or what you're up to, you can whip out a card.

Snail and E-Mail Lists

You never know who might be in a position to do something for you or your book. Freelance publicist Jim Eber advises, "Make a list of every single person you know and keep it going." Keep your lists current. Bring your Empty Book with you wherever you go, and get snail and e-addresses from everyone—friends, colleagues, media people, booksellers. Build your fan base. Receiving an e-mail or a postcard or a flyer for your book or an event can remind people how great you are and prompt them to invite you on a show, write something about you, come to your event or buy your book.

If you have a big and potent mailing list, you can help spread buzz by giving your people regular updates when anything happens to you or your book. You can let everyone know when you're on TV or radio or in a magazine or newspaper. All in all, great mailing lists make it easier to solicit help and spread the word.

Your Author Questionnaire

Your publisher probably gave you an author questionnaire soon after you completed your deal. Filling it out may seem like a trivial afterthought amid the wild excitement of landing a book contract. Wrong. You are handing your publisher a veritable toolbox that can be used to start revving up the publicity, marketing and sales departments.

Here are some of the questions you may be asked, with a brief explanation of why your publisher is asking them:

1. Where have you lived?

Local interest is a great way to generate marketing, publicity and sales. The more places you've lived, the more places you can "go local." It's much easier to get a story in the local media than in the national media. And local attention can help build your press kit and make you more credible to those large national media outlets.

2. What is the summary of your book?

Here comes your old friend: The Pitch. Trot her out in her Sunday best. Your pitch will be used for everything from your catalog copy, to the pitch your salespeople use to get bookstores excited about carrying your book, to your publisher spreading the word at a cocktail party.

3. What was the inspiration for your book?

You might not realize it, but the genesis of your book could serve as a great hook for media. The more drama, the better.

4. What interesting things happened during the writing of your book?

Again, anything that the media can sink their teeth into will help get coverage for your book. Think widely and weirdly here. You never know what's going to grab someone's attention.

5. Who is the audience for your book?

And what other classic or popular books have a similar audience? What useful comparisons would you suggest? Your answers to these questions will supply the sales force with the positioning they need to sell your book. Riffle through the competition and audience sections of your proposal. You want to provide the sales force with a succinct, easy comparison to introduce booksellers to your work.

6. What current books directly compete with yours?

Your publisher needs to know about any and all directly competitive books. If you don't provide this information, you're doing yourself and your publisher a huge disservice, because booksellers are sure to ask, "How is this different from or better than such-and-such?" Supply these titles and explain how your book is *both* different and better.

7. Where have you appeared in the media?

Throw a wide net here. Write down every appearance/mention, regardless of whether or not it relates to your book. If you've done a lot of media, don't just mention a few of your biggest hits. Try to put down everything. It's so much easier to approach those who already know about you. And you never know what tiny mention in the *Podunk Gazette* could lead to a segment on the *Today* show.

8. What well-known people might provide blurbs?

Make your list an exhaustive one; your publisher may know all sorts of famous people. If you have a top-five list, mark those names with asterisks so your publisher will pay special attention to them. And make it clear if you rub elbows with any of these people.

9. What publications should receive a free copy of your book?

Start with newspapers and magazines, and then move on to associations and organizations whose newsletters or other publications might help get the word out. Include any contact names you may have.

10. Do you have lecture or seminar experience?

This is not a moment to be shy about your speaking skills. Do you get standing ovations? Glowing testimonials from people who've hired you or seen you speak? Let your publisher know. If you already give lectures on the subject of your book, supply the names of your lectures and the places where you've spoken. It's also helpful to create short synopses of these lectures, along with places where you might give them once your book comes out.

11. Do you have any other comments or suggestions?
Here's the place to show your publisher how motivated you are—how much you want to help, what you've done that didn't make it into the rest of your questionnaire—as well as your game plan. Susan Edsall, author of *Into the Blue: A Father's Flight and a Daughter's Return*, ended her questionnaire this way: "I've already contacted 500 organizations by e-mail and letter and gotten significant positive response. I recognize that your publicity people are champions at garnering major media. I hereby volunteer to bird-dog the smaller but highly motivated audiences that you realistically don't have the time to chase down. I see it as my job and responsibility to support your publicity department in continuing to generate and follow through on this interest."

Like your book proposal, your answers to the author questionnaire should sound as much like your speaking voice as possible. The more engaging the answers, the more engaging the author—or so the publisher will assume.

Blurb Wrangling

Next on your agenda is tracking down blurbers or adding to the ones you've already got. Your editor should help, but even if she doesn't, work overtime at this particular task. As we've said before, a great blurb from the right person gets you instant respect. And who doesn't want instant respect? As Jonathon Keats, author, freelance journalist and member of the National Book Critics Circle awards committee, says, "For a critic, blurbs are hugely important. If I get galleys of a book by someone I've never heard of, a good blurb is pretty much the only thing that makes me pay attention, acknowledgments next. Blurbing is also really important from the standpoint of readers who haven't heard of you, but have heard of the person giving you the blurb."

It's in your best interest to get the blurb machine moving as quickly as possible. If you get a blurb early enough, you can put it on your galleys. Remember, galleys will go out to select reviewers, so if they see those great blurbs, their eyes will light right up.

Unless you have a connection to a person, there is a good chance that 300 manuscript pages that show up uninvited will end up in the recycling bin. For this reason, it's best to go after the people you know in the manuscript stage and wait for galleys to approach those you don't. Either way, write personal thank-you notes for all blurbs as soon as they come in. When you get finished copies of your book, send a personalized signed copy to each blurber.

Since you've already made blurb lists (see Chapter 9), you have a leg up. Go over that original list with your editor and agent. Ask them for a list of authors they work with and look for potential blurbers there. Did you get any leads in your publisher meeting? Now is the time to follow up and nail them down.

Many people feel shy and uncomfortable approaching well-known writers and authority figures. That's normal. But if you approach a well-known person in a respectful, sweet-natured way and make it easy for them to say yes, you'll be amazed how often you'll get results. When we were putting together *Satchel Sez*, we had a tough time getting blurbs. We'd made a great list of potential blurbers, and we were going after them hard. Phone calls, e-mails, faxes. But we couldn't get even a whiff of a blurb. Finally, through an editor who had shown interest in our original proposal, we made contact with TV sportscaster Bob Costas. We sent our stuff to him with a very nice letter. And guess what? He not only blurbed, but wrote a beautiful foreword.

Platforming

In the old days, if you had something you wanted to say to the public, your platform was a stump in the town square. Obviously, the world has become much more sophisticated, but you still have to find a platform if you want to be heard. And whether it's becoming an expert, writing articles or developing a one-man show, you have to find exactly the right one for you and your book.

Use these months before your pub date to fully develop your platform so that you get the ear of the whole town and not just one lonely loony passing by. It takes a long time to get people to listen, so the more time you allow yourself, the better.

Janis Jaquith, author of *Birdseed Cookies: A Fractured Memoir*, has a particularly quirky writing style. She was worried that people would shy away from her unique voice when her book came out. "I decided to write commentaries for the radio," she told us, "so that people could get used to my voice . . . in both senses of the word." With this platform in place, she then went on to publish her book.

Here's another idea. The media are always looking for experts to consult. Make yourself one. Think about Phillip McGraw, a.k.a. Dr. Phil, who became Oprah Winfrey's in-house expert on human behavior. His appearances were so successful that he got his own show. And all this media attention paved the way for his books to jump to the top of the *New York Times* bestseller list. So if you can realistically frame yourself as the leading person on anything from alien abduction to dachshund grooming, you have a good chance of getting some attention.

If you don't feel comfortable as an expert, there are lots of other ways to draw attention to yourself and your book. Daniel Handler created a fictitious character named Lemony Snicket, and then, under that name, wrote *The Bad Beginning*, the first of his young adult novels collectively called "A Series of Unfortunate Events." He then devised events in which he plays the accordion, manipulates nutty props and generally puts on a wild and crazy show. These events draw hundreds of kids and parents to see, not Daniel Handler, but Lemony Snicket.

Mike Daisey created a one-man show called *21 Dog Years* about his experiences working as a customer service representative for Amazon. It premiered in a grungy pit in Seattle, but eventually found a home off-

SPEAKING AGENTS

One of the fastest ways to build a platform is to speak in front of large groups. (It's also a way to make some money.) But tracking down the contacts you need to get yourself speaking gigs is a grueling grind that takes particular expertise.

The good news is, there are people who do nothing but this. They're called speaking agents. The bad news is, many of them want you to be *already* speaking to large groups of people with a published book in hand before they'll take you on. With the right package, however, including a top-quality press kit, photograph and videotape of yourself, and a list of past and future speaking events you've set up on your own, you can at the very least whet a speaking agent's appetite, if not get one to bite. And once you've interested someone, you can keep following up as your profile grows.

Broadway in New York City. This platform led Mike to a publishing contract that turned his show into a book. He continues to tour his show around the world—and to keep selling books.

WORKING WITH YOUR PUBLICIST

So far, we've been talking about things you can do on your own to let the world know about your book. Now it's time to introduce you to your publicist, who typically will be assigned to you approximately six months before publication.

Notice the word *assigned*. You will not get to pick the publicist of your choice. And while you don't have to go on vacation with her, you do want to form a cohesive unit that will get the media ball rolling. And keep it rolling. Because one big media hit can translate into readers running to bookstores. And it's not just media that your publicist goes after; she'll also be speaking to booksellers to set up store events. Elaine Petrocelli, owner of Book Passage in Corte Madera, California, says, "There are certain publicists we trust implicitly." If your publicist communicates enthusiasm about what you've written, this enthusiasm can ripple out into the universe. Roberta Rubin, owner of The Bookstall in Winnetka, Illinois, adds, "One of the best ways to get me excited about your book is to have a publicist be excited about it."

To get your publicist on board, you need to prove to her that you know your stuff and are willing to go out there and strut it. Do you know how to reach your readers? As we've said before, this is one of the most important questions you will have to answer if you want to sell lots of books. And it's one you hope your publicist will be grappling with on a daily basis. You want to make her job easy by providing, in an organized, friendly fashion, the information you've already compiled. For example, make a media wish list out of your research and present it to her on day one. Are there any updates or additions? Have you made any contacts that will help your publicist turn these wishes into realities? Keep this wish list in a prominent place so that you can look to it for inspiration and cross wishes off as they come true—a very satisfying experience.

Once you've given your publicist the overview on your marketing and publicity strategy, be clear about what you're comfortable with and what you're not. Are you afraid to fly? Are you nervous about doing "shock jock" radio? Shows whose political agenda you don't agree with? "I never mind authors who have preferences and dislikes," says Pru Rowlandson, head publicist at Canongate Books. "It's easy to work with people if they tell you in advance what they will do and what they won't."

It's important to have an ongoing dialogue with your publicist. This doesn't mean calling every half hour to ask if she's sent your book to Oprah. It means coming up with creative ideas for her to take out into the world. It also means being able to respond honestly and graciously to your publicist's suggestions ASAP, since many media offers require immediate responses.

A publicist's reputation is dependent on whether or not what she promises in an author is what the media actually get. So if your publicist tells the *Today* show that you're a smart, attractive, articulate, responsible person and you turn out to be a curmudgeonly, slovenly, inarticulate bum who arrives an hour late, the *Today* show won't return her calls the next time she has a "great" author she wants to book. That's why you and your publicist should get together as soon as possible. "It's much easier," Pru continues, "to 'sell' someone once you've met them and you can confidently say that they're great personalities and good talkers. Also, if they aren't, that's useful, too, because there's no point setting someone up for something that they are completely unsuited for."

Sadly, publicists are saddled with many books to promote simultaneously. And while you don't want to be a thorn in your publicist's side, you do want to maintain a constant happy presence in her mind. One excellent way to do this is to create a streaming source of perfect pitches that your publicist can hand right over to the appropriate contact. Another way to stay in touch, while producing results, is to give her regular updates on new developments through e-mail and the occasional phone call if something particularly great or horrible happens. As many-time author Phil Bashe says, "In fairness to publicity staffs, they can't possibly become as expert in a given field as the writer. That's why it's the author's responsibility to supply them with everything they need and more—starting with extensive lists of specialized media outlets for reviewing the book or perhaps suggesting topics for feature stories and radio interviews. Make their job as easy as possible. They appreciate the effort and will go the extra mile for you."

What if you do all these things but are left high and dry by your publicist? Has she still not gotten that *New York Times* book review? First of all, no publicist can control whether or not you get such a review. Secondly, it's necessary to understand that the best way to get word out about your book may not be through the traditional routes of reviews, a book tour or getting on *Oprah*. Look, if your book on incontinence gets reviewed in *Seventeen*, chances are that very few of your potential readers are going to see it. But if it gets a simple mention in *AARP: The Magazine*, you may strike gold. The point is, you want your book to be featured where your readers will learn about it. You need to be sure that your expectations make sense—that you're not wanting your publicist to do a job that doesn't fit your book description.

If you find that your publicist is pitching to media outlets that don't address your audience (or address only one small part of your audience) or is setting up events at places where your audience doesn't go, speak up gently and make a compelling case for who and where your audience actually is. Rainelle Burton, author of *The Root Worker*, a coming-of-age novel about an African American girl, had this experience: "On my book tour, my publisher targeted only an African American audience. I thought the book had more mainstream appeal, as it does not fit the popular notion of an 'African American book.' With the exception of one book club that showed up at a bookstore, only four or five African Americans showed up in five cities despite publicity in black community newspapers."

If someone requested material directly from you or you made direct contact with someone in the media, always follow up a week or so later to make sure they got the material from your publicist. If you simply gave your publicist a list of people you don't know and who don't know you, add the name of a good friend to your list and see how long it takes for him to receive something. If he doesn't get it, ask your editor and agent for advice on how to rectify the situation.

If your publicist is not making anything happen, period, then it's time to review the situation. You may find yourself with a wet-behind-the-ears publicist who doesn't yet have the roster of connections that make senior publicists so effective. Let us make clear that young doesn't equal bad. A young publicist can be a highly motivated go-getter who wants to prove herself. But lack of action, from a novice or seasoned veteran, is a red flag. Discuss your thoughts with your editor and agent to see what must be done.

If you still feel that you're not getting the pub love you deserve and need, it might be time to hire an outside publicist.

On Hiring an Outside Publicist

When our book *Satchel Sez* came out, it became clear that our in-house publicist had neither the time nor the sports contacts to handle our promotion. So we went out and found Duffy Jennings, a former publicist for the San Francisco Giants. This guy knew everyone who was anyone when it came to baseball. He turned out to be worth every penny we paid. And he got us everything from an appearance on Armed Forces Radio (which goes out to millions of people in dozens of countries) to a boxed mention in *Sports Illustrated*, the holy grail of sports publications. We ended up getting over a hundred thousand dollars worth of publicity (it costs this for an ad in *Sports Illustrated* alone) for $2,500. Interestingly, this also freed up our in-house publicist to concentrate on the areas he knew best, such as pitching us to local radio shows all over the country. So, even if your assigned publicist is as good as can be, she might have many, many books to promote and not enough hours in the day to do justice to them. And sometimes the right independent publicist is the midwife you need to give your book a proper birthing.

There are no tests or degrees or unions or bar exams required to become a publicist. Anyone can call herself a publicist. But it's very, very hard to be a *good* publicist. The good ones have extraordinary media contacts, the smarts to know the perfect show, magazine or newspaper in which to place a piece about you and your book, the timing to know when to make the move and the ability to spin your story differently for each target. Good publicists almost always charge a lot of money, anywhere from $1,000 to $25,000 (or more if they stay on past your initial launch), depending on the scope of the job and the level of their experience. Every publicist works differently. Some get paid by the hour, some by the job, some by the market. It's up to you to get a lot of quotes, do some haggling (if you're haggle-friendly) and strike the best deal you can.

Keri Levitt of Keri Levitt Communications, a top publicity firm in New York City, has this advice for hiring a publicist:

- Make sure the person has a background and expertise in your field. This way, you know she has the necessary connections to publicize your book.

Another additional benefit of hiring someone who works specifically within your field is that her connections may prove helpful even beyond publicity and contribute to building your business or book.

- Ask the publicist for names of media contacts that are appropriate for your book. Be wary if these aren't quickly forthcoming.
- Ask to see examples of the publicist's work to verify that they're in line with what you have in mind. And be sure to check clippings; if they're all from a year ago or more, look elsewhere. A publicist's press kit should be as up-to-the-minute as her contact list.
- Ask for a proposal outlining your publicist's objectives so that you can be sure you're on the same page. There should also be a detailed list of initiatives, along with the publicist's plans to accomplish them over a period of three to six months.
- Be sure to get an activity report at the end of each month, detailing all communications up to that time. Even if you part ways after a couple of months, you'll know when and to whom your book was pitched.

PLAY NICELY TOGETHER

If you have an in-house publicist, be careful about hiring an outside publicist. If there's an outside publicist whom your in-house publicist has worked with and liked, interview him as well. It's imperative that these two people get along. If they don't, you could end up spending more time putting out fires than getting the PR you desire . . . and deserve.

Once you've hired an outside publicist, make sure everyone is clear about who's doing what. You don't want your in-house publicist just dumping her work in your outside publicist's lap. Again, you can ask your agent to help you with this bit of intricate diplomacy. In the best of all possible worlds, the publicist you hire and your in-house publicist will have complementary contacts and skills so that your work is landing in the hands of twice as many of the right people. If they don't know each other, be sure you all speak together. While most publicists are sweet, lovely humans, some of them are prickly and sensitive about guarding their territory and their contacts. Make sure everyone feels open and generous. If you can, take both publicists out to lunch and discuss how you can all best work together. At the very least, arrange a get-acquainted conference call.

We also recommend asking for referrals. And whatever you do, don't pay the entire fee up front. Break up the payments so you can be sure the person you hired does the job she said she would do.

Your Press Release

Your publicist will probably create your press release, but that's no reason you shouldn't put your two and a half cents in. You've been pitching your book longer than anyone else. By this time, you should know what grabs people's attention and what turns them off. However, your publicist is a trained professional who knows what the media respond to. Hopefully, working together, you can create a press release that educates, excites and entices.

A primo press release remains pretty constant. First off, it should never be more than the front and back of a page. If, for some reason, you can't fit everything you need on this page, you can switch to legal-size paper. But don't go to a second page. Secondly, it should include the following elements:

1. The name and address (and perhaps the logo) of your publisher at the top of the page.

2. Underneath, at the upper left, the words "For Immediate Release" along with the date.

3. Under the publisher's logo, at the upper right, the contact name, phone number and e-mail address of your publicist.

4. The title of your book and your name underneath it.

5. Your pitch in the form of a paragraph or two. You want your press release to be clear, concise, compelling without revealing too much. Calla Devlin, a publicist at Chronicle Books, says, "It's really important to avoid absurd, over-the-top descriptions that so many succumb to. Let your book speak for itself in a way that's accessible and in a journalist's voice. Avoid superlatives."

6. Edited-down versions of blurbs. If you've managed to get a great blurb from a well-known person who can really speak to your subject, feature that one up top. Journalists who don't know you may know the blurber.

7. Edited-down versions of any great reviews.

8. A small, self-contained chunk from your book, particularly if it's a novel or a work of creative nonfiction. Something that illustrates the points in your pitch. Something that shows you off to your best advantage and makes the reader excited about your book.

9. Your bio, reduced to one paragraph, with any pertinent information that might make you an interesting interview. Again, this is NOT a boring recitation of your professional life. That said, if you've got BIG credentials, trot them out. If you don't have a particularly impressive bio, blurbs become all the more important.

10. Any relevant information about speaking or seminars.

11. Your ISBN (the number assigned to your book for retail purposes).

While your publisher will do only one press release, you might be called upon to write many of them in the course of publicizing your book. Be sure your press releases are always up to date. You could get a great review in *The New York Times* that isn't in your publisher's release. If your book sells to Hollywood, you'll want to include that information front and center. Over the next months and years, you can use your own releases to get more media and alert the press to your events. You can also personalize them for particular media outlets or journalists.

Consider that journalists, reviewers and other media get hundreds and hundreds of press releases in the course of a week. Yours has to stand out immediately or it will end up in the garbage.

Your Press Kit

Fortunately, you already have a number of the elements you need for your press kit. Now it's all about assembling them into one professional, visually smart package that makes you look good. Larry Mantle, host of public radio's *AirTalk with Larry Mantle* on the NPR affiliate KPCC-FM in Los Angeles, says, "Having a nice package really helps. Something that's professionally presented, that doesn't look homemade. How it looks really does make a difference. I get 50 to 70 books a week. So I often have only 20 seconds to spend looking at a press kit."

PEARLS FROM A PUBLICITY PRO

Lynn Goldberg, CEO of Goldberg McDuffie Communications, one of the leading PR agencies in publishing, shares some thoughts on capturing the media's attention:

- Press releases are generally viewed as formulaic. That's why customized letters and handwritten notes are so important.
- Press kits are essential for broadcast media. They need a package with topics for discussions and show ideas. Here's where the Q&A can be very important. It's a terrific place to pull out an author's ideas and show the consequences of these ideas.
- For fiction, the voice is key. I often have authors do anecdotal bios that are a page unto themselves. These don't begin "I was born . . ." Instead, they feature what is unique or surprising about the authors and how their background has informed their work.
- For nonfiction, you need a good journalistic lead. It could be about current events or a recent survey. But don't overreach or make extraneous connections. Instead, distill the information in a thoughtful way so reviewers will pick your book out of the pack.
- If you have a how-to book, provide user-friendly nuggets like lists and tips.
- The media are not anxious to hear from authors directly. Once you've sent your press kit off, follow up prudently. You want to be a helpful resource, not a pest.
- The good news? The media like ideas. They are thirsty for them.

On the inside flaps of an attractive folder should be some variation of the following:

1. Your press release
2. A full bio (like the one you included in your submission to publishers)
3. Author photo
4. Reviews/blurbs
5. Articles about you
6. Q&A
7. CD, audio or videotape
8. A one-paragraph description of what you can offer as a speaker or workshop leader

Since you're still in the prepublication stage, your reviews (if you have any) will be only from trade publications such as *Publishers Weekly*, *Booklist*, *Kirkus* and *Library Journal*. That's fine. The great thing about a press kit is that you can keep adding to it as more raves come in. So if you're worried that your press kit looks a bit skimpy to begin with, just know that it will keep growing as your book garners more acclaim.

All articles and reviews should be cleanly reproduced, with the name of the publication and the date it appeared displayed clearly. And your Q&A should include the questions you'd like to be asked by the media along with your very pithy one-paragraph answers.

Even with a major publisher, your publicist may create only a press release, not a full press kit. So the latter may fall to you. But pass your finished kit by her to make sure it's up to snuff.

A GOOD AUTHOR PHOTO IS NOT AN OXYMORON

An enticing author photograph can really help your book. Which is why it's so important to include an attractive, professional photo in your press kit. This doesn't mean you have to look like a model; it just means you have to look your best, whatever your best is. Book critic Jonathon Keats says, "Author photos are an often overlooked opportunity. As much as nobody wants to say it, a good photo really matters in terms of getting a feature. Reviewers actually ask about this on the sly."

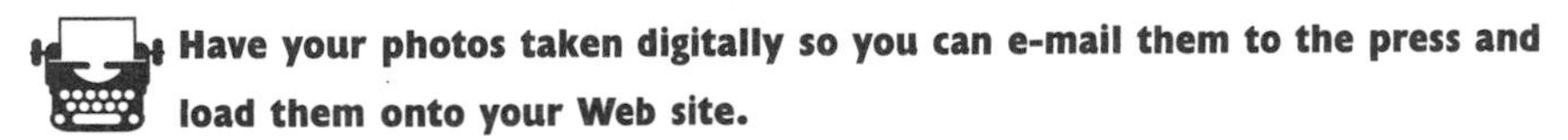

Have your photos taken digitally so you can e-mail them to the press and load them onto your Web site.

Don't be cheap. A six-year-old Polaroid that makes you look kind of cute will not do. Whether you're going for a head shot, a full-body shot or something in between, it's usually worth the money to go to a professional photographer with a studio and lights. Your agent or publisher may know a good one. If not, ask around or look on the Internet. Make sure you see each photographer's portfolio. Most of all, find a photographer you're comfortable with. This will make for more natural photos.

Make the most of your photo shoot. Do a whole series of poses: serious to goofy, sexy to thoughtful. This way, you have a number of choices for the media. Interesting, beautiful or unusual photographs have a way of ending up in "pick of the week" sections of newspapers because editors are always looking for eye-catching visuals. Sometimes a small appropriate prop can be fun, as long as it doesn't dominate the picture. When the aforementioned Mike Daisey was photographed, a friend brought in a toy dog bone since his story was called *21 Dog Years*. Mike put it in his mouth and made a crazy, wide-eyed dog face. It became the poster for his show. Then the cover for his book. Then a much-published photo in newspapers and magazines around the country. Simple prop. Used beautifully.

If you're super photogenic, don't be shy about sending your picture out with ALL promotional materials. And if you have several different and fun shots, include more than one smaller photo on the inside of your press kit as well.

If you don't feel comfortable in front of a camera, bring a friend to loosen you up or have a glass of wine to relax. Try engaging in a conversation as you're being photographed. But if you absolutely cannot bear the thought of your mug on the cover of your book, you can forgo a photo. Remember, a bad picture is worse than none at all. Note how David's horrid poses, combined with the hideous use of unsightly shadows, create an almost epic degree of badness:

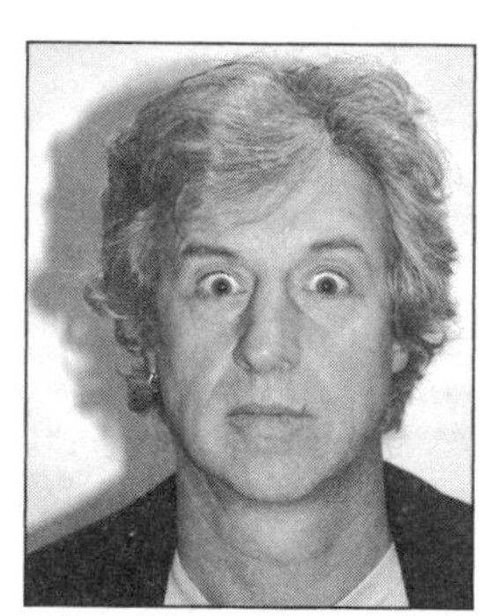
Bug-eyed.

Comb-over w/ cheese.

Deep and shadowy.

Focus-challenged.

Painful smile.

Shaggy.

A PRETTY PICTURE'S WORTH AN IN-STORE EVENT

Author photos can make booksellers take notice. Barbara Morrow, co-owner of Northshire Books in Manchester Center, Vermont, told us this story: "An unknown author named Prill Boyle wrote a book called *Defying Gravity: A Celebration of Late-Blooming Women.* She sent us a copy of the book along with a press packet that included a great author photo. She is an attractive woman, and she looked like she would present herself and her subject well. We didn't know who she was (she had no track record), but I decided to bring her in to do an event. She was so appealing, and she presented herself and her material so well. Fifteen people showed up, and the amazing thing was that everyone bought books. That hardly ever happens."

This story shows just how powerful a good author photo can be. On the flip side, though, Barbara adds: "Authors who send pictures that look deadly dull do themselves a disservice by including them in their press packet."

THE VIDEO/CD/DVD THING

If you've appeared on TV or radio and you were able to be your brilliant, charming, lovely self, you'd be crazy not to put together an excerpt of one or more of your appearances on CD, DVD and/or videotape. This will make a fantastic addition to your press kit. It can also serve as your publicist's calling card for more TV and radio spots, speaking engagements and any number of other events.

Just make sure you have a top-quality copy of your appearance(s). Do not include out-of-focus, grainy footage of you reading somewhere, or third-generation junk. You want crisp, sharp footage that makes you look scintillating, deep, funny and/or brilliant. Running time should be under five minutes, total. Do yourself a favor and begin the tape with you, not a long lead-in from whatever program you happened to be on. No one has time for the boring parts. However, if it was a national show, it's good to start with its logo or a few seconds of Katie or Matt or Regis saying, "In the next half hour, we'll be talking to (insert your name here) about his fabulous new book."

If you haven't appeared on television but you just know you're a natural, try recording yourself reading or doing a Q&A. If you happen to know someone who has professional camera and editing equipment, this can be done dirt cheap. Regina Louise, author of the memoir *Somebody's Someone*, is a particularly dynamic and charismatic person. Before her pub date, she hired a filmmaker to put together a short documentary about her life and her book. It included clips of Regina reading from her book like the consummate performer she is, and it made for a great selling tool.

Make your packaging impeccably attractive. And make sure the CD, DVD, video or audiotape itself has your name, the name of your book and all contact information clearly displayed.

Presentation Doctor/Media Coach

If you're shy, inexperienced and/or anxious about the prospect of appearing in the media, a good presentation doctor or media coach can help you feel comfortable with yourself and your message. Some of these people come from the world of publishing, some from the world of public relations, some from the world of acting/directing. A good presentation doctor/media coach will evaluate your presentation skills, determine your strengths and weaknesses, and help you with everything from your appearance to eliminating unconscious nervous tics, to relaxation techniques, to making eye contact from something as simple as what to do with your hands, to something as complex as comic spin. A good coach will also help you find your message, hone your pitch and learn to deliver it in graceful, potent, 15-second sound bites.

David has been a media coach for years. One of his most effective techniques is to have you videotape yourself making a presentation or doing a mock interview. Then play the tape back for yourself. This way, you'll see all of your Achilles' heels, step by step, frame by excruciating frame. Then you can work to eliminate them and accentuate your strengths (yes, you've got to look for your strengths, too). It's shocking how often authors unconsciously tap their fingers, twiddle their thumbs, fiddle with their collars, and say "Uh" every seventh word. And they don't even know they're doing it!

If exposing yourself to a professional is so scary that you never, ever want to hire a media coach, consider this: A little humiliation in front of a nonjudgmental professional is much easier to take than watching yourself stutter, phumph and fidget in front of millions of Americans.

More Galley Action

If your publisher prints bound galleys, get as many sets as you can! Often, your publisher will give you as few as five sets because bound galleys are very expensive to produce—even more expensive than your book itself. But if you ask early enough, you can often get more. Because you have so few sets—rarely more than 15 to 20—you want to make sure to use your galleys judiciously.

If your publisher won't give you the number of galleys you want, you can always order more and pay for them on your own. But you have to let your publisher know before they place their galley order. Make sure to find out when this will happen early on and put it on your Master Calendar so you don't miss the date.

Who are the people you most want to have an early look at your book? Often these are blurbers or long-lead journalists, i.e., those who work at monthly magazines. If there are booksellers you know well, get your galleys into their hands, too, since booksellers are great at creating buzz. And if you have particularly strong connections with any prominent loudmouths, it's worth sending them galleys.

Be sure to include a personalized letter with each set of galleys. This is much like your press release, the main difference being that you want to start out your letter by connecting to the person you're gifting with your galleys, just as you did with your query letter. If you were referred by someone, put that person's name in the first line. If you read an article by the person that relates to your book, get this info right up front so it's clear why you're sending galleys. Again, the more you know about the person you're approaching, the better. You also want to be sure that you coordinate with your publicist so that you're not duplicating work.

Another great reason for galleys is the possibility that your book has movie/TV potential. Galleys can be a terrific way to court Hollywood before your book has actually come out. You will also need galleys if you've retained the foreign rights to your book. This way, foreign publishers can get an early look at your book. Make sure you and your agent get enough galleys to send to subagents/publishers overseas.

Hooks and Angles: Stoking the Media Fire

Even if you have all the perfect publicity materials, they'll go only so far if you don't have a wide array of hooks in your vest. A hook, simply put, is something on which an article, an interview or an appearance can hang. Hooks should be custom-built for the media you're courting. Oddly, many times your hook will be about some interesting facet of your personality, your hobbies, your vocation, your background or your heritage and not about your book. Sometimes you can slant a story about a time of the year (Mother's Day, Christmas, World Series), a news event, your relationship with your wife.

The fact is, the media business is like a two-headed snake that feeds on itself. If one hook grabs the interest of a local newspaper journalist who then features your book in his column, this story may then beget a feature on the local news, which may beget a feature on a national TV show. That's why you should always be looking for trends that relate to your book. Scour the news sources: *The New York Times*, NPR, TV network news, and so on. Keep track of what's being said and written about your subject so you have specific ammunition for your pitch. Now's the time to pull out your running list of journalists who are reporting on subjects similar to yours. Spin your story in such a way that it's an inspired editorial fit for the publication you're pitching. For example, if your book is about Mae West, you might spin an article to politically minded *Mother Jones* about West and censorship, since it would relate to current attempts to censor Internet content. For fashion-centric *Vogue* magazine, you might pitch Mae West as a fashion trendsetter whose effect is felt to this day. For advice-obsessed *Cosmo*, you might talk about how Mae West can spice up your sex life.

THE MAN WHO WORE THE WRONG PANTS

An author we know who wrote a gripping, difficult book had one of the most counter-intuitive hooks in recent memory: "I'm a golfer. There I said it. I'm not ashamed. Although I'd rather you didn't use my real name. But my book couldn't really have anything less to do with golf."

This author told his publicist about his love of golf. She knew of a particular journalist who was also a golfer. She pitched the idea of doing an article about the two golfing together, and to everyone's surprise the paper loved it. When the writer and journalist arrived at the course, which happened to be particularly stuffy, the author was informed that he was wearing pants, shirt and shoes strictly forbidden by the club. You can imagine the field day the journalist had with this! "The article turned out great," the author told us. "It was really unique and funny. I can't tell you how many people now ask me about my pants." He ended up selling lots of books and getting a piece that looks great in his press kit.

You never know when your idea will fit in with someone's upcoming issue. Just be sure to let your publicist and/or publisher know what you're up to. They won't be happy if you're simultaneously pitching the same place.

The first places you want to hook into are long-lead magazines, i.e., ones that are published monthly or less frequently. These magazines plan their issues six months ahead of their publication dates. So if you want to get an article in such a magazine near your pub date, you need to pitch early and often.

Movie Deal as Mega-Hook

My book is being made into a movie. In our experience, few things make people's eyes light up faster than hearing these words. Even the *rumor* of a Hollywood deal can create enormous buzz. And the boost in sales if your book actually ends up on the screen can be life-altering. As Pulitzer Prize winner Jeffrey Eugenides said (with his tongue firmly planted in his cheek), "For me, the key to getting on the bestseller list was first to have my book turned into a movie, then to get a bunch of pretty good reviews. That's it."

If you get a sniff of interest from Hollywood before your book hits the shelves, spread the buzz. Let everybody know. Get your agent and everyone at your publishing house excited about the movie possibility. Buzz with a capital "B" is exactly what happened to J.T. LeRoy's book *Sarah*, about a teenager's troubled relationship with his mother. Suddenly word buzz-sawed through Hollywood that both Angelina Jolie and Courtney Love wanted to play the role of the mother. The news was reported in arts and entertainment sections of local newspapers, on TV and in major national magazines. It escalated to the point that it was reported in the media as a cat fight between two Hollywood vixens. This heat fueled rampant speculation: Who is J.T. LeRoy? What is *Sarah*? Why are these starlets fighting for this role? In the end, it was one of the factors that helped make LeRoy's book a success and paved the way for his next book, a collection of short stories. Of course, it didn't hurt that he wrote a stellar book.

"Having your book turned into a movie is like seeing your oxen turned into bouillon cubes."
—John le Carré

Should you be lucky enough to have your book optioned and then made into a movie or TV series, use each step of the often very long process to spin stories and pitches, to get some public love for your book. Cinematic flirtation and rumor, the contract terms being agreed upon, the script being written, the director and actors being hired, the cameras rolling, the grand opening, the release of the DVD and video—every one of these events is a potential buzz builder. But since the chance of an optioned book becoming a TV show ranks right up there with getting into Harvard, there's all the more reason to capitalize on *any* Tinseltown action you do get.

THE BEAUTY AND POWER OF NETWORKS

Movie deal or no movie deal, great media response or no media response, there are people who will be interested in your book. You just have to connect with them. Some of these people you already know—like your friends and family—and you'll want to get them talking about your book right away. Some you may know through someone else, so take the time to track them down. Some are now colleagues—authors who have written books that are complementary to your own and who can help you down the path they've already trod. Some you may only share common interests with.

But *all* of these people can help make your book a success. You just have to take the time to network with them. The sooner, the better.

Networking with Your Network

Truman Capote had this advice for young writers: "Socialize. Don't just go up to a pine cabin all alone and brood. You will reach that stage soon enough anyway." People you already know are possible advocates for and buyers of your book. And these people are connections to everyone else they know, and all those people are connections to all the people they know, and on and on, in one big Kevin Bacon six-degrees-of-separation-type deal.

Do you know anyone who knows anyone in the media, from mogul to peon? Comb all your various databases. Cousins, second cousins and in-laws. Colleagues, friends, near-friends and acquaintances. Fellow union, PTA or club members. Hairdressers, mailpeople and bartenders are good to have in your loop. You never know, your hairdresser might cut the hair of the local anchordude on TV. Your mailperson may deliver to the woman who writes the local gossip column.

Ask all of them to keep their ears open, their eyes peeled and their mouths spreading your good word.

Your Book's like My Book

Start looking for authors who have written books complementary to yours. Begin by going back to books you know and love on your subject or in your genre. Again, you want to choose books that are similar to but not directly competitive with yours. If you approach a writer as a huge fan of his work and now a fellow author, you could end up not only with an advocate but with a future blurber and friend as well.

As you did when you scouted your competition, start with an Internet bookstore, looking for the "People who bought this book also bought . . ." icon. You know the drill by now. Make your list. Check it twice. Find out everything you can about the writers. Make sure you've read their books thoroughly. When you contact them, praise them in specific, real, emphatic yet not bum-kissing ways. If they let you, pick their brains about what worked for them when their books came out. The pitfalls to watch for. The tricks of the trade. People to talk to. Folks to avoid. You may learn things that make all the difference between a breakout book and a dud.

David was lucky enough to get a great blurb for his book *Chicken* from Jerry Stahl, bestselling author of numerous books including the novel *I, Fatty* about silent film star Fatty Arbuckle. The blurb came through his publisher, but David went out of his way to write Jerry a nice letter thanking him. When Jerry came to San Francisco, David went to his event. He bought Jerry's book *Plainclothes Naked* and made sure he was last in line so he could have a conversation while Jerry signed it. They e-mailed back and forth, and eventually David asked if he could set up an event with Jerry to promote *Chicken* in his hometown. Jerry not only said yes, but turned David on to an editor at a national magazine to whom he could pitch articles. All of this happened because David responded to Jerry's initial blurb. Now David tells everybody what a great guy Jerry is and how great his books are, hoping in some small way to repay his generosity.

> *"The successful networkers I know, the ones receiving tons of referrals and feeling truly happy about themselves, continually put the other person's needs ahead of their own."*
>
> **—Bob Burg**

Also, look for similar books that are being released at approximately the same time as yours. Writers with books similar to yours may be great to do events or pitch articles with. Who knows, maybe you can corral several writers and get a little Lollapalooza thing going. Doing stuff with other writers can make an event become an Event and help you feel a lot less alone, as well as being a lot of laughs.

Network with as many authors as you can. Author events, writers' conferences, book fairs, festivals and expos are all great ways to meet authors. Buy their books and get them to sign your copies. Join the fraternity/sorority of authors. And mingle!

NETWORKING WITH PEOPLE WHO HAVE SIMILAR INTERESTS

Thea Kotroba, buyer and event coordinator at Chester County Book and Music Company in Westchester, Pennsylvania, talked to us about bestselling thriller writer Lisa Scottolini: "She doesn't rely on her publisher. Instead, she networks with every group she can get into. That's one of the reasons her books end up on bestseller lists." You need to do as Scottolini does: network with your potential audience. Poke your nose around. Look for people, places and things that relate to your book. If you've written a mystery, start attending mystery writers' conferences and haunting mystery bookstores. If you've written about rats, start contacting rodent lovers. Now is the time to integrate and infiltrate the various worlds that your book could inhabit.

Master marketer Nancy Levine, coauthor with her philosopher dog Wilson of *The Tao of Pug* (a humorous reinterpretation of the *Tao Te Ching*, accompanied by adorable pug photographs), used the months leading up to her publication to get to know the players in the pug kingdom. She contacted pug rescue organizations and hung out at dog parks and pug events. She put up an early version of her book on her Web site, had WILSON FOR PRESIDENT buttons made and started getting pug people prepared for the launch of her book by sending out e-mails to pug nuts around the country. By the time her pub date arrived, she had a panting pug public palpitating. Of course, it didn't hurt that she brought Wilson with her wherever she went.

Search through all the worlds in which your book belongs, so it can find a home there. Nowadays, one of the best ways to find these worlds is through the World Wide Web, which leads us to . . .

Cybersizing: Setting Up a Web Site

"A good Web site can help you develop a following. It's a way of staying in touch with people and letting them know what you're doing." That's the opinion of LikomaIsland.com founder Bradley Charbonneau, whose company designs many a writer's Web site. "You can constantly change it and update it, redesign it with a fresh new look."

Do not make a boring, insipid, nasty-looking Web site. Even if there's not much stuff on it, make sure it's good-looking, stylish and easy to navigate. Again, better to be great and minimal than sloppy and maximal.

It will save lots of time and money if you come up with a model, just as you did for your book. Investigate other Web sites, particularly other writers' sites. See what works and what doesn't, not just visually but also from an architectural and navigational point of view. You don't want a beautiful Web site that says nothing about how to buy your book. The more you know

10 REASONS TO SET UP A WEB SITE

1. People all over the world can go to your site, read about your book and presumably click on a link that will take them to an e-tail outlet where they can buy it.
2. If people ask about your book, you can tell them, "Check out my Web site." It's an instant-gratification, ever-changing ad for you and your book.
3. You can post high-quality pictures that media all over the world can download. This will save you enormous time, money and energy. It's a big pain sending pictures all over the place. Even if they're not precious family photos.
4. If a reader, researcher or member of the media is searching the Web for information regarding your subject, your site could very well show up, leading to additional business or review attention.
5. You can say anything you want on your Web site. Sometimes you can't do that in your own book.
6. You can publicize your events on your Web site, put up radio interviews, post video of yourself reading parts of your book and give away free stuff.
7. You can post other writing that is not yet published.
8. A great Web site is a work of art that enhances the value of your book. It makes publishers feel that you're a true partner in their sales and marketing efforts.
9. You can start buzz about your next project.
10. You'd be stupid not to.

10 WAYS TO MAKE YOUR WEB SITE SUCCESSFUL

1. Get a domain name that makes sense: www.firstnamelastname.com is good, or www.titleofyourbook.com. Or both. You can make one redirect to the other. Make sure every e-mail you send contains your Web address—it's a tiny reminder of where people can find you and your book.
2. Put your Web site in the back of your book, and include a link on your site so people can buy it.
3. Get your Web site listed as a link on other people's sites. Link other people on your site. Search engines such as Google create the hierarchy of Web sites that appears in any search by looking at how many links a visitor uses to get to a particular site. The more links or the more popular the link, the higher your ranking. If you can get yourself linked to a well-trafficked site, all the better. FYI: You can learn a lot about how people are getting to your site using statistics-tracking software. Some of this software (ask your Web designer which of the large number of companies that offer it is best) is both free *and* good. You just want to be sure that the software you choose shows how visitors came to your site—via which search engine, which search words and which exact link.
4. Get as many friends and e-friends as possible to go to your Web site. In fact, you should go onto your own site as much as possible. As above, this will help your site occupy a higher spot when you go to a search engine and put in a key word search. You can also set up your e-mail account so that your e-mails go through your site.
5. Make it sticky. Give visitors a reason to visit your site, but also give them a reason to stick around awhile. Post a photo gallery. Other writing. A blog. Video clips. And give people a reason to come back again. Keep it up to date and fresh with new cool stuff.
6. If anyone interviews you for print, ask to have your Web site included in the interview somewhere. If you get interviewed on TV or radio, mention your site on air.
7. Put free stuff on your Web site, like an autographed bookmark to the visitor who answers the Question of the Day or a signed free book to the person supplying the best Quote of the Week.
8. Include links to e-bookstores such as Amazon, bn.com and your local Book Sense bookstore.
9. Create a Book Club Guide (with Q&As for discussion) or a monthly newsletter.
10. Make your Web site candy to the eye and good fun.

what you want, the better your chances of getting it. Assemble all your elements carefully and have them all ready before you hire a Web designer. The easier you make it for her, the fewer hours it will take and the less it will cost you. But at a minimum you should include your press release, samples from your book, a calendar of events, blurbs, reviews and interviews, links to e-books and contact information.

Fauzia Burke, president of FSB Associates, a pioneering Web marketing firm that specializes in books, says, "The most important aspect of an author Web site is its quality in design and content. Many authors hire the cousin of a neighbor who's in high school because it's less expensive. The look is often immature, unprofessional and poorly designed. Authors need to understand that a Web site is their resumé to their readers. An immature site reflects poorly on the author's style and the quality of his or her work."

Try to find someone who will bring state-of-the-art know-how to your Web site, along with a great sense of style. When you're searching for a designer, check out other Web sites they've made and ask if they've ever done author sites before. If you have a small or minimal budget, contact design schools and find people who've just graduated. Out-of-work tech people. Freelance designers. Obviously, many of these can be found on the Web. Many are highly qualified. Some will barter with you.

Before you plunk down your credit card, ask a techy friend where to register the domain and find reliable Web hosting, a service that provides the space for your Web site. As Bradley Charbonneau says, "You can own your own domain name, but you rent the apartment your site will live in." If you're not a Web pro, you'll never be able to figure this out because the ads for these services are intended to confuse you. Hosting for $5 might even have better features than for $20!

Once your Web site is launched, get feedback from everybody who will look at it. Ask your team to make their invaluable suggestions. Keep tweaking it until you get it just right. Update it regularly. Nourish it, and it will be good to you. As with everything you do in pursuing your book, make your Web site a representation of the best of you. Take your time and do it right.

E-Marketing: A Gift to the Shy

You're lucky. You live in a time when you can do so much marketing and research and promotion from the luxury of your own home. Over the Internet. Reaching people all over the world. In your robe and slippers with really bad hair. If you don't know how to use the Internet or don't have a computer, we heartily suggest you come join us here in the 21st century. It's a lot of fun.

E-marketing can be particularly beneficial if you don't feel comfortable promoting yourself in a public way. Caroline Leavitt, author of eight novels including *Coming Back to Me*, is just the sort of person who's benefited greatly from the Internet. "People told me to network with other writers, and I never did," she says. "I'm very shy. Now that we have the Internet, it's a lot easier. And I've made valuable contacts. Publicity, promotion, blurbs and friendship, which is the most important of all. Who but another writer understands what you're going through?"

In the months leading up to publication, you want to make the most of e-marketing. Begin e-mailing as soon as your book is accepted. Identify key words that explicate your book. Do a search for each of these words. In various combinations. When we were marketing *Satchel Sez*, our key words were:

- Satchel Paige
- Leroy Paige
- Baseball
- Negro Leagues
- Black History
- Integration
- Barnstorming
- Dizzie Dean (a peer of Satchel's)
- Bill Veeck (the man who first brought Satchel to the major leagues)
- Buck O'Neil (a former teammate of Satchel's and a well-known raconteur)

Locate and contact civic, business and social organizations, enthusiasts, hobbyists, colleges/universities/professors to see if they would be interested in hosting an event or inviting you to speak. It's simple to reach professors because their e-mail addresses are easily accessible through their college or university Web sites. Who knows, one e-mail six months before your book comes out may result in your book ending up on a class syllabus. If your book ends up on a syllabus, that means *all* the people in the class have to buy it. This is a good thing.

Keep files as you contact interested groups, individuals, experts and novices. The wonderful thing about the Internet is that one pertinent Web site can lead you to another, which can lead you to another, and on and on. And so much can be done for so little by so many in the e-world.

E-FRIENDS FROM INDIA TO INDIANAPOLIS

About six months before his book *Chicken* came out, David started doing searches on the Internet, eventually sending out over 10,000 e-mails to organizations and individuals who might be interested. He was relentless, spending 10, 12, 14 hours a day, sometimes pulling all-nighters. He made e-friends from India to Indianapolis, South Vietnam to South-Central Los Angeles, Rome, Italy, to Rome, Texas. Eventually he contacted a professor at a university in the Deep South. They e-mailed back and forth, and the professor read a set of David's galleys. David said he'd love to come talk to the professor's classes when his book came out. The professor said he'd like that, and David figured that would be that—he'd never hear from the guy again. But just to keep himself in the back of the professor's brain, David kept e-mailing him. Kept him up to date on what he was doing. About a year later, the professor asked David if he was still interested in coming to talk to his students. David said he absolutely was. They arranged dates. The professor flew David down, and he had a blast. He talked to four or five classes, and the students were fantastic. David sold a bunch of books. Plus they gave him a very nice stipend. And he had hooked the whole thing up in his jammies, from the comfort of home.

TO TOUR OR NOT TO TOUR

If you're not shy, and you're excited about getting out on the road to promote your book, great. But you may find that your publisher isn't interested in supporting your efforts. They may have initially told you that they were going to send you out on a tour, but the next time you brought it up, they had no memory whatsoever of their sweet-breathed promises. Or maybe your publisher never promised a tour. The question you must now face is: Are you sure you want to tour with your book? It takes hard work and expertise to set up a tour. Money and time, energy and effort, and almost certain frustration. Will you be able to attract media? Will you really sell books by doing events? How will you get people to show up? What if no one does?

Many publishers feel that unless you're able to garner media attention, a tour that comprises bookstore events is not worthwhile. But before you make a decision, consider this: You may get a real sense of completion when you stand up in front of an audience and read your work aloud. When you go on a tour of bookstores, you also get a great education about yourself, your audience, your book and the entire process of writing and publishing. It's a fantastic feeling to see your book on display. To be introduced to people who are actually interested in your book. To read your words out loud, to sign your books and to engage with those who are actually selling your book.

But if you're going to take the plunge and do it, do it right. Trust us, there are few things sadder than a miserable, poorly attended event.

Setting Up Your Events

First you have to decide where you want to go. Where do you have a built-in audience? Where can you get media attention? Where are the places you'd like to visit? For the most part, if you select random places where you have no support or no chance of getting media attention *before* your event, you'll get very few people to show up. This can deflate even the healthiest ego after a couple of stops. And take a chunk out of your wallet.

Once you decide on your destinations, it's time to pick your venues. If you plan on doing events in bookstores (and we highly recommend that you do if bookstores are where your audience hangs out), try to do a combination of independents and chains (in different parts of the city, if possible). Look them up on the Web. Try to get a feel for the different stores before you call. Check out their event calendars.

To set up events, contact the event coordinator at least three months in advance. This will give you plenty of time to promote your events and allow bookstores the necessary time to get you into their calendars. Be sure to have your pitch down cold so that you can tell the person on the phone in under a minute who you are, what your book is and why she should have you in her store. For example, if you can put together a mailing list of friends, family and colleagues in the area, let her know. Tom Campbell, co-owner of Regulator Books in Durham, North Carolina, says, "If you have a mailing list with fifty names on it, and you tell us lots of them will come to an event, that's great. It's hard to just blindly put out publicity about an unknown book and expect people to show up. If we know an author will bring in people, there's a very good chance we'll book them to do an event."

Use the next minute to explain why your event is particularly suited to that bookstore. Let them know you've done your research.

Also make a variation on your press release that is specifically designed for book events. Have this ready to fax or e-mail as a follow-up or as an introduction if you aren't able to get through on the phone. Be sure to include any information about why your event will sell books, specifically, whether a local book group will be attending, you're bringing in a musical group with a following or you have connections to the local media. All these efforts will make your case much stronger. Jennifer Ramos, director of promotions at Vroman's in Pasadena, California, puts it this way: "If the author can convince me he's going to be very active in promoting, getting press, getting people to come to the event, that really helps." Putting on events actually costs bookstores money. So if they don't sell a requisite number of copies (anywhere between 15 and 40, depending on the size of the store and how much promoting/marketing they do), it's not worth it for them.

Don't forget about libraries, which often have wonderful author events and series. Sally Reed, director of Friends of Libraries, USA, says, "Try to set up events with libraries in whatever city you go to. Call up each library's program office and ask to do a signing. If they don't have a program office, ask for the local Friends of Libraries group." Also, try to get a local bookseller to sell your books at those events.

Keep very careful notes on what venues you're going after and who the event coordinator is. Leave a message the first time you call if the person is not available. But don't wait for her to call you back. Be sure to follow up.

Obviously, if you're putting together a tour, you have to line up your events geographically so you have enough time to get to them. Check your Master Calendar, and slot in your events accordingly. Also be sure to check with your publisher before you set up any events. They'll need time to get your books to the location—at least a couple of weeks and often more. Plus, if your publisher is helping you with your tour, there are very strict rules about how many venues you can do in one city, as well as how to set up events with the chains. If they're not sending you on tour, ask them if they can help out with media or chip in a night at a hotel.

PUTTING THE FANNIES IN THE SEATS

Many authors assume that just because they have an event in a bookstore, flocks of wild readers will show up. This is not so. Even at the biggest and best bookstores, with newsletters that go out to thousands, you can have an empty house. Sharon Kelly Roth of Books & Company in Dayton, Ohio, says, "I don't think authors understand how much work goes on in putting together an event. Every Monday, I send out press releases to thirty-nine contacts for eight events. With the high price of books these days and the enormous effort it takes to put on events, it's even more crucial for writers to make sure lots of readers attend their events." But guess who's ultimately responsible for putting the fannies in the seats? You, the poor slob who wrote the book! And don't be fooled if you're on a publisher-sponsored book tour. Think you can just lie back and watch your readers stroll on in? Wrong again!

Gary Frank, owner of The Booksmith in San Francisco, says this about contacting him for events: "Convince me. People think because they have a book out they'll automatically have a crowd. That is definitely not the case. It's really hard to get people to come out. We've had very successful events with unknown authors, but it's always because they made the effort to get people here. Of course, media coverage helps a lot. We have so little money to spend on promoting events."

The first thing to do in your epic struggle to get people to show up is to pick the brain of the bookseller or event coordinator where you're presenting. Provided there is one. And that he'll let you into his brain. Work with him to come up with a list of concrete things you can do. Let him know you'll do whatever it takes to get people there the day of your event.

Among the things to ask are:

- What successful things have other authors done?
- What media should I contact?
- Will you be sending information to calendar listings? If not, do you have names and numbers I can send to?
- Will you write and send out a press release?
- Do you know any organizations I should approach?
- Will you make a flyer?

If you're doing events and you want people to show up, you need media attention. It's time to pull out those old hooks and start fishing. Make a press release or flyer for your event. Saturate all local media with it. Journalists. TV and radio producers and hosts. Calendar listings in daily and weekly papers. Everything. Everybody. Everywhere. Start about a month before your event to let them know you're coming. Send out another press release 10 days to a couple of weeks later. Then a final notice three days before your event.

Present your information in the form each media outlet requests. Find out when they want it. And give it to them then. It's very difficult, but if you can, and it's appropriate, get them on the phone and pitch your little heart out.

In addition to media, contact special-interest groups, societies, organizations and enthusiasts who would be interested in your topic. Marilyn Paige, the Barnes & Noble CRM, told us about Rachel Simon, author of *Riding the Bus with My Sister*, a book about her relationship with her disabled sister. "Rachel did some research and found out there was a huge

A ROGUES' GALLERY

Remember those wacky, interesting, fun, sexy or unusual photographs we encouraged you to take along with your regular author photos? Well, use them when you send your event info to all the calendar sections of the local newspapers and weeklies. Having an outstanding, compelling, jump-off-the-page picture can make all the difference between you and your book getting featured prominently and getting tossed onto the slag heap of wasted opportunity. Here are some fun photos we took:

No place to hide.

We want YOU.

How to treat a coauthor.

The wacky world of publishing.

What, us worry?

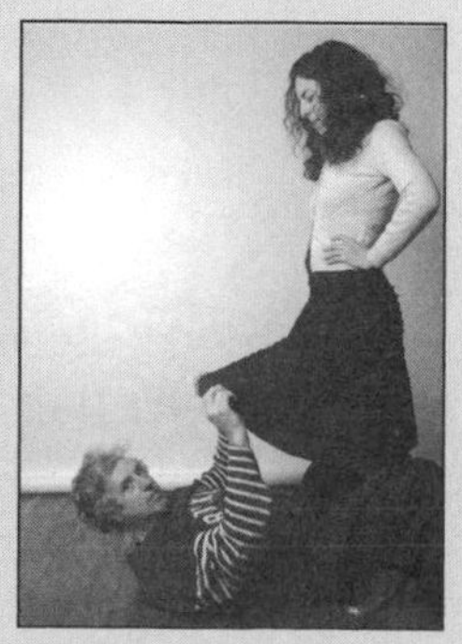

What have we here?

THE POWER OF THE SMALL TOWN

Paulina Springs Book Company in Sisters, Oregon (population 911), was the only store of the dozens we contacted that had any interest in doing an event on our book *Satchel Sez.* We'd been told that books about baseball don't draw crowds, so we just assumed that Paulina Springs didn't know any better. We got to Sisters at 4:40 on a Saturday for our 5:00 event, and apart from Kate Cerino, the owner of the bookstore, none of the Sisterites were there. Our expectations, already low, plummeted as we spied the 30-some empty seats sadly facing the lonely microphone. We walked out to find a place to get a cup of tea, and as we strolled around Sisters, we noticed that no one was around. It was like a *Twilight Zone* episode. We began to wonder if we were about to be abducted by author-starved aliens.

Well, imagine our surprise when we returned at 5:00 to find Paulina Springs Book Company packed with 50 of its 911 occupants. Our jaws hit the floor. Those melancholy chairs were now brimming with Sisters' readers, all waiting for us to say something insightful and witty. We scanned the crowd, and it suddenly hit us that there were only two people under the age of 60. Exactly our target audience—old enough to remember Satch. Afterwards, the crowd asked great questions, and many of them shared their own stories. It was America at its best, oral history flying all around us. Near the end, the oldest man in the room, who looked 90 going on 120, raised his hand. In a voice weathered with age but still going gangbusters, he told us that he had been a batboy for Satchel Paige when he was 15 years old. He stole the whole show in about 20 seconds.

We signed book after book, with some people buying two or three. It was our most successful event on that tour, monetarily and emotionally. Obviously, Kate Cerino knew

network of siblings of the disabled. She contacted them and they turned out in droves."

Contact libraries, community centers, unions. Put up flyers. Drop off flyers. Press flesh.

Contact professors and grad student/teaching assistants at local colleges and universities. Invite them to your event.

If you're writing about a particular religion, ethnicity or sexual orientation, there will be seminars, art festivals, parades and book fairs where you'll find your readers discussing, mingling and/or partying. For example, if your book is of Jewish interest, there are well-regarded Jewish book festivals that run between the High Holidays and Hanukkah. They draw large exactly what she was doing. Later on, we asked her for her thoughts on why the event worked so well:

PYPIP: Why did you buck conventional wisdom and bring in an event revolving around a deceased, fairly obscure historical figure?

KC: Someone in the store heard David being interviewed by Scott Simon on National Public Radio and thought it would make a good event.

PYPIP: The subject of the book was an African American. How many African Americans live in Sisters?

KC: Probably under five. But I don't really think about it like that. We try to do great events; the people who come know it's going to be interesting. Like all independent bookstores that have managed to survive, we have loyal customers and they support us.

PYPIP: Your event was the most successful on our tour. And there are only 911 people in the whole town!

KC: Well, that's a little deceiving. There are about 10,000 people who live in and around Sisters. But I think Paulina Springs Book Company is in many ways an intellectual center. Besides, Sisters is a very special town with a lot of smart, interesting people.

PYPIP: Do you think publishers sometimes underestimate small-town bookstores' ability to sell books and stage successful events?

KC: Most definitely! We have a very hard time getting publishers to send their authors here. We just hope they realize that independent bookstores in smaller towns can put on great events and sell lots of books. We really make sure to get the word out so people know who's coming.

crowds of avid booksellers and buyers, and they'd be a great place to get some face time with your audience.

Dig around. Shake the trees. Rustle the bushes. Plant the seeds. And if in the end you're not convinced that you can get strangers to come out to bookstores, make the most of your friends and family! Husband and wife Jenoyne Adams and Michael Datcher, authors of *Resurrecting Mingus* and *Raising Fences: A Black Man's Love Story*, had what they called a "living room tour" for their books. They had friends and family around the country host events to which they'd invite other friends and family. It was a smashing success. Not only did they sell lots of books, but they couldn't have had a more captive audience.

DOING EVENTS IN SMALL TOWNS

If there's one place your publisher is sure NOT to book an event, it's in Smallsville, USA. In fact, publisher tours are defined by how many "cities" they include. The thing is, Smallsville often knows how to pack 'em in. In big cities, you're competing against multiplex movie theaters, five-star restaurants, pyrotechnic musical acts, the symphony, poetry slams, nightclubs and the opera. It's hard to get noticed if you're not a famous person. It's difficult just to get word out that you're having an event. But in small towns there's a chance that you're IT. Better to get 50 people in Smallsville than a drunken yahoo and some lunatic with too much time on his hands in Big City, America.

HITTING LOCAL BESTSELLER LISTS

If you can get on *one* national bestseller list for *one* week, your book will be a bestseller for the rest of its life and you will forever be a bestselling author. A national bestseller is not limited to books that land on the *New York Times*, *USA Today*, *Book Sense* or *Publishers Weekly* bestseller lists. Hitting the lists in large newspapers like the *Los Angeles Times*, the *San Francisco Chronicle* and the *Denver Post* count, too. You need far fewer sales to get on these lists. And if you do, suddenly your stock as a writer goes up, people take you more seriously and your press kit has a new pizzazz. People just love to throw the term "bestselling author" around—whether they're hosts of speaking events, booksellers or your mom. So how do you get to the Promised Land?

David, whose *Chicken* made the *San Francisco Chronicle* bestseller list, recommends planning as many bookstore events in as many different venues that report to bestseller lists as possible within one specific week. By befriending employees in bookstores, by asking the local sales rep of your publisher or your publicist, you can find out which stores report to bestseller lists within that region. In cities outside New York, it's typically the biggest, most prestigious bookstores (but can be smaller ones as well). These are the stores where you want to be sure to have events.

Unfortunately, if you live in New York City, you will not be able to pull off the "eventing onto bestseller list" program. The reason is that your "local" bestseller list is in *The New York Times*, which really *is* a national bestseller list in that it polls bookstores around the country.

Alan Lew and Sherril Jaffe wrote an award-winning *and* bestselling book called *One God Clapping: The Spiritual Path of a Zen Rabbi.* Alan is an excellent speaker and longtime resident of San Francisco, a city with a national bestseller list. So, the week his book came out, he and his publisher saturated the area. He did events in and out of bookstores, but wherever he did them, from community centers to synagogues, he had booksellers set up tables and sell his books so they would count on the bestseller list. He orchestrated everything so that he had a number of different media appearances the week before and the week of the events. It was a tremendous amount of work and took a lot of coordination. But it was all worth it when that weekend *One God Clapping* landed on the *San Francisco Chronicle* bestseller list.

EVENTS IN CRAZY PLACES

Please, we beg you, don't limit your events to bookstores. Keith and Kent Zimmerman, coauthors with Ralph "Sonny" Barger of *Ridin' High, Livin' Free: Hell-Raising Motorcycle Stories*, know just what we're talking about. "Signings need to be directed toward your audience, and that might not be via a conventional bookstore. For us, it's a Harley-Davidson dealership, a giant motorcycle rally, a cross-country road trip/signing campaign."

If you have a cookbook, consider having an event at a bakery or a restaurant where your book could sell long after you're gone. If your book is about birds, maybe you could do a bird walk benefit for your local Audubon Society in some gorgeous spot. If your book is about childbirth, you might do an event at a local Lamaze clinic. If you have a book about dogs, host a doggy beauty show at a local park.

Martha Manning, author of *Undercurrents*, a memoir about clinical depression, spoke at numerous gatherings of local mental health associations. Larry Dossey, author of *Healing Words*, a book about the healing power of prayer, spoke both in churches and at medical schools. Kirk Read, author of *How I Learned to Snap*, a memoir about growing up gay in the South, did a monthly reading series at a gay men's health clinic. Jamie Byng, publisher of Canongate in the U.K., was bringing out *Loaded* by Robert Sabbag, a book about drug smugglers. Jamie thought it would be wild to bring several notorious ex-smugglers together and tour them in nightclubs and cool, happening venues. Thus was born the Smuggler's Tour. Their talk of high times and fast living was chaired by the author. Needless to say, the tour was a huge success and made *Loaded* a bestseller in the U.K.

If you have a book that's hard to make an event out of, you can do what we did. Look for a hole in the market—something people want and/or need—and make up an event around it that's tangentially connected to your book. Then do it wherever anyone will have you.

Who knows where it may lead you? For us, it led straight to writing this book!

SELLING BOOKS AT NON-BOOKSTORE EVENTS

If you decide to do an event somewhere other than a bookstore, you have to figure out how to get and sell books there. It's tempting to buy books from your publisher at your discounted rate (typically 50%) and then resell them at full price. You make a lot more money per book than your standard royalty, and it may seem a lot easier than figuring out the logistics of getting someone else to sell them. For example, if your book sells for $10 in a bookstore and you buy copies for $5 apiece from your publisher, you can make $5 a book. Whereas, with a standard 7½% royalty, you'll make 75¢ a copy.

If you're strapped for cash, this may be your best route. Otherwise, you're better off either bringing in a local bookseller or having a sponsoring organization buy books. Why?

- Most contracts technically bar the resale of books bought at the author discount (though most publishers look the other way at this very common practice as long as the author isn't buying books in very large numbers).
- You will make contact with a bookseller, which can lead to other events and general support of your book.
- A sponsoring organization that's buying books may decide to put information about your book in its newsletter or gift store (and if it buys in large enough quantities, it's going to get a higher discount, too). Ultimately, the organization will be motivated to get people to the event so that it won't be left with a stack of books.

If you're asked how many books a bookseller or organization should order, always overestimate without being pie-in-the-sky. It's a form of torture to witness people asking to buy a copy of your book only to have them be turned away because there are no more to sell.

ABSENT BOOKS AND THE POWER OF PERSISTENCE

After getting herself booked into a big event, a first-time author contacted the assistant publicist at her publisher's to make sure plenty of her books would be showing up. As a backup, she actually lugged 20 copies of her book with her. When she got there, she contacted the person in charge of books and was horrified to learn that her publisher had not only been a nightmare to deal with, but hadn't sent any of her books. "After the event, I quickly sold all my copies. Imagine my chagrin when reader after reader came up to me the whole rest of the weekend and asked where they could buy my book. I called my publisher and they said, 'Well, we didn't set up the event in the first place, so . . .' As if I'd done a bad thing by setting up my own event. When I got home, I called the head of publicity and expressed my displeasure in a rational but passionate way. To my amazement, he apologized and sent me a free box of my books. I never had that problem again."

Another first-time author wanted to do a book event in New York City. Her publicist told her that this would be impossible—that New York stores are the hardest to book. Well, this author had a lot of friends there, so she decided to rent a small theater and fill it herself. Then she asked if her publisher would sell books there. They said no, a bookstore would have to do that. Well, she asked, what bookstore would they recommend? No bookstore would do it, they said. Using the PYPIP Guide to Perseverance, the author called bookstore after bookstore in New York City. No luck. Finally, she went into the Barnes & Noble on Fifth Avenue and talked to Carla Oliver, the community relations manager. Her great pitch persuaded Carla to come sell her books at the theater. It was a very successful event, and afterwards Carla invited the author to do an event at her store. It seems no one had told Carla that it was impossible for a first-time author to hold an event in New York City. "What a great sight it was," the author recalls, "to see my book in the beautiful display that Carla created in the window of the original B&N, right there on Fifth Avenue."

If you're not personally lugging books with you to an outside event, don't just assume your books are going to magically show up. MAKE SURE the books have been sent and will arrive on time. What's worse than not having enough books at an event? Having NO books. It happens.

Writers' Conferences, Book Festivals and Fairs

As part of your tour or your continual event schedule, locate and contact any and all appropriate public events—conferences, festivals and fairs—where writers and readers gather. If you can get yourself on a good panel and things go reasonably well, you will certainly sell some books. And you don't have to generate the crowd yourself. All you have to do is show up, do your job, be your fabulous self and sell tons of books.

Of course, you'll also meet many writers from all over the country. It's important to meet other writers. Famous, infamous or unknown. Watch them closely. See what they do well. See what they don't. Go to as many events as you can. Help out if you feel up to it. People who put on these events appreciate your willingness to help and may well invite you to future events.

Bruce Lane ran the South Carolina Book Festival for many years and learned a lot about what kinds of authors shine at such events. If you want to get into a festival, we suggest following Bruce's advice: "Be persistent but not annoying, aggressive but friendly, confident but flexible. In short, be willing to fit in to what I'm doing with the festival overall—remember, a book festival features lots of writers, not just one—and trust that when the event rolls around, you will have every opportunity to promote yourself and your work, no matter which time slot, day or strange panel discussion you may be assigned."

Some writers make careers of conferences, festivals and fairs and go back to the same events year after year. Bruce has insight into why people get asked back: "Authors are welcomed back because a) they're prolific, so

RAISING A BUNCH OF MONEY AND SELLING A BUNCH OF BOOKS

Remember Regina Louise, author of the memoir *Somebody's Someone* about growing up in the foster care system? Regina timed the opening of her own nonprofit organization to coincide with the release of her book and hosted a gala event for 400 people. Local dignitaries, clients of the salon she runs, friends, admirers and social butterflies were invited. So were a dozen young women who were currently in the foster care system. During the event, Regina asked these young women to come up on the stage. One by one they talked about their dreams in life. There wasn't a dry eye in the house.

Regina then read from her book and showed her documentary (see pages 259–60). She raised a bunch of money for her charity while everyone had a ton of fun and ate great food (much of which was donated because it was a fund-raiser). She also sold all 250 books that her local bookseller brought to the event. You can be sure the bookseller became an instant fan and mouthpiece for Regina and her book.

they always have something new to promote, b) they understand and appreciate the festival and what we're trying to accomplish, c) they're not prima donnas and do not think of themselves as celebrities (we suffer no egos here), and d) they're like family. 'D,' of course, is the most important factor, with 'C' running a close second. The writers who take time to get to know folks, chat endlessly and play well with others—those are the ones who get asked back. The ones who zip in and out as if this is a business transaction, well, one appearance is quite enough, thank you."

Lastly, Bruce has this advice for writers on panels: "A good panelist needs to be witty, intelligent and a good listener. Listening to the other panelists and the moderator is by far the most important aspect. There's nothing worse than an author who's clearly sitting there like a spider, waiting for a chance to read from his new novel or tell some long, prepackaged story. Panels are only interesting when they're spontaneous, which is why I think the best panelists come with an open mind."

"It's My Party!"

Many authors count their book parties among their all-time favorite events. A book party can be a great way to begin your tour. This is where you announce your book to the world, celebrate yourself as a writer and thank all those who've helped. It can cost a lot and have little value in terms of book sales, but the right party at the right time can raise your profile . . . and be a blast.

For the most part, publishers no longer pay for book parties. Not even the invitations. Certainly, let your publisher know about your party and ask if they'll contribute, but don't count on it.

Throw your own book party only if:

- You're independently wealthy.
- There's a chance of luring the press with a newsworthy cause.
- You have a fun theme around which you can construct a party.
- You can get a company or organization to sponsor the party.
- You can tie it into a charity event.
- You can turn your party into a "must" event.
- You can get a local or national celebrity to be the host.

Jack Boulware, author of *San Francisco Bizarro*, co-creator of the San Francisco literary festival Litquake and veteran book-party thrower, says, "If you make your book party more of an event, it stands a better chance of getting press attention. Get a press release out with plenty of advance time. And an image that can be printed in papers and magazines." We also recommend inviting a local bookseller to sell books. Get a band, a musician or DJ.

Meg Cohen Ragas and Karen Kozlowski wrote an illustrated social history of lipstick called *Read My Lips*. Being the fabulous gals they are, they asked a liquor company to sponsor their event, which was held at the Georgio Armani store in downtown San Francisco. It worked. Everyone got free booze in a gorgeous setting, and the local press covered the party.

PREPARING FOR YOUR FIRST INTERVIEW

You've already done the bulk of your prepub publicity, set up events and distributed your galleys (if you had them) far and wide. You've pitched articles and created buzz locally and nationally. You've contacted bookstores all over creation. You've flagged down book groups and organizations that might be interested in your subject. You've pitched yourself and your book to other writers, journalists and media people.

Then it happens. You've got your first interview. Your book hasn't even come out yet, and you're nervous because this is the FIRST ONE. How do you tackle your jumpy stomach? What do you do if your brain freezes? What if someone attacks you? How do you get your agenda across while appearing to answer the questions you're being asked? What if your fear of being exposed as an inarticulate buffoon leads to acting like an inarticulate buffoon?

First and foremost, there are three things you can do immediately to avoid looking b-a-d:

1. Rehearse,
2. Rehearse, and
3. Rehearse.

Almost everyone is going to ask you: "So what is your book about?" You must have a pithy, fascinating answer that lasts under a minute. Sound familiar? If it doesn't, start popping the ginkgo biloba. This is, of course, YOUR PITCH! This will be the backbone of your media presentation. Write and rewrite and practice and repractice. Don't just do it by yourself into the mirror. Do it for friends. Do it for relatives. No matter how comfortable you are in private, the natural instinct when you're on the spot is to freeze up and squirm. And the first step toward overcoming that instinct is to have the pitch for your book down so cold you can do it in your sleep. Which will help when you have to do a radio interview at 4:15 in the morning.

When you're rehearsing, have a friend do things to trip you up. Ask you the questions you fear most. Misquote facts. Practice doing your job. Listen carefully, tell your stories, sell your book and have as much fun as you can.

Reread your book. Funny how, after all that time away from it, you can forget a lot of what you wrote. Once you've refreshed your memory, come up with several additional stories from your book. And the process of writing it. Or any fascinating bits of information, if that's appropriate. These are all weapons in your entertainment arsenal, and you will need them. Again, rehearse them until they're second nature.

Have a clear agenda. This will include talking about any events you've lined up. And what's funny, interesting, unique and special about your book. You want to entice without giving away the whole story. If you can easily slip your title into the piece, by all means do so. But do NOT force it; you will almost always come across looking tacky and self-serving.

Study the interviewer beforehand if you can. Or if your publicist has lined up the event, find out what the show or journalist is like. Listen to the segments that precede yours. This can be a great way to get an easy laugh, through what professionals refer to as a "callback," a comic reference to something that has already transpired. Portland radio journalist Daria O'Neill says, "If it's a TV or radio show and you've seen or heard some of it prior to your appearance, absolutely bring up the content of an earlier moment if it can be tied in at all. This will a) endear you instantly to the hosts/listeners/most avid viewers, and b) make you seem like a necessary segment of a greater whole."

Start getting ready 15 minutes before your interview is scheduled to start. Stretch your body out. If you know any yoga, do some; if you don't, learn some. Do some deep breathing. Go over your pitch and your stories once again. Picture yourself having a great time. Being funny, relaxed, totally in control.

If you're doing a live interview, bring a glass of water with you. For dry mouth, of course. But also to give you a moment to compose yourself if you need it.

Most people think being interviewed is all about talking. They're wrong. Being a good listener is as important as being a good talker. Be present. The best interview almost always have some wonderful improvisation in them. Being in the moment makes it possible to react spontaneously to anything that comes your way. And it's so much easier to be relaxed and spontaneous if you're well prepared with material you know like the back of your hand.

But no matter how much you're prepared for being interviewed, you cannot possibly be completely prepared. Yes, of course, control what you can control, look good, be well-spoken, have a pitch you love, some stories you're confident in and an agenda that makes sense. But once it starts, be open to the fun that presents itself. Don't freak out if something goes wrong or you make a mistake. Sometimes the most human, endearing moments come from snafus and boo-boos. Laugh at yourself and show you don't take the whole thing too seriously. A little good-natured self-deprecation goes a long way.

One more word: passion. Hopefully that's what has been fueling your book the whole time, and that's what will make you a good interview. Your passion, in the end, is what will sell your book and make you an interesting, captivating speaker.

Craft your passion.

Rehearse your passion.

Then let your passion flow.

Diana Jordan, whose show *Between the Lines* airs on the AP Radio Network, puts it this way: "Of course, you have to be able to say what your book is about. You have to nail it. But I want to have an animated dialogue with someone who's relaxed and confident, who knows his topic inside and out. People like that don't just know the basics; they know the nuances, and they have a great breadth and depth of knowledge. But, most of all, I'm looking for passion. I want them to communicate their passion. The driest of subjects can come to life that way."

10 ESSENTIAL RULES FOR BEING A GOOD INTERVIEWEE

1) Maintain good posture.
2) Don't play with/pick at sleeve, hair, face, fingers.
3) Make eye contact.
4) Breathe deeply.
5) Have lots of energy without being manic.
6) Don't force a smile.
7) Don't panic if something goes wrong. Try to play with it.
8) Keep your sense of humor—no matter what.
9) Listen carefully.
10) Have fun.

BUILDING BUZZ

In a sense, everything you've been doing from the time your book was accepted has been to generate and maintain buzz. But what is buzz? Where is it? And how do you get some of it?

Buzz is ethereal. It flits about, coming and going with seemingly random whimsy. If you could bottle it, you'd be a kazillionaire. Some people can create it. Sometimes it appears to have a mind of its own.

Just one word at the right time from the right person at the right place can create huge buzz. Buzz can be sparked by a celebrity, a dignitary, a member of the literati or the aristocracy, the right reviewer or your big-mouthed Aunt Sally. We all know that an appearance on *Fresh Air*, *Oprah* or the *Today* show can make a whole career. When David Sedaris went on NPR and read his story about being an elf at Christmas in a department store, the response was so overwhelming that it launched him into bestsellerdom.

> *"The difference is slight, to the influence of an author, whether he is read by five hundred readers or by five hundred thousand; if he can select the five hundred, he reaches the five hundred thousand."*
>
> **—Henry Adams**

Because buzz is so much like the wind, there is no one way to create it. And you never know which of the things you're doing will be the thing that makes the buzz that launches your book. Maybe it's the book fair you attended, the postcard you sent to your college roommate, the e-mail you whisked off to your favorite local columnist.

SELLING FOR FREE: THE ULTIMATE BUZZ BUILDER

Seth Godin's book *Permission Marketing* posited the idea that if you want to grab someone's attention, you first need to get permission with some kind of bait. Free bait. That's why this marketing guru extraordinaire decided to offer up a third of his book for nothing. Guess how many people asked for that free sample? A whopping 175,000. And then a healthy percentage of those 175,000 went on to buy the book.

With *Unleashing the Ideavirus*, he took his idea one step beyond. He decided this one would cost $0.00. That's right, he gave the whole thing away for free over the Internet. As a result, the book has been downloaded over two million times. Sounds nuts, until you consider that Godin's consulting business skyrocketed because he was successfully getting his ideas out to lots and lots of people.

Seth had to keep on figuring out ways to one-up himself. Since he couldn't lower the price any further, he decided to make packaging part of his hook. The result was *Purple Cow*, which came in a custom-designed milk carton. Again, the book would be free, but the carton plus shipping and handling cost a mere $5. If you're trying to imagine bookstores selling books in milk cartons, you've underestimated Seth's brilliance. He bypassed bookstores altogether. Instead, he hooked up with the hip business magazine *Fast Company* and sold the books directly through them as a special one-time promotion. In five days, they sold 5,000 copies. This got the buzz jumping and buyers flocked to Seth's Web site, where he now offered an unusual deal: 12 copies for 60 bucks. You either had to buy a dozen or none at all. This multicopy deal encouraged buyers to circulate copies to colleagues and friends. Which, of course, spread buzz like butter. Within 14 days, Seth had sold his entire 10K first printing.

Yes, it's hard to make money selling books for free. And if you want to be published by a major publisher and you were to ever suggest such an idea, they'd look at you like you're from Bizarro (Seth both self-publishes and works with major publishers, depending on the nature of the project). But Seth has this wisdom to share about why you should at least consider the possibility of dangling free bait no matter what your book: "If you're writing a book to make money, you're doing the wrong thing. Every once in a while, someone wins. But every once in a while someone wins the lottery, and that's not a reason to buy a ticket. Similarly, to pray to get on *Oprah* is absurd. The reason to write a book is to spread ideas. If your ideas spread, you can do so many things. That's why you need to find as many ways to give as many copies of your book away as you can afford."

But one common denominator we've noticed is that buzz seems to follow people who are willing and able to stand out from the crowd, think outside the book box, take a few calculated risks.

Andy Behrman, author of *Electroboy*, a memoir about his struggle with manic depression, is a king of buzz. He plastered Manhattan's Upper West Side with posters of his book. Someone from *The Rosie O'Donnell Show* saw them and invited him on as a guest. That week, he sold thousands of copies of his book.

Since you never quite know whence the buzz will come, cultivate it constantly. Those who wait for buzz to find them often wait forever. Every once in a while, you get lucky with some free buzz, but most of the time you have to earn it.

If you're fortunate enough to get a little buzz, spread it around like a busy little bee pollinating a field full of fertile flowers. Tell your editor, your publicity and marketing people, your agent and all the assistants, your boss or your secretary, your friends, family, your mailing list and, of course, your team. Let them know that you're counting on them to spread the word.

Often we humans wait until a bandwagon is already moving before we jump on board. If you do get buzz from a raving review, a boffo endorsement, a gaudy blurb or really any interest WHATSOEVER in your book, jump on it and run with it until the cows come home and you've milked them for all they're worth.

PART III

Getting the Word Out

CHAPTER 11

LAUNCHING YOUR BOOK AND KEEPING IT ALIVE

"No one interested in being published in our time can afford to be so naïve as to believe a book will make it merely because it's good."

—RICHARD CURTIS

Okay, you did it. All your inspiration, perspiration and determination have finally paid off. Your book has come kicking and screaming into the world, and it's time to enjoy the kudos of your peers. Time to kick back and party. Right?

WRONG!

Now the real work begins.

Now you have to get people to actually BUY your book.

Through a combination of events, national and local media coverage and appearances, creative marketing, connections with organizations and corporations and word you spread, you want the big beautiful buzz storm you've been generating to peak on your pub date. Here's why: Your book is considered new for just three months. After that, it's old. In a year or two, unless you do something to prevent it, your book can die an early death. So you have to pack everything you can into those first three months. And we mean EVERYTHING.

So how in the world do you do this? Did you start spending every possible minute marketing and promoting your book three weeks before your pub date? Well, come your pub date, you've got to double that. How do you double every possible minute? It's amazing what a cocktail of caffeine, adrenaline and desire can do.

Revisit your old publicity and marketing plan. Whip out that wish list. What has worked so far? What hasn't? Have you more clearly redefined your audience? Have you found that your children's book, *Mr. Poopy Pants*, is extremely popular with college students? Have you discovered that Mobile, Alabama, is mad for your book on crawdads? Have you realized that you'll have to find a way to promote your book on cross-dressing lacrosse goalies of the 1940s outside bookstores?

Creating the buzz necessary to successfully bring your book into the limelight is a bit like juggling 14 balls of all different weights. Some of the lighter balls might not come down for a very long time, while you'll be catching and tossing the heavier ones every single day. By pinpointing exactly what you need to focus on, you can figure out which balls need immediate attention and which can hang in the air for a while.

Throughout this book, we've endeavored to lay things out chronologically; in this chapter, that's impossible. Many of these tasks come at you too fast; often they arrive all at once. But we've got to start somewhere, so let's begin in your own backyard.

LOCAL LOVE

Take your book with you to the grocery store, to your favorite restaurant, to baseball games. Go back to those mailcarriers, barbers and barkeeps. Local authors, social gadflies, event organizers, gossipmongers. These are all great sources of local buzz. Can't you just hear it?

"Did you know that (insert your name here) just wrote a book? It's in all the stores."

"You don't say? (Insert your name)? You've got to be kidding. Are you sure it's the same person?"

"Oh, yeah. The book's called (insert your book title)."

"Really? (Insert your name) wrote (insert your book title)? I'm shocked. Is it any good?"

"Yeah, actually it is."

And that's how buzz gets started.

Throw that book launch party we gently suggested you plan back in Chapter 10. See if you can get your friends to fete you at get-togethers to which they invite all their friends.

BOOKSTORE LOVE

Bookstores are certainly not the only places you want to sell books, but you do want to make the most of them. This can mean everything from befriending bookstore employees to making sure your books are in stores and signing them if they are, to getting your book prominently placed in stores, to having events and getting lots of readers to come and buy your book.

Make your hometown the epicenter of your bookstore efforts. If you can get a good blast locally, the aftershocks will sometimes result in sales at bookstores hither and yon. You know those relationships you've been cultivating with all the people at your local bookstores? By attending events? By buying books? Well, now it's time to pick the fruits of your labors. Time to get booksellers jazzed about your book. And don't just talk to the managers. Try to talk to everyone in the store at one time or another, from the events people to the people ringing up your book at the cash registers. Show them all in your charming, humble yet aggressive way that you're going to help them sell a lot of copies.

Let your local bookstore know that you'd love to speak to book clubs and at conferences or events. Ask about any local critic or reviewer you can send a book to. Any journalist who might do a story about your book. A radio show that might have you on.

But don't stop there. Anytime you go someplace outside your hometown, whether it's for publicizing your book, attending your Uncle Rodolfo's wedding or beaming in for the annual Star Trek convention, make time to visit local bookstores. As many as you can. Introduce yourself. Sign stock (insider lingo for "copies"). David sent a personalized postcard to every bookseller who participates in Book Sense, introducing himself and his book *Chicken*, and thanking booksellers for their support. Several stores invited him to come and read as a result. Other writers we know have packed their cars with books and traveled across the country, introducing themselves in person to booksellers from coast to coast.

While most booksellers are delighted to meet authors, a few curmudgeonly sorts won't want to give you the time of day. Odd as it seems, they may treat you like a hungry mosquito on a muggy day. Just remember, in the words of Don Corleone: It's always business, never personal.

HOW DO YOU GET TO MADISON SQUARE GARDEN?

Bob Nelson, book marketing guru and author of *1001 Ways to Reward Employees*, was in New York City on business. He was staying in a seedy hotel across from Madison Square Garden, but he took an extra day to promote his book. He ripped out the bookstores section of the Yellow Pages in his hotel room, went out and hailed a cab, and asked the cabbie to take him to as many of the bookstores as possible in the 10 hours before his flight. As Bob went into one bookstore, the cabbie determined the next closest one, and so forth throughout the day. Once inside each bookstore, Bob introduced himself. He checked and signed stock. He spoke with the bookstore manager and tried to generate excitement about his book. "Most authors don't like to visit bookstores where their books may not be available," Bob says, "but I love doing it! It's a chance to make a sale. Just being there says 'I cared enough to show up' and 'Gee, if you had some copies of my book, I could have signed them for you.'" Bob paid $220 to visit 27 bookstores in Manhattan that day. Five years later, he was back where he initially hailed that cab, this time speaking at Madison Square Garden about his book.

Use bookstores nicely and make it easy for them to use you. Thank everyone. By being a friendly, helpful, sweet professional, you can go from having one lonely copy to having a prominently displayed stack that gets reordered whether you're there or not.

The Power of Independents

While we absolutely advocate pursuing bookstore chains, it's imperative to get independent bookstores excited about selling your book, because this is something you can do on your own without the help of your publisher. At many independents, employees are encouraged to write little reviews of books they're enthusiastic about and make picks of their favorite new releases so they can suggest books to readers who might not be aware of them.

In fact, a number of years ago, independent booksellers got together and created Book Sense, an organization with a list of recommendations by independent booksellers from all around the country. Both the list and a display of the picks of the month are front and center in the hundreds of bookstores that participate in this program. And one of the best ways to get your book on this list is to ask your independent booksellers, locally and wherever you travel, to send in a recommendation for your book. The more recommendations you can get, the better your chances of landing on the list.

Stock Tips: Signing Books

When you walk into a bookstore, wait for a lull in the storm, then introduce yourself to the staff as the author of your book and ask if they have any copies you can sign. John Evans, co-owner of Diesel Bookstore in Oakland, California, advises, "Authors will come in and say things like 'Do you have such-and-such a book?' But it's *their* book. Better to be straightforward. Be positive and an advocate without being condescending or pushy."

It's so gratifying when your name comes up in a computer, your book magically appears in front of you and you get to sign copies of it. We urge you not to deprive yourself of this thrill. And it's very good for business. Marilyn Paige, the community relations manager of Philadelphia's biggest Barnes & Noble, says, "Yes, absolutely, sign stock! This kind of face time is very important. And it can possibly lead to an event."

While you're in a store, make sure that the number of books on the shelves jibes with the number of books in the store's computer. Bookstores will not reorder your book if they think they have them already on hand. And while you're at the computer, see if there's a way to ask if they'd be willing to order more copies of your book. Here's what Bob Nelson did: "In three out of four Waldenbooks, an employee would say, 'Well, the computer says we have four copies. Let's go see if we can find them.' They wouldn't be on the shelf. The clerk would say, 'Let me go check in back.' And after 20 minutes he'd return with two copies. When you've gotten the same thing from 43 Waldenbooks, you know something's wrong. I'd say something like 'If all your books are ordered centrally, and your computer says you have books in stock but they aren't actually on the shelf for someone to purchase, it seems to me you will never reorder this book!'" Because he went out and asked, his book went from two or three copies in 60 Waldenbooks to three to five copies in 140 stores—and on automatic reorder when the number of copies dropped below five. Bob would then focus his attention on another bookstore chain or on the independent bookstores.

It helps to have a postcard in hand when you go around to bookstores. This makes it easy for booksellers to look up your book. If you don't have a postcard, or your postcard doesn't list any blurbs or reviews, bring your

When you sign books, not only do you get to meet store employees, but you'll also get a little sticker on your book that says AUTOGRAPHED COPY. The value of your book rises, and that little sticker twinkling on your cover really draws people's attention. Plus, if you sign your books, there's a good chance the booksellers will display them nicely somewhere. They'll also be less likely to return them.

handout. If a bookstore doesn't have your book, this can help you seduce them into buying it.

If the store doesn't have your book and the clerk you're talking to isn't the person who orders books, you may need to take a step up the ladder. If you do this right, you can turn what seems like a setback into an opportunity. Sometimes just showing up and making polite conversation will get your book ordered. We know authors who've walked into independents and chains looking for their book, been told there were no copies in the store and had clerks take it upon themselves to order some on the spot. The authors didn't even have to ask. It's cool walking out of a bookstore knowing that copies of your book are already winging their way toward your readers. For more on selling your book to bookstores, see Chapter 12.

Bookstore Real Estate: Placement in Stores

You know those big display windows that stare at you as you walk into a bookstore? The ones full of blockbuster bestsellers and the bestsellers of tomorrow you never heard of today? Or those books that beckon to you from front display tables? Or by the sides of cash registers? Often they're in these center-stage positions because a publisher paid for them to be there. This is an example of *co-op marketing*, a joint venture in which publisher and bookseller combine to promote your book.

This whole cop-op marketing business begins with your publisher deciding to spend marketing dollars on your book—not something that happens frequently. Booksellers have to agree that this is a title worthy of a prominent space in their stores. This is a big decision for them because they make so little on each book, and they don't want to have a dud in their window. Michael Powell, owner of Powell's Books in Portland, Oregon, says the average net profit is between 0% and 2% per book. And often there are losses. This is why booksellers have to be sure that the books they accept co-op dollars on are going to fly off the shelves.

Sometimes a bookstore and your publisher will decide these co-op dollars should be spent to promote holidays or other themes (pets, politics, back-to-school) or perhaps your upcoming event in that store. Your publisher sweetens the bookstore's pot by helping to defray the costs of getting in calendar listings, doing mailings, sending out press releases or making and displaying signage.

This special treatment not only improves your location in the bookstore, but also increases the number of copies the store will order. And the more the bookstore orders, the more they try to sell your book.

Let's imagine there are 100,000 books in a bookstore. In all likelihood, 90,000 are single copies displayed with only skinny spines showing. Of the remaining 10,000, 7,000 are *The Da Vinci Code.* Okay, not exactly. Point is, multiple copies of a small number of bestselling titles make up those 10,000 books. Of these, let's say 5,000 are placed face out in the stacks. Of the remaining 5,000, maybe 4,965 are on display tables. Of the remaining 35, let's say 25 are near cash registers and 10 are in the window. That's .0001%. So you can see why competition is so dog-eat-dog for this space. Let's face it, many a book buyer has walked into many a bookstore just to "browse" and walked out with some cool-looking book whose cry of "Buy me!" from the window or a display table couldn't be resisted. You want that book to be yours.

But here's the sad truth. It's unlikely that your book will be getting any of that sweet co-op money. Still, there are a number of ways to get out of the slums and onto the Rodeo Drive of bookstores. First off, go in and sign books. And after you've signed, ask the bookseller if your book can be placed in a more prominent position.

Secondly, don't just assume that your publisher will never give you co-op money even if it wasn't forthcoming at the time of publication. Come up with hooks to convince your publisher that these dollars are worth spending. Remember how we talked about bookstores loving tie-ins to holidays, anniversaries of events, special months (Black History Month, National Poetry Month or Children's Awareness Month)? Find out what bookstores are promoting on their windows and tables. Notify your publisher and see if you can go along for the ride. Also be sure to ask your publisher if any of the chains are doing particularly well with your book. If, for example, it's going bonkers at Borders, you'd be smart to ask your publisher if a co-op situation with them might make sense.

Don't go into a bookstore and move your book to a more prominent location without asking first. No one will be able to find it if it's not on the shelf where it's supposed to be. And then, if someone asks for it, the bookseller will look it up on the computer, will see that it's in stock and won't reorder it. So, in the end, no one will be able to find it or buy it and the bookstore will never order it again. However, you can rearrange copies (or the one copy, as the case may sadly be) of your book so that your cover is facing out.

You can also call bookstores around the country and dazzle them with your amazing hook. If you get a nibble with your hook, follow up with an e-mail or fax of a tailored press release. Give them the information they need to determine that your book is display-worthy. While you're at it, suggest an event if it seems at all doable.

Lastly, do events in stores. This will get your book in the window and/or on a display table. And having signage up for your book when the event is announced is like having a semipermanent ad in place.

MAKING AN EVENTFUL EVENT

You've already put in all the work to set up your events, to invite the media to cover you and to contact friends, relatives and other interested parties. If all goes as planned, you'll show up at your event and the throngs will be waiting with open arms. You'll be witty, smart, articulate and thoughtful, and you'll get a standing ovation and sell boxes of books. You'll get invited to speak at other events all over the country. A movie producer who just happens to be in the audience will option your book and make a boffo film.

The chances of all this happening are minuscule. However, if you do the necessary work to get the word out, if you prepare an event that perfectly suits you and your book, if you show up on time and smell good, you can make any number of these things happen. Dan Rhodes, author of *Timoleon Vieta Come Home*, met his wife at one of his readings!

What to Do, What to Read

Author escort Crofton Diack of Portland, Oregon, told us, "I get authors who show up at events and ask me, 'What should I read?' And in my head I'm always thinking, 'Are you kidding? Kinda late for that question, isn't it?'"

Preparation is key. And you should be thinking of your event as a show. As Melissa Mytinger, marketing manager of Cody's Books in Berkeley, California, says, "In this day and age, people expect authors to be entertainers. That's an unfair expectation. If you don't feel entirely comfortable in front of an audience, forgo bookstore readings and talks. It's *okay*!" But if you're up for it, then embrace your inner entertainer. Even if your presentation is about something as serious as death and taxes, or as dry as the history of the Gobi desert, more people will come (and, more importantly, buy books) if your event is entertaining. Chances are, you're not going to charge money for your show. Your payment comes in the form of book sales and word of mouth. As an added bonus, you're also getting your books in the stores, having them prominently displayed and revving up booksellers. So, as you put together your show, do your research and go to see as many events as you can. See for yourself what works and what doesn't.

Your show should be tailored to what you do, who you are, what your book is, where you're performing and what you're comfortable with. Melissa adds, "The best presenters are people who enjoy what they're doing. Lots of authors don't, and it really shows. If your publicist hasn't done Events 101 with you, insist on it. If this doesn't work, or if you don't

HAVE A BALL! GET YOUR FREAK ON!

No matter how goofy or out of left field an idea may seem, if it gets you positive attention, it counts as a good one. And if it has nothing to do with your book? Who cares? Every little bit helps:

Walking around a book convention dressed in a sandwich board.

Sitting up in a tree for months to protest the slaughtering of our environment.

Holding a rock-and-roll spelling bee.

All of these have been done to great success. Jonathan Ames, author of the novel *Wake Up, Sir!*, arranged a boxing match with another artist. He trained hard, got himself in rip-roaring shape and approached the bout with a seriousness that turned the event into a happening. Hundreds of people showed up, he and his opponent had a tremendous fight and the media ate it up with a fork and spoon. Even though Jonathan "lost" the bout, he won a ton of press as the literary author who took up the bloodiest of sports.

FYI: His books have nothing to do with boxing, but this didn't stop the press from mentioning and praising his work.

have a publicist, talk to other writers or experts who have toured and pick their brains about what to do and what not to do. You should also do a little research about the store you're doing an event at. Just take ten minutes and look through their Web site, see what kinds of events they've done in the past, get a feel for the place."

You may not be a professional comedian, a master storyteller or a highly trained entertainer. But if you display your passion, people will leave your event feeling excited about you and your book. Remember, passion is contagious. Make sure everyone at your events catches yours.

LOOKING, FEELING AND SMELLING GOOD

People are often confused about what to wear to an event. There are no fashion "shoulds" here. It's more important to feel comfortable in your favorite outfit than to go out and buy something that makes you feel as if you're not in your own skin.

Just as you need to feel comfortable when you walk into the room, so it helps to create a feeling of comfort around you as you do your event. Do you prefer to sit or stand? Do you prefer a cup of green tea to water? Are you more comfortable mingling and talking before the show or going off on your own and gathering your thoughts?

Susan Wooldridge, author of *Poemcrazy*, has these words of advice about events and appearances: "Make sure you've got the right shoes. You want to feel spiffy. You also want to get there a bit early and create a little of your own atmosphere. I sometimes bring my own lamp or flowers. Something to create a setting. And I try to sit quietly and ground myself beforehand."

Have your hair nicely coiffed. Don't wear clothes that are so tight they make you feel uncomfortable. Again, avoid nervous fidgets, tugs, picks and pulls. Yes, check your zippers and/or buttons. Give yourself a once-over twice in the mirror. Bring a fashion-friendly friend to check you out. Or, if the vibe is right, ask the host to give you a final inspection. If done with sufficient charm, this can be very endearing.

KEEP IT SHORT

Unless you're doing a workshop or you're the greatest reader ever, 15 minutes of reading is perfect. Leave them wanting more. Your whole event, including Q&A (more on that in a moment), should last approximately half an hour—even if it seems like everything is going well and people are loving it. After a certain point, people drift away and then they don't buy books. You can always hang around afterwards and chat if you want.

STALL A LITTLE

Whatever you do, DO NOT start on time. First of all, a certain percentage of people show up late. Second, it gives the audience time to bond in their admiration and respect for you. Third, it's just gauche to start on time. That's why they call it *fashionably* late.

The general rule of thumb is that one should start an event not less than 5 and not more than 10 minutes after the announced starting time. Sometimes a store employee will want to start right on time. Ask nicely, without being a pain, if you can wait a couple of minutes—you're sure some friends are going to show up.

MANAGE YOUR INTRODUCTION

Have someone introduce you. Make sure she tells the audience that you'll be signing books after the event. Also make sure the same person comes on afterwards and thanks everyone and reminds them that you'll be signing books.

Some people at bookstores go to great lengths to write introductions for writers. Some do not. Here's a generic introduction you can use if your introducer is unprepared:

"(Insert your name) has been a (put in relevant work information here) for many years and has written (insert your writing credits if you have any). This is his/her first/second/whatever book. (Title of book) has been called (short, pithy quote from a review or endorsement). She/he has also (insert any additional interesting information here—awards, colorful jobs, etc.). There will be a brief question-and-answer period, and the author will sign books afterwards. And now, ladies and gentleman, please welcome (your name)."

START WITH A STORY

Begin your event with a story, an anecdote or a joke. This will give you a chance to connect directly with your audience. Your story could be about how you came to write your book and get it published. About the subject of your book. Or about something completely different. But it must be entertaining, funny, inspirational, witty, honest, revealing or deep. You should have a couple of these stories prepared, written and practiced. Write them out longhand on index cards; this will help you remember each word. Also, you can take the index cards with you during your performance. Even if you don't need them, they're a wonderful binky.

Be open to a spontaneous anecdote that presents itself. What happened to you on the way to the event. What you read in the paper that day. Something that's occurring in the moment. Melissa Mytinger says, "Make speaking extemporaneously your goal. Yes, it's a skill, but it's one that can be learned and developed, and it will make your event so much better if you can do it well. This is certainly no substitute for writing a great book, but writers can work hard at and improve their public-speaking skills."

It's important during your event, as indeed it is in life, to be in the moment, aware of your surroundings and in tune with any comedy and/or tragedy that's happening while you're speaking. We once witnessed writer/comic/actor Kevin Meany ("Uncle Buck") at an event. Observing that a man had fallen asleep in the audience, he quietly placed the microphone under the man's schnoz, and the sounds of the guy sawing logs echoed through the room. The whole place cracked up. No, it had nothing to do with what he was talking about, but Kevin made lots of fans that night.

Pay attention to what's around you. You never know what might get a laugh. Is a life-size cutout of Captain Underpants next to the podium? Point him out! Have some fun! It will loosen everyone—you, included—right up.

LEAVE 'EM GUESSING

You want to give the audience a real flavor for your book, without giving too much away. Many savvy authors like to read just up to a climactic scene and stop just before the climax. If your audience wants to know what happens, they have to buy the book. You should probably read a little from the beginning, unless there's some compelling reason not to. This will give people a context. Then read a couple of self-contained passages that do not need much setting up. Do not tell the whole story of your book. Better to think of it as reading a couple of short stories.

> *"How many readings can you go to and hear the same lament: 'I am deep and I am in pain. It is raining outside.'"*
> **—Greg Gatenby**

Try to memorize as much of your presentation as you can. Then, when you go up and have the book with you, you'll be able to make periodic eye contact with the audience.

Always bring a copy of your book with you to any event. We were at the L.A. Book Fair when suddenly a crazed publicist came by screaming, "Does anyone have a copy of Oliver Sack's new book? He's reading in five minutes and he lost his copy!" And there was the bestselling author of *Awakenings,* following the bellowing publicist and looking very much like a man who mistook his wife for a hat. They finally found a copy but actually had to buy it!

Take your time. Pick out places in your reading where you can pause and look out at the audience. Vary your rhythm and tempo. Find places to go fast and places to go slow. Places to be loud and places to be soft. Bruce Lane, ex-director of the South Carolina Book Festival, adds: "This may seem obvious, but more writers than not sound bored and emotionless when they read, as if they've done it a million times or just never got past that singsong 'reading in front of your high school English class' method. So it's exhilarating to hear writers read their own works with a joy and excitement that almost makes you feel they're hearing their own words for the very first time."

Do not ignore the importance of a Big Finish. You want to go out with a bang. Something that's tragic, or hysterical, or lyrical. It should be you at your best.

But again, DO NOT give away the ending of your book.

OUTSIDE-THE-BOX EVENTING

Don't be afraid to step outside the box and do something totally unexpected. But make it reflect the nature of your book. Beth Lisick, author of *Everybody into the Pool,* does many of her readings with a live band behind her—a perfect complement to her hip stories about pop culture. Jamie Oliver, a.k.a. The Naked Chef, cooks fabulous dishes from recipes in his cookbooks at his "readings." Gayle Brandeis, author of *Fruitflesh: Seeds of Inspiration for Women Who Write,* created events that perfectly reflected the content of her guide to writing: "Because *Fruitflesh* is very much about tapping into the body, the senses, as a source of creativity, I offered hands-on experiences, sensory meditations with fruit, at the beginning of my readings. I thought that engaging the audience's senses would help draw them into the heart of the book more quickly. People seemed to appreciate that."

THE QUESTION & ANSWER

One of the biggest problems with the Q&A is that it's hard to get started. Many times, people feel shy about asking questions. Nobody wants to be first. Usually, once you get the ball rolling, people will ask interesting questions, and if done right, the Q&A can be the highlight of the event as the give-and-take between audience and author can be seriously provocative and quite exciting to boot.

To avoid an awkward silence after you ask, "Does anyone have any questions?" prepare your own questions for yourself. Raise your hand and say something like "I have a question. Is this book based on something from your real life?" "Why, thank you, that's an excellent question." And then whip out your clever, witty, charming answer. Again, adding a laugh will loosen everyone up.

Jen Reynolds, director of publisher relations and events at Joseph-Beth in Cincinnati, has another great suggestion for starting off a Q&A: "Ask the audience what they'd like to hear about." If silence reigns after this question, you can again make some suggestions yourself: Would you like to hear about the inspiration for this book? What the research was like? How long it took to write? How my parents feel about the book? Am I available? Sharon Kelly Roth, director of public relations at Books & Company in Dayton, Ohio, adds: "Many people in the audience are aspiring authors looking to get published. It's therefore important to talk about the process or journey of writing. How did you write your book? How did you get published? People are hungry for this knowledge." Peppering your Q&A with these bits of info will keep it spicy.

Whatever you do, don't let the Q&A go on too long. Nothing takes the steam out of an event like a Q&A that drones on and on. One of the most difficult moments in an author's life is watching potential readers walk out the door before buying a book.

CUTTING OFF THE LONG-WINDED

Some people are so enchanted by the sound of their own voice that they'll use any excuse to harangue the world. And often, once they get started, they just will not stop. One of them may even show up at your event and start a filibuster during the Q&A session. It's your job to cut him off and shut him down without alienating him or anyone else. This is just as hard as it seems. If a person talks for more than a minute and hasn't come to a question yet, ask him if he can phrase his comment as a question. If, after another 30 seconds, he still hasn't gotten to a question, politely tell him you have to move on but you'll be happy to answer any question he may have after the event.

This may seem harsh, but we've seen sad lonely loudmouths put huge crimps in wonderful events. And your audience will appreciate and respect your ability to set limits.

HAVE A PLAN B

The PYPIP Guide to the Unexpected clearly states that anything can go wrong at any time. It is therefore imperative to have a Plan B. And probably a Plan C. Let's say your book is about an adult subject and a bunch of kids are in the audience. Or there's a room full of people waiting, but you know more are on the way. Or your books aren't there yet. Or someone else on the bill is late. You may have to stall, or stretch, so you need something you can rely on to help you out in a pinch.

If you have any unusual talents, such as birdcalls or playing spoons, be prepared to dust them off to help you fill time if you have to—or to throw in for fun when nothing else seems to be working. Recite a classic poem. It's so great to have something like that to fall back on, and if done properly it will endear you to your audience.

While doing an event in New York, Dan Rhodes (author of the short-story collection *Anthropology*) was faced with just such a conundrum. The event had been advertised to start at 7:30 in one place and at 8:00 in another. So at 7:45 there was a big crowd waiting, starting to fidget, getting a little antsy. But he knew there would be people coming at 8:00. What to do? Well, Dan Rhodes was a man with a Plan B. He had prepared a wonderful short story from Jane Austen's *Juvenilia*. Familiar, yet totally unique. So he was able to trot out his party piece and keep everyone beautifully entertained until the 8:00 crowd strolled in.

TAKE TIME TO SIGN BOOKS

When you're signing, it's important to give everyone who buys your book a little piece of you. Look people in the eye and ask them something about themselves. Ask how they found out about your event, about your book. This will give you an idea of what kind of publicity and marketing techniques are effective. Your readers are precious gems, and you want to find out all you can about them. Be grateful and sweet and humble. These are people who actually took time out of their lives to come out and see you, then stuck around afterwards and paid good money to buy your book and have you sign it for them. If they tell five people, and those people tell five people, and those people tell five people . . . well, you see where we're going with this.

That being said, you want to walk that fine line between keeping the queue moving and giving everyone the individual attention he wants. If there's a small line, this won't be a problem. But if there's a long line (and we should all have this problem), you want to give people their moment in your sun and then gently guide the next person into place.

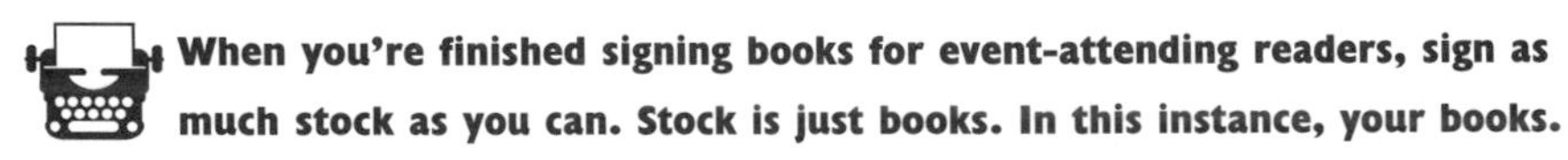

When you're finished signing books for event-attending readers, sign as much stock as you can. Stock is just books. In this instance, your books. Again, if you've signed it, they probably won't return it. And returns are the scourge of the writer.

WHAT TO WRITE WHEN YOU SIGN

Many first-time authors are confused about what to write when they sign someone's book. First and foremost, find out if your buyer wants you to dedicate your book to him or if he simply wants your signature. People who collect books often want only your signature, because it increases the value of your book. If your buyer does want a dedication, be sure to spell his name right. Some authors have a standard dedication they like to use; others like to make things up spontaneously. Some authors give advice; others write pithy and funny lines. Judy Budnitz, author of the short-story collection *Nice Big American Baby*, draws cartoons. Obviously, do whatever suits you, but know that a lot of buyers want something personal—something that shows you connected with them. Undoubtedly, you will feel on the spot at this moment. So it's good to have a couple of prepared options that you can personalize.

EVENT JITTERS

If appearing in public is just too much for you, all is not lost. You can still invent an event that suits you and your talents.

Remember J.T. LeRoy, author of *Sarah*? When he started his literary career, he was called upon to do a public performance. It was a nightmare. He was so nervous, he threw up. He didn't want to do it again. His friend, well-known author Mary Gaitskill, suggested he have other people read his writing at events. So he asked friends and fellow writers to read his stories in public. And it was a raving success. In fact, the events became so popular that he now has famous actors doing them. From Winona Ryder to Tatum O'Neal to Matthew Modine, wonderful voices have brought J.T.'s words to life and made his readings must-see events.

Doing an Event with a Book That Can't Be "Read"

Let's suppose you have a book that doesn't lend itself to a reading. A medical text or a statistical analysis of postwar swallow migration. You can't very well go into a bookstore and read facts and stats. Well, you could, but what would be the point? So: what to do? Luckily, you've got a lot of options. Arrange a debate with someone whose views oppose yours. Ask a local luminary or journalist to interview you (another way to get journalists interested in your book). Give a lecture about your topic. But not a dull, drab academic lecture. A fun, charming, well-rehearsed, informative, passionate lecture. A demonstration or workshop might work. Or a slide show (if the images are A-1). If you're addressing a medical issue, a generous Q&A session where you answer everyone's questions about your topic may be just the ticket.

Joann Eckstut, Arielle's mom and the author of *Room Redux: The Home Decorating Workbook*, gave interior design classes at bookstores. Not only did she draw book buyers, but she attracted new clients as well.

Sharon Kelly Roth of Books & Company says, "We've had authors who write about antiques invite people to bring in an antique for them to appraise. That's a big hit with customers. One customer found out that the lamp she paid $1,500 for was actually worth $25,000. Just remember, make it fun and they will come!"

Bill and Rachel Parker, authors of *A Gynecologist's Second Opinion*, knew it wouldn't be easy to do events in bookstores for their opus. With their usual wit and aplomb, they illuminated their thoughts on books that don't lend themselves to readings:

Bill: "Having events in bookstores for medical books can be deadly—"

Rachel: "No pun intended—"

Bill: "Thank you. Because nobody shows up. The best thing for me is going to medical conventions. Doing medical shows. Writing medical articles. Becoming a media expert. If you give good advice and plug the book at the end, shows are happy to do it."

EVENTS 101: A CHECKLIST TEAR SHEET

When you show up at your event, it's easy to get sucked into the vortex of nervous excitement and lose track of taking care of business. Here's a checklist of stuff you should do to make your event all it can be. Xerox it and take it with you.

1) Have fun.
2) Look sharp and smell good.
3) Arrive 30 minutes before the announced starting time.
4) Introduce yourself to as much staff as possible.
5) Make sure they're going to introduce you correctly and announce that you'll be signing books.
6) See if there's anything in the room you can comment on.
7) Do a physical/vocal warm-up.
8) Rehearse your major points and opening just before you go on.
9) Check your zipper and/or buttons. Bring a fashion helper, or use the mirror or host (if appropriate) to give you a final once-over.
10) Bring a beverage to the podium with you.
11) Introduce yourself with a joke, anecdote and/or story.
12) Make eye contact.
13) Don't let hair hang in your eyes. Avoid fidgeting, tugging and/or picking.
14) Have lots of energy, but don't be manic.
15) Take your time.
16) Be intimate, but make sure everyone can hear you.
17) Vary volume, pace and intensity.
18) Don't give away the ending.
19) Once the Q&A stars, don't let an audience member go on for more than a minute. Cut off the long-winded politely.
20) When you're finished, make sure the audience knows where you will be signing books.
21) Try to connect with everyone who has you sign your book.
22) Sign stock.
23) Thank everyone for having you.
24) Get business cards from everyone. It's a great way to sign up people for your mailing list.
25) Have fun.

This strategy has worked out well for Bill and Rachel's book, which is now in a second edition.

What If No One Shows Up?

Read this sentence carefully: An event at a bookstore is a good thing, even if nobody comes to it.

If you happen to have an event and no one shows up, and you're standing in front of a table loaded with your books and there's a room full of empty chairs where your readers should be, and your publishing career is flashing before your eyes and you feel like the loser of the universe, it may not seem like a good thing.

And yet it is. Here's why. The booksellers will have a bunch of your books in their store. They may make a sign or poster or flyer and put it up in their store. They may contact the local paper, which may announce the event in its calendar section. They may put you in their own calendar, which they may send out to their mailing list of readers. They may send out a mass e-mail, informing their people of your book and your reading. They may put the event on their Web site, and you can put the event on your Web site. And, hold on to your hat, the store may actually put your book in the most coveted spot in the joint, the Boardwalk of the bookstore kingdom: THE FRONT WINDOW. The place everyone has to walk past to enter the store. So, even if no one comes to your event, your name and your book may be seen by hundreds, maybe even thousands, maybe even hundreds of thousands.

Plus, they may give you a nice pen or a lovely paper bookmark. You will almost certainly be given a free beverage, hot *or* cold. Don't count on it, but you may even get a free muffin.

Plus, you will probably get to meet the events coordinator and, if you're smart, a bunch of the people who work at the store. The people who, you know, sell your book. If no one shows up, you'll have a lot of time to bond with all of them. If you do it correctly, and keep a lovely attitude, you can make everyone feel better, and you can, believe it or not, sow the seeds for the hand-selling of your book.

Caroline Leavitt, award-winning author of *Girls in Trouble*, has this to share: "I went to a bookstore reading and no one showed up. No one! Three people from the bookstore felt sorry for me and sat down in the chairs (they had put out 50 chairs because they expected a crowd) and sat there with their name tags on while I read. Afterwards, Michael Dorris, author of *A Yellow Raft in Blue Water*, soothed me and told me how he read in front of four people once and the cops came in mid-reading and arrested three of them, who happened to be bank robbers on the lam."

Thank You, Thank You

Again, get business cards from everyone who's working your event. After the dust has settled, make sure you're very generous with your thank-yous. When you get back home, send cards (or postcards of your book) to everyone who helped. John Evans, owner of Diesel Bookstore in Oakland, California, told us: "The people who really make an impression are those who are respectful. Acclaimed British author and Whitbread prizewinner Jeanette Winterson went directly up to each person (including the person at the counter) and said, 'Thank you so much, I really appreciate all the work you've done.' Five years of booksellers' recommendations came out of that."

Jen Reynolds, director of publisher relations and events at Joseph-Beth in Cincinnati, expressed similar sentiments in this story: "Jimmy Carter was the greatest. He was very clear about what he wanted: a chicken salad sandwich. That was it. And afterwards he dropped us a note right away, thanking us, saying he appreciated the event and our efforts. I was blown away. People often come in on edge and complaining, making demands. And then I think of Jimmy Carter, how easy he was, and he was the *president*, for goodness sake!"

A TOUR OF YOUR BOOK TOUR

If you're lucky, your publisher will set up a book tour for you. It may be a 5-city tour or it may take you to 20 hot spots. This tour will be arranged by your publicist, who will organize your bookstore events (and maybe even set up events at book festivals). She will make sure books arrive at each location. She will provide each bookstore with promotional posters and make sure you end up in its newsletter. She will confirm your listing in each local paper's calendar section. She will send your book and press release to local and national media. She will try her hardest to coordinate a landslide of attention to hit just before and all during your tour. This may include reviews, interviews, puff pieces, you name it. Without your even lifting a promotional finger, you stand the chance of getting a lovely itinerary filled with lots of juicy interviews and events.

Of course, your publicist isn't a magician. Even with publisher-driven tours, there may be spots where you have little or no media attention. Or the media that were contacted may have to bow out due to late-breaking news. Even though your publisher will do all sorts of amazing things for you, don't forget to supplement these efforts in any and every way you can.

Very few authors get sent out on tour anymore, so make sure you're in great shape, fully rested, with your battery completely charged, at the very top of your game. Pick out a couple of great outfits that can be easily packed and repacked without having to be ironed and reironed. Travel light. It's a huge pain lugging big bags.

Despite all the wearisome traveling, the grueling grind of being dragged hither and thither signing stock at store after store, all the maddening glad-handing, all the utterly draining interviews (sometimes, if you're lucky, five or six in a day where you have to say all the same things but make it seem like it's the very first time you've ever said them), you will *still* be expected at the end of the day to go to a venue and deliver a slamming show so that a room full of strangers will want to lay down their hard-earned money to buy your bouncing baby book.

Michael Perry, author of *Population: 485*, has this to say about touring: "It's tough to describe a book tour. It's intense, not in a heavy-lifting sort of way, but in a sort of nonstop way. You're always driving or talking or trying to find a radio station or a television station or a hotel or a departure gate. Your life boils down to showing up and talking. Showing up and talking. Over and over. But every stop, people listen and smile, and then say gracious things. I've spoken with several other authors during the course of the year, and they all confirmed what I feel: Writing is a mostly solitary existence and we prefer it that way, but when we see someone in a chair at a reading it reminds us that a reader is someone who gives us his time, and this leaves us frightened and deeply grateful. So to everyone in the chairs, thank you so much."

After the high of a show, it can be depressing to end up in a lonely hotel room feeling alienated and alone, with nowhere to go and no one you know. Bring a great book or two with you. Bring a journal to write in. If you've got a blog on your Web site, write up the day's events. Work out. Eat some healthy food. Take care of yourself physically, mentally and emotionally. Be ready for what's coming and make the necessary adjustments as you go.

Luckily, provided you're in the best shape of your life, you have the right attitude and you make an extra special point to HAVE FUN, there's a huge upside. Being on a publisher-driven tour bestows upon you a higher status than if you're just Joe or Jane Author walking in off the street. This status should lend you some extra-special face time with people at bookstores. Cherish these contacts and make the most of them. They could be a lifeline for the rest of your writing career. Ditto when you're interviewed by local and national media. Get cards from everyone both for thank-yous and for future follow-up.

You'll also get to rub elbows with your public far and wide. Yes, you have a public, and this is them. Treat them like gold, and they will make you golden. And beef up your mailing lists while you're at it.

Touring is a giddy mixture of delight and drudgery. But in the end, you'll improve your event and your presentation skills. You'll accumulate great war stories. You'll come home a more successful, experienced, respected author.

Phone, minibar and room service are often not covered by your publisher. You don't want to end up paying $10 for 12 macadamia nuts, no matter how good they were.

An Escort Is Not What You Think

Most likely, your publisher will hire an escort for you when you go to another city. Before you get all excited, an escort is someone who picks you up at the airport and takes you to your hotel; drives you to your event, your interviews, the local bookstores; introduces you to local bookstore owners, managers and employees; helps you sign books; shows you the local ropes and hips you to the local lingo; and generally makes your life much easier. As is true with every profession, there are oustanding escorts and there are terrible ones. What makes for a great escort? All you need to do is meet Ken Wilson. He's not just good; he's an escort god. Ken works out of Los Angeles. In under four hours, he'll take you to 15 bookstores from Santa Monica to Hollywood to the Valley. He knows everyone's name at every bookstore and how many kids and dogs each bookseller has. He knows how to pitch and position a book in a quick, skillful 30 seconds. With great style and wit.

Should you be lucky enough to meet Ken or any of his escort colleagues, be sure to befriend them. Pick their brains, learn from them, observe and absorb. Push them to take you to each and every bookstore

THE SEVEN HABITS OF HIGHLY EFFECTIVE WRITERS

Escorts meet A LOT of authors and, unlike publishers, get to see them in action day after day. One of the best, Crofton Diack of Portland, Oregon, put together these pearls of wisdom about what successful authors have in common:

- They can distinguish between the creative side of writing their book and the selling of it. They've learned how to let go of the child that is their book so it can be released into the world and flourish.
- They make lots of time to prepare, and they take advantage of that time to plan and map out their strategy. Sending out postcards and e-mails to everyone who might be interested in their book. Sending out advance copies and doing prep work in cities where they're doing events.
- They have good agents. Having a good agent and having a good relationship with that agent are important. An author who shall remain nameless wrote a book that wasn't even that good, but he has a great agent who really helped push it by telling everybody about it. Got him a big advance, a big tour. Sold the movie rights. That agent made a huge difference in this author's book being successful.
- They look good. I took around one supposedly big celebrity who looked like a slob and smelled like a bum. And honestly, that's all anyone remembered.
- They know how to create a connection between their own image and their book's image. Through the way they look, the stories they tell, the stuff they read, they let the audience see the connection between them and their book.
- They take good care of themselves when on a tour. They stay rested and sharp. When people are tired, they tend to go on autopilot. I've seen it happen. When an author's not fresh and looks like he's just going through the motions, it's a terrible thing.
- They get people from their publishing team—their agents, their editors, their publicists—to come see them in action. Authors should really make an effort to get those people out to see them so they can help spread the word.

in the area. Remember, this could quite possibly be your one shot at this town in your three-month, winner-take-all window. Take advantage of this precious opportunity while it exists and get maximum mileage out of your escort.

Escorts tend to be a chatty group. It's very likely that your treatment of your escort will become drive-time conversation with the next author under his protection. Not to mention telephone gossip fodder for your publicist (who is your escort's contact at your publisher's). So be generous with your gratitude. And when you're tempted to throw a hissy fit because some producer keeps you waiting or a journalist blows you off for a bigger story, take a deep breath and remember that you want your escort to make—not break—your reputation.

Satellite Tours

Publishers sometimes send authors on "virtual" radio or TV tours. These are called satellite tours, and they're set up and run by companies who specialize in this handy form of publicity. Satellite tours require you to sit in one room only. You'll be interviewed over and over again by different stations around the country (or, in some cases, you may do one taped segment that's then sent out to stations).

What's the point of a satellite tour? Why would your publisher decide to spend the dough on such a thing (and these do cost money)? Calla Devlin, marketing and publicity coordinator at Chronicle Books, says, "Satellite tours are great when you want to saturate the marketplace in a short period." They can, if they're done right, get you seen by hundreds of thousands of readers—which is why you might want to consider hiring a company to set one up for you if you can't convince your publisher that it's a good idea. But let us repeat ourselves: Satellite tours *do* cost money.

Satellite TV interviews can be particularly awkward because you can't see the person who's interviewing you. It's tough to connect with someone when there's no eye contact. All the more reason to listen carefully.

THE SKINNY ON LOCAL AND NATIONAL MEDIA

If your book comes out with a good publisher, and you're lucky, your publicist will arrange press coverage—reviews, interviews and features in national and local magazines, newspapers, on radio and TV . . . all coordinated with your tour and/or with the publication of your book. Sometimes an interview will be a *phoner*, an interview on, you guessed it, the phone. Sometimes you'll be asked to go to a radio or TV studio where you'll be interviewed live or on tape. There might be an audience, or you might be alone with the interviewer and the crew. You might be part of a panel of interesting or uninteresting people who have something or nothing in common with you (David was once interviewed on a panel with Yoko Ono!). Sometimes the interviewer will come to your home. Sometimes the interviewer will take you to a location. And sometimes—the worst—you'll sit in a room with just a camera or a microphone, unable to see the person who's interviewing you. As we said, this is when you really need to listen carefully to the questions and keep up your energy while still being intimate with your unseen listener (something you may want to rehearse with a friend or presentation doctor).

But just because you have a publicist working on getting you media, don't think you shouldn't be trying to get large media love all on your own. Your publicist may not make the effort to get you on *Good Morning America* because she wants one of her bigger-profile authors on the show. Re-identify what media attention you want. In revisiting your media wish list (see page 249), focus on national media but do not neglect local media. Identify clearly what exactly is unique and timely about your book, and track down anyone who does appropriate pieces. Radio interviewers, book reviewers, human-interest journalists, gossip columnists. Woo them. Give them a hot-off-the-press copy of your book. The right article at the right time in the right publication can be a big boon to sales. And even if it's not exactly on point, it can still be added to your press kit—plump her up so she's thick and powerful!

Publicist Jim Eber says this: "You have to work your way in sometimes. Nobody knows why certain things will make it. Anne Byrn's *The Cake Mix Doctor* wasn't on a national show until ten months after the book was out. The author hit her own Southern backyard first. Media begets media, and now that book has well over a million copies in print. Tape from even the crummiest cable show can help. The media doesn't have to be great. You do."

Back to Pitching and Hooking

The publication of your book may be earth-shattering news in your house, but believe it or not, it isn't to much of the rest of the world. You have to make it so. You have to figure out how to feed your story to the media so it's easily digestible. Just as you're trying to reach a particular audience, so is each media outlet. This means that your book about the difficulties of aging may help AARP sell more magazines, but it has to be spun to their specifications in terms of tone, style and point of view. Often this means hooking up with a larger story than your own. Keep putting your book and your ideas out there. You never know when *Newsweek* will be doing an exposé on your subject. But if you go in assuming that you just want a review or feature, it will lessen your chances.

One author we know is an avid listener of NPR's *Talk of the Nation.* She noticed how, every single day, Neal Conan does a teaser for the show in the form of a few questions followed by a short pitch. So when her book came out, she sent an e-mail to a producer at *Talk of the Nation* in this exact form. Boom! A month later, she was on the show. The more you key in to a particular media outlet's gestalt, the better your chances of landing that show, magazine or newspaper. But again, make sure you get a list of who your publicist is going after so you don't tread on her toes or have her trip over your feet.

SCHMOOZORAMA: GETTING TO THE MEDIA YOU WANT AND NEED

It's time to pull out your now-weathered PYPIP Guide to Connecting and Schmoozing. Journalists and producers, like agents and authors, appreciate it if you've taken the time to look at their work. Let them know what you liked about it, then show them how your book fits right in. If you've accumulated all the information you can and you have the appropriate schmoozing skills, try to get the targets of your media wish list on the phone. Sometimes there's an underling in a big company whom you can turn into an ally. Don't forget, the receptionist of today is often the honcho of tomorrow. If you're lucky enough to get through to the person you're trying to reach, make sure you ask her if she has a moment. If she doesn't, ask where you can send your material so she can look it over at her leisure. If she does have a moment, let her know about any personal connection and/or why she's the right person to contact about your work. Then give her your fully refined under-one-minute pitch. DO NOT GO ON AND ON. If she wants to know more, let her ask. Listen very carefully if she has anything to say. Write it down.

After you speak with a producer, journalist or receptionist, get your material into their hands as soon as humanly possible. Have your press kit ready to go BEFORE you make the call. The less time that elapses between hanging up that phone and finding your package on their desk, the better.

Guess what's next. Go ahead, guess.

FOLLOW-UP.

Again with the thank-yous! If anyone interviews you, or writes about you, or helps in any way to get the word out about your book, slap a thank-you note on them. When people feel appreciated, they're much more likely to want to do something with you again.

GOING BACK TO THE WELL

Do not be put off if you don't hear back from the media outlets you contact. Even if a lot of time goes by. Do not assume your ideas and updates are going unnoticed. You never know what's happening on the other end. Do not assume that no one's interested.

Keep plugging and grinding, coming up with cool new ideas that someone can use to feature you, your subject or your book.

The more you put out there, the better your chances of getting something back. Bob Nelson, author of *1001 Ways to Reward Employees*, is the ultimate plugger and grinder. He sent out pitches to Costco's magazine, *Connections*, for over five years. Never heard much back. Then suddenly he got a call. They were doing a cover story on him for an upcoming issue and could they send a photographer from Los Angeles to take some photos? When he asked how this all came about, they told him they had kept the material he'd sent them over the years, loved it all and found themselves continually pulling from it when writing for their readers—who also loved his stuff. They had a file folder five inches thick of material Bob had sent them. By the way, the *Connections* issue that featured Bob on the cover went out to over 4.5 million business owners.

The Medium of Media

Each form of media has its own rules and idiosyncrasies. But before we give you tips tailored to each one, here are some general rules:

- Before you're interviewed, try to watch or listen to the show or read the work of the journalist. This will help eliminate surprises.
- Show up 20 to 30 minutes early.

- Don't eat right before you're interviewed, unless part of your shtick is regurgitation. If you're being interviewed over lunch, eat light and be sure to wipe your mouth regularly.
- Have a beverage close at hand. Again, this is not only for dry mouth, but also for use as a prop if you need to stall.
- Do a physical warm-up beforehand: yoga, stretching, jumping jacks.
- Just before you're interviewed, prep yourself; go over your key points and your pitch.
- Try to establish a personal connection with your interviewer; asking a few questions of your own can loosen both of you up.
- Gently ask the interviewer beforehand to mention your book, your Web site and any events you have coming up.
- Before you go on a show, ask for a copy of your performance. Always bring a blank audiotape, videotape or CD with you in case they won't provide you with one. And be sure to pick it up on your way out. For print, be sure to ask the interviewer to have the publication mail you a hard copy of the issue your interview appears in.
- If you're in the same room as a host, make eye contact. The more you can focus on having a real conversation, no matter how nervous you are, the better the interview will be.
- Be aware of everything that's going on around you. For TV and radio, almost always someone will signal the host 30 seconds before your segment is done and they have to go to a break. When you see that signal, know you have to wrap up.
- Try not to be combative or argumentative. Unless that's your persona and it will help sell your book.
- Don't mention the name of your book over and over again. However, for TV and radio, if your host hasn't mentioned it at all, be sure to say the name at least once.
- Don't say, "You'll have to read my book to find out" or "People always ask me that question." It can seriously alienate your interviewer and make you seem self-serving.

ON THE AIR WITH LARRY MANTLE

Larry Mantle, host of public radio's *Airtalk* (on NPR's L.A. affiliate KPCC-FM) and one of Southern California's most beloved radio interviewers, shared some of his insights from years of talking to the famous, the infamous and dozens of first-time authors:

PYPIP: What can a first-time author do to attract your attention?

LM: Demonstrate that you really know the show. If you're a fan and you know who you're pitching to, this can make a huge difference. Make your pitch highly personalized. In addition, relating your book to something that's going on in the world can make a big difference. The more of a hook you have, the better.

PYPIP: What makes for a good interview?

LM: You've got to know the style of the host and what the audience is used to hearing. I'm on public radio, so we like depth. Do your research. Past interviews are often available online. Study the list of guests.

PYPIP: What makes radio different from other media?

LM: Radio is intimate. The best interviews feel like the subject is talking to one person. And, in fact, typically a listener is alone in a car or at home. Never say "you listeners." Always assume you're talking to an individual. Also, radio is driven by imagination, so you want to provoke a listener's creative imagination. Terry Gross is a great interviewer because she introduces you to a world that may be entirely different from your own. She gives you an insight into what it would be like for you to be doing what her guest is describing. She uses words to open up your mind and make the subject personal. I want the audience to say, "You drew me in." I want the listeners to feel like they're riveted, in the same room, overhearing an intimate conversation.

PYPIP: Any general tips for authors going on the air?

LM: I prefer the person I'm interviewing to have high energy without being overwhelming, funny without being shticky, intelligent but accessible. If it's too complex, it's boring. If it's too simple, it's dull. No abstract concepts, just real stories that people can relate to. In the best interviews, it's like the audience is eating greens, but they feel like they're popping Gummy Bears.

- Make sure you have a clear understanding of what kind of language they want you to use if you're going on air. How sophisticated, racy or old is the audience you're speaking to? Tailor your interview accordingly. Especially if it's live.

- Don't give one-word answers unless you're doing it for a specific reason (to create comedy, for example).
- Get contact information from the interviewer, the producer and/or the host before you leave.

RADIO

Are you live or taped? Make sure you ask! If you're being taped and you make a mistake or don't like the way you expressed something, you can start over again. If you're live and you make a mistake, you've got to have fun with it. Live or taped, be sure to develop a nice relationship with the microphone. Before you go on, find out how far away or how close you should be. If, God forbid, you should have to clear your throat, cough or burp, avert your mouth from the mike.

If you're interviewed over the phone, even if you're in your bathrobe, make sure you're warmed up both physically and vocally. Pace the room so you can get the blood moving. You might also want some privacy so you can be more relaxed. Have notes you can refer to. DO NOT use a phone that has call-waiting (unless you can suspend it). If it's a live radio interview, don't have the show on your radio at home. Don't be surprised if the call doesn't come in on time. Very often, live radio runs late. In fact, there's a good chance you'll be bumped to another day. Also, there's a chance you'll hear the show over the phone just before your segment. Listen closely for anything you can refer to during your segment.

Try not to speak in run-on sentences. It's hard for listeners to take the information in if they can't actually see you speaking.

There's a subspecies of the radio world whose bread and butter is meanness. If you find yourself in an interview with a "shock jock" who attacks you viciously, you have several options: 1) have fun with it, 2) act wounded and hurt, or 3) attack back. If all three make you want to puke, be sure to tell your publicist that you don't want to do this sort of thing.

TELEVISION

If you're appearing on TV, a makeup artist/hairdresser will sometimes help you look beautiful. Some men are loath to let someone put makeup on them. If you fall into this category, it's time to get in touch with your feminine side. You have no idea what those TV lights do to your skin. If you're on a low-budget show that doesn't supply a makeup artist, at the very least

WHO'S THE BOSS?

Develop the art of slipping your critical information into the answer of any question you're asked. It's very difficult to do this and make it seem natural. That's why it helps to practice with your team and in front of a video camera. But if you can in essence run the interview, you will often be much happier with the results. Of course, it's a fine line between running an interview and running roughshod over the interviewer. Both the interviewer and your audience will want to feel that you're a good listener. So always be sure to respond to questions, even if you end up taking the questions in new directions. It's also important to be open to whatever avenue your interviewer leads you down, because you never know what fun is lurking down there. A question out of left field may result in an animated, engaging conversation that has a greater effect on book sales than your normal shtick.

apply a thin layer of powder to get rid of the shine. And a little color in the cheeks and some mascara wouldn't hurt.

Watch that posture on TV! Yes, appear comfortable and relaxed, but try your best not to slouch and look like a human question mark. If you can, chat with the host beforehand. Don't assume, however, that just because the host is chummy before the camera's on, he'll be chummy on air.

Sometimes you'll find yourself in front of a live studio audience. Make sure to include them from time to time (with eye contact and/or gestures) as you speak. For example, if it's a show that has a Q&A, you can refer back to a previous question an audience member asked. This can go a long way toward gaining their support.

Find out before your interview where the producers would like you to look. Unless you're a seasoned professional, it's almost always better NOT to look at the camera.

PRINT

Arrange for print interviews to be held someplace where you're comfortable. Have the reporter come to your home or meet you at a coffee shop or somewhere outside that you enjoy. Just make sure there's not a lot of background noise so your quotes are accurate. Also, journalists need what are called "color" paragraphs, i.e., writing that describes the setting or mood where the interview takes place. So if you pick the right spot, you can get more ink. And even if no one's taking your picture, look as good as you can.

As with TV, don't assume that journalists who get very chummy and intimate with you are doing this to be your friend. Sometimes they're just trying to get you to say something you'll wish you hadn't said. Do not, even off the cuff, say anything to a journalist that you don't want plastered all over creation. Even if you tell a journalist that something is "off the record," you may find that your wishes aren't always granted.

Be prepared to be misquoted and know that there's absolutely nothing you can do about it. Don't start sending letters to the editor (unless a journalist has written something that will cause physical harm); you'll most likely come off as a whining boob.

If someone from the media comes to photograph you for a newspaper or magazine, do yourself a favor and employ the techniques described in the last chapter, i.e., bring a friend, engage in conversation, keep physically loose. Be a cooperative subject, but if you're asked to do something you're not comfortable with (like putting on a dumb hat or removing your shirt), JUST SAY NO.

Get contact information from everyone who interviews you and stay in touch. Add each name to your e-mail list and send regular updates. You never know when one of them might need a story quickly on your topic. Also, people who still have you in mind may help you out with contacts within their organization. Editors who might be interested in one of your ideas. Producers at shows that might be interested in you.

Keeping Track and Keeping It Real

If you're extremely fortunate, you'll be interviewed over and over and over again. Sometimes on the same day. Starting at four A.M. And guess what? People will ask you the same questions over and over and over again.

Not only do you have to have great answers for all these questions, but you also have to make them seem fresh as a daisy every time they pop out. You have to make it seem as if the interviewer is asking you insightful, intelligent, really-makes-you-think questions. Even though you've answered them over and over and over again.

One way to keep it fresh is to consciously reconnect with the origin of the idea, the seed of your passion. Another is to constantly try to improve your stories. Weed out weakness; add strength. Whether it's changing the words or tweaking the delivery, by attempting to make it better, you will keep a little edge in your stories. Whenever you improvise a great line, write it down afterwards so you can use it again.

If you're being interviewed back-to-back-to-back, it's difficult to keep track of what you've already said and what bon mots you delivered in your last interview. If you end up repeating yourself or doing something stupid, admit you're an idiot. In small, appropriate doses, self-deprecation can actually be sweet. Remember, if you handle it right, a mistake can lead to the best moment in your interview.

Evaluate your presentation after every interview and see what you can do to make it even greater. Keep it real. The late great George Burns put it his own way: "Sincerity is the most important thing in life. Once you can fake that, you've got it made."

Getting Snarked

If you're getting any media attention, you will sooner or later get smacked upside the head with some snark. Snark is ugly, mean nastiness for its own sake. Sadly, in this cynical age, some people mistake snark for journalism. They may use you and/or your book for target practice as they pepper you with potshots.

If you're a member of the human race, it's hard not to take this personally. David was repeatedly snarked when his book *Chicken* came out. Not for the quality of his book or writing, but because his nose was too big and his eyes were too close together. And this was from highbrow papers like the London *Times*. After resisting the urge to book a big block of time with a plastic surgeon, David realized that this was more about the need to sell papers than about him.

Back to author Dan Rhodes (*Timoleon Vieta Come Home*) for a moment. He actually puts his snark to work by using it as fodder for comedy. He keeps a running list of some of the nastiest things ever written about him and his books, and then reads the highlights as entertainment at some of his events.

Heidi Julavits, editor of the hip, intellectual San Francisco journal *The Believer*, defined snark in her manifesto on it as "hostility for hostility's sake." She sees snark passing for literary criticism more and more, as book critics become more concerned with being "funny and smart and a little bit bitchy" than saying anything about a book's merits and deficiencies. (*The Believer* has since launched "Snarkwatch," a fantastic Web post dedicated to identifying these kinds of hostile reviews. See Appendix I.)

If you're worried about bad reviews, you're not alone. But there are several tried-and-true methods for dealing with them. Your first option is not to read them. There's a lot to be said for this approach. After all, they're just some people's opinions. And you don't want their voices in your head the next time you sit down to write something. If you want constructive criticism, you can always find smart, fair people who'll give it to you.

Some writers have a trusted friend or colleague read the reviews first and just pass on the nice and/or instructive bits. This makes sense, too. You don't get that critic's voice in your head, but you still learn from constructive criticism and register the nice things people are saying, filtered through a friendly protective voice.

Some writers read their reviews and take them with a very large grain of salt while extracting whatever useful information they can from them. Again, this makes a lot of sense, but it's a tactic fraught with difficulties. For one thing, it's not easy to find that grain of salt when you need it. So, as much as you say you won't take it personally, it's almost impossible not to. On the flip side, it's wise to take raves with a small bit of salt as well.

Some writers read their reviews and memorize the worst bits, rage against the cruel world, grow bitter and never produce that masterpiece they were meant to write. We consider this a last-resort option.

But just know this: If you write a book, you will get bad reviews. Just like every writer—great and not so great—before you. So next time you get bashed, pilloried, dismissed, railed upon or savaged, don't despair. Instead, embrace the words of Oscar Wilde: "The only thing worse than being talked about is not being talked about."

GIVING AWAY BOOKS: YES, THAT'S RIGHT, *GIVING* THEM AWAY

It may seem slightly insane, but giving away books can be a very, very good thing. Of course, we do not advocate any willy-nilliness in regard to the giving away of your books. As you might suspect, the important thing here is not just *that* you give your books away, but *to whom* you give them.

Conversely, everyone you know will want a copy of your book. Most people are unaware that authors have to buy their own books. Writing a book, getting it published and then having to buy it back to give it away can cause a slightly woozy feeling. Explain this to everyone within earshot when your book comes out.

However, there are many, many people you should give your book to. If you were able to finagle free books for publicity and marketing purposes in your contract, now's the time to use them. While you want your publisher to send your book and publicity package to as many people as possible, sometimes it helps if it comes directly from you. Don't scrimp when there's a chance to get an interested party excited about your opus. Newspapers, magazines and radio stations, colleges and independent bookstores, book groups and libraries, loudmouths and busybodies. Movie agents, directors, producers and actors. Other writers. Teachers. Special-interest groups related to your book. Academic researchers. Web sites. Experts in your field or related fields. A potential love interest.

"Someday I hope to write a book where the royalties will pay for the copies I give away."
—Clarence Darrow

Bill and Rachel Parker, authors of *A Gynecologist's Second Opinion*, had this to say on giving away books:

Rachel: "We used to be stingy about books—"

Bill: "I was terrible. I hoarded the books. I kept thinking, 'If you want a book, why don't you go buy one?' Now we give books away all the time."

Rachel: "We send them out to everybody."

Bill: "And it's really helped to spread the word."

Our publisher, Peter Workman, has this rule: "For every one book you give away, you sell three."

Words to live by.

E-MARKETING REDUX

Again, the Internet and World Wide Web can help generate great marketing and promotional love. So much of the media-getting, and the event-planning, and the contacting-similar-authors, and the alerting/galvanizing of groups with similar interests and of course the following-up can be done after you take that 30-second commute from your bedroom to your computer. And the beauty of the Internet is that it has a life of its own. Let it take you where it will. Push and ride it for all you and it are worth. Remember how we talked about maintaining a robust e-mailing list? Not only can you give regular updates to everyone on your list, but with any luck those people will send to other people, who will send to other people, who will send to other people. This is what is known as a viral e-mail. An important distinction: This is the kind of virus you want to spread as opposed to the kind that crashes your hard drive and leaves you in a puddle on the floor.

In addition to casting your net wide, you can also use it to pinpoint buzz. Phil Bashe, author and coauthor of numerous books (many in the health category), has this e-advice: "The Internet provides authors with endless opportunities to get their books noticed. Around the time of publication, I write one or two personalized letters a day to relevant Web sites, alerting them to my new book and explaining why I believe their audience would benefit from knowing about it. They're usually extremely receptive." Take a look back at your Web research and Web contacts, and do as Phil does!

BOOK CLUB HEAVEN

From *Oprah* and *Good Morning America* to *USA Today* and your Aunt Grizelda's living room, there has been an explosion of book groups in America. To court your run-of-the-mill neighborhood book club, many publishers now put reading guides in the backs of books; they may even directly contact individual book clubs that have an interest in a particular kind of book. There's no reason you shouldn't do the same. Engaging with book groups—in person, over the phone or on the Internet—can be a great way to get your book bought, read and talked about. Often they'll be tickled pink if they know the author will speak to them. And remember when we told you to post discussion questions about your book on your Web site? Well, here's where they can pay off big time. Caroline Leavitt, author of *Girls in Trouble*, says, "I did EVERYTHING to get my book out into the world. I offered to talk via speakerphone or e-mail to every book club I could find."

You can track down book groups on the World Wide Web, in chat rooms, through bookstores and by asking everyone you know. You'll be really surprised how many you can unearth all on your very own. So hop on the bandwagon and enjoy the hayride!

AWARDS AS BUZZ

A great way to get buzz is to be nominated for or win an award or to get a fellowship or a grant. It's odd, but perfectly human, that when we see an award next to a person's name, we automatically think better of him. Enter your book for as many awards as you can afford (awards typically have "reading fees," or application costs that run from $10 to $50). Apply for fellowships and grants.

Lists of awards, grants and fellowships, with specifications and deadlines, can be found on the Web and in writers' magazines. *Poets & Writers Magazine* is a particularly great place for prize listings. (See Appendix I for more info.) There are also certain awards that your publisher needs to nominate you for. But don't assume your publisher will automatically do so. You need to make a list of any relevant awards and gently nudge and follow up with your publisher to make sure they're on it. Also, for some awards, you can be nominated in more than one category. This may cost your publisher more money, and if you don't push them, they simply won't do it. But if you ask, you'll almost always receive. And this can make the difference between your becoming an award winner and remaining an also-ran.

KEEPING YOUR BOOK BALL ROLLING

Yes, your book is new for only three months. But even if it doesn't jump off the shelves when it's new, don't despair. A book can catch fire six months, a year, even decades after it's published. Virginia Woolf's *Mrs. Dalloway* hit the bestseller lists 80 years after it was written. Why? Because she inspired and was a character in Michael Cunningham's Pulitzer Prize winner *The Hours*, which then became a movie starring Nicole Kidman as Virginia Woolf.

Always be thinking of new angles and hooks you can pitch to the media. Rick Beyer, author of the collection of fascinating historical tales called *The Greatest Stories Never Told*, is a serious hookmeister who knows how to keep a book in the public eye. He regularly comes up with new hooks for radio interviews, a technique he has had particular success with. Whether it's Presidents Day, Memorial Day, Thanksgiving or graduation, Rick writes terrific pitches with great, original hooks that his publicist can simply forward on to her radio contacts. Here's a sample of his Presidents Day pitch:

> Did you know that . . .
>
> George Washington was not the nation's first president, but was actually number 8?
>
> While John Wilkes Booth assassinated President Lincoln, his brother saved the life of Lincoln's son?
>
> President James Garfield was shot by a lawyer but killed by the ineptitude of his doctors?
>
> Author Rick Beyer is ready to fill your audience in on these and other fun tidbits of presidential history. He is the author of *The Greatest Stories Never Told: 100 Tales from History to Astonish, Bewilder and Stupefy*. Rick has appeared in more than 100 radio and television interviews, entertaining audiences with fascinating little-known stories from history.

Continue to update your contacts. Media constantly need nourishment. You just have to find the meal to feed the beast. For example, pay close attention to the news. If some hot story develops that's related to your book, even tangentially, placing an op-ed piece in the right publication can be a boon for your book. Andrew Exum, author of *This Man's Army: A Soldier's Story from the Front Lines of the War on Terrorism*, noticed a nationwide debate heat up on whether or not there would be a new draft. He quickly wrote an op-ed on the subject. Next thing he knew, he was in *The New York Times*. It's easy to find e-mail addresses for editorial sections in newspapers all over the world, either in the paper itself or online.

Don't Say No

If you're sick and tired of pounding the pavement for your book, especially doing small, dinky stuff that never seems to pay off, let us inspire you with a story. Susan Wooldridge, author of *Poemcrazy*, was asked to attend an event where, essentially, she'd be sitting listening to others make speeches all day. But the keynote speaker didn't show. So guess who filled in? That's right, Susan became the keynote speaker in front of several thousand people and took them by storm. "It ended up being marvelous and has led to workshop after workshop, even another keynote. Say 'yes'! I regret the things I canceled or that I didn't go to."

Develop a Long-Lasting Community

Most importantly, become an enthusiastic part of the community in which you now reside, the world of books and authors and publishers and agents and promoters of the arts. Bruce Lane, former director of the South Carolina Book Festival, says, "We really do watch out for each other. And if you stick with that group—even in the face of poor sales, vanishing publicists or empty spaces on store shelves where your books ought to be—you will, at the very least, be respected."

Paperback Publication: More Beautiful the Second Time Around

Sometimes a publisher will bring a book out in hardcover and then, a year later, bring it out in paperback or sell the paperback rights. One of the great things about having your paperback come out a year after the hardcover is that now you have a second chance to get it right. Even if your hardcover didn't do well and your publisher isn't doing much with the launch of your paperback, in the eyes of the media and the world at large this is a fresh start. You can learn from your mistakes and capitalize on all the contacts and knowledge you've gained in the year since the hardcover came out. You can set up events at places you couldn't get to the first time around. And it's a particularly good time to book events at colleges, libraries and community centers, because students (and readers who frequent libraries and community centers) are far more likely to pay $15 than $25 for your book.

You'll also want to let those who have already interviewed you know about the release of your paperback. Laura Schenone, author of *A Thousand Years over a Hot Stove*, did just that through a mass e-mail. Several radio producers e-mailed her right back to say they'd rerun the show she was on or expressed interest in having her back.

It's also a good time to renew your quest to get more media attention. Reviewers who passed on reviewing your book in hardcover might take a crack at it when the paperback comes out. Make sure you go back to your media wish list and try, try again. Pursue any and every newspaper, magazine, radio and TV show/journalist who might be interested in your book.

PAPERBACK GOLD

Many books have a much richer life in paperback than in hardcover. And there's no better example of this phenomenon than Anita Diamant's novel *The Red Tent*, which takes place in biblical times and is told in the voice of Jacob's daughter Dinah.

To begin with, Anita is a walking advertisement for the PYPIP promotional techniques and can-do attitude. When *The Red Tent* came out in hardcover, it sold in the neighborhood of 10,000 copies. For Anita, this was a rather disappointing neighborhood, because she knew there was a big bountiful audience just waiting for her book. So when her publisher told her that her book was going to be remaindered and that what didn't sell would be shredded, she took this shudder-inducing moment and turned it into an opportunity. She convinced them to use those books instead as a promotional tool for the paperback edition, which was coming out shortly. They agreed.

Anita decided that she would begin her efforts with what she identified as her core audience: female Reform Jewish rabbis. Her publisher agreed to send her book to 500 of these women. The response was good. So Anita then cast her net a little wider and sent her book to another 500 rabbis, male and female alike. These mailings became the epicenter of the quake that would spread throughout the Jewish community and rumble into the general population.

Anita followed up this effort with relentless speaking engagements and readings at Jewish book fairs, synagogues and community centers. Her publisher, smelling success, continued to spread the word to religious leaders of many denominations. They also approached book groups, offering discounts to bookstores that ordered in quantity for these book groups.

Through Anita's constant diligence and relentless effort, *The Red Tent* has to date sold more than 2.4 million paperback copies. From the slag heap of the remaindered and shredded to the bestseller list. How sweet it is.

New Edition Is Not a Boy Band

After your book has been out awhile, you'll think of things you wish you'd added or deleted. Or perhaps the world has changed in some significant way. For nonfiction books, particularly reference books, you can rectify anything that needs changing by writing an updated edition. This may give your book fresh legs to walk another mile.

When Arielle's book *Pride and Promiscuity* first came out in the U.K., it did very well in the holiday season. So her publisher decided to commission an artist to create original illustrations for the paperback edition. This definitely added spice to make it extra nice.

Turn Your Book into Some Other Cool Thing

One-person shows. Greeting cards. A line of T-shirts. Making something else out of a book can really help you expand your audience. And it can be profitable and fun.

Let's take the example of turning your book into a one-person show. Even an unknown play by an unknown writer, put on at a small but respected theater, is more likely to get reviewed than an unknown book by an unknown writer from the biggest publisher. It could also help raise its profile as a possible movie or TV project.

If you prefer the idea of turning your book into a product, go back to the research drawing board. Just as you looked for agents, editors and publishers, look for licensees, manufacturers or whoever else produces the kind of stuff you'd like to make. You'll use the same techniques to approach these companies as you have all along. And if you succeed, you may be able to develop a whole line of products, each of which will raise your visibility another notch and hopefully put some gold in your pot.

AND IN CONCLUSION . . .

The more you think about the rules of marketing and publicity, the more you realize there are no rules. We've laid out some basic principles you can apply. Given you some simple and some sophisticated tools to use. But in the end, you never know which thing will lead to the thing that will lead you to the thing that gets your book the attention it so richly deserves.

The one truth we know for certain about publicity and marketing is that your chances of getting into the spotlight increase exponentially with every intelligent, passionate, properly directed drop of energy you put into it. And because you never know which bit will send your book over the top, be sure not to quit five minutes before the miracle!

CHAPTER 12

THE FINE ART OF SELLING

"Writing books is a whole lot easier than selling books."

—John Grisham

It is a truth universally acknowledged that in order to sell books, someone has to buy them. After all your work—thinking up your book, writing the thing, generating publicity—it's now time to figure out how to get your readers to lay down some cold hard cash.

There are as many ways to sell a book as you and your sales reps can invent and pull off. From the utterly obvious: bookstores, both independents and chains. To the slightly less obvious: drugstores, home improvement centers, flower shops, catalogs, mass merchandisers, warehouse clubs. To the Internet: your own Web site all the way up to Amazon. And to the downright bizarre: from the subway or a public square to a haberdashers' convention. But in order to make those sales, you're going to need books. "What?" you say. "Won't I have books?" Of course you will, but how many you have will be determined by your print run.

"HOW MANY COPIES DID YOU SAY?"

Authors are generally mystified by the seemingly arbitrary size of their first printing. This is decided, in part, by what happened at the sales conference, as well as by the orders that come in as a result of the work of your sales reps. For example, one of the crack members of your sales team is in charge of the Barnes & Noble account—the largest bookseller in the nation. A Barnes & Noble order is, in many cases, more important than any other and will also help determine your first printing. But even if your sales rep delivers a dazzling pitch, the B&N buyer in charge of your category may still place a low order.

The price of your book plus the size of your first printing are, for most publishers, the determining factor for the publicity and marketing budget for your book. So your first print run has a significant impact on what kind of support your book will receive.

If you think you have the stomach for it, find out how many copies of your book your publisher is going to print initially. But keep in mind that a publisher can't print 20,000 copies of your book if they project sales of only 5,000. And since their projections are hardly scientific, they are doing the best they can to estimate demand. But if you feel your publisher is underestimating the number of copies your book will sell, try to convince them otherwise if—and only if—you have solid facts to back up your claim. For example, if you have a book on medieval animal husbandry and you have good sales figures for a similar book, by all means pass these along. Have you convinced the head of the animal husbandry department at Texas A&M to include your book on her syllabus this year? Will this result in 2,500 copies sold in one fell swoop?

If you feel that your publisher isn't paying enough attention to the demand for your book, speak up, speak loudly and speak often. In publishing as in life, windows of opportunity present themselves rarely and shut with alarming speed. If your window opens, do everything you can to dive through before it closes.

Don't despair if your initial print run is smaller than you anticipated. Your publisher can go back and repitch to get more orders if you get good reviews or media coverage, or if your book is selling well in other markets. More good news: If your book flies off the shelves after a small first printing, you may quickly go into a second, third and fourth printing, and this gets people very excited. *The Artist's Way* by Julia Cameron started out with an inital printing of under 10,000 copies. It took two years before this book about the daily practice of becoming an artist started to take off. Now, 12 years later, there are more than two million copies in print! Joel Fotinos, publisher of Tarcher (the company responsible for *The Artist's Way*), put things in perspective: "Of course, publishers, like agents and authors, like to start out with a big first printing. But the business being the way it is these days, that doesn't happen very often. I've had some books with first printings of 5,000 to 7,000 copies that went on to sell 15,000, 20,000, 50,000 or more copies. Those books are particularly gratifying, because they're the books that found their audience despite the many roadblocks in their way."

In this competitive market, with the price of printing and paper and the risk of returns being what they are, publishers often *under*- rather than *over*estimate the number of copies they'll sell. So you may find yourself in a situation where readers want your book but aren't able to buy it because the publisher didn't print enough copies. This is particularly gnarly when you have a four-color illustrated book, which was probably produced overseas and takes months to reprint.

One author had this tale of woe. His beautifully illustrated history book was published one September with a modest first run. The author worked his tail off to secure reviews, radio interviews and speaking engagements. And lo and behold, his book starting selling really well. It was listed in numerous holiday gift roundups in newspapers across the country. Thanksgiving rolled around, the beginning of the holiday shopping rush, and suddenly his book was no longer available. Because it was produced overseas, no more copies could be had until January. So, in what should have been the best season for selling his book, he had to sit and watch as the demand he had created went unfulfilled.

At the height of demand, the author and his agent took a measured but persistent approach, but by that time it was too late. In retrospect, when the book first started getting good reviews, they should have gone to the publisher and rattled whatever cages they needed to in order to get more books printed.

BACK TO THE BOOKSTORE

We've talked about chains, independents and discount retailers. Chain bookstores are owned by large corporations. The two largest chains are Barnes & Noble and Borders. Independent bookstores are more often owned by individuals and/or small companies. A subcategory here is independents that have branched out into several locations. Then there are the discount retailers like Costco, Target and Wal-Mart.

Now it's time for some surprising numbers. It seems almost counter-intuitive, but the fact is, even though discount retailers account for over 50% of all book sales, they carry only a fraction of the titles carried by more traditional bookstores. Discount retailers tend to concentrate on bestsellers and reference books; by comparison, only 3% of B&N's total sales are bestsellers. For many independents, this percentage is even smaller. So if you're the next J.K. Rowling, many of your sales will come from Costco. However, you're going to have a very hard time getting your 500-page epic poem about a heroic apricot into these discounters.

"Where is human nature so weak as in the bookstore?"
—Henry Ward Beecher

Many authors are confused about how to approach and work with the various kinds of bookstores. Below, we'll go into detail with regard to chains and independents to dispel all confusion and quell your anxieties.

Ch-Ch-Chains

The evolution of the bookstore has led to the creation of chains such as Barnes & Noble and Borders. Not only do these chains make thousands of titles available, but they also offer great sales on fantastic books, hold

WHERE BOOKSTORES BUY BOOKS

Oddly enough, most bookstores order many of their books not from publishers, but from wholesalers. As a reminder, wholesalers are companies that stock books for publishers (so that bookstores can order them with ease) but do not actively go out and sell them.

Ingram is the largest wholesaler of books to booksellers in the country. And booksellers like to do business with them because they can do one-stop shopping and receive one bill. In general, bookstores tend to order front-list books directly from the publisher. Then, when a book becomes backlist, they go to Ingram.

There are also a whole host of other wholesalers. For example, Baker & Taylor is a major wholesaler that primarily services libraries. And then there are numerous regional wholesalers.

Since it's so much easier, why don't booksellers order *all* their books from wholesalers? The reason is, publishers give booksellers a better discount than wholesalers do. So bookstores end up paying more money for books they buy from wholesalers.

author events and help to kick-start new writers' careers through special programs like B&N's Discover Great New Writers program and Borders' Original Voices. They've also created a reader-friendly, kid-happy environment where you can get a cappuccino, a fine baked good and read anything you want in peace, browsing to your heart's delight, basking in all those books.

The best way to understand a book chain is to picture it as a big brain with many tentacles ending in pods. The big brain is the central headquarters. The pods are the individual stores, each with a similar look and feel. Headquarters does most of the ordering of books and makes most of the decisions about where they're placed in the stores around the country. Indeed, just about everything that happens in the individual stores is determined by headquarters personnel. So whenever you deal with chain bookstores, you must realize that many times you'll have to go to the big brain to get what you want. Although the stores may have some autonomy, their hands are often tied when it comes to buying books or scheduling readings.

Worried that your book is selling like gangbusters in far-flung locations, miles and miles away from headquarters? Put your mind at ease. Headquarters scours sales reports daily from the biggest to the piddliest pod. And if they see that your book is moving, they'll beef up orders accordingly.

Some chains, like Barnes & Noble, have buyers who order only for particular regions. Sometimes, the regional buyer even has the power to buy for the entire country. Say, for example, you've written a southwestern cookbook. Chances are, the regional buyer for the Southwest has a much better sense of your book's potential than the head buyer based in New York. So your sales rep may pitch this buyer instead of the national cookbook buyer.

If, however, you have an Italian cookbook, chances are your rep will want to go straight to the main buyer. This one person is responsible for nearly every cookbook buy for the entire chain. If she thinks Italian cooking is on the outs, you're in trouble. Want to convince her otherwise? Making contact with her is extremely difficult because, as you can imagine, every author and every publisher in this category would like to speak with her. As a result, attempts to contact a buyer can actually do more harm than good. What you *can* do is get to know the salespeople who go out and sell your books to the chains, and give them the ammunition they need to convince the buyer that Italian food is where it's at.

You can, of course, approach individual stores in a chain and get to know the people there. The manager at your local outpost of a chain can become a big ally. In fact, he can contact headquarters and suggest that they carry your book or tell a regional buyer to take a serious look at it.

And if you're lucky enough to get a VIP on the phone, make sure your passion-fueled pitch is on the tip of your tongue. As Carol Hoenig, marketing national events specialist for Borders, says, "Sometimes I see a book and think, 'I don't know . . .' but then the author wins me over with his passion. A lot of times, it's the author's passion that moves me to buy a book."

Declaration of Independents

Independent bookstores tend to be more mom-and-pop (though by no means necessarily small) operations, started by an individual or a family with a great passion for books. Melissa Mytinger, the marketing manager of Cody's Books in Berkeley, California, says, "Our staff throughout the store are well read, and they're encouraged to express their opinions. We do take chances on smaller books. Small, university and independent publishers are welcome here." This is why it's so important to make connections with people in these bookstores. They can buy and sell your opus one book at a time.

A MAN AND HIS PASSION

If you want to experience the height of independence, visit Powell's Books in Portland, Oregon. Starting in the '70s in an old car dealership, Michael Powell and his father Walter, a retired painting contractor, created a bookstore with an unorthodox modus operandi. They put used and new books, hardcover and paperback, all on the same shelf. They hired knowledgeable and dedicated book lovers as staff. And they stayed open 365 days a year.

Today, Powell's Books is one of the world's largest bookstores and one of the most successful independent e-bookstores serving customers around the globe. But they'll carry your book even if you published it at Kinko's. Because Michael Powell is, as he says, "committed to giving all worthy books, big or small, easy or difficult, a chance to meet their readers and win them over."

HOW TO GET YOUR BOOK IN THE DOOR

To help you understand the world of retail, we interviewed some of America's most beloved independent booksellers about how to get in their stores. See if you can identify some common themes . . .

- Elaine Petrocelli, owner, Book Passage, Corte Madera, California: "The best way to approach a bookseller about carrying your book or holding an event is to shop there and to express your enthusiasm so that they know you're part of their community."
- Carole Horne, head buyer, Harvard Bookstore, Cambridge, Massachusetts: "Be nice and low-key. Don't insist on talking to a manager or a buyer. The worst thing you can do is be pushy and rude, and yet so many authors do just that. Low-key and nice: good. Pushy and rude: bad."
- Nancy Peters, co-owner, City Lights Bookstore, San Francisco: "Introduce yourself briefly and leave a catalog or flyer and ordering information. Of course, buying a few books never hurts!"
- Margaret Maupin, trade buyer, The Tattered Cover, Denver, Colorado: "A great thing to do is come in and say you're going to be on the local news on Saturday at noon and you'll mention that people can buy your book at our bookstore. You should also say you're going to link our bookstore to your Web site."
- Sydne Waller, head buyer, Chapter 11 Books, Atlanta, Georgia: "It seems so obvious, but it's much better to be nice and polite. Too many authors hound me in a nasty way. I always wonder, 'Why do you think this behavior will succeed?'"
- Linda Bubon, co-owner, Women & Children First, Chicago, Illinois: "Sometimes having someone else introduce your book for you can be more effective. Ask your friends or another writer who has had some success."
- Valerie Lewis, co-owner, Hicklebee's, San Jose, California: "Many authors think they're the first ones to come in here and pitch a book. You've got to understand that I have boxes of books waiting for me to read. The best way to approach us is to come in and say, 'Hi, I'm a local author and I've written a book, and I'd love you to sell it here. What's the best way for me to follow up?' And be sensitive. When someone takes a giant step toward you, you tend to take a giant step back. Approach gently."
- Jill Bailey, buyer, BookPeople, Austin, Texas: "Do not show up unannounced. Be respectful of people's time. Do your research. Make sure you're talking to

the right person. And get to the point. Sometimes people send me ten pages of quotes without giving me a real sense of what their book is about or letting me know how to get in touch with them. Make it easy to find you."

- Ty Wilson, buyer, Copperfield's Books, Sebastopol, California: "It's better to call first than to just walk in cold. That way, you don't put instant pressure on the buyer. Be upbeat. It's better to soft-sell. Your pitch has to be content-oriented. The more articulate you can be about your book, the better."
- Roberta Rubin, owner, The Bookstall, Winnetka, Illinois: "Attitude is so important. Authors have to be sensitive to what's going on in the store when they come in. If I'm in a good mood, and it's not crazy, I'm much more likely to be receptive. But please, don't pester me. Don't make me feel like I'm a publisher. I'm a bookseller."
- Rick Simonson, buyer, Elliott Bay Books, Seattle, Washington: "If I were to give a one-word answer, it would be: patience."
- Frank Sanchez, head buyer, Kepler's Books, Palo Alto, California: "The best way to present your book for consideration is to call and set up an appointment. I review most titles coming into the store, and the things I look for, besides content, are physical quality of publication and a willingness to work with us. Many authors I speak with are understandably enthusiastic about their book, but they need to be realistic as well. Getting books into the store is just a first step."
- Deb Covey, buyer, Books & Company, Dayton, Ohio: "Walk in with your book in hand and a good press release, not just a mock-up. Attitude is also very important. Some authors come in all cocky; they don't understand that we're inundated with books. It really helps to be honest and open and friendly."
- Debby Simmons, inventory and distributed products manager, Deseret Book Company, Salt Lake City, Utah: "We're in a niche market, so it's really important to do your research and make sure your book fits in with what we sell. Then bring or send us your book with a press release, and make sure you follow up."
- Tom Campbell, co-owner, Regulator Books, Durham, North Carolina: "Walk into the store with your book in hand and show us the goods. It's important that your book fit in with our store. We're a general bookstore, but we don't sell romance novels, for example."
- Andy Ross, owner, Cody's Books, Berkeley, California: "Here's the best thing you can say: 'I will send all my friends to your store if you stock my book.'"

The best independent bookstores are the beating hearts of their neighborhoods. Plugged into what's happening all around them, they're centers of learning and knowledge and fun. They know their readers, and their readers trust them to know what books are new and great. Gary Frank of San Francisco's Booksmith describes his relationship with his neighborhood: "We're in the Haight-Ashbury, so we have a lot of quirky stuff here. That's one of the things that makes independent bookstores unique—we cater to our neighborhood. In terms of how I order my books, I look at lots of catalogs, and book companies come and pitch me their list. And then I use my instinct and my knowledge of the community."

SELLING BOOKS IN UNEXPECTED PLACES

Special markets are places you wouldn't normally expect to sell a book. Doctors' offices, hair salons, the backs of cereal boxes. But if you do it right, you can sell lots of books to these special places. Sometimes a book can do very poorly in bookstores yet sell thousands of copies to special markets. *The Recovery Book* by Al J. Mooney, M.D., and Arlene and Howard Eisenberg sold minimally in bookstores but did fabulously with hospitals and treatment programs and nontraditional groups. This book now has over 240,000 copies in print.

Hilary Liftin, the author of *Candy and Me: A Love Story*, was smart enough to include a resource guide to candy stores in her book. When the book came out, her publisher contacted all those stores to find out if they wanted to give copies away to customers as an incentive to buy candy. Now many of these stores sell her book, and she's featured on several of their Web sites.

Some special markets make immediate sense, but some require more imagination. For example, maybe your book about humor in the workplace can be sold to Southwest Airlines as an employee giveaway since Southwest considers humor to be a job prerequisite. Maybe your book about famed flatulence artist Le Petomane would make a great special promotion for Beano.

When you're talking retail, categories vary seasonally. Is your book appropriate for graduation or Mother's Day? Christmas or Easter? The kick-

WACKY PLACES TO SELL YOUR BOOK

Some special markets are *beyond* special. They're places where you'd never in a million years think you could sell books. And yet, if you're bound and determined, books can be sold there.

Heru Ptah, author of *A Hip-Hop Story*, self-published his novel and decided to take to the streets of New York City. Well, to the subways, actually. His goal was to sell 50 books a day. At $10 a pop. In all, he sold over 10,000 copies. One night on the subway he sold a copy to Jacob Hoye, who just happened to be the director of MTV Books. Jacob took the book home and devoured it. He loved the book so much that he acquired it for his publishing house.

Susan Wooldridge will sell her book *Poemcrazy* anywhere. One summer she was in Scotland to enjoy the Edinburgh Theatre Festival, the largest arts festival in the world. She noticed that a little square tucked away far from the crowds was getting a lot of foot traffic, so she made a space for herself there and sold a bunch of her books—right on the streets of Edinburgh.

off of football season or Halloween? Just think about how stores change merchandise according to the time of year. How can your book work into their schedules?

Jenny Mandel, director of special markets at Workman, says this: "Special market sales are the forgotten stepchild of publishing because people don't understand them. They can be bigger than independents and chains, and these opportunities to sell books are more and more valuable. But they are extremely hard to come by. You face a lot of rejection."

It's hard to sell to special markets with anything but a finished book, because people want to see the final product. But in the meantime there's no reason why you shouldn't ask to meet with a special sales person at your publisher's. Prepare a list of companies you think your book would be appropriate for as a tie-in or as a giveaway. Don't forget the obvious. Include mail-order catalogs. You may also want to prepare pitch letters tailored for each company that you can hand over to the appropriate person. It's back to the old PYPIP formula: 1) make a connection, 2) personalize your pitch, 3) provide information about you that will entice buyers.

If you're going after a special sale yourself, follow the advice of Frank Fochetta, director of special sales and custom publishing at Simon &

Coming to your publisher with a special sale in tow will make you very popular and may infuse the special sales department with new enthusiasm. You may also find that you've talked your way into a larger first printing.

Schuster: "Before calling on a potential buyer, learn as much as you can about the company and its Web site. If the company is nearby, go to its offices to pick up its literature. If you can afford the time and money, go to trade shows and talk with the company's salespeople. Try to make an appointment with your particular prospect, who is likely to be the product manager or, if you're dealing with a consumer products company, the brand manager."

Even if your publisher puts only minimal effort into special sales, there's no reason you can't take the ball and run with it. As Jenny Mandel says, "Nothing about special markets is rocket science. It's all about staying after it. Usually you don't get a callback, or you find out the book's been passed on to someone else. It's a scavenger hunt."

One of the tricks with special sales is locating the right person to target within a company. And then it's all about follow-up. Jenny has this final advice: "This job is really about finding the needle in a haystack. The best thing authors can do is go out and see what kinds of special markets would be interested in their book. There has to be a place for their book. It has to fit."

THE WORLD WIDE WEB

Web sales have changed the book business. And not just with regard to books with subject matter that might make buyers uncomfortable about purchasing them in a store. While your publisher will handle sales to the big Internet bookstores, there's no reason why you can't scour the World Wide Web for an array of smaller sites that could sell your book. These might be for organizations, foundations, online catalogs and smaller online bookstores, many of which sell through Amazon. Here's yet another opportunity to roll out that pitch. Re-tailor it so these sites know why your book will sell there.

Not only have Amazon and bn.com become great ways to sell books electronically, but they've also become every author's way of monitoring sales. Amazon has a feature called the Amazon Sales Rank, which rates

TALES OF AN AMAZON JUNKIE

One author was obsessed with tracking the sales of her book. "I actually stopped calling it a book," she told us. "I started calling it a unit. I just couldn't stop checking my Amazon ranking. It was all I cared about."

At first, her book wavered in the high five figures, but then she was asked onto a big national talk show to discuss her "unit." After the piece aired, her book started to spike on Amazon. It climbed to 2,000, then 200, then all the way up to 26. "I was dancing around the house as if I'd just been crowned Queen of the World," the author told us. "It was one of the happiest moments of my life, and for *one* brief shining moment I thought I was a success." Well, of course, then came the crash. The next day, her unit started free-falling, bum over teakettle, back past 50. Tumbling terribly to 100. Slipping and sinking beyond 250. Dropping through 1,000. When the dust settled, it was back down in the high five figures.

Soon thereafter, a local book group chose her book to read and discuss. "I know it seems a little vain and strange, but it changed my whole attitude. I had such fun with the book group. Those women were so nice. They loved my book. And I had such a blast talking about what was so near and dear to my heart. I stopped looking at my ranking every waking minute of every day, and my book ceased to be a unit. I realized that my bouncing baby had become a big, grown-up lady, that she was beautiful and that I loved her dearly. *Love* her dearly. That day, I went from being a failure to a success. In nobody's eyes but my own."

your book in comparison to other books they sell, with #1 being the best-selling book. It's hard to know how your book is selling, so it's extremely tempting to check the status of your book on Amazon regularly. Okay, hourly. Okay, every 30 seconds.

Truth be told, Amazon rankings may or may not relate to the overall sales of your book. If you're on the *Today* show, you might see your book fly up through the ranking system—a good indicator that it's selling well around the country. On the other hand, your book may sell well on Amazon but not do particularly well elsewhere. Or, conversely, you may have a book that's selling fabulously in hip-hop shops around the country but ain't doing diddly-squat on Amazon. That said, if you were to pop in on us unexpectedly, you'd be sure to find Arielle glued to the screen, checking the rankings of one of her books.

If you want to beef up your presence on Amazon, bn.com and other e-bookstores, urge friends and colleagues to post a five-star review of your book. The more, the merrier. And the earlier, the better. In addition, you and your friends should go to the Amazon listing for other similar or related books. Once there, look for the section labeled "Our customers' advice . . ." and recommend your book.

LOVELY, LUSCIOUS LIBRARIES

There are just under 120,000 libraries in the United States, and you want your book in as many of them as the traffic will allow. You can do readings at libraries. You can put together panels where you discuss your topic with other writers. And librarians can be a great source of word-of-mouth buzz if they know about your book. You simply cannot underestimate the power of the librarian. Remember Michael Moore's story about how *Stupid White Men* finally got published? His book was saved from the recycling bin by the networking power of librarians.

"I have always imagined that Paradise will be a kind of library."
—Jorge Luis Borges

One of the other great things about libraries is that no matter how offbeat your subject is, there's sure to be a librarian who has a collection it will fit right into. Libraries also tend to be great buyers of regional books. If you have a book that concentrates on a specific area, be sure all your local libraries know about it. Go to them. Befriend them. Show up at events and fund-raisers. When the moment is right, be prepared with your pitch, promotional material and book.

BACK TO SCHOOL

Getting your book taught in elementary and high schools or at colleges and universities can result in blacklist manna. Some publishing companies have marketing departments and sales reps specifically devoted to targeting schools across the country and around the globe.

If you feel your book is worthy of course adoption, rejigger your pitch accordingly and get it post-haste to the appropriate people at your publisher's (ask your editor who handles this type of sale). Ideally, they will send a flyer to every applicable department in the country (although it's expensive to buy these lists, so your publisher may start with one particular group). If they don't, guess who has to? You. Internet searches are your best bet for tracking down colleges and universities. It helps immensely if you have a track record of lecturing and/or presenting at well-known schools. You can use this pedigree to lure prospective academics to buy your book, put it on their reading lists and maybe bring you in to lecture.

ROTTEN RETURNS

Remember when we talked about returns in Chapter 7? They're about to rear their ugly heads again. In this day and age, when a bookstore's margin of profit per title is tiny, booksellers often exhibit very little patience when it comes to waiting for a book's success. If a title doesn't sell within a few months, it goes back to the publisher with its tail between its legs.

While most returns fall somewhere between the 10% and 25% mark, returns can run as steep as 75%. If, God forbid, you should have returns, know that you're in excellent company. Almost every book suffers from returnitis.

If you want to know how many of your books are being returned, check your royalty statement, which lists sales, returns and reserves. (For more on reserves, see page 171.)

THE REMAINDER TABLE

If your book is shortly coming out in paperback or if it's not selling well, your publisher may take the copies they have on hand and remainder them because of the steep cost of warehousing them. Remaindered books are sold at such deep discounts that neither you nor your publisher makes much money from the sale.

If this happens to you, don't freak out. Check the remainder table at your local bookstore. What do you see? Lots of bestselling authors? Books that were on the *New York Times* bestseller list? Yes!

Remaindering happens whenever a publisher prints beyond the demand, so you're in very good company. Often, the *best* of company. Only when you're remaindered can you say, "I saw my book sandwiched between Philip Roth and Toni Morrison!"

THE LAST WORD ON ROYALTIES

One of the most common questions we hear from first-time authors is "When do I get my royalties?" Most often, even after you've earned out your advance, there's a long lag time between the moment your book is sold and when you get your cut. Sometimes this can take up to a year, and occasionally, with a smaller or disreputable (gasp!) publisher, you may never see one royal penny.

If and when you receive statements, you want to know how to decipher the gobbledygook. In fact, some royalty statements seem purposely gobbledygookish to confuse authors about how many copies their book has sold.

Note that your royalty statement will probably reflect sales that occurred a number of months ago. Be sure to check the end date of the royalty statement so you know exactly what period it covers.

A good royalty statement should include:

- The number of copies sold, returned and held in reserve
- The number of copies sold at a high discount, as exports, through mail order and all the other types of sales detailed in your contract
- Sub rights income (for foreign sales, book club, audio, serial rights, etc.)
- Sales made in the particular period of the statement as well as total sales to date

If your statement does not include this information, ask your publisher or agent. It's your right to know.

Once you've gathered everything you need, it's time to check the accuracy of your statement. This is a huge pain, and yet it's very important. The royalty statement is put together by someone in the accounting department at your publisher's who undoubtedly works on many royalty statements; therefore, human errors crop up. One decimal point in the wrong place can be the difference between a trip to the Bahamas and an evening at Chuck E. Cheese. Daniel Greenberg, co-owner of the Levine Greenberg Agency, was nitpicking his way through a client's royalty statement when he discovered an error. After he checked it several times, it was clear his client was owed just shy of $100K!. Imagine the client's delight when he received that phone call. You may not have as meticulous an agent, if you have one at all, so hone your own nitpicking skills. Here's how:

1. Ask your editor or the appropriate person in your publisher's royalty/ accounting department how many books were in print up to the end date of your royalty statement. Then add up the total number of books sold, returned and held in reserve. Is that number close to the in-print-number ballpark?

2. In all likelihood, your contract stipulated a "reasonable" reserve for returns. Does the reserve for returns on your royalty statement really seem "reasonable"? If your book has been out for more than a couple of years, this number should be small and based on the number of returns from the last royalty period.

3. Most contracts have escalating royalties. This is one of the biggest trouble spots in royalty statements, especially if your escalators are not typical. Publishers sometimes continue to calculate your royalties at the original rate. So pull out your contract and make sure that if, for example, your royalty rate is supposed to go up after 5,000 copies, this is reflected in your statement.

4. Does your statement account for all sub rights sales? Does it list exactly who the sales were made to? If your book sold to Italy and you want to know how it's doing there, you can request those royalty statements as well.

It doesn't happen often, but occasionally there will be an irreconcilable discrepancy between the number of copies you think you've sold and the number of copies your publisher claims they've sold. This is usually an accounting/mathematics problem; however, publishers have knowingly underreported sales of books. If you find yourself in either situation, you may have recourse. If your contract includes a stipulation stating that an accountant of your choice should be allowed to examine the publisher's books (see page 174), now is the time to ask for an audit. Be sure to hire an accountant who has experience with publishing audits. Contact the Authors Guild if you have trouble finding the right person.

During this audit, your accountant will actually get to look at how many orders have been placed by bookstores, distributors and other sales channels. By delving deep into the publisher's numbers, he'll be able to determine exactly how many books have sold and exactly how much money you're owed. While this may be a last resort and can possibly result in strained relations, sometimes it's the only way to make sure your publisher SHOWS YOU THE MONEY!

KEEP THE SALES TRAIN ROLLING

Books can lead long, healthy lives or they can disappear in the blink of an eye. In the end, keeping your book in print and continuing to sell is up to you and you alone. The techniques we've described in this chapter should be used as guidelines for you to develop unique and ongoing ways to sell your book. From bookstores, universities and libraries to conventions to pet stores, yoga centers, beauty salons and candy stores, the whole wide world is a fertile breeding ground in which you can plant the seeds from which the sales of your book will grow.

Happy sales to you!

CHAPTER 13

PUBLISH YOURSELF

William Blake. James Joyce. Virginia Woolf. Rudyard Kipling. Edgar Allan Poe. Ezra Pound. Mark Twain. Gertrude Stein. Walt Whitman. Carl Sandburg. Beatrix Potter. What do these celebrated authors have in common? They all self-published books. Yet self-publishing is seen in certain circles as the illegitimate cousin of the book world. Janis Jaquith, an NPR commentator and self-published author of *Birdseed Cookies: A Fractured Memoir*, says, "When I announced to my writer friends that I was planning to self-publish, you'd have thought I'd just announced that I had syphilis or something. Such shame! Such scandal! I'm glad I didn't listen to the naysayers, because I've had a ball with this."

The fact is, self-publishing *can* be a ball. It can also launch you into superstardom and turn you into a millionaire (okay, rarely, but still . . .). That's precisely what self-publishing did for the now ubiquitous Tim and Nina Zagat and their restaurant guides, for John Bartlett and his familiar quotations, and for many, many others.

IT'S UP TO YOU

As the publishing business becomes increasingly corporate, record numbers of writers are turning to publishing their books themselves. Two of the great things about self-publishing are: 1) You can make your book exactly how you want it. Your cover, your title, the size of your book, its contents—everything is yours and yours alone to decide. 2) You get to keep a lot more of the profits. (If, of course, there *are* any.)

Here are some other reasons to self-publish:

- You've written a book about a specific subject that publishers consider too narrow. Or too regional. Or too whatever. A social history of albino squirrels in the Ozarks, for example.

- You've written up your family history or the lifetime of a loved one that will be of great interest to Aunt Coco or Cousin Momo and a handful of other blood relations, but no one else.
- You want a book to use as a promotional tool for your business or as a calling card for yourself as a writer or artist. But you don't want to have to wait a year or more to get it published through the more normal channels.
- You really want to publish a book, but you just don't have the right kind of personality to market it to an agent and/or publisher and you have some money to lose.
- You already have a relationship with a specific organization, retailer or company that has the ability to sell your book.
- No matter how much you rewrite, or how hard you market yourself, you just can't find anybody to work with you. You know there are readers who will buy your book, and you're sick and tired of relentless rejection at the hands of shortsighted, narrow-minded agents and publishing houses.

If you decide self-publishing is the road you'd like to go down, this chapter will serve as your map. But realize there will be much to learn. So as you get farther and farther down your own self-publishing path, you will almost certainly have to be a research maven and find out every-

THE JOYS OF SELF-PUBLISHING

Lisa Zamarin is a visual artist and a writer, but her mainstay is graphic design. Even though she had suggested to many writers that they self-publish and had designed many books, she had never considered doing her own. That is, until a well-known writer read one of her pieces and asked why she'd never published her own book. She decided to make a book that would combine her passions for writing, art and graphic design. She wrote the text, created the artwork and designed the cover and interior. "When I finally got the books back," she said, "I could barely stand to open them I was so scared. But of course I did, and I was so happy. They turned out really well. And those books are so precious to me." Her book, *The Things I Remember Forgetting*, is as beautiful to look at as it is precious to Lisa.

THE HORRORS OF SELF-PUBLISHING

One self-published author was convinced he could easily sell 5,000 copies of his book. He knew there was a sizable audience for his humor book, and he thought all he had to do was write a good book, get it printed and put up a Web site that would have his reading public flocking to him. After six months had passed and no such flock appeared, he was struck by a sad but sobering thought: He would have to market, publicize and sell his book, too. These were not activities that came easily to him, nor was he particularly interested in developing those parts of his personality. The result? Three years later, he can't even stand to go into his basement because 4,500 books are crying in the corner.

thing from how to fit 2,000 copies of your book into your 450-square-foot studio apartment to how much it costs to ship your book to Kalamazoo. We also suggest buying two important resource guides: 1) *Literary Market Place*, which in the publisher's own words is "the worldwide resource to the book publishing industry" and lists all kinds of crucial industry services that you'll need to know about along the way, and 2) self-publishing guru Dan Poynter's *The Self-Publishing Manual*, which will supply you with all the nitty and gritty you will ever need.

THE MANY FACES OF SELF-PUBLISHING

These days, you have many self-publishing options. You can don all the hats: publisher and printer finder, production manager, cover designer, marketer, distributor, shipper and doer-of-everything. Or you can hand all those hats to one of the new print-on-demand publishers. Or you can end up anywhere in between.

The better you understand what kind of book you want to make, the easier it will be to determine which self-publishing path to pursue. Are you content going to your local copy center, making a mess o' copies of your manuscript, slapping on a cover and stapling them together? Do you want a spectacularly elaborate photo-filled opus that's printed on the finest paper money can buy? Or are you simply looking for a way to make your book look like the average trade paperback from Random House? Investigate as many different kinds of books as you can. See which ones appeal both aesthetically and functionally. Make a list of the qualities you want in your book. As you do, your book will come into clearer and clearer focus.

If you choose the do-it-all-yourself route, you'll learn every aspect of publishing, which will be great training for selling future books, either on your own or to an established publisher. (In the latter case, you can use the insight you've gained to evaluate the publisher's treatment of your work.) But if you decide you can't do it all, there are many different kinds of companies that can help you self-publish. Some will lay out and print your book. Others will also edit your book, design your cover, file your book with the Library of Congress, file for your copyright, obtain a bar code and ISBN, make press kits, bookmarks, postcards and brochures, even sell you padded shipping envelopes! The whole megillah.

All, of course, for a fee.

VANITY PUBLISHING

In days of yore, vanity publishing and self-publishing were virtually synonymous. Not anymore. In fact, you want to stay as far away from this form of "publishing" as humanly possible.

But what exactly is vanity publishing? Our definition is as follows: it's when you pay a company to publish your book (which includes the cost of designing, laying out and printing) but—and here's the major catch—you get NO royalties on books sold *and* you give away ALL the rights to your work. In other words, you not only give up the rights to your own work, but you actually pay someone to take them from you. This payment could be in the tens of thousands of dollars. And if you thought that, at the very least, these "publishers" would work hard to sell lots of copies of your book, you'd be sorely mistaken. These "publishers" make the bulk of their money by overcharging you for production costs (and then by overcharging you for publicity and marketing materials). There is no incentive for a vanity publisher to sell your book. And bookstores will most certainly be leery of these sharks in sheep's clothing.

Please understand that just because you pay a company to help you publish your book doesn't mean you're dealing with a vanity publisher. Vanity publishers are strictly limited to those who take all rights to your work and give you no royalty.

THE MAN WHO DIDN'T DO HIS RESEARCH

We know a man who's a well-known figure in his esoteric field of pharmacy studies. The man knew absolutely nothing about the publishing business, but he wanted to take his passion for his expertise and put it into print. He surfed the waves of the Web and found a company that called itself a "publisher" in his neck of the woods, and without checking around or finding out about any other options, he "signed up" with the company. He was told it was typical for the author to pay for the costs of publishing, but that he would easily earn back this money once he was selling books. They showed him the math, and it all looked very promising. They asked for half the payment on signing of the agreement and half on finished books. He made his first payment, and things seemed to be moving ahead. He received a cover design and saw sample page layouts. He was starting to get excited, thinking about giving his book to colleagues.

Sometimes it was hard to reach his contact, but he assumed there were many authors to contend with. Then, when the date passed for finished books with nary a book in sight, his contact gave a legitimate-sounding excuse and told him they'd definitely be ready in two weeks' time. Two weeks later, still no books. He called again. More excuses. Finally he received a half-dozen copies of his book, and he was filled with a profound joy until the "publisher" said they needed the final payment. When he asked about the rest of the books, they said they were currently being shipped and would arrive within a week. Overexcited by his books in hand, he cut the check. Guess what? The rest of his books never arrived. He left numerous messages and never got a call back. After a couple of weeks, he called and the number was no longer in service.

So, if you go down the self-publishing route, make sure you get lots of references and that you don't make any payments until you get what you were promised. Don't become a cautionary tale.

PRINT-ON-DEMAND PUBLISHING

If you plan on publishing a small number of books (say, 200 copies or less) or need to limit up-front costs, you'll probably want to explore print-on-demand publishing. POD publishing allows for printing books one at a time for a nonprohibitive cost. The nonprohibitive part is what makes it so exciting. Two of the biggest POD companies, iUniverse and Xlibris, are partially owned by publishing titans Barnes & Noble and Random House, respectively, in part for market research purposes. Clearly the big boys, along with everyone else, are interested in the future of print-on-demand.

Fortunately, you can take advantage of this technology and the services provided along with it at the new crop of POD companies that are popping up like mushrooms in a wet field. These companies can minimize your up-front costs and greatly simplify the self-publishing process. They will edit and copy-edit your manuscript, they'll design your cover and interior, they'll assign it an ISBN and bar code, they'll help you market and publicize your book, they'll obtain distribution for it, and more. But you keep all rights to your work.

Each company has different packages you can choose from. But, generally speaking, for as little as $500 you can have many of your basic self-publishing needs covered. For a few hundred dollars more, you can get editorial services and help with marketing. And for under two grand you can get help with every aspect of the publishing puzzle.

Sounds good, right? It is. But there is no free lunch. POD publishing has major downsides that offset the advantages of self-publishing, i.e., making your book exactly what you want and keeping more of the profits. For example, as a rule (and there are exceptions), POD publishers:

1. Provide only templates for you to choose from when it comes to your cover and interior. This will significantly limit your chances of having an original-looking book, if that's what you're after.

2. Determine the price of your book. This is determined by the page count, not by your audience and what they will pay. So, if your book is 150 pages, it will be sold for the price they've set for all 150-page books, even if you know your audience will pay more.

3. Determine the discount of your book when it sells to booksellers and other outlets.

4. Determine the discount at which you buy books. You're often given 5 to 10 books for free, but the rest you have to purchase. Some POD publishers offer higher discounts the more books you buy. But some don't, and their discounts are low. For those that do offer discounts, they can start as low as 20% for under 10 copies and escalate to 80% for over a thousand copies. Since these discounts can change, be sure to do comparisons before you choose a POD publisher.

We do not suggest using a POD publisher if you're planning on producing more than 200 or so books, because even with a high discount you'll make much bigger profits if you print books yourself. The exception here would be if you simply don't want to handle all the other stuff and are willing to give up profit for help with the process. If this is the case, go with a POD publisher that gives an escalating discount based on the number of books you buy.

Each POD publisher does things a little—or a lot—differently. Before deciding on which one to go with, make a list of what is most important to you and make your choice based on those criteria. (For a list of the largest and most reliable POD publishers, see Appendix I.)

BECOMING YOUR OWN PUBLISHER

If you decide it's in your best interest to be your own publisher, you have much to learn. There are many people to track down. Bargains to hunt. A mammoth amount of research ahead. But there will also be a lot of rewards to offset your risks.

Balancing Your Budget

Being your own publisher requires a potentially significant (depending on the size of your checkbook) up-front investment, so it's time to yank out those math skills and figure out your costs. Creating a budget begins with our old friend research. Here are some of the places your money will go:

- Editor/copy editor
- Cover designer
- Layout
- Permissions
- Lawyer (to check text so you don't get sued and/or to set up company for tax purposes)
- Author photo
- ISBN
- Printing
- Shipping
- Marketing (ads, postcards, tchotchkes)
- Publicity (hiring publicist; paying for book tour or events)
- Web site

To give you a ballpark sense of a self-publishing budget, we will now introduce you to our favorite imaginary author, Sid Sickamore, who was looking to self-publish his 200-page tour de force *Legumes! Legumes! Legumes!*, a narrative history with recipes for the legume enthusiast in all of us. We'll be following Sid's self-publishing saga through this chapter.

Although Sid had written a wonderful book about the history of legumes, along with tips for planting and cooking, he's not much of an editor (and frankly, we know no one who can impartially edit his own work), nor is he a designer. Fortunately, Sid is a great self-promoter and, by God, he loves legumes. He took his pluses and minuses into account when he researched what his self-publishing budget would end up being. With $5,000 to spend on his book, he couldn't go crazy throwing around his samolians, but he had a little room to play in. Here's what he came up with as his options:

Editor/Copy Editor

Option 1: $250 (from Sid's friend Nancy, who once worked as a copy editor for *Garbanzo Monthly*)

Option 2: $400 (from a reputable editor in town whom Sid tracked down through his local writing group)

Option 3: $2,000 (from a professional former senior editor at Random House found on the Internet)

Cover Designer

Option 1: $0 (from Sid's artist son, who agreed to help his dad in exchange for using the car whenever he wants)

Option 2: $150 (from a recent graduate of the local art college)

Option 3: $5,000 (from a favorite designer/artist at *Rutabaga Quarterly*, the price of which includes an original illustration of a legume)

Interior Designer

Option 1: $0 (from Sid's wife, who's a Pagemaker whiz)

Option 2: $250 (from a local bookseller who does this sort of thing on the side)

Option 3: $3,500 (from a designer recommended by a small local publisher Sid found through the Publishers Marketing Association)

ISBNs and Bar Code

$300

Author Photo

Option 1: $0 (Sid's favorite photo from his 50th birthday party)

Option 2: $250 (from a writing seminar contact who does a lot of author photos)

Option 3: $750 (from the photographer who shot his daughter's wedding)

Permissions for Photos/Illustrations

Option 1: $0 (for 12 public-domain line drawings)

Option 2: $250 (for one shot from a photo agency like Corbis)

Option 3: $500 (for 10 photos from the Legume Society of America at $50 apiece)

Option 4: $750 (for all of the above)

Lawyer/Accountant

Option 1: $0 (from an accountant pal in Sid's drum circle in exchange for gardening help)

Option 2: $500 (from sister's best friend's nephew, who just graduated from law school)

Option 3: $1,200 (from "the best lawyer in town")

Printing

Option 1: $1.01 per book (for a trade paperback with standard 50lb paper)

Option 2: $1.04 per book (for trade paperback with a little bit nicer 60lb paper)

Option 3: $2.47 (for trade paperback with standard paper and an 8-page color insert)

Web Site

Option 1: $59.95 (from Sid's 12-year-old next-door neighbor, in exchange for the new Die Alien Scum! video game)

Option 2: $500 (from a local Web designer recommended by florist friend who just had a Web site made for her store)

Option 3: $5,000 (from a high-end Web designer who specializes in author sites; found through Web research)

Shipping Supplies

$47 for 50 boxes in two different sizes (one that holds 16 books and another that holds 32 for bulk sales and shipments to wholesaler/distributor)

$52 for case of 300 padded envelopes for individual sales (which comes down to 17¢ per book)

A LESSON IN SUPPLY AND DEMAND

Roger Gilbertson and a partner started a company related to building robots and developed an expertise with shape-memory alloys, an obscure and unique way of creating motion without motors. One day a visiting mentor, having listened to Roger talk on the phone, commented that he had just answered the same set of questions for the third time that day. The mentor said, "You should write this all down and sell it to people instead of giving it away for free." Roger sat down and wrote up a detailed explanation of a number of his robot-building projects: "It was so esoteric that it didn't even seem worth it to go with a publisher. I went to Kinko's and made stapled xeroxed copies with card stock covers."

Roger then ran an ad in monthly electronics magazines for *The Muscle Wires Project Book*. For $39.95, buyers would get the book *plus* a kit of the hard-to-find alloys in wire form, manufactured by a supplier that Roger had known for years. In the publishing industry, this is known as a *book plus*. There were no other sources for this information, and very few for the materials, so Roger knew he could determine the price. In fact, he was making $20 per book. "The really cool thing I learned was that not one person (in over 1,000 books sold) complained, because the information was so vital. No one cared that it was xeroxed. They were getting inside info."

Still, the scientist in Roger kept him researching. On the printing front, he decided to switch to web press (a process in which printing is done on large rolls of paper) with perfect binding, a glued back and a soft cover. He printed 10,000 copies. On the presentation front, he hired a professional graphic designer to design a new cover. He also went to hobby stores and found out what they'd like to see on the cover. He got information on key words and phrases that should be in the top half-inch of the cover to help attract readers. He found out that hobby store owners liked "third edition" to be highlighted in

Shipping Costs*
$6 for smaller-size box of books
$11 for larger-size box of books
*Because authors typically charge for shipping and handling above and beyond the cost of their books, the costs here are limited to shipping to a wholesaler or distributor.

Marketing
Option 1: $100 (for 500 business-card-size legume magnets)
Option 2: $150 (for ad in *Legume Lovers Monthly*)
Option 3: $185 (for 1,000 postcards made via online postcard company)

the top corner. And he added a gold sticker on the cover for the gold medal one of his robots won, because he knew this would stand out in hobby stores.

The only things Roger wasn't too happy about were the boxes and boxes of books that filled his apartment. He partially solved the problem by building furniture out of them. But with later editions of the book, he decided to switch his printing to a new POD technology called DocuTech. "Now we simply order 500 books at a time. It looks better than web press. We still have the perfect-bound, full-color cover, and the interior is a crisp laser-printed original. Plus we can update the contents quickly as the technology advances so we can keep the book up to date."

Printing wasn't the only piece of the self-publishing process that required a learning curve. Distribution was Roger's number one headache, and it required a lot of trial and error. "I knew this book was for electronics and hobby stores. But in the days before the Internet and Amazon, the book distribution scene was entirely different. Books were sold only through a few giant national distributors. I found one to sell to these places, and it was a nightmare. They'd buy five or six copies, and then they'd return four and order six more." Though the distributor was a bust, Roger persevered. He got his book into these stores by going in and introducing himself and learning what each store wanted and needed. He then got lists of stores around the country and sent off a press kit. He also got into catalogs by tracking down the buyers and giving them his well-honed pitch. His company was a very early Internet user and had its first Web page up and running in December of 1996, long before the rest of the world caught on.

In 15 years, Roger has sold over 40,000 copies of a book whose subject most of us have never even heard of. His is a true self-publishing success story.

Publicist

Option 1: $0 (Sid, being a mega self-promoter, knows he could do this himself.)

Option 2: $2,500 (from publicist on the Legume Board)

Option 3: $10,000 (from publicist found through the acknowledgments in Sid's favorite book)

Events

Option 1: $0 (if Sid decides to do them only locally)

Option 2: $500 (for book party at home for 150 people)

Option 3: $2,500 (for book tour of the Midwest)

What should Sid do? Obviously, some choices were made for him. The high-end cover designer would have wiped out his whole budget in one fell swoop. But other choices were less obvious, and they all came back to this question: What kind of book did Sid want to make? We'll see exactly what and how he chose as he came to each fork in his publishing road.

Need help funding your project? Check out the grant info in Appendix I and/or subscribe to *Poets & Writers Magazine*, which lists all kinds of grants and awards available to writers.

Getting Back to Basics

Knowing your competition, audience, publicity, marketing, sales and special markets is perhaps even more crucial when you're publishing yourself than when you're working with a publisher. These essential areas influence the kinds and number of books you should print. We will lay out some of the specific issues that affect a self-published book, but it would probably be prudent to read the PYPIP competition, audience, publicity and marketing, sales and special markets sections in Chapter 2 to see how they impact your self-publishing decisions.

THE COMPETITION

It is always difficult to get a self-published book into stores (even if you go with a POD publisher that comes with distribution). And another book too similar to yours will greatly increase the difficulty factor.

Sid found another book on the history of legumes, but it was targeted to ag students and didn't include any gardening tips or recipes. He felt his book would reach out to a more popular audience and that, in fact, this other book was not in direct competition.

YOUR AUDIENCE

The more accurately you can ascertain the size of your audience and where you can find them, the less likely you are to have boxes of your sad unsold book in your basement.

Sid knew that 5,000 legume enthusiasts attend the National Legume Convention every year, and he felt he could sell books to approximately 300 of them. He also knew that several thousand farm stands and farmer's markets across the country have no prejudice against self-published books.

After contacting two dozen of them, he was confident he could sell another few hundred to his audience at these outlets. Also, by asking around, he found out that many in his audience would like a nice-looking book, not only for themselves, but to give to their friends as presents.

MARKETABILITY

It's one thing to identify your audience; it's another to inform them about your book. Getting your book into newsletters and publications and onto radio shows is vital.

Sid had to figure out how to get his book into the hearts and minds of legume lovers. If he could do it through legume chat rooms, by reaching legume lovers over the Internet and by working farmer's markets all over creation, it would make his job much less expensive. However, taking out expensive ads in *Legume Magazine* or traveling the country to speak to legume groups would eat up his budget in no time.

WHY ME?

As we've said, turning yourself into a person of interest to the media is one of the key ways of getting continued press. If you're not an "expert," or if you have no angle to draw attention to yourself, it will be difficult to generate the excitement needed to make a splash.

Luckily, Sid had spent his life collecting humorous legume anecdotes. He also had a custom-made legume suit, which drew crowds whenever he wore it and which had landed him in the local paper on several occasions. So he devised a few legume lectures that he could give everywhere from secondary schools and agricultural colleges to public libraries and gardening centers.

SELLING YOUR BOOK

Another big challenge is getting distribution so that you can actually sell your book to the public at large. As an individual, you can reach out to only so many places. However, one key store (and it doesn't have to be a bookstore) can mean a sold-out printing, so selling to the right places is as important as selling to many. On the other hand, many self-published authors have created such a strong Internet presence that they don't need to sell in stores at all.

How was Sid going to sell his book? Would he sell it out of his living room? Through his Web site? Use a distributor who would take a chunk of his nut? Would he go with greengrocers? Was a supermarket chain going to sell his books in the vegetable section? Could he talk nurseries into selling them by the cash register? Fresh produce markets? Could he succeed at the very difficult job of convincing bookstores to carry his book? Sid knew he had to zero in on those places with the most interest in legumes if he was going to land at least one bigger bulk sale. He also liked the idea of signing on with a distributor for bookstores, since calling up hundreds of stores across the country seemed overwhelming.

PITCHING YOUR BOOK

You better have a great pitch, because without the support of a professional sales force you're working without a net. Your pitch is your tool to entice distributors, bookstores, specialty stores, the media and the guy sitting next to you on the plane.

Sid knew his challenge was to make a book about legumes seem interesting to his core audience: rabid legume-heads. But he thought he had something to say to a wider audience. So he perfected his pitch to the point where he could pique the interest of even the most die-hard legume hater.

FINDING A MODEL

Because of the prejudice against self-published books, the importance of finding a model that generates genuine excitement is accentuated. Demonstrating how your book will attract the audience of a book that's already been successful (but is not exactly like yours) will help you convince stores to carry your book and people to buy it.

Sid had a great model in the classic *Totally Tomatoes*, a book that combined a narrative with recipes (though no gardening tips). In addition, he used as backup the recent spate of one-subject histories, including *Cod: A Biography of a Fish That Changed the World*, *Salt: A World History* and *Vanilla: Travels in Search of the Ice-Cream Orchid*.

Writing Your Book All by Your Lonesome

Keep envisioning your book. Imagine your audience. See yourself selling and signing your books. Now it's time to start writing.

Some of the advantages of self-publishing are that you get to set your own pace. You don't need to steer your book down a path your editor insists upon, and you don't have to worry about delivering a manuscript that won't be accepted. But you still might want to hire an editor or writing coach with whom you can hash out your plan (see Chapter 2 for hiring details). And as you near completion of your manuscript, hiring an editor is crucial for making sure your book is up to professional standards. Just take a moment to consider how much an objective, professional eye can help your book. If you think your manuscript is perfect just the way it is, let us be blunt: It almost certainly isn't. It's the rare book that doesn't benefit from a good stiff edit.

Ideally, you will hire someone who is capable of both editing and copy-editing your book. Someone with the ability to assess overall content, narrative flow and voice, as well as to correct any of the grammatical and typographical errors that give self-published books everywhere a bad name. It's an immutable law of human nature that no matter how many times one person scans a document, errors will be missed.

Sid opted for a reputable editor he found through his local writing group. He met with her and felt that her experience at a small publishing house and her interest in gardening made her the right person for the job. She gave him both an hourly price and a price for the whole job, and Sid opted for the latter. The editor seemed like a meticulous person who would spend more time than her fee projected.

If you don't have the money to hire a professional editor, your next best bet is to create an editor by committee. Ask friends and colleagues to read your book. The best readers are those who fit within your audience profile; they are the people who would actually buy your book and have read other books like it. If you don't have any friends who fit the bill, join a writing group and/or writers' chat rooms. Tracking down organizations or associations in your field will be your next step.

Self-publishing doesn't exempt you from needing to clear permissions for artwork, photographs, poems or other writing that's not your own. The last thing you want is someone coming after you because you used something for which you have no permission. See Chapter 8 for more info on permissions.

Your Pub Date

When you're preparing a writing schedule for yourself, the best deadline may be a date of publication for your book. Don't be arbitrary. The season, the simultaneous release of competitive titles and any pertinent anniversaries or historical dates should all be considered when setting your pub date.

Because you're publisher-less, you don't have to worry about competing with bigger titles on your publisher's list. But you still have to compete with all the other books coming out all over the country. Troll the Web to see what books are due out. And this is where your subscription to *Publishers Weekly* (see Appendix I) will be extremely helpful. *PW* not only reviews a wide range of books one to three months before they come out, but for each season they also preview many publishers' upcoming releases. Try to position your pub date so that your book won't compete with other, bigger books that are similar to yours.

Sid chose to launch his book the week of the National Legume Convention. He felt that this would help spread the word and that if local papers were doing stories on the event, he might be able to get press as a "legume expert" and author of a new book on legumes. The National Legume Convention takes place in the third week in April. Sid liked this date because as spring springs, farmer's markets start to emerge from hibernation and people start to plan their gardens.

See Chapter 9 for more information on pub dates.

If you can (and you've got the $175 entry fee plus airfare and hotel), attend the Book Expo of America, a.k.a. BEA. This yearly event is the trade show for the publishing industry. There you can collect catalogs from many, many publishers to ascertain what books will be released in the upcoming season/year. Plus it's a huge schmooze fest, and you can bring home a ton of free books.

Getting Down to Business

As you hurtle toward your pub date, you must establish a name for your company and obtain a post office box, ISBNs and bar code. You must also register your copyright and your book itself with the Library of Congress.

THE NAME GAME

If you survey the shelves of a bookstore, you'll see that almost every book has a company name and/or logo on its spine. Your book needs these, too. You and your company should not have the same name, because this will scream "self-published"—and not in a good way. Again, because of the prevailing prejudice against self-published books by reviewers, book business professionals and booksellers, it's important to make yourself as legit as possible. And making it seem as if there's a company behind you will help immensely.

Sid chose the name Garden Variety Press. He liked the wordplay, but more important, he felt that it sounded like a specialty gardening publisher. This was just what he was after. He chose one of his favorite legumes, a trionfo violetta pole bean, as his logo. And he bartered with his drum circle accountant pal to set up his "sole proprietor" business in exchange for help planting a new vegetable garden.

For most self-published authors, a sole proprietorship is the kind of business to set up. In a sole proprietorship, you ARE the business. What the business makes, you make. What the business owes, you owe. It wouldn't hurt to get some expert advice from a lawyer or an accountant as you begin building your publishing empire, though.

POST OFFICE BOX

You do not want your own home address on your book. Not only will it make you look both rinky and dinky, but it could also be dangerous. (Imagine a crazed legume nut showing up at your door in the middle of the night.) You can get a P.O. box at your local post office.

COPYRIGHT

Your book is automatically copyrighted once you write it, but you still need to register it with the Library of Congress. All legitimate publishers register their books, and you should, too. Registration should be in the author's name. This can be done for a mere $30.

LIBRARY OF CONGRESS CATALOG CARD NUMBER

If you're self-publishing for the first time, you won't be eligible for Cataloging-in-Publication (CIP) data from the Library of Congress, a tool that makes it easier for librarians to shelve books. But you can apply for a Library of Congress Catalog Card Number, also called a Preassigned Control Number (PCN), which enables librarians to actually find and order your book. The only catch is that the Library of Congress has to believe that your book will be of interest to libraries before they assign you a number, so there's no point applying if your book is not appropriate for libraries. But don't be lazy here. Librarians all over the world use the cataloging system, so having a PCN can be beneficial.

PCNs are free (except for the copy of your book you're required to send when it's published) and assigned before publication, so that the actual number can be printed on your copyright page. Be sure to apply three months before your pub date. (For information on acquiring a PCN, see Appendix I.)

ISBN AND BAR CODE

An International Standard Book Number (ISBN) is like your book's dog tag. It allows instant identification, and your book should always be wearing one. If you want to sell your book outside of small mom-and-pop shops, you will need not only an ISBN but a Bookland EAN bar code. You can't buy just one ISBN, though. They come in groups of 10 and are currently $225 if you're not ordering a rushed service. If you go through the ISBN Web site, bar codes are currently $25 each. But if you do your research on the Web and buy bar codes separately, you can get them for less.

FYI: If you do a hardcover and a paperback edition of your book, each one needs a separate ISBN, so the extra numbers can come in handy.

The Look of Your Book Inside and Out

You don't want people to diss and dismiss your book because it looks amateurish. Research great-looking books so you have a standard against which to measure. (For a list of great-looking books, see page 72.)

If the interior of your book is very simple, it's possible to lay it out on your own. But if you decide to hire a designer, you may want to use the same person for both the cover and the interior. Or you may want to go with a flashy, splashy cover that costs a pretty penny and a more straightforward interior design done by yourself or a less expensive designer. This decision comes down to talent, money and the kind of book you want to make.

Sid's book, overall, required a relatively simple design, save for his photos, line drawings and recipes. But, as we said, he wanted his book to look good enough to be purchased as a gift. After seeing the professional, up-scaley look of the work his local bookseller friend had done for several other self-published authors, he decided to hire her.

COVER DESIGN

In order to help your designer do her best work, show her covers that are similar in look and feel to what you want. In fact, you may want to see if you can hire the cover designer of one of the books you love. Cover designers usually have their names printed on the back of a book, on the back flap or on the copyright page. Many can be tracked down through an Internet search. Check out AIGA's 50 Books/50Covers Award at www.aiga.org, which includes each designer's information.

Sid debated and debated whether to hire the person who designed the cover of his all-time favorite gardening book, but he simply didn't have the money. So he went down to the local art college and found an amazingly talented senior who agreed to work with him. She got to build her portfolio. Sid got a great cover.

Don't forget about your spine! Unless your book is displayed face out (an unlikely scenario), this is the only thing potential buyers will see in stores. Make it colorful. Put a picture on it. Make sure your title is legible and stands out.

COVER INFORMATION

You want not only a great-looking cover, but one that includes all pertinent information. It's important for you to figure out exactly what is going to appear on the front and back of your cover (and on the front and back flaps, if you decide to print hardcovers). Besides your ISBN and bar code, your cover can include a plethora of information, from category, blurbs and cover copy to author photo and bio, and anything else that you feel will draw readers in.

Category. A crucial detail that you may want to put on the corner of your book's back cover is its category. Since the right category allows bookstores and libraries to shelve your book correctly, it's not surprising that the best way to decide on a category is to walk the aisles of bookstores. You'll see where yours fits best.

Sid was a little sad and surprised that there was no category specifically devoted to legumes. So he decided on two categories: gardening and food writing.

For more info on categories, see page 229.

Blurbs. Beautiful blurbs have a way of allaying potential skepticism about a self-published book better than almost anything. These are stamps of approval.

Sid worked very hard at getting blurbs. He landed one of America's top legume experts as well as the author of *The Bean Cookbook*, both of whom said his book belonged in the hands of vegetable lovers everywhere.

For more infor on blurbs, see pages 72 and 246–47.

Cover copy. Trot out your A-game pitch for this all-important opportunity to show how professional and appealing you are. Most people who aren't in the book business don't really care which publisher published a book; they just want something that satisfies their needs, and they look to the jacket copy to see if a particular book fits the bill. They will most certainly be judging your book by the promise you make on the cover.

Sid spent a day reading jacket copy at his local bookstore, paying particular attention to books that would be shelved near his. Then he went to some specialty gardening stores and asked what information they thought was necessary. Once he'd done several drafts, he had his editor edit his copy. In the end, he felt he'd put together something that was enticing, inviting and informative. And he knew he'd written great cover copy when he read it to his writing group and they broke into spontaneous cheers.

Author photo. Yes, a good author photo can sell books. So, if you choose to put a photo of yourself somewhere on your cover or flaps, make sure it's flattering, high-quality and nicely reproduced.

Sid wanted to use a snapshot that he thought made him look sexy. Unfortunately, it was grainy and he had a mullet in it. Luckily, his wife convinced him that having an out-of-focus, cheese-ball author photo was bad. She talked him into hiring a photographer he met through a writing seminar for $250.

For more info on author photos, see pages 233 and 257–58.

Bio. In order for your self-published book to look professional, you need a short bio of yourself on the back of your book or on the back flap if you have one. If the bio is on the back cover, it should be short: your credentials, any awards and where you live. In addition, you can have a more complete bio inside your book. Either way, your bio should help answer the "Why Me?" question we referred to earlier.

Sid originally wrote a long, flowing bio. But when he studied author bios in successful books by larger publishers, he realized he'd rather use the precious cover space for buyer-enticing information.

Pricing Your Book

The price of your book will also go somewhere on its cover. But how much to charge? Do market research. Look at the prices of similar books. Nobody is likely to buy an overpriced book. Some schools of publishing say it's an edge to go slightly under the typical retail price. However, do your research well, because certain kinds of books can bear high prices. And they're not necessarily expensive books to produce. It's a supply-and-demand situation. If there's demand for your book but little or no supply, readers may be willing to pay more.

Aside from comparison titles and competition, it's standard for both large and small publishers to charge 8 to 10 times what it costs to produce the book.

Sid researched comparative titles and asked booksellers, greengrocers and farm stand proprietors who might sell his book what they would expect it to retail for and what kind of discount they'd expect. Of course, he wanted to be sure he wouldn't lose money on each book he sold. He knew that a number of bookstores and wholesalers would ask for a discount of 50% or more. This meant he had 50% or less left to cover printing, marketing, shipping, returns and giveaways. Not to mention any profit! But things worked out. His market research told him he could charge $15—allowing him some wiggle room.

Printing Your Book

Once you've written and designed your book, it's time to print it. But how much will you have to pay? According to self-publishing guru Dan Poynter, that's like asking how much a car costs. The format of your book, the kind of paper, the number of colors and the number of copies—all these factors will determine price. And the more you print, the cheaper each book will be.

Many printers specialize in specific kinds of printing: big or small print runs, one-color, two-color or four-color printing. (See Appendix I on how to find reputable printers.) Make a list of printers who do the kind of book you want. Get price quotes that itemize the cost of each element (e.g., paper, binding, cover, illustrations). That way, you and your printer are sure to end up on the same page.

Once you've found your printer and begun the process, be sure to ask for page proofs so you can make sure all mistakes are eliminated before your book is printed. But you can forgo bound galleys; it's much less expensive and a lot easier to simply send out finished books. If you're concerned about sending potential blurbers an unbound manuscript, just take it to your local print shop and have them bind it for you.

At first, Sid thought he wanted to do an old-fashioned kind of printing called *letterpress*, but when he saw how much it would cost, he decided to save some money for his Web site and go with a *photo-offset* process. He then began his printer search in earnest. His goal: to find a printer who would also do a bang-up job reproducing his photos.

FORMAT AND SIZE

Unless you're aiming to get your book into supermarket racks—which is highly unlikely—you'll probably want to go with a *perfect-bound trade paperback*. This is a standard quality trade paperback book. Hardcovers may feel more substantial, but you probably want to get more bang for your buck—as does your audience. If your book is lavishly illustrated and made for coffee table viewing, or if your audience habitually buys hardcovers, then . . . maybe. But most of the time you'll be better off publishing it as a paperback.

If you want to keep even more money in your pocket, you'll want to go with a standard-size book, the most common of which is 5.5" × 8.5" for a trade paperback and 6" × 9" for a hardcover.

Sid was originally thinking about a hardcover, because this format felt classier to him. Especially when slightly oversized. He became very attached to this idea, but when he saw how much it would cost and how difficult it would be for a bookseller to fit this size on a shelf, he decided to go with a standard trade paperback but with nicer-than-average paper.

THE RIGHT PAPER

There are so many paper types, a person could spend weeks going through the alternatives; fortunately, most printers offer you only a few options. Typically, uncoated book stock is your best choice for a standard, non-illustrated book. It's decent quality for a good price. But if you're doing an illustrated book—especially a four-color one—you'll want to bump up your paper quality. Ask to see heavier papers as well as coated papers.

Sid was printing his book in one color (black-and-white), but since he had a number of beautiful photos that he wanted to show off, he decided to upgrade to a heavier paper.

FIRST PRINT RUN

How many books should you print? The industry standard is to print as many books as you think you can reasonably sell in the first year. A thousand copies may sound like very little—until you actually try to sell them. Even though the unit cost is cheaper when you print more, again, you do not want to be stuck with boxes and boxes of unsold books. On the other hand, you're not just going to sell books, you're also going to give quite a few away. These will go to family, friends and booksellers, as well as to reviewers and others in the media. Designate around 10% of your print run to giveaways.

When will you get your books? Four to eight weeks from when the manuscript arrives at the printer.

Sid didn't want to overestimate, because his wife had made it perfectly clear that she wouldn't stand for boxes of books in her basement. So Sid made sure to ask each printer what they would charge for *reprints* (which should be cheaper on a per-book basis than a first printing) in the hope that he'd sell out his first print run and go on to second, third and fourth printings. Between the 300 he thought he could sell at the National Legume Convention, the 1,000 he thought he could sell to specialty stores, the 200 he was hopeful would go to booksellers, the 200 he planned to give away and the other 500 he thought he could sell over his Web site, Sid came to the conclusion that 2,000 was a good starting point.

Always keep an eye on your stock and always know how long it will take to reprint your book. Then do your best balancing act to figure out when to reprint. This isn't easy (big publishing houses have employees devoted solely to this task), nor are there hard-and-fast rules to follow. But if you keep meticulous records of how many books are going out the door (and how many are coming back in from returns), you should develop a sense of when you need to place orders for more. Try never to be caught without books to sell when people are looking to buy them.

DOCUTECH

If you're planning on printing fewer than 100 books and you're not interested in the services that a print-on-demand publisher supplies, take a look at DocuTech. This is essentially a super fast, double-sided laser printer that spits out your pages so that they can then be bound. However, DocuTech has a number of limitations:

- You need to keep your page size to 8.5" × 11" or some derivative thereof, for example, 8.5" × 5.5" (8.5" × 11" paper, cut in half width-wise). Otherwise, the unit costs will be exorbitant.

- You can't print on any kind of special paper. All printing is done on laser paper.
- You can print only in a trade paperback format, unless you choose to have your books bound elsewhere. Again, this ends up being a pricey proposition.

DocuTech can be found at many office supply chains as well as at select printers and copy shops.

The Shipping News: Costs and Supplies

If you're going to sell your book yourself, you have to be ready to ship your books all over the world. Stamps, envelopes, labels, all that mess. It takes time, organizational skills and lots of heavy lifting. You can reduce your shipping costs by joining the Publishers Marketing Association and/or the Small Publishers Association of North America (see Appendix I), but you certainly won't eliminate them. So once again, do your research on the Web, in bookstores and libraries, and with other self-published authors. Shop around. And make sure your goal is to have your books arrive at their destination right on time.

As Sid studied the shipping issue, he was daunted by the idea of packaging and mailing individual books himself and became intrigued by the idea of a wholesaler. Then he found out how much of his money a major wholesaler would take and thought maybe selling books out of his home wasn't such a bad idea after all.

Selling Your Stock

One of the biggest hurdles in successful self-publishing is figuring out how to actually sell copies of your book. In other words, how in the world is someone in North Carolina going to buy your book if you happen to live in North Dakota?

If you're your own sales force, it's up to you to convince people to buy it. And this is enormously hard work. Selling takes a ton of time and involves a lot of rejection. But it can be done. You just have to see the world as one big bookselling opportunity. You must be prepared to sell your book out of your car. At the library. At your job. At the Laundromat. At the airport. At the mall. At your college reunion. At conventions, expos and fairs. Everywhere.

And just like any major publisher, you have to have sales materials. In the book biz, one of the essential sales pieces is the tip sheet, which lets potential sales outlets know why your book is worth selling. A typical tip sheet includes the title of your book, a short pitch, any relevant models or comparison titles, blurbs/press, price and format (for additional information, see page 237). Make your own tip sheet and keep it with you at all times. You never know when a good sales opportunity will arise.

In addition to selling generally everywhere you go, you'll want to look at the specific sales venues outlined below. We'll start with the one place we know you can sell your book: your own Web site.

A WICKED WEB SITE

A Web site is an easy, effective way to make you seem big-league (if it's done well, of course). But, more important, it may be the only way for people to find out about your book, let alone buy it. You can sell books directly over your Web site, or you can link up to amazon.com or bn.com (see below).

Sid was tempted to hire his 12-year-old neighbor to design his Web site, but he decided to spend $500 bucks for a local Web designer. He knew the Internet was going to be a key sales tool for his book. He studied lots of author Web sites and sites geared to the garden hobbyist for ideas to pass on to his designer. And he chose to buy two domain names: www.gardenvarietypress.com and www.sidsycamore.com in anticipation of becoming a household name.

For more on developing a top-notch Web site, see pages 267–69.

INTERNET BOOKSELLERS

One of the easiest and fastest ways to get your book up and running is to get accepted into the Amazon and Barnes & Noble programs to sell it over the Internet. Both programs have straightforward application systems. Amazon's can be found under "Advantage" in the Books section of their Web site. B&N's can be found under "Publisher and Author Guidelines" in the Services section of their site. Amazon's program requires a $29.95 annual fee. They buy your book at 55% off the cover price (which they have the final say on). Typically, they will order two to five books as a first order. B&N's program has no annual fee. And you determine the discount and the cover price. But the better the deal you give, the better your chances of having your book carried. B&N will typically order one to two books as a first order. They also warn that it could take two to four months to find out if you're accepted into the program.

Though there is no guarantee that you will be accepted into either program, if your book is not pornographic or blatantly offensive and has the requisite requirements (ISBN, EAN bar code, etc.), then you should have a very good chance of getting your book onto at least one of these sites. And if you can get both, all the better.

Because Sid was not keen on the whole shipping-from-home thing, he decided to set up accounts with amazon.com and bn.com with links on his Web site to both. One day he sent out a mass e-mail to his mailing list featuring the link to Amazon. And two weeks later he did the same with B&N. He had been told that both companies track books carefully and are likely to order more if they notice an upsurge in sales.

DISTRIBUTORS AND WHOLESALERS

If you don't want to sell and ship to bookstores on your own, there are distributors that will do this for you. For a fee. These companies will go out and try to sell your book to stores and specialty markets. They are the equivalent of a publisher's sales force and typically take between 60% and 65% of your cover price. (Remember, they have to resell your book for around 50% off the cover price.)

There are also wholesalers, who will not actively try to sell your book but will stock it so that booksellers around the country have easy access to it. Many booksellers don't want to have to place individual orders to individual publishers. It's much easier for them to do one-stop shopping.

Unfortunately, Ingram, the largest wholesaler, won't accept books from publishers with fewer than 10 titles per year. But many other wholesalers—both national and regional—are approachable. They typically take between 50% and 60% of your cover price.

Distributors are understandably harder to land than wholesalers since they put more effort into selling. As always, you need to have the proper materials and pitch to make these companies believe they will end up making some money and are not just acting as a large storage unit. By joining the Publishers Marketing Association and/or the Small Publishers

Association of North America, you can get the dope on who's good to work with, who pays up and who doesn't.

After much fact-gathering and careful consideration, Sid decided that in addition to selling books from his house, he'd do his best to find a local wholesaler in order to give himself a leg up with the local bookselling community. He figured once the sales started rolling in, he'd cut himself a sweet deal with a great distributor.

For a comprehensive list of book distributors and wholesalers, see *Literary Market Place.*

It is not unheard-of to wait up to four months to get paid by a wholesaler. Do not count on immediate cash in your pocket!

BOOKSTORES

As strange as it may seem, you'll probably have the most difficult time selling your book into bookstores. But both the independents and chain stores have their pluses as well as minuses when it comes to selling a self-published book.

Independents. Not only are independent bookstores much easier to approach than chains, but they're more likely to stock your book and will typically ask for a lower discount—more like 40% than 50%. The problem is, unless you have a distributor, you'll have to call each and every bookstore on your own. This could take several thousand calls, since there are 1,900 members of Book Sense alone (see page 378).

Of course, you want to approach all your local independent booksellers. Most independents want to help local authors and are willing to take at least one copy if it fits in with the books they sell. Which leads to an important piece of advice: Know your stores before you approach them. Independents are not beholden to a corporate office, so they each have their own individual flavor and color. If you don't live near a bookseller, go on the Web. Most independents have their own sites. Study them and then, when you visit the booksellers, show them why it makes sense for your book to be on their shelves. Arielle Gronner of Powell's Books in Portland, Oregon, suggests having the answers to these questions ready when approaching her bookstore: "How will people know about the book?" "Who will be looking for it?" "Is there a marketing plan?" "Are you working with a distributor or wholesaler?"

To learn more about independent booksellers, go to the Web site of the American Booksellers Association (ABA), which lists its members by state. Also check out the Web site for Book Sense, a marketing campaign created by the ABA to help independents, which also lists participating members. (See Appendix I.)

Sid has spent his life rooting around in bookstores. He goes to readings regularly and knows most of his local booksellers by first name. So it's not surprising that he received a nice bit of local bookseller love when he published his book. One bookstore featured his book in its newsletter, and two others invited him to do workshops. He also took the postcards he had made and sent personal notes to every bookstore with a gardening section (which he found out by doing Web searches). As a result, one bookstore that was putting together a summer event with several gardening authors invited Sid to speak.

Chain stores. The great thing about these stores is that if they order your book, it will have national distribution or, at minimum, distribution throughout an entire region. This means orders in the three and four figures—a bonanza when you're used to dealing in ones and twos. The downside is that it's very difficult to get your self-published book into a chain. In most cases, individuals in chain stores cannot sell your book there, no matter how much they would like to. All they can do is recommend your book to the head buyer.

But while the chain stores are difficult to penetrate, they are not *im*penetrable. You will have to go through corporate headquarters, where you can contact:

- The person in charge of small press relations, or
- The person in charge of your specific category, or
- The person in charge of your region

Marcella Smith, director of small press and vendor relations at Barnes & Noble, had this to say: "Yes, B&N orders self-published books. The author usually contacts us by calling and then sends materials—the finished book and the marketing plan for review by the buyer. We order self-published books under the same conditions as we order all books. Does the title have sales potential in a general trade bookstore? Is it competitive in the marketplace? Is there a marketing plan? If it's a nonfiction book, does the author have credentials in the subject? If it's fiction, has the author been published in magazines or journals?"

Sid knew the manager at his local Borders quite well and asked him if he'd be kind enough to give him the gardening buyer's info. Because Sid was so nice and because he gave the manager a signed copy of his book, the manager told him what he needed to know. Sid put together a great package of all the stuff he'd been up to, sent it off and followed up every two weeks until he heard back.

For more info on chains, see page 337.

Distributors, wholesalers and most bookstores work on a commission basis, i.e., they can return your books anytime they want. So be sure to remember that a sale isn't really a sale until a reader buys it and doesn't return it!

LIBRARIES

If you think libraries would be interested in your book, then you've got a great opportunity to sell a mess o' books. There are just under 120,000 libraries in the United States, but as always, you'll have to do your homework to find out which ones your book actually belongs in. If it's library-friendly, you'll want to check out the distributor Baker & Taylor, since the bulk of their sales are made to libraries. Also, go to the "Facts About Libraries" section of the American Library Association's Web site (see Appendix I) to find out how to locate libraries around the country.

One of the many nice things about libraries is that they generally expect lower discounts than bookstores. These discounts typically range from 10% to 45%.

Over the years, Sid had made friends with a number of librarians across the country who share his love of gardening books. He sent letters to them all, asking for help in approaching libraries with good gardening collections. They, in turn, sent e-mails contacting their library friends. So far, Sid's book is in over two dozen libraries.

For more info on libraries, see page 346.

OTHER SALES CHANNELS

Certainly you want to place your book in bookstores and libraries if you can, but don't limit yourself to these venues. You can sell thousands of copies of your book without it ever seeing the inside of a bookstore. For example, if your book is about golf, do a tour of golf club pro shops and give them your pitch. If your book is about cats, contact local and national cat shows and pet stores. The fact is, there are thousands of places to sell a book besides bookstores.

If you can line up a bulk sale to one specialty retailer, you have one of the best self-publishing situations possible. Your profits will be much bigger than what you'd receive if you went with a publishing house. And the work associated with this kind of self-publishing is minimized. You have to ship books to far fewer locations. You don't have to spend your life going from store to store, trying to sell your book. You can use this sale to open many doors that would typically be hard to access. And these kinds of special sales are typically nonreturnable. The only downside is that the discount demanded is usually higher than that at your average store. Even so, if you're fortunate enough to line up a big special sale and get a purchase order before you print your books, you're in a great position to make some serious coin.

In order to nail a sale of this kind, you've got to approach the right person within the right company. If you're dealing with a chain, you'll want to go through corporate headquarters. This way, you'll have a better chance of getting into all their stores. If, however, you hit brick wall after brick wall, try regional or individual managers. Develop a relationship with them and see if they can help you.

Sid was convinced he could get into a big gardening chain. But no matter how many times he called, he just couldn't get anyone on the phone. So while he hasn't yet been able to garner a big bulk sale, he has taken to concentrating his efforts on other places where his audience hangs out: the friendly world of farmer's markets, farm stands and fresh produce markets. By networking, he has contacted over 500 of them and the benefits are starting to pay off. Last week, he got an order for a dozen books from one farm stand, 30 books from a bean farmer who sells at farmer's markets across Southern California and 5 books from a local produce market.

For more info on special markets, see pages 342–44.

Publicity and Marketing

Since we wrote the publicity and marketing sections of this book with the assumption that you may not get any help from your publisher even if you have one, we suggest you go back and read Chapters 10 and 11. Obviously, there will be parts that don't apply to self-publishing, but there won't be many. Here's the stuff that you'll want to pay particular attention to:

- How to make great handouts
- How and when to hire a publicist and media coach
- How to create a press release/kit
- How to put together a promotional video/CD
- How to pitch articles to magazines and newspapers
- How to network
- How to e-market
- How to dream up angles and hooks
- How to set up tours and events
- How to give away books
- How to keep your book alive and well
- How to throw a cool book party
- How to generate lots of local love
- How to say nice pleases and thank-yous

The minute Sid settled on a cover, he had some postcards made. He handed them out like calling cards wherever he went and sent them all over the country—to colleges, libraries, gardening groups and stores. However, he also made sure to develop a great press release, which he used regularly when he pitched story ideas to both local and national newspapers, radio shows and TV. It was slow going, but Sid was invited onto a really good local cable-access show. This was exciting, because he knew he'd be able to use this tape to entice local news programs. In fact, when bean season rounded the corner, he got a TV station to do a short piece about him and his local farmer's market.

A number of newspapers, including *The New York Times,* have a policy whereby they will not review self-published books. However, they will mention self-published books in the body of an article. So don't waste time and money sending books to the book review sections at major papers, but do try to find a news angle through which your book can be cited or about which a feature article can be written.

CONTACT PERSON

In some instances, it may be to your advantage to create the illusion that you're not self-published. That's why it's a good idea to find someone who will act as your media contact or screener. Another possibility is to invent a company and publicity person and play the part yourself. We know it sounds ridiculous, but again, it's much easier to say nice things about someone who's not you. When you're pretending to be your publicist, you can rave shamelessly about what a great writer you are. Take this route only if you have the requisite personality, verve and nerve.

Another alternative is to have an answering service or separate phone line with an answering machine. Record an outgoing message that says the name of your company (use a friend so that the voice is different). Then call the person back yourself.

Sid's wife volunteered to be the voice on his business machine. And when she was home, she picked up the line with a nice "Garden Variety Press, may I help you?" This made Sid's heart sing with joy every time he heard it.

PLATFORM

We've talked about how much publishers love authors who have a platform, because it's so much easier to promote their books. Well, if you're a self-published author, you have an even greater need for a platform. And the bigger it is, the more chance you have of garnering media and speaking directly to your core audience. This can translate into serious book sales.

Sid decided to do a gardening workshop at his local Learning Annex; he thought this would help him develop his workshop/lecture so he could take it on the road. He also spent a day on the Internet researching universities and colleges with agricultural departments. He looked through their virtual catalogs searching for any course that directly or tangentially related to legumes. He then sent off 50 e-mails to the professors with a description of his book and workshop. He ended up with a fully paid trip to an agricultural college, a $1,000 stipend and the chance to sell his book to 250 ag students.

DIRECT MAIL

If you're thinking about investing in a direct-mail campaign, two pieces of advice: 1) Don't use random lists, which will most certainly result in minuscule sales. Make sure to buy mailing lists that are made up of your core audience. 2) The key to direct mail is repetition, so one postcard isn't likely to do the trick. Direct-mail campaigns are expensive, and few people respond. If you use direct marketing, you may have to sell your book at a higher price, so that even a very small response rate will result in profits.

After exploring the costs of direct mail, Sid decided to pass on this marketing device for the moment. He figured, being a cockeyed optimist, that once he hit 5,000 sales, he'd give it a shot.

If you decide to launch a direct-mail campaign, network with other authors who have used this technique so you know which mailing list companies are reputable and which are not.

CREATING COMMUNITY

Once you've decided to be your own publisher, join the Publishers Marketing Association, the Small Publishers Association of North America and/or a local self-publishing association. (See Appendix I.) These organizations provide all sorts of help and guidance. And because they have hundreds of members, they are able to provide discounts on things like shipping, much as AARP provides discounts to seniors. They'll also set you up so you can take credit cards, and they'll give you the latest info on wholesalers and distributors.

Sid not only joined PMA and SPAN, but also formed his own local self-publishing group because his town had none.

Revising Your Book

One of the great things about self-publishing is that you can keep making your work better without having to get permission from your publisher. Use this asset to your advantage. First give yourself a nice break from your book—at least a month or two—and then dive back in and read it for errors or updates.

Sid dreamed of the day when the words "third edition" would appear on his book. In the meantime, he was content to plan all the changes he'll make, like changing the "W" to a "B" in his final chapter title, which currently reads, "My Favorite Wean." And adding a recipe that he came up with while on an exotic bean trip.

MAKING IT BIG

Andy Kessler had a great idea for a book about the securities industry that was fortunately (and unfortunately) extremely timely. He signed with an agent, who liked his idea but told him a conventional publisher would never buy it due to the necessary time frame. Andy needed a finished book on shelves within three months, and it would be at least nine months to a year before a publisher could get it out. When he asked why they couldn't do a rush job, he was told they won't put in the extra dough to rush a book to press unless you're famous or you're writing about something of major national importance.

Instead of throwing up his hands and cursing his bad luck, Andy decided to take charge. He started researching printers on Google. He hired an editor for $35 an hour. He found a couple in Florida (Andy lives in California) to design his book cover. He hired a well-known illustrator to do the cover. He tracked down a printer in Boston who could print 1,000 hardcovers in 10 days. He purchased his ISBNs. He set up his page on amazon.com. And he did all this in a matter of weeks:

- End of December: Had idea for book titled *Wall Street Meat.*
- January 1: Started writing book.
- January 31: Finished book.
- March 17: Book for sale on amazon.com.

Books arrived. Andy wasn't happy with the quality of the spine, so he found a new printer who gave him a stitched rather than glued binding. These books arrived four weeks later. In the meantime, he was getting orders. By the end of the first day, he had 50 orders via Amazon. Soon they were coming 100 at a time. Soon a human being from Amazon called Andy and ordered 500 books. And soon he was out of his first printing.

Selling Your Book to a Publisher

If you're selling at a rate of 5,000 copies or more a year, you may want to consider trying to interest an agent or going directly to a small or midsize publisher. Many major publishers have trouble selling 5,000 copies of their books a year, so it's pretty impressive if you've done this all by yourself. Hopefully, by the time you've sold this number of books, you've become an excellent pitchman, you've received some hot press, you've gotten yourself into some good stores, you've created your own platform and/or you've got a great Web business going. All of these things will entice agents and publishers.

Seeing how well everything was going, Andy searched on Google and found the number of the business book buyer at Barnes & Noble. He called, but didn't hear back. Then he started researching airport bookstores. All this time, he was shipping books out of his garage. This was getting tiresome, so he found a distributor in Maryland who would give him 40% of the cover price on all books sold (he was currently getting 45% with Amazon) and get his books to Amazon, Ingram and Baker & Taylor. They said they would be his sales force, but in reality they didn't do anything to help sell his book; they just handled the shipping and payments. But Andy says, "I would do it all again with them because beyond Amazon no one was going to deal with me directly."

Through a previous contact, Andy landed an interview on CNBC. The next morning, he got an e-mail from the business book buyer at B&N, asking, "How many copies do you have and how quickly can we get them?" Around November, an airport book chain followed suit. Andy says he knows he could have had a bestseller if he'd done it right. But he adds, "Still, I never could have done it on my own. It would have been too much work."

During all this activity, Andy was contacted by the editorial director of HarperBusiness, a division of HarperCollins: "He dropped some lowball number that I didn't accept." Then Andy got a call from a new agent, who said: "Let's do this right. We'll have an auction." The agent generated a ton of interest, and HarperBusiness ended up buying the paperback rights to the book—plus a new book—for far more than they originally offered. And Andy even managed to convince Harper to accelerate its typical 12-to-18-month schedule on the new book.

To check out more of Andy's story and to learn more about his book, go to www.andykessler.com.

THE BOTTOM LINE

It's very easy to spend a lot of money when self-publishing. But it really is possible to do a lot on a limited budget. If you're wondering what Sid was able to do with his $5,000, here's his final budget:

Editor: $400
Interior design: $150
Cover design: $250
ISBN/bar code: $300

Author photo: $250

Permissions: $500 (for public-domain illustrations and photos from the Legume Society of America)

Lawyer: $0

Web site: $500

Printing: $2,080

Shipping supplies: $100 (This figure is for initial costs only, since Sid will be able to charge his customers for shipping and handling.)

Marketing: $185 (for postcards only)

Publicity: $0 (Sid decided to go it alone, at least at first.)

Events: $0 (Sid's wife is throwing him a party, so he's not including this cost in his budget!)

Total $4,715

We live in an exciting time. Almost anyone with some cash on hand can write a book, self-publish it and get it sold all over the world through the Internet. And with hard work, perseverance and a little luck, you can put your passion into print all by yourself.

As for Sid, you'll be happy to know that he got himself named Bean Expert on the Food Network. He's now in his third printing of *Legumes! Legumes! Legumes!* And he's just gotten an offer from a major publisher for his next one: *The Ultimate Bean Book.*

CHAPTER 14

OKAY, WHAT'S NEXT?

"Writing is like prostitution.
First you do it for the love of it, then you do it for a few friends, and finally you do it for money."

—MOLIÈRE

When the dust settles, give yourself props on your enormous accomplishment. You wrote a book. You got it published. People bought it—maybe a lot of people, maybe fewer than you hoped. But no matter what, you put your passion into print. Bravo for you.

So, what now? Is it time to think about writing another book? Isn't that what authors do? Well, actually, not all of them. Harper Lee wrote only one book: *To Kill a Mockingbird.* Who knows why she didn't write another, but we like to think that she did something similar to the patented PYPIP Post-Publishing Experience Exercise and thought better of it.

Now it's your turn to do the same. Think about your own book—everything from your first I've-got-an-idea moment to your appearance on the *Today* show (or at your mother's reading group). Then make two lists. A FUN list. And a PAIN list. Put all of your publishing experiences into one of those lists. That's right. Relive the fun, then relive the pain. Which list is longer?

The Zimmermen, the Glimmer Twins of publishing and the authors of numerous books, remind us of some of the things we love about being an author: "Reading a post on the Internet from a reader who was helped out emotionally or inspired by reading your work. We've had men read our books aloud to their fathers as they lie dying in the hospital. Seeing people buying the book. Getting published in other countries is cool, too!"

Jemiah Jefferson, award-winning author of three books including the vampire novel *Wounds*, reminds us of some of the difficult parts of being an author: "I have had my cover ideas ignored. I've had the titles of my books changed—and then gotten no publicity budget. They ignore my corrections on the proofs, and of course I don't get paid very much. Just because you have good intentions and skills and whatnot doesn't mean anything. It's a crapshoot almost as vicious as Hollywood. The only advantage is that you don't have to go to Hollywood."

If, after careful consideration, you decide to write another book, make two more lists. Your RIGHT list. And your WRONG list. Yes, everything you did right and everything you did wrong.

Critically evaluate your choice of agent, publisher, editor. Now think about your relationship with each of them. Review how you handled publicity, marketing, sales. Reread your book and see how it holds up.

At this point, you may feel the urge to disappear to Cucamunga. Resist the urge! Force yourself to think about what you can do next time to enhance and expand upon your earlier successes. How can you eliminate your mistakes and avoid the pitfalls of publishing? Can you write a better book? Take advantage of more promotional opportunities? Make your events better? How can you get into more book festivals and writers' conferences? What can you do to get Hollywood interested? Can you figure out how to get reviews and interviews?

To paraphrase an old Chinese proverb: *Those who do not learn from the past are stupid.*

DON'T MAKE THE SAME MISTAKE TWICE

Did you enjoy working with your publishing team? (Or, if you self-published, was your team of one enough?) Did they get the job done? Again, you don't have to be in love with them, as long as they did right by you. Conversely, you may have the sweetest, nicest agent and/or publisher in the world, but sweet and nice don't feed the baby. We highly recommend having a where-have-we-been, where-are-we-going talk with all of them. Ask which parts of the process went well for them and which didn't. And vice versa. Many people will avoid confrontation at any cost and thus leave an agent or publisher without resolving any differences or voicing their disappointments. We always advocate open discussion before jumping ship. It can lead to a better, more successful relationship if you decide in the end to work with them again.

At the same time, always keep your eyes, ears, nose and mind open to what and/or who is out there. Meet with everyone you can. You never know when you might need them or they might need you. If you decide it's time for a change, consider this before you do anything rash: It's much easier to find a new agent or publisher when you already have one. Of course, if your old agent or publisher doesn't want to work with you anymore, you won't have this option; you'll have to go out and find a new one. And if you're talking to new agents or publishers, don't rag on your old ones. If you have nothing nice to say, keep yer big yap shut—you cannot imagine how interconnected all these people are.

At the same time, try to get as much information from the new people as possible *before* you make a move. Ask other writers about their representation. Keep a list of people you might want to work with, and try to meet with as many of them as you can.

LOOK AT THE NUMBERS

Before you start thinking about what your next project will be, it's important to take a serious look at how your book has done in the marketplace. Unless it's sold like hotcakes, this can be a depressing task, which may explain why many authors don't do it. But if writing another book is something you want in your future, then do it you must. Have you earned out your advance? Was your publisher happy with your sales? Has your book gone through multiple printings?

The cold hard truth is this: If your first book didn't sell as many copies as expected, your publisher will be less inclined to do another book with you. And if your sales were both disappointing *and* meager and you go ahead and write a second book, the big accounts like Barnes & Noble will more than likely order no more copies (and maybe fewer) than they sold your first time out. This can be a huge drag, especially if you're convinced that your new book can do much better.

When you choose an idea for a second book, be aware of this reality. You have to either fight it or circumvent it. You can fight it with a pitch that has a promise so persuasive that it turns everyone's eyes into slot machines cranked and landing on dollar signs. Or you can circumvent it by writing a book in a totally different category. For example, if your first book was a reference book, your second book could be a novel. When an author's books are in such divergent categories, booksellers don't compare numbers. If neither of these choices makes sense for you, you can always push forward knowing that you will receive a smaller advance (if you got an advance at all) and that you may get the same number of copies out as your first book sold. Maybe shop this new book to a smaller publisher who would be satisfied by those numbers. But no matter what, don't fool yourself into thinking that the numbers will have no effect on your next sale.

HAVE THE NEXT IDEA READY

Make sure you always have a few excellent ideas in your pocket. Just in case the gods shine down upon you, and right out of the gate your book takes off and you're suddenly hothothot.

But even if your book doesn't fly off the shelves, you never know where or when opportunity may knock. Look, even if you wrote a book that few people bought, if it got some decent reviews or won an award or if, in fact, it was a really great book, someone somewhere will probably want to publish your next one. Or maybe you'll be at a book conference and you'll meet an editor who casually mentions how much she wants a book just like the one you've been pondering. If you've got a good pitch, or maybe even a proposal that you can send out, you may just have your second book contract.

For those of you looking for a career as a professional writer, we turn once again to the Zimmermen: "Here's some advice we never got but learned through the process of getting published. When your book is published and turned in, don't just stop there and wait for it to be released. You should be working on your next project. Then, besides that, you should have one or more additional projects in development. As a professional writer, you must always be a book or two ahead of what's in the stores. That keeps you fresh and eliminates being the needy writer in case that book doesn't do as well as you thought it would. You're already on to the next thing. Don't be a one-trick pony. Have various interests so you can come up with new ideas. Challenge yourself by writing about many different worlds. If you just put out one book and it doesn't do well, then your self-esteem suffers. But if you're aggressively chasing new projects all the time, the possibilities are expanded. Don't be overly precious about that one published piece. Move on right away! While it may be your masterpiece, it's still only one book. We see too many writer friends hanging their reputations as writers on one work."

If full-time writing isn't your thing but you know you want to pen another book down the line, it's still important to keep the idea mill churning. Either way, the question will always be:

What to write?

Sequel? Or Give It a Rest?

Many people want to do sequels to their first book. A good way to gauge the validity of Your Book, Part Two, is to see if anyone wants you to write it. If no one's calling, you better have a convincing argument. Because a sequel is 99% about the numbers.

This is not to say that you should just give up on the idea of a sequel, but make sure it's the project that you MUST do next. Sometimes people do themselves a disservice by writing a sequel without a compelling reason to do so. You don't want to repeat yourself, and you don't want to dilute your first book. On the other hand, if you have a good idea for a sequel and feel passionate about writing it, why not?

Another idea is to wait on your sequel. Write another book first about an entirely different subject and come back to a sequel later, if it's justified. It may be a good thing for you mentally and emotionally to write about something else.

Writer for Hire

If you're looking to make writing a career, you might want to take a break from your own projects and instead hook up with a celebrity, a person with a great story or an expert who wants to write a popular book. Cowriters can earn good money, learn a lot and have fun. Sometimes you'll want to go after a person of particular interest yourself. But sometimes you can get your agent or editor to help you track down someone you can write a book with. Or you may want to get in touch with packagers (see page 36) and publishers who could potentially hire you as a writer. Jessica Hurley, who's teamed up with authors and packagers on a number of book projects, has this advice: "Unless you're getting paid handsomely, I wouldn't recommend ghostwriting. It's really frustrating when you don't get credit for all the hard work you put into a project. A great compromise is to get a 'with' or 'and' credit on the title page. If you don't believe in your worth as a writer, nobody else is going to, either."

If you decide to become a hired gun, use the patented PYPIP research techniques to find and woo the people who could hire you.

Put on Your Idea Cap

If you've ruled out a sequel and aren't interested in writing for anyone but yourself, then it's time to draw on your passion, your skills and your new understanding of how this madcap business works. What sections of your book did people most respond to? What did people find most interesting? What part of your pitch attracted the most media attention? What did you have the most fun talking about? Revisit old lists and try to match up your new ideas with your past successes.

Once you've narrowed down your ideas to a few, it's time to . . . return to Chapter 1! And start all over again.

Remember that you're an already published author, with a network of readers, media, booksellers, other writers and people who share your interests. So, once you've found your idea, start spreading the word. Gary Frank of The Booksmith in San Francisco says, "I like it when an author keeps me abreast of what he's working on, how his new book is coming. It gets me excited, so when his book does come out, there's already a little buzz around it. And a small bookstore can start a book on its way to becoming a bestseller. It happens over and over."

WHEN TO SEND

Now that you have a track record, *when* you send your material out will influence the sale of your second book—big time.

Let's start on a positive note. If you had success with your first book, it's likely that your publisher will want to sign you on for another sooner rather than later. But don't count on this feeling lasting forever. Strike while the iron is hot. Windows of opportunity take a long time opening but close in a second.

If you didn't have the success you or your publisher dreamed of, buck up. You might have to wait a bit, but your opportunity may be closer than you think. Watch the news, continue to get out into the world, network, research and keep writing. Read the publishing trades. Search for your window—and then open it yourself.

TH-TH-TH-THAT'S ALL, FOLKS!

As we put our baby to bed, we reflected back on how it all started. After we'd both put our passions into print and written our books on our heroes, Satchel Paige and Jane Austen, our publishers told us there was no way to publicize our beloved babies. So we dreamed up an event called Putting Your Passion into Print. We got on the phone and cold-called enough bookstores to set up our own tour. *Et voilà!* We were on the road. A funny thing happened. Putting Your Passion into Print became our passion. And now it's in print.

"Without passion, man is a mere latent force and possibility, like the flint which awaits the shock of the iron before it can give forth its spark."

—HENRI FRÉDÉRIC AMIEL

We hope we've created a tool kit that will help you invent your own way of putting your passion into print. And we'd love to hear all about how you did it. Please e-mail us at www.passionintoprint.com and tell us your stories.

See ya at the bookstore!

Appendices

APPENDIX I

RESOURCES

PUBLICATIONS

- ***Annual Guide to Literary Agents,*** edited by Kathryn S. Brogan (Writer's Digest Books)
- ***Annual Novel & Short Story Writer's Market,*** edited by Anne Bowling (Writer's Digest Books)
- ***Booklist***
  P.O. Box 607
  Mount Morris, IL 61054-7564
  Tel: 888-350-0949
- ***The Chicago Manual of Style*** (University of Chicago Press)
- ***Jeff Herman's Guide to Book Editors, Publishers, and Literary Agents: Who They Are! What They Want! How to Win Them Over!,*** by Jeff Herman (Writer, Inc.)
- ***Kirsch's Guide to the Book Contract: For Authors, Publishers, Editors and Agents,*** by Jonathan Kirsch (Acrobat Books)
- ***Kirsch's Handbook of Publishing Law: For Authors, Publishers, Editors and Agents,*** by Jonathan Kirsch (Acrobat Books)
- ***Literary Market Place (LMP): The Directory of the Book Publishing Industry***
  www.literarymarketplace.com
- ***Poets & Writers Magazine***
  See ORGANIZATIONS OFFERING INFORMATION ON GRANTS.
- ***Publishers Weekly***
  360 Park Avenue South
  New York, NY 10010
  Tel: 646-746-6758
  Fax: 646-746-6631
  www.publishersweekly.com

  To subscribe, call 800-278-2991 or 818-487-4557.
- ***The Self-Publishing Manual,*** by Dan Poynter (Para Publishing)

  For more information on self-publishing by Dan Poynter, go to *www.parapublishing.com*

ONLINE PUBLICATIONS

- ***Publishers Marketplace***
  www.publishersmarketplace.com
- ***Hollywood Creative Directory***
  www.hcsonline.com

WRITERS' COMMUNITIES

- **Bread Loaf Writers' Conference**
  Middlebury College
  Middlebury, VT 05753
  Tel: 802-443-5286
  Fax: 802-443-2087
  http://www.middlebury.edu/academics/blwc/

- **Squaw Valley Community of Writers**
  P.O. Box 1416
  Nevada City, CA 95959
  Tel: 530-470-8440
  www.squawvalleywriters.org

Here are three great virtual writing communities:

- *www.readerville.com*
- *www.mediabistro.com*
- *www.bksp.com*

Spotted some snark? Report it at:

- *www.believermag.com/snarkwatch.*

If you're looking for a coauthor with an expertise in a particular area, you may want to try the American Society of Journalists and Authors' writer referral services at:

- *www.asja.org*

NONRESIDENCY MFA PROGRAMS

- **Antioch University, Los Angeles**
  Admissions Office
  400 Corporate Pointe
  Culver City, CA 90230
  Toll-free: 1-800-7-ANTIOCH
  or 1-800-726-8462
  Tel: 310-578-1080 x 100
  http://www.antiochla.edu/programs_mfa.shtml
  www.antioch.edu

- **Bennington College**
  One College Drive
  Bennington, VT 05201
  Tel: 802-440-4452
  Fax: 802-440-4453
  E-mail: *writing@bennington.eduwww.bennington.edu*

- **Goddard**
  123 Pitkin Road
  Plainfield, VT 05667
  Tel: 1-800-906-8312
  http://www.goddard.edu/academic/MFAcreativewriting.html
  www.goddard.edu

- **Warren Wilson College**
  MFA Program for Writers
  P.O. Box 9000
  Asheville, NC 28815-9000
  Tel: 828-771-3715
  Fax: 828-771-7005
  E-mail: *mfa@warren-wilson.edu*
  www.warren-wilson.edu

ASSOCIATIONS

- **American Library Association (ALA)**
  50 East Huron Street
  Chicago, IL 60611
  Toll-free: 800-545-2433
  www.ala.org

- **American Society of Composers, Authors and Publishers (ASCAP)**
  ASCAP Building
  One Lincoln Plaza
  New York, NY 10023
  Toll-free: 800-95-ASCAP
  Tel: 212-621-6000
  www.ascap.com

- **Association of Authors' Representatives, Inc. (AAR)**
  676A Ninth Avenue, #312
  New York, NY 10036
  www.aar-online.org

- **Communication Arts**
  110 Constitution Drive
  Menlo Park, CA 94025
  Tel: 650-326-6040
  www.commarts.com

- **Directors Guild of America (DGA)**
  www.dga.org
  Go to DGA Members' Directory to track down who represents which director.

- **Independent Book Publishers Association (PMA)**
  627 Aviation Way
  Manhattan Beach, CA 90266
  www.pma-online.org

- **Screen Actors Guild (SAG)**
  5757 Wilshire Boulevard
  Los Angeles, CA
  90036-3600
  Tel: 323-954-1600
  www.sag.org

- **Small Publishers Association of North America (SPAN)**
  P.O. Box 1306
  Buena Vista, CA 81211
  Tel: 719-395-4790
  www.spannet.org

Here are a number of booksellers' associations:

- **American Booksellers Association (ABA)**
  828 South Broadway
  Tarrytown, NY 10591
  Toll-free: 800-637-0037
  Tel: 941-591-2665
  Fax: 941-591-2724
  www.bookweb.org

- **Association of Booksellers for Children**
  4412 Chowen Avenue South
  Minneapolis, MN 55410
  Toll-free: 800-421-1665
  Tel: 612-926-6650
  Fax: 612-926-6650

- **Book Sense**
  www.booksense.com

Christian Booksellers Association
P.O. Box 62000
Colorado Springs, CO 80962-2000
Toll-free: 800-252-1950
Tel: 719-265-9895
Fax: 719-272-3510

Great Lakes Booksellers Association
P.O. Box 901
208 Franklin Street
Grand Haven, MI 49417
Toll-free: 800-745-2460
Tel: 616-847-2460
Fax: 616-842-0051
www.books-glba.org

Independent Mystery Booksellers Association
Clues Unlimited
123 South Eastbourne
Tucson, AZ 85716
Tel: 520-326-8533
Fax: 520-326-9001
www.mysterybooksellers.com

Mid-South Independent Booksellers Association
6130 Bluebonnet Pond
Kingwood, TX 77345
Toll-free: 877-357-0757
Tel: 214-557-5620
Fax: 281-361-6977
www.msiba.org

Mid-South Independent Booksellers Association
2309 NW 120 Street
Oklahoma City, OK 73120
Tel: 405-751-5681

Mountains & Plains Booksellers Association
19 Old Town Square, Suite 238
Fort Collins, CO 80524
Toll-free within region:
1-800-752-0249
Tel: 970-484-5856
Fax: 970-407-1479
www.mountainsplains.org

Mystery Writers of America
17 East 47 Street
New York, NY 10017
Tel: 212-888-8171
Fax: 212-888-8107
www.mysterywriters.org

New Atlantic Independent Booksellers Association
2667 Hyacinth Street
Westbury, NY 11590
Toll-free: 877-866-2422
Tel: 516-333-0681
Fax: 516-333-0689
www.naiba.com

New England Booksellers Association
1770 Massachusetts Avenue, #332
Cambridge, MA 02140
Toll-free: 800-466-8711
Tel: 617-576-3070
www.neba.org

Northern California Independent Booksellers Association (NCIBA)
The Presidio
P.O. Box 29169
37 Graham Street

San Francisco, CA 94129
Tel: 415-561-7686
Fax: 415-561-7685
www.nciba.com

- **Pacific Northwest Booksellers Association**
  317 West Broadway #214
  Eugene, OR 97401
  Tel: 541-683-4363
  www.pnba.org

- **Romance Writers of America**
  16000 Stuebner Airline, Suite 140
  Spring, TX 77379
  Tel: 832-717-5200
  Fax: 832-717-5201
  www.rwanational.com

- **Society of Children's Book Writers and Illustrators**
  8271 Beverly Boulevard
  Los Angeles, CA 90048
  Tel: 323-782-1010
  Fax: 323-782-1892
  www.scbwi.org

- **Southeast Booksellers Association**
  1404 South Beltline Boulevard
  Columbia, SC 29205
  Tel: 803-252-7755
  www.sebaweb.org

- **Southern California Booksellers Association**
  301 East Colorado Boulevard
  Pasadena, CA 91101
  Tel: 626-791-9455
  E-mail: *scba@earthlink.net*

- **Upper Midwest Booksellers Association**
  3407 West 44 Street
  Minneapolis, MN 55410
  Toll-free: 800-784-7522
  Tel: 612-926-5868
  E-mail: *UMBAoffice@aol.com*

ORGANIZATIONS OFFERING INFORMATION ON GRANTS

- **The Authors Guild**
  31 East 28 Street
  New York, NY 10016-7923
  Tel: 212-563-5904
  Fax: 212-564-5363
  E-mail: *staff@authorsguild.org*
  www.authorsguild.org

- **Funds for Writers**
  www.fundsforwriters.com

- **National Endowment for the Arts**
  1100 Pennsylvania Avenue NW
  Washington, DC 20506
  Tel: 202-682-5400
  www.nea.gov/grants/apply/Lit.html

- **PEN American Center**
  588 Broadway, Suite 303
  New York, NY 10012
  Tel: 212-334-1660
  Fax: 212-334-2181
  www.pen.org/awards/awards.htm

- **Poets & Writers, Inc.**
  72 Spring Street, Suite 301
  New York, NY 10012
  Tel: 212-226-3586
  Fax: 212-226-3963
  www.pw.org

- **Writer's Digest**
  www.writersdigest.com

INFORMATION FOR SELF-PUBLISHERS

Print-on-Demand Publishers

- **Author House**
  1663 Liberty Drive, Suite 200
  Bloomington, IN 47403
  Tel: 888-519-5121
  www.authorhouse.com

- **Ikon Publishing**
  Cambridge, Ontario, Canada
  Tel: 519-624-9735
  E-mail: *info@ikonpublishing.ca*
  (best known for their illustrated and highly designed books)

- **iUniverse**
  2021 Pine Lake Road, Suite 100
  Lincoln, NE 68512
  Toll-free: 800-AUTHORS (288-4677)
  Tel: 402-323-7800
  www.iuniverse.com

- **The Writers' Collective**
  780 Reservoir Avenue, Suite 243
  Cranston, RI 02910
  Tel: 401-537-9175
  Fax: 401-537-9175
  www.writerscollective.org
  (does not accept all manuscripts)

- **Xlibris**
  436 Walnut Street
  Philadelphia, PA 19106-3703
  Tel: 888-795-4274
  E-mail: *info@xlibris.com*
  www.xlibris.com

To acquire your PCN, go to:
- *http://pcn.loc.gov*

To acquire your ISBN, go to:
- *www.isbn.org*

For a list of reliable printers, go to:
- *http://www.isbn.org/standards/home/isbn/us/printers.asp*

Publishers Marketing Association
See ASSOCIATIONS.

Programs for Self-Published Writers

- **Barnes & Noble Author & Publisher Guidelines**
  www.barnesandnoble.com/help/pub_wewant_tosell.asp?linkid=9&userid=3U6yjPwA48&cds2Pid=946Titles@bn.com

- **Amazon.com Advantage**
  advantage@amazon.com.
  www.amazon.com/exec/obidos/subst/partners/direct/direct-application.html

APPENDIX II

SELECTED PUBLISHERS

Abbeville Press
137 Varick Street
New York, NY 10013
Tel: 212-366-5585
Fax: 212-366-6966
www.abbeville.com

Abrams
100 Fifth Avenue
New York, NY 10011
www.abramsbooks.com

Abrams
Tel: 212-206-7715
Fax: 212-645-8437

Stewart, Tabori & Chang
Tel: 212-519-1200

Adams Media
57 Littlefield Street
Avon, MA 02322
Toll-free: 800-872-5627
Tel: 508-427-7100
Fax: 800-872-5628
www.adamsmedia.com

Amacom
1601 Broadway
New York, NY 10019
Toll-free: 800-714-6395
Fax: 518-891-3653
www.amanet.org/books

Andrews McMeel
4520 Main Street
Kansas City, MO 64111
Tel: 816-932-6700
www.andrewsmcmeel.com

Avalon Publishing Group
245 West 17 Street
New York, NY 10011-5300
Tel: 212-981-9919
Fax: 212-375-2571
www.avalonpub.com

Avalon Travel/Seal Press
1400 65 Street, Suite 250
Emeryville, CA 94608
Tel: 510-595-3664
www.travelmatters.com
www.sealpress.com

Carroll & Graf, Marlowe & Co., Nation Books, Thunder's Mouth Press
245 West 17 Street
New York, NY 10011-5300
Tel: 212-981-9919
Fax: 212-375-2571
www.carollandgraf.com
www.nationbooks.org
www.thundersmouth.com

Shoemaker & Hoard
3704 Macomb Street NW, Suite 4
Washington, DC 20016
Tel: 202-364-4464
Fax: 202-364-4484
www.shoemakerhoard.com

Barron's Educational Series
250 Wireless Boulevard
Hauppauge, NY 11788
Toll-free: 1-800-645-3476
www.barronseduc.com

Beacon
25 Beacon Street
Boston, MA 02108
Tel: 617-742-2110
Fax: 617-723-3097
www.beacon.org

Berrett-Koehler
235 Montgomery Street, Suite 650
San Francisco, CA 94104
Tel: 415-288-0260
Fax: 415-362-2512
www.bkconnection.com

Bloomberg Press
Tel: 609-279-4600
www.bloomberg.com

Candlewick Press
2067 Massachusetts Avenue
Cambridge, MA 02140
Tel: 617-661-3330
www.candlewick.com

Chronicle
85 Second Street
San Francisco, CA 94105
Tel: 415-537-4200
Fax: 415-537-4460
www.chroniclebooks.com

Disney/Hyperion
77 West 66th Street
New York, NY 10023
Adult: 212-456-0100
Children's: 212-633-4400
www.hyperionbooks.com

Grove/Atlantic
841 Broadway
New York, NY 10003
Tel: 212-614-7850
Fax: 212-614-7886
www.groveatlantic.com

Harcourt
www.harcourt.com

New York office:
15 East 26 Street
New York, NY 10010
Tel: 212-592-1000

California office:
525 B Street, Suite 1900
San Diego, CA 92101
Tel: 619-231-6616

Harlequin
Tel: 416-445-5860/212-553-4200
www.eharlequin.com

New York office:
233 Broadway
New York, NY 10279

HarperCollins
www.harpercollins.com

HarperCollins/HarperResource/
William Morrow/ReganBooks
10 East 53 Street
New York, NY 10020
Tel: 212-207-7000

HarperSanFrancisco
353 Sacramento Street, Suite 500
San Francisco, CA 94111-3653
Tel: 415-477-4400

Zondervan
5300 Patterson Avenue SE
Grand Rapids, MI 49530
Tel: 616-698-6900

Harvard Common Press
535 Albany Street
Boston, MA 02118
Tel: 617-423-5803
Fax: 617-695-9794
www.harvardcommonpress.com

Health Communications
P.O. Box 266498
Weston, FL 33326
Tel: 954-360-0909
www.foodandhealth.com

Holtzbrinck
www.holtzbrinck.com

St. Martin's/Picador/
Bloomsbury
175 Fifth Avenue, Suite 300
New York, NY 10010
Tel: 212-674-5151
www.stmartins.com
www.picadorusa.com
www.bloomsbury.com

Farrar, Straus & Giroux
19 Union Square West
New York, NY 10003
Tel: 212-741-6900
www.fsgbooks.com

Henry Holt
175 Fifth Avenue
New York, NY 10010
Tel: 212-886-9200
Fax: 212- 633-0748
www.henryholt.com

Palgrave Macmillan
175 Fifth Avenue
New York, NY 10010
Toll-free: 800-221-7945
Tel: 212-982-3900
Fax: 212-777-6359
www.palgrave.com

Tor
175 Fifth Avenue
New York, NY 10010
Tel: 212-388-0100
Fax: 212 388-0191

Houghton Mifflin
222 Berkeley Street
Boston, MA 02116
Tel: 617-351-5000/212-420-5800
www.houghtonmifflin.com

John Wiley & Sons

Wiley
111 River Street
Hoboken, NJ 07030
Tel: 201-748-6000
www.wiley.com

Jossey-Bass
989 Market Street
San Francisco, CA 94103-1741
Tel: 415-433-1740
www.josseybass.com

Kensington
850 Third Avenue
New York, NY 10022
Tel: 212-407-1500
www.kensingtonbooks.com

MacAdam Cage
155 Sansome Street, Suite 550
San Francisco, CA 94104
Tel: 415-986-7502
www.macadamcage.com

McGraw-Hill
2 Penn Plaza
New York, NY 10021
Tel: 212-512-2000
www.mhcontemporary.com

The New Press
38 Greene Street
New York NY 10013
Tel: 212-629-8802
www.thenewpress.com

New World Library
14 Pameron Way
Novato, CA 94949
Tel: 415-884-2100
www.newworldlibrary.com

W.W. Norton
500 Fifth Avenue
New York, NY 10110
Tel: 212-354-5500
www.wwnorton.com

Overlook Press
141 Wooster Street, Suite 4B
New York, NY 10012
Tel: 212-673-2210
www.overlookpress.com

Oxford University Press
198 Madison Avenue
New York, NY 10016-4314
Tel: 212-726-6000
www.oup.com

Penguin Group (USA)
375 Hudson Street
New York, NY 10014
www.penguin.com

Avery/Prentice Hall/Berkley/Dutton/Gotham/New American Library/Penguin/Perigee/Plume/Portfolio/Putnam/Riverhead/Rowland Books/Tarcher/Viking
Tel: 212-366-2000

Children's Books
Tel: 212-414-3600

Dorling Kindersley
Tel: 212-213-4800

Perseus Book Group
www.perseusbookgroup.com

Basic/Civitas/Counterpoint/Da Capo/Public Affairs
387 Park Avenue South
New York, NY 10016
Tel: 212-340-8100

Running Press
125 South 22 Street
Philadelphia, PA 19103
Tel: 215-567-5080

Westview
5500 Central Avenue
Boulder, CO 80301
Tel: 303-444-3541

Phaidon
180 Varick Street
New York, NY 10014
Tel: 212-652-5400
www.phaidon.com

Random House
1745 Broadway
New York, NY 10019
Tel: 212-782-9000
www.randomhouse.com

Ballantine/Random House/
Bantam/Dell/Broadway/
Doubleday/Clarkson Potter/
Crown/Harmony/ThreeRivers/
Dial/Knopf/Pantheon/Prima/
Villard/Vintage/Anchor

Red Wheel/Weiser/Conari
368 Congress Street
Boston, MA 02210
Tel: 617-542-1324
www.weiserbooks.com

Rizzoli
300 Park Avenue South
New York, NY 10010
Tel: 212-387-3400
www.rizzoliusa.com

Rodale
Rodale Books
33 East Minor Street
Emmaus, PA 18098-0099
Tel: 610-967-5171/212-697-2040
www.rodale.com

Routledge
270 Madison Avenue
New York, NY 10016-0602
Tel: 212-216-7800
Fax: 212-564-7854
www.routledge-ny.com

Rugged Land
401 West Street
New York, NY 10014
Tel: 212-334-8228
Fax: 212-334-5749
www.ruggedland.com

Scholastic
557 Broadway
New York, New York 10012
Tel: 212-343-6100
www.scholastic.com

Shambhala
300 Massachusetts Avenue
Boston, MA 02115
Tel: 617-424-0030
Fax: 617-236 1563
www.shambhala.com

Simon & Schuster
1230 Avenue of the Americas
New York, NY 10020
212-698-7000
www.simonsays.com

Atria/Fireside/Free
Press/Pocket/Scribner/S&S/
Washington Square Press

Sourcebooks
1935 Brookdale Road, Suite 139
Naperville, IL 60563
Tel: 630-961-3900/212-414-1701
Fax: 630-961-2168
www.sourcebooks.com

Sterling
387 Park Avenue South
New York, NY 10016
Tel: 212-532-7160
www.sterlingpub.com

Ten Speed Press, Celestial Arts, Tricycle Press
P.O. Box 7123
Berkeley, CA 94707
Toll-free: 800-841-BOOK
Tel: 510-559-1600
Fax: 510-559-1629
www.tenspeed.com

Time Warner Book Group
1271 Avenue of the Americas
New York, NY 10020
www.twobookmark.com

Warner Books
Tel: 212-522-7200

Little, Brown
Tel: 212-522-8700

Oxmoor House
Tel: 205-445-6560

Workman Publishing
708 Broadway
New York, NY 10003-9555
Tel: 212-254-5900
Fax: 212-254-8098
www.workman.com

Algonquin
Artisan
Storey
Workman

APPENDIX III

STANDARD PERMISSION FORM

[Name of copyright holder] authorizes [your name] and his/her publisher, [name of your publisher], and its licensees, to use the following [photograph, article, poem, recipe, pages, lines, etc.] from [title of book, poem, song, article, etc.] to use in [title or tentative title of your book] by [your name] in all versions and media and in the advertising and promotion thereof throughout the world. As full consideration for the contribution and all rights therein, [your name] shall pay [name of copyright holder] a one-time fee of ——— dollars ($———) due within thirty (30) days of publication of the Work.* [Name of copyright holder] waives any claim [name of copyright holder] may have against the aforementioned parties, their licensees, and assigns based upon such use, including any claims for copyright infringement or violation of any right.

[Name of copyright holder] warrants that [name of copyright holder] has the right to grant the above rights, that the work does not infringe upon the copyright, or other rights, of anyone. [Name of copyright holder] agrees to indemnify the author, [publisher's name] and its distributors, customers and licensees against all costs and expenses, including reasonable attorney's fees, that may result from any alleged breach of the aforesaid warranty.

____

Signature

____

Typed or printed name

____

Date

*Delete this sentence if there is no fee involved.

APPENDIX IV

OUR PROPOSAL FOR THIS BOOK

Putting Your Passion into Print

By Arielle Eckstut & David Sterry

Open This Book and Discover How to:

- Find a Top-of-the-Heap Idea
- Come Up with a Blockbuster Title
- Write a Door-Opening Query Letter
- Create An Airtight Proposal
- Find the Perfect Agent, Editor and Publisher for You
- Get People to Actually Buy Your Book
- And Much, Much More

SUMMARY

A 61-year-old grandmother in Iowa, a 43-year-old academic in Boston, a 21-year-old surfer in Laguna Beach. What do these people have in common? THEY ALL WANT TO WRITE A BOOK! But how to get a book successfully published remains a mystery to most aspiring authors. Literary agent/author Arielle Eckstut and author/pitchman David Sterry demystify the publishing process and reveal the secrets of putting your personal passion into print.

During a recent coast-to-coast tour of their workshop of the same name, people across the spectrum of the publishing process—even published authors with agents—attended Arielle and David's workshop and came out with a whole new arsenal of bookselling weapons. Booksellers and attendees alike had only one complaint: they wished they had a book to take home with them containing all the information they had learned. Indeed, there is a profound need for a soup-to-nuts guide that illuminates each step of the bookselling process, answering every question a writer could ask. A book that addresses the particular concerns of today's authors. A book by those in the publishing trenches who know the tricks of the trade. A book that will speak to the literary fiction writer, the new age guru, the romance novelist and the high-tech businessman alike

Putting Your Passion into Print will be this definitive tome. Written in a lively, encouraging and humorous tone, it will inspire the millions who want to get a book published.

AUDIENCE

In the days when a book cost as much as a farm, only the rich or the religious could even dream of producing a book. Well, things have changed. Now any Tom, Dick or Martha has the chance to get a book published. From those who fantasize about appearing on *Oprah*, to Goth Ann Rice wannabes, to the heir to the Atkins diet throne, this book will appeal to a wide (and growing) audience. Our audience breaks down into the following categories:

- *Workshop and Conference Goers:* These are the people who populate writing workshops from Bread Loaf to Squaw Valley to the multitude of local Learning Annexes around the country. These people write predominantly literary fiction, genre fiction, creative nonfiction and children's books. They are avid readers. They often have professional writing experience and some publishing knowledge. Many have finished manuscripts in hand. What they don't have are agents or publishers.

- *Academics Who Want to Reach a Popular Audience:* There are tens of thousands of academics out there who feel their work merits more than 12 readers. They are looking for a way to bring their work out of the ivory tower and onto the streets. Usually, these folks have little to no knowledge of trade publishing, nor have they developed a voice that will speak to Jane Q. Public. Academics will find this book particularly suited to their needs because we address questions like: Under what circumstances does it make sense to hire a writer or editor to help with style and readability? What are universal tips to "popularizing" academic work? How can you parlay your academic success into a hefty book contract?
- *Professionals with a Message:* Just like academics, many professionals have a dream of getting their message out to those outside their immediate grasp. They also know that there's no better business card than a book. From management consultants to interior designers to tae kwon do instructors, this book will help professionals take their expertise to the page and bring them business in return. We'll also show professionals how to develop a platform based on what is unique about their business and how to use this platform in each stage of the bookselling process.
- *Hobbyists with a Mission:* Whether their passion is beer, Jane Austen or tracking down their family's genealogy, many hobbyists dream of writing books about their personal obsessions. These obsessions can make for excellent books because usually thousands, if not millions, of others are obsessed with these subjects as well. However, hobbyists often know the least about putting a book together of any of our potential audience. They may not be readers at all, and they may have very little professional or writing experience. These are the people who will want to read this book from cover to cover, so that we can hold their hands through each step of the process.
- *Mystery Mavens, Romance Lovers, Sci-Fi Freaks and Other General-Genre Junkies:* These folks have usually read hundreds of books within a genre. And now they're at the point where they believe they are ready to write their own. Unlike the workshop junkies, they've never put pen to paper. Like the hobbyists, they need all the help they can get.
- *Students and Educators:* When we have brought our PYPIP workshop to colleges and universities, the attendance and interest has been overwhelming. So many students want to write books and get them published. But hardly any academic programs provide this kind of information. After attending our workshop, several professors have already told us that as soon as we have a book out there, it will be required reading for all their graduate students.

- *Published Authors Who Want to Do It Differently with Their Next Book:* Originally, we never would have thought that these people would be our audience. But our workshops proved otherwise. So many authors have had publishing experiences that either did not live up to their expectations or didn't live up to the publisher's expectations. These people want a chance to do things differently the next time around. This book will help them answer the myriad questions they may have, including: Should you have taken a lower offer from a more creative and passionate publisher? Did you start your marketing and publicity efforts as early as you could? Is a sequel your best option, or should you come out with something entirely different?

Our audience also includes people who will come to the book with specific questions: What is the proper format for a proposal? Do you need a subtitle? How do you write a query letter that someone will read? How do you write a bio that blows your own horn without making you sound like a blowhard? When does it make sense to self-publish? How do you get an agent you've queried to return your call? How do you get your editor/publisher to invest in the promotion of your book? What do you do when your agent/editor makes a suggestion that you're uncomfortable with? How do you make sure you don't get stuck with a cover you hate? Should you hire an outside publicist? How do you get on a bestseller list? All this, and so much more, will be at our readers' fingertips in *Putting Your Passion into Print.*

COMPETITION

After doing an extensive search, three things became clear:

- Almost every competitive book concentrates on only one aspect of getting a book published, whether it's finding an agent, writing a book proposal or publicizing your work. You'd have to buy at least three books to get the amount of information supplied in *Putting Your Passion into Print*! Who would spend $45–$75 when they could spend under $20?!
- Competitive books also tend to divide between those writing fiction and those writing nonfiction. We believe the essential principles apply across categories (though where there are differences we will have sections or boxes in the book with tips for addressing each), and we've found that many writers want to write *both* fiction and nonfiction. Again, the issue of buying more than one book vs. one book arises.

- There is only one nicely packaged book out there, and this one has a Vintage-esque feel that will scare off those with more practical than literary sensibilities. All the other books have the look of a resumé primer published by Adams or McGraw-Hill; in other words, they look like amateur PowerPoint presentations. They're bland, they use only text (with the exceptional stock photo here and there) and they're plain ugly! Maybe you shouldn't judge a book by its cover, but that doesn't mean you won't buy a book because of one. We believe the packaging alone could make our book a category killer.

Now for the three truly competitive titles. They are:

1) *How to Get Happily Published* by Judith Applebaum (HarperCollins, first published in 1978; latest edition, 1998). The information in this book is very good. Applebaum's voice is clear and authoritative but not intimidating. This book has sold over half a million copies and is now in its fifth edition, proving that there is a huge audience out there for our book. But as good as the information in this book is, we feel it has a number of significant drawbacks.

- *Bad packaging:* "Zzzzzzz" is all we can say about this dud of a cover. It has absolutely no presence on the shelf. And if you're just looking at spines and can't see the "fifth edition, half a million copies sold" seal (which is the case 99% of the time), your eye would never seek it out. The size is 5 × 8, which reinforces its lack of presence. The text itself is 242 pages, but 82 of those are on self-publishing. This means Applebaum spends only 160 pages on the entire process of getting a book published from idea through and past publication! As a reader on Amazon wrote, "Great book—if you want to self-publish. Otherwise not so helpful."

- *Dated material:* It's almost 25 years old. Yes, it was updated in 1998, but the lion's share of the book has not changed since it was first published. The problem is, publishing is not the same as it was 25 years ago. Hence the information has a dated feel about it even though there are a number of current anecdotes sprinkled throughout.

- *Poor organization:* We had to look in three different places before we found Applebaum's tips on writing a good query letter—one of the most-asked questions by those trying to get a book published. And to go back to the datedness of the material, the author never actually gives tips on writing a query letter to an agent—only on writing them directly to book editors. Since nary a book editor looks at query letters these days, we felt that this was a case of giving not only dated information, but bad information as well.

- *Slim on e-information:* So much has changed since the proliferation of e-business. From marketing to research, to selling your book, we'll show you how to make your computer your best friend. And while the Applebaum book does have some information about the Web world, we will cover it in much greater depth and breadth.
- *Limited expertise:* While Applebaum is a publishing veteran, she has never developed and sold books on a day-to-day basis nor has she written books on a wide variety of subjects (this is her only book). She's written primarily about the industry or worked as a book publicist. With three books under our belt (and counting), Arielle's experience developing and selling dozens of titles day in and day out and David's experience as a professional pitchman, we have many more publishing bases covered.

All in all, we believe with up-to-the-moment information, a great package, a larger word count, easier navigation and our upbeat voice to give people encouragement, we've got a book that will be the standard for generations to come.

2) *The Shortest Distance Between You and a Published Book* by Susan Page (Broadway, 1997). This is another book with good information and a clear format. But we think our book has much more to offer than this one.

- *Limited packaging:* This is the book with the delightfully literary cover. It's nice to look at, but we believe it appeals to the female buyer and to those with *New Yorker* sensibilities (the font is the giveaway). We want these people, too, but we also want to reach out to a much broader audience.
- *Limited scope:* While this book covers a wide range of issues, it does not cover them in detail. *PYPIP* will leave no stone unturned, so writers will never have to go out and buy another book on the subject, no matter what genre they write in or what dilemma they face.
- *Limited experience:* Page has only been on the author side of the publishing equation. She's never tried to sell, edit or publicize any book other than her own. We, on the other hand, are both an agent and a professional pitchman. We know the ins and outs of selling from doing it every day for the past 30 years combined. However, we also have the personal author experience and can empathize with our readers every step of the way.

3) *From Book Idea to Bestseller* by Michael Snell, Kim Baker and Sunny Baker (Prima, 1997): This book is not stocked in any independent bookstore in the Bay Area, nor is it on powells.com. We assume it has been remaindered and is on its way

out of print (it is listed on Amazon, but Amazon lists remaindered books as still in print).

Lastly, *Putting Your Passion into Print* will be unique because we are a married couple who continues to capture the media's attention (see next section). The playful banter, which is so much a part of our collective voice and makes our events so much fun, will in turn make *PYPIP* not just the definitive book on the subject, but also the most entertaining.

THE AUTHORS

Arielle Eckstut is a literary agent with James Levine Communications, Inc. She worked in their New York office for seven years before opening up JLC's West Coast office in the Bay Area in 2000. Arielle represents numerous bestselling and award-winning authors and has sold millions of dollars worth of books. She made her first publishing deal at the age of 23 for $300,000. Ever since, she has made it her mission to nurture and develop the talent of those she represents while never losing sight of the art of the deal.

After almost a decade of acting as midwife to other people's creations, Arielle coauthored two of her own books: *Pride and Promiscuity: The Lost Sex Scenes of Jane Austen* (Simon & Schuster, 2001) and *Satchel Sez: The Wit, Wisdom, and World of Leroy "Satchel" Paige* (Crown/Random House, 2001). She was finally able to experience, firsthand, the excitement (and disappointments) involved in making a book. Going through the publishing process strengthened her skills as an agent and gave her a much broader perspective on the world of publishing.

Arielle is a graduate of the University of Chicago, where her major required her to ask a "grand question" and to back up this question with six essential texts. While many doubted the sagacity of such a major (What job will you get? How will you be able to pay for health insurance?), it turned out to be the perfect preparation for a life in publishing. By reading texts so closely and examining every last detail, Arielle was able to understand what makes for a great book. She continues to bring this attention to detail to all her work.

Arielle has also baked pastries for Madonna and the President, cut karyotypes and performed improvisational comedy at the Edinburgh Festival, Fringe.

David Henry Sterry is the author of the *San Francisco Chronicle* bestseller *Chicken: Self-Portrait of a Young Man for Rent* (ReganBooks/HarperCollins, 2002) and coauthor of *Satchel Sez: The Wit, Wisdom, and World of Leroy "Satchel" Paige* (Crown/Random House, 2001). He is also a published poet.

David started his acting career as a stand-up comedian, at the Holy City Zoo, the Punchline and the Comedy Store, performing with everyone from Robin Williams to Milton Berle. As an actor, he has worked everywhere from Lincoln Center to the Magic Theater, with everyone from Will Smith (in *The Fresh Prince of Bel Air*), to Michael Caine, to David Letterman (*Cabin Boy*) to Zippy the Chimp. He has been a TV pitchman for companies such as AT&T, Levis and Isuzu, performed in over 500 commercials, winning 4 Clios. He starred in Children's Television Workshop/ HBO's Emmy-winning *Encyclopedia* and was the emcee at Chippendale's Male Strip Club in New York, winning Cabaret Performer of the Year. His plays have been performed at P.S. 122, the West Bank Café and the Duplex. He has written screenplays for Disney, Fox and Nickelodeon Pictures. He is also a presentation doctor who goes into companies and works with their executives on how to improve their presentation skills.

David has also worked as a soda jerk, a barker, a cherry picker, a chicken fryer, a building inspector, a shoe salesman, a bike messenger and a marriage counselor. He graduated from Reed College and loves his woman, his cat and any sport involving a ball.

Why We're the Best People to Write This Book

To successfully write a book on how to get published, you've got to cover all the bases. While anyone can do the research, it's much better if the authors themselves have an insider's knowledge of a wide range of publishing experiences and access to the top professionals in every area of the world of books.

Arielle is an agent who not only sells books but spends an extraordinary amount of time on editorial development, editing, packaging, publicity and marketing, and many other aspects of the publishing process. Over 75% of her clients are first-time authors (90% of whom go on to be second-, third- and fourth-time authors) so she knows the trials and tribulations of the novice. She has worked with dozens of people from a wide range of backgrounds, such as doctors, MFA grads, moms, professional writers, academics, amateur scientists, baseball nuts and interior designers. And because she herself is an author, she understands the frustrations, joys and pitfalls a writer goes through each and every step of the way.

David is a bestselling author who knows the nuts and bolts of how to put together a book from soup to nuts, proposal to bestseller list. His years as a professional actor, pitchman and presentation doctor have given him a unique understanding of how people should market and present themselves so they can shine like the stars they are.

Publicity and Marketing

Because of our unique background and training in improvisation, stand-up comedy, emceeing, acting and presenting, along with our years of writing and agenting, our appearances are not just informative, they're also fun. And the fact that we're a married couple, with our own style of playful banter, sets us apart from all the other stars in the literary firmament.

- Events

  When we did our Putting Your Passion into Print: The Pacific Northwest Tour, we were overwhelmed by the reception. The tour taught us all about the art of the event, from the independents to the chains, from the big city to the small town, from universities to book fairs. It also taught us how much fun we have together in front of an audience.

- Print

  There are numerous opportunities for print publicity for *PYPIP* beyond the review attention we hope the book will garner. For one, to coincide with publication, we will pitch original articles to magazines that target their particular audience or subject matter on how to get a book published. Secondly, we recently realized that our personal story seems to be of interest to the general public and could help sell our book. We were featured in *New York* magazine a few weeks ago and then called by *Good Morning America* as a result. This response showed us how remarkably easy it should be to market us as an interesting couple with a unique take on the world. And the fact that our story as a couple begins with putting our own passion into print will be the cherry on top.

- TV

  Again, our story as a couple combined with our experience as performers (we're both extremely comfortable in front of a camera) and our clear presentation of the information contained in *PYPIP* will help us gain the interest of the *Good Morning Americas*, *Oprahs* and local morning and afternoon shows of the world.

- Radio

  Radio is one of our favorite publicity mediums, and we have a wealth of experience in this area. We have appeared repeatedly on National Public Radio, with Scott Simon, Rene Montagne, Neal Conan and Larry Mantle. We have also done local radio from Hawaii to Portland to New York to Los Angeles, honing our on-air skills to become masters of the sound bite and the extended story-telling information-giving format.

- Appearances

  Collectively or individually, we have appeared at, on, with or in (among others): *The New York Times, Washington Post, SF Chronicle* bestseller list, *Portland Tribune, Los Angeles Times, New York Daily News, The Oregonian, Baltimore Sun, New Orleans Picayune, St. Louis Post Dispatch,* the Associated Press, *Sacramento Bee, Dallas Morning News, Chicago Tribune;* Reed College, San Francisco State University, Sonoma State; *New York* magazine, *Sports Illustrated, Details* magazine, *Cooperstown* magazine of the National Baseball Hall of Fame, *Pages* magazine; Sally Jesse Rafael, *The Other Half* (with Dick Clark), *Mornings on 2, Northwest Afternoon at 4, Good Morning Central Oregon;* NPR's *Morning Edition, Weekend Edition, Talk of the Nation, AirTalk with Larry Mantle, The Gil Gross Show,* ESPN Radio, *BookTalk, Between the Lines, Radiozine, Cover to Cover, Mancow & Muller, Lydia & Gunther, The Bob and Tom Show;* Book Passage, Cody's, A Clean Well-Lighted Place for Books, Elliot Bay Books, Eagle Harbor Books, Powell's, Book Soup, Paulina Springs Book Co.; Barnes & Noble in Philadelphia, Berkeley, Vancouver, Seattle, Colma, Fremont and Bend; San Francisco Public Library (Lila Wallace Reader's Digest Writers on Writing series); the Edinburgh Fringe Festival and Lincoln Center.

- The Radio Show

  When we brought Putting Your Passion into Print onto National Public Radio's *Talk of the Nation,* the switchboard lit up with calls from one corner of America to the other. In fact, *Talk of the Nation* was so inundated with calls that they brought Arielle back later in the week to answer follow-up questions. We were subsequently approached about the possibility of launching our own Putting Your Passion into Print call-in radio show and are now working to have the show up and running in conjunction with the release of the book. We will pitch the show as "*Car Talk* meets Publishing" and will approach Barnes & Noble as a sponsor. We expect the show to start as a segment on an already nationally syndicated NPR show or as a weekly in the San Francisco Bay Area out of KQED or KPFA. Each week will feature a different expert from some segment of the book world: from editors to illustrators, booksellers to agents, book doctors to lawyers, along with a wide range of writers of nonfiction and genre fiction, children's books and cookbooks. We'll have segments like the Pitch of the Week, where an audience member gets to pitch his book on the air in two minutes or less, a Name That First Line contest and a Worst Rejection Letter of the Month. *Putting Your Passion into Print: the Radio Show* will, of course, give us a regular platform to reach a broad-based demographic.

MANUSCRIPT SPECIFICATIONS

We see *Putting Your Passion into Print* in a trim size of at least 6" X 9" and a page count of approximately 500–600, including references and index. Each chapter will include:

- Boxes (or some kind of call-out visual) with dos and dont's, tips and reminders, FAQs and our personal favorite: the "Think Outside the Box Box."
- Sample writing from query letters, proposals, pitches, etc.
- Stories and advice from those within the publishing industry. We plan to interview over 100 people, including authors, agents, editors, media escorts, publishers, publicists, marketing, sub rights and sales directors, booksellers, publishing lawyers, Hollywood book agents and more.
- Workbook elements for helpful exercises such as our title word chart.
- Templates for sample letters to agents, editors and booksellers for each stage of the game.

There is also the possibility of adding a software component to this book as Jeff Herman has done with his *Guide to Book Editors, Publishers, and Literary Agents*.

ENDNOTE

A suburban mom from suburban England, a southern lawyer, a new-age guy who talks to God. What do these people have in common? Their grandchildren's grandchildren's grandchildren will never have to work a day in their lives because they *put their passion into print*. And this, too, can be true for the millions of authors—aspiring and otherwise—who read this book!

SAMPLE MATERIAL

LOCATING AND QUERYING THE RIGHT AGENT FOR YOU

You've found your passion, located your model, perfected your pitch and completed your nonfiction proposal or novel. You've also determined that you want to go for a big-time publisher so you can receive money up front—an advance (see p. XX)—for your book.

Now you need to query an agent.

For those without a personal referral (which will be about 99.9% of you), don't despair! We have a system that is as close to foolproof as you'll get.

[REMINDER: Yes, there are millions of aspiring authors and only a few hundred agents. But while you need an agent, it's fair to say that an agent needs you even more. Without authors, agents wouldn't be in business, and we all know the reverse is not true. It's also important to realize that every single agent has passed up or passed over a project by an unknown author that went on to sell hundred of thousands of copies. This is precisely why nearly every agency—whether they claim to or not—looks at query letters. Just keep saying to yourself: THEY NEED ME MORE THAN I NEED THEM! Because nobody wants to be remembered as the agent who passed on Harry Potter or *The Catcher in the Rye*.]

Personalizing Your Letter

The key to catching any agent's attention is to personalize your query letter. How do you personalize a letter to someone you don't know? The first thing you'll need to do is make a list of the books you love that have something in common with your book. Do not pick books that are in direct competition with your own, but ones that draw the same audience, that you have read thoroughly and that you have strong feelings for. For example, say you're writing a cookbook on vegetarian Thai cuisine. There may already be a book out there on this exact subject. But rather than choose this book for your list, choose your favorite vegetarian cookbooks and your favorite Thai cookbooks (that are not exclusively vegetarian). We'll explain why shortly.

How do you find books like yours? A few years ago, you would've had to wade through *Books in Print*. But now, just log onto amazon.com and you'll amass a list in no time. Amazon is extremely helpful even if you think you know what's already out there. In the search field, plug in key words (like "vegetarian" and "Thai") and see what comes up. Or if you already have a book you love and want to use on your list, put that into the search field. Once you've found a book that looks like a good match, scroll down until you get to the feature that says "people who bought this book also bought . . ." This will point you in the direction of potentially dozens of other books on your subject that you can then buy or check out at your local library or bookstore. Once you've located 5 to 20 books of this nature, take your project notebook with you to the bookstore. Then look in the acknowledgment sections to see if the authors have thanked their agent or editor. Make two lists: one of agents, the other of editors. This way you can call the editor's office and ask for the name of the agent if none is listed. The names of these editors will come in handy later as well (see Chapter XX).

[TIP: No agent or editor listed in the acknowledgments? All you need to do is call the main number for the publisher and ask for the sub-rights department. (All major publishers have Web sites that list their numbers. These numbers are also provided in the publishing guides listed in the Appendix.) Tell them you're interested in acquiring the film or television rights to the book and need to know who the author's agent is. No one will ask who you are or why you need to know. If on the off chance they do, just make up a production company name!]

Once you've culled a list of agents—the more the merrier—find out everything you can about them. Many agencies have Web sites that list the bios of the individual agents who work there. Another great resource is *Jeff Herman's Guide to Book Editors, Publishers, and Literary Agents,* which lists personal and professional information about individual agents (see Appendix). Find out what other books the agent has represented. Study these books. Figure out how your book relates to the other books and other authors this person represents. Find out if the agent has ever written a book, as many agents have. Read agents' books to find out about their personal likes and dislikes—in other words, *their* passions. Do they have a dog? Are they a vegetarian? A soccer player? A nature lover? A world traveler? Depending on the subject of your book, you may be able to use this information to personalize your letter. For example, a vegetarian world traveler might be just the right agent for your vegetarian Thai cookbook!

What most authors don't realize is that agents are an essentially anonymous piece of the publishing puzzle. They don't get much credit outside the industry. Guess how many literary agents the average Jane can name? None. So anything you can do to make an agent feel acknowledged, smart, interesting or special will go a long way.

If you don't do your research, chances are, you'll send your sci-fi novel to a sci-fi hater, your illustrated history of tea to a coffee drinker, your Christian self-help book to a die-hard Buddhist. The fact is, most people do NOT do their research. This means that if you do, you've put yourself leagues ahead of your competition.

Continue your research until you've put together a list of at least 10 agents who appear to be legitimate matches for your book. These are all people who have done similar but not identical books. Do not send your Thai vegetarian cookbook proposal to an agent who has already done a Thai vegetarian cookbook. Most agents will not want this conflict of interest. And any agent who does is not the agent for you.

[BOX: An agenting story from Arielle. One day, I got a query letter with lots of children's stickers and rubber stamps covering the envelope. It was both playful and goofy and caught my attention immediately. Susan Wooldridge, the person who wrote the query, had most certainly done her homework about me. She found out I grew up right by Columbia University in New York City and then went on to the University of Chicago. She also found out I was a poetry lover. It turns out Susan had grown up right by the University of Chicago and went to school at Columbia. And her book was about how writing poetry can help us get to the root of our creative selves. I certainly can't remember the exact words of this letter, but I remember the connection she made with me and how she used our similar histories to peak my interest in her book. Indeed, I sold this book. It's called *Poemcrazy* and is now in its 18th printing.

Soon after *Poemcrazy* was published, I got another query letter. This one was from someone who had no connection to me—except that she had read and LOVED *Poemcrazy*. She wrote a beautifully detailed letter about reading the acknowledgments in Susan's book, telling me what she thought was so special about *Poemcrazy* as well as how her book was both similar and different. She made a very convincing case for why the agent for *Poemcrazy* should also be the agent for her book, *Fruitflesh*. And she convinced me. *Fruitflesh* came out last month and became a Book Sense top 10 bestseller (see PUBLICITY), and she just won the Bellweather prize juried by Barbara Kingsolver, Toni Morrison and Maxine Hong Kingston for her first novel!

Neither of these women had ever written a book. There was nothing particularly special about their resumés, and their books were not obvious bestsellers. But the work they put into researching agents turned them both into successful published authors. Follow their lead, and you won't be agentless for long.]

WRITING YOUR QUERY LETTER

Now it's time to actually write your query letter. The query letter is one of the most important pieces of the publishing puzzle. A smart, interesting, well-crafted personal query letter can open many doors for you.

A query letter consists of three parts:

Connection with the Agent

Using your research, you need to make your case for why a particular agent is the right person to represent your material. You'll also want to add any possible personal connections you may have discovered (you both graduated from the University of Wisconsin, own three pugs or spent your youth in Florence). Make specific references to books the agent has represented or written. Tell him or her what you liked about the book and why your book is similar to the successful books he or she has represented. Here are three different styles of sample paragraphs:

1) In researching literary agents, I saw that you represented two of my favorite books, *Poemcrazy* and *Fruitflesh*. I have used these books both personally and professionally in my psychotherapy practice. What particularly impressed me about these books is the incredible amount of heart they display. What brave women Susan and Gayle are to reveal their lives in such intimate detail! I can't tell you what an inspiration both women have been to my patients and me. I believe that my book, *Writing for Your Life,* shares some of the essential qualities of *Poemcrazy* and *Fruitflesh,* but is rooted in my experience as a clinical psychologist. Because both Gayle and Susan acknowledged you so effusively, and because my book shares many of the same fundamental beliefs as these, I hope that you'll be interested in reviewing my proposal.

2) After seeing you acknowledged in *Hooligan Killers,* I logged onto your Web site to check out what other books you represent. I was happy to see so many books that I have on my shelves and that I admire thoroughly. I am a particular fan of *Goalie on a Rampage* and *Sweepers Gone Mad*. But what impressed me the most was your love of Manchester United, as I myself am a Red Devil fan from the days of Bobby Charlton and Georgie Best. At 20, I moved to England and played for Newcastle United's Under 21 Club. I've written a novel about my time as an American soccer player in England, so it made my day to find an agent who shares my love for the game. I hope at the very least you'll get a kick out of reading *The Referee Assassin.*

3) I recently bought a copy of your book, *Monkeys in the Bible*, and I read it cover to cover in one night. I loved the chapter where you had the orangutan come down from the mount with Moses and the Ten Commandments. I'm telling all my friends in the scientific community about your book, and some of us quote lines back and forth from it. My favorite is: "When Moses slipped on the banana peel, one of the tablets broke and suddenly, instead of 13 Commandments, we only had 10." I also saw on your Web site that you have agented many popular science books, including *Bees Bees Bees* and *Men Are Dogs, Women Are Cats*. I myself am a leading primate biologist, and I have written a proposal for a book about monkeys based on my award-winning research in Kenya called *Everything I Need to Know I Learned from My Monkey*. Thanks for your time, and I can't wait to read your next book.

[TIP: Don't be fooled into writing a dull, boring query. Yes, be professional (see p. XX), but make sure the letter reflects your own personality and style. Show the agent you'll be great to do business with.]

The Pitch

Take the flap copy you have meticulously crafted (see p. XX), and condense your pitch to one paragraph. This means getting your story down to its essential ingredients and making them exciting. Here are two examples of great paragraph-length pitches:

1.

> My book is called *Why God Won't Go Away?* and it asks the age-old question: Did God create the brain, or did the brain create God? It's based on my long-term study at the University of Pennsylvania in which I used high-tech imaging techniques to examine the brain functions of Buddhists meditating and Franciscan nuns praying. And my answer to both questions, based on my study and research, is a resounding Yes!

This is a pitch for a bestselling book Arielle agented called *Why God Won't Go Away* by Dr. Andrew Newberg, Dr. Eugene D'Aquili and Vince Rause (Ballantine/Random House, 2001).

2.

> My book is extremely unpleasant, for it tells a terrible tale about three unlucky children. Even though they are charming and clever, the Beaudelaire siblings lead lives filled with misery and woe. In this short book alone, the three youngsters encounter a greedy and repulsive villain, itchy clothing, cold porridge, a disastrous fire and a plot to steal their fortune. My book is best described as "*Home Alone* meets Edgar Allan Poe," and it's called *The Bad Beginning,* the first in a series of unhappy tragedies about the brave, resourceful, talented Beaudelaire children as they suffer one cruel blow after another, surviving by the skin of their teeth and the pluck of their mettle.

This is an example of how we would have pitched the wildly successful young adult book *The Bad Beginning* by Lemony Snicket (HarperCollins, 2001).

Your Bio

In a paragraph, tell the agent what is interesting about you and why you're the person to write this book. This is not about a dry job resumé. This is a wet, fun-filled paragraph that lets the agent know how great and yet modest you are, and why you and you alone are capable of pulling this book off. If you've been published anywhere else, this is a good thing to add. If you've won any awards, include them. It doesn't matter what the award is, as long as you won it. No need to add it's from junior high school—the award alone will do. And feel free to put in any information that shows you've got the savvy to publicize and market your book. In one of our seminars, a successful businessman told us he had been homeless for several years. We told him to put this in his query letter because it helped show what an unusual and resilient person he was—and it was a great story for publicity. Can't you just see him on *Oprah*! Clearly, this is the kind of information that doesn't go on your CV, but again, it would set you apart from the hordes of others trying to get a book published.

[TIP: The more professional your presentation, the better off you are. Use high-quality stationery, folders and visuals. Be sure to have someone else proof your letter. And whatever you do, spell the agent's name right. Remember that God is in the Details!]

FAQs:

Q: Should I send query letters to more than one agent?
A: Absolutely. The more competition you can generate for your book, the better off you are.

Q: If I get interest from one agent, should I tell the others?
A: Oh, yes. If anyone expresses any interest at all, notify the rest of your list. Make them know they're going to miss out on a good thing if they don't jump on board fast. This is a variation on the old Peter-Paul gambit, in which a person plays one potential buyer off the other to jack up the price of whatever is being sold.

Q: How long should my query letter be?
A: The whole thing should fit on one page, unless you have a very good reason for it not to.

Q: Should I send a whole manuscript with my query letter?
A: Do not bombard the agent with material. That is a good way to get your material shredded and trashed. Just send a query informing them of what material you have available (see p. XX), and let them tell you what they want.

Q: Should I send a self-addressed stamped envelope?
A: Yes. And be sure to include a phone number, an e-mail address and a snail mail address. Seems pretty basic, but you'd be shocked how many people leave out this information.

CHAPTER-BY-CHAPTER OUTLINE

1. Writing the Right Idea
    - Preparing a Tool Kit
    - Finding a Support Team
    - Looking at Salability
    - Making Friends with Your Local Bookseller
2. Building Your Book
    - Locating a Model
    - Titles and Subtitles
    - Finding Coauthors, Cowriters and Ghostwriters
    - Crafting Your Pitch
    - The Nuts and Bolts of the Nonfiction Book Proposal
    - Your Fiction Manuscript (with a subsection on poetry)
3. Selling Your Book to an Agent
    - Finding the Right Agent for YOU
    - Writing a Killer Query Letter
    - The Art of the Schmooze (with a section on secretaries and assistants)
    - Follow-Up
    - Picking an Agent (if you have a choice and what to do if you don't)
    - Maximizing Your Agent
    - How to Be the Dream Client
    - Rejection
4. Selling Your Book to a Publisher
    - Picking Editors/Publishers
    - The Waiting Game
    - Choosing the Right Editor/Publisher for YOU
    - The Deal (auctions, advances, rights, contracts and more)
    - Rejection
5. Self-Publishing
    - Should You or Shouldn't You?
    - With Whom?
    - The Look of Your Book
    - Distribution
    - Pitfalls
    - Advantages

6. Writing Your Book
    - Making a Schedule
    - How to Work with Your Editor Effectively
    - Differences of Editorial Opinions
    - Writing Is Rewriting
    - Permissions
    - Illustrations/Photos
    - Title
    - Legal Questions

7. Prepublication
    - The Look of Your Book (the cover and interior)
    - Blurbs
    - Setting up a Tour (with or without your publisher)
    - Prepublication Print, Radio and TV
    - To Hire or Not to Hire an Outside Publicist
    - Getting Media Savvy (coaches, rehearsal, etc.)
    - Publicity Kits

8. Post-Publication Publicity
    - Making the Most of Where You Live (bookstores, media, etc.)
    - Bookstore Placement
    - Getting Yourself on TV and Radio and in Print
    - Buzz
    - Getting on a Bestseller List
    - E-Marketing (a gift to the shy!)

9. Keeping Your Book Alive for the Long Term
    - Movie Deals
    - Course Adoptions for Colleges and Universities
    - Speaking Agents
    - Conferences
    - Revisions
    - Special Marketing Opportunities

10. Figuring Out Your Next Project
    - Sequels
    - Not Making the Same Mistakes Twice
    - Do You Need a New Agent or Publisher?
    - Maximizing Your Success

ACKNOWLEDGMENTS

We are so grateful to the dozens who have helped us write this book. Numerous authors and publishing people put in their two cents, and we simply could not have done this without the information and advice they ponied up. Unfortunately, our acknowledgments would be as long as this book if we gave props to each and every person. So, instead, we've settled for thanking the "team" behind this book and then listing everyone who graciously agreed to be a part of it either by telling us their stories or by lending us their words.

First, we'd like to thank the team in order of where they came into the picture. Jessica Gillard, our seriously gifted and talented former Reed intern (who is now in the publishing business herself), came up with the title for this book and helped us put together our first PYPIP tour. Our wonderful colleagues/friends at the Levine Greenberg Literary Agency, Jim Levine, Daniel Greenberg, Melissa Rowland, Miek Coccia, Elisabeth Wooldridge, Melynda Bissmeyer, Jenoyne Adams, Elizabeth Fisher and Lindsey Edgecombe have supported us from beginning to end. In particular, Jim Levine has been the dad our book never had, giving us ideas and fantastic feedback, making sure our book was nurtured, well fed and tucked in nicely. Margaret E. Boyle contributed her big brain, her hard work and her eternal good nature. Danielle Svetcov always came through in a pinch. She is an *übermensch,* top-drawer researcher, fantabulous writer and generally all-too-talented human being. Jessica Goldstein has been a constant and generous supporter, and this book would never have been born without her. Chris Baty was kind enough to let us make an example out of his exemplary proposal. Suzie Bolotin has been the kind of editor you think exists only in your wildest dreams. She asked all the tough questions while making sure all the t's were dotted and the i's were crossed. And she's read this thick tome too many times to count. She is also a truly loving, sweet, good-natured, good-humored person. Lynn Strong is a copy editor with a capital "C." She fine-tuned this manuscript in an awe-inspiring manner. Megan Nicolay provided invaluable assistance (and fellow commiseration) at every turn. Nicki Clendening is the rare publicist who takes the time to get to know her authors and then uses this knowledge in creative, savvy ways. Bruce Harris spent a good chunk of his time sharing his wisdom. Peter Workman and the rest of his team simply couldn't be more creative, smart, together, fun, talented and lovely. We feel eternally grateful and lucky to be working with what we always heard and now believe is, indeed, "The Workman Magic."

Many thanks as well to:

David Allender
Jonathan Ames
Peter Andersen
Tamim Ansary
Jill Bailey
Philip Bashe
Andy Behrman
Rick Beyer
Jack Boulware
Gayle Brandeis
Armin Brott
Linda Buban
Judy Budnitz
Fauzia Burke
Rainelle Burton
Katy Butler
Jamie Byng
Tom Campbell
Elise Cannon
Kate Cerino

Bradley Charbonneau
Amy Cherry
Doris Cooper
Amanda Cotten
Deb Covey
Mike Daisey
Dennis Dalrymple
Michael Datcher
Karen Davidson
Paul Davidson
Barbara DeMarco-Barrett
Calla Devlin
Crofton Diack
Anita Diamant
Mauro DiPreta
Larry Dossey
Jill Dulber
Jim Eber
Susan Edsall
Hallie Ephron
Jeffrey Eugenides
John Evans
Andrew Exum
Frank Fochetta
Joel Fotinos
Gary Frank
Paul Gamarello
Roger Gilbertson
Mary Gleysteen
Seth Godin
Lynn Goldberg
David Graham
Arielle Gronner
Eve Grubin
Carol Hoenig
Carole Horne
Khaled Hosseini
Jessica Hurley
Sherril Jaffe
Janis Jaquith
Jemiah Jefferson
Duffy Jennings
Diana Jordan
Jennifer Josephy
Raphael Kadushin
Caryn Karmatz-Rudy
Jonathon Keats
Dan Kennedy
Shawna Kenney
Andy Kessler
Wayne Kirn
Bob Klein
Thea Kotroba
Karen Kozlowski
Annik LaFarge
Bruce Lane
Alice LaPlante
Caroline Leavitt
Nancy Levine
Keri Levitt
David Levy
Alan Lew
Valerie Lewis
Beth Lisick
Emily Loose
Regina Louise
Gwen Macsai
Steve Malk
Jenny Mandel
Martha Manning
Larry Mantle
Margaret Maupin
Damian McNicholl
Leslie Meredith
Dottie Mitchell
Geoffrey Moore
Barbara Morrow
Barbara Moulton
Maria Muscarella
Melissa Mytinger
Jill Nagle
Jan Nathan
Bob Nelson
Andrew Newberg
Jan Nelson
Carla Oliver
Daria O'Neill
The Onion
Marilyn Paige
Rachel Parker
William Parker
Karen Perea
Liz Perle
Michael Perry
Nancy Peters
Elaine Petrocelli
Kathy Pories
Michael Powell
Joe Quirk
Suzanne Rafer
Meg Cohen Ragas
Jennifer Ramos
Vince Rause
Kirk Read
Sally Reed
Jen Reynolds
Dan Rhodes
Marion Rosenberg
Andy Ross
Sharon Kelly Roth
Pru Rowlandson
Roberta Rubin
Bob Sabbag
Brandon Saltz
Frank Sanchez
Laura Schenone
Joan Schwieghardt
Susan Shaw
William Shinker
Debby Simmons
Rick Simonson
Marcella Smith
Matthew Snyder
Neil Sofam
Jerry Stahl
Jane Anne Staw
Valerie Tomaselli
Sydne Waller
Jodi Weiss
Karen West
Jun Chul Whang
Sun Chul Whang
Crystal Wilkinson
Ken Wilson
Ty Wilson
Rosalind Wiseman
Susan Wooldridge
Carolan Workman
Katie Workman
Lisa Zamarin
Keith Zimmerman
Kent Zimmerman

We also thank these people (both alive and long dead), who we've never had the pleasure of speaking with but whose inspirational stories or words were essential to our book:

James Boswell
Prill Boyle
Alan Burns
Alan Coren
Christopher Paul Curtis
Daniel Handler
Heidi Julavits
Jonathan Kozol
Anne Lamott
J.T. Leroy
Hilary Liftin
Ray Magliozzi
Tom Magliozzi
Kevin Meany
Michael Moore
Heru Ptah
Alice Sebold
Rachel Simon
Gene Wilder
David Williamson

INDEX

M

N

Q

R